ROYAL COMMISSION ON TRADE UNIONS AND EMPLOYERS' ASSOCIATIONS 1965-1968

CHAIRMAN: THE RT. HON. LORD DONOVAN

REPORT

Presented to Parliament by Command of Her Majesty
June 1968

LONDON
HER MAJESTY'S STATIONERY OFFICE
£1 0s. 0d. net

Cmnd. 3623

A

The estimated gross total expenditure of the Commission is £113,500. Of this sum £13,100 represents the estimated cost of printing and publishing this Report, £22,700 the estimated cost of printing and publishing the Minutes of Evidence and Written Evidence, and £8,100 the estimated cost of printing and publishing Research Papers. The sum of £8,667 has so far been recovered by the sale of Minutes of Evidence and £7,068 by the sale of Research Papers.

Expenditure of the Government Social Survey Department on research undertaken by it on behalf of the Commission is not included in the above total.

THE ROYAL WARRANT

ELIZABETH R.

ELIZABETH THE SECOND, by the Grace of God of the United Kingdom of Great Britain and Northern Ireland and of Our other Realms and Territories QUEEN, Head of the Commonwealth, Defender of the Faith to

Our Right Trusty and Well-beloved Counsellor Terence Norbert, Baron Donovan, a Lord of Appeal in Ordinary;

Our Right Trusty and Well-beloved Counsellor Alfred, Baron Robens of Woldingham;

Our Right Trusty and Well-beloved Edwin Savory, Baron Tangley, Knight Commander of Our Most Excellent Order of the British Empire;

Our Right Trusty and Well-beloved Harold Francis, Baron Collison, Commander of Our Most Excellent Order of the British Empire;

Our Trusty and Well-beloved:

Sir George Pollock, Knight, one of Our Counsel learned in the Law;

George Woodcock, Esquire, Commander of Our Most Excellent Order of the British Empire;

Hugh Armstrong Clegg, Esquire;

Mary Georgina Green;

Otto Kahn-Freund, Esquire;

Andrew Akiba Shonfield, Esquire;

John Thomson, Esquire, upon whom has been conferred the Territorial Decoration;

Eric Leonard Wigham, Esquire;

Greeting!

Whereas We have deemed it expedient that a Commission should forthwith issue, to consider relations between managements and employees and the role of trade unions and employers' associations in promoting the interests of their members and in accelerating the social and economic advance of the nation, with particular reference to the Law affecting the activities of these bodies; and to report:

Now know ye that We, reposing great trust and confidence in your knowledge and ability, have authorised and appointed, and do by these Presents authorise and appoint you the said Terence Norbert, Baron Donovan (Chairman); Alfred, Baron Robens of Woldingham; Edwin Savory, Baron Tangley; Harold Francis, Baron Collison; Sir George Pollock; George Woodcock; Hugh Armstrong Clegg; Mary Georgina Green; Otto Kahn-Freund; Andrew Akiba Shonfield; John Thomson and Eric Leonard Wigham to be Our Commissioners for the purpose of the said inquiry:

And for the better effecting the purposes of this Our Commission, We do by these Presents give and grant unto you, or any four or more of you, full power to call before you such persons as you shall judge likely to afford you any information upon the subject of this Our Commission; to call for information in writing; and also to call for, have access to and examine all such books, documents, registers and records as may afford you the fullest information on the subject and to inquire of and concerning the premises by all other lawful ways and means whatsoever:

And We do by these Presents authorise and empower you, or any of you, to visit and personally inspect such places as you may deem it expedient so to inspect for the more effectual carrying out of the purposes aforesaid:

And We do by these Presents will and ordain that this Our Commission shall continue in full force and virtue, and that you, Our said Commissioners, or any four or more of you may from time to time proceed in the execution thereof, and of every matter and thing therein contained, although the same be not continued from time to time by adjournment:

And We do further ordain that you, or any four or more of you, have liberty to report your proceedings under this Our Commission from time to time if you shall judge it expedient so to do:

And Our further will and pleasure is that you do, with as little delay as possible, report to Us your opinion upon the matters herein submitted for your consideration.

> Given at Our Court at Saint James's the eighth day of April, 1965, In the fourteenth Year of Our Reign.

By Her Majesty's Command.

Frank Soskice

NOTE:

Mr. G. Woodcock was admitted a member of the Privy Council in June 1967.

Miss M. G. Green was appointed a Dame Commander of the Most Excellent Order of the British Empire in January 1968.

Mr. E. L. Wigham was appointed a Commander of the Most Excellent Order of the British Empire in June 1967.

CONTENTS

ROYAL COMMISSION ON TRADE UNIONS AND EMPLOYERS' ASSOCIATIONS

1965 - 1968

REPORT

To the Queen's Most Excellent Majesty

MAY IT PLEASE YOUR MAJESTY

We, the undersigned Commissioners, having been appointed by Royal Warrant " to consider relations between managements and employees and the role of trade unions and employers' associations in promoting the interests of their members and in accelerating the social and economic advance of the nation, with particular reference to the Law affecting the activities of these bodies; and to report "

HUMBLY SUBMIT TO YOUR MAJESTY THE FOLLOWING REPORT.

Chapter I

INTRODUCTION

PREVIOUS INQUIRIES

1. We are the fifth Royal Commission to be appointed to inquire into questions affecting industrial relations in the last hundred years.

2. The first was appointed in February 1867 under the Chairmanship of Sir William Erle, to inquire into and report on the organisation and rules of trade unions and employers' associations and their effects on industrial relations and on trade and industry. Its final report was made in March 1869. During the interval it issued ten reports of the evidence it had collected. The final report was not unanimous, being signed by seven Commissioners out of ten. The dissenting report was signed by the other three. Two of the seven Commissioners who signed the majority report dissented on certain particular matters. The reports of this Commission led to the enactment of the Trade Union Act 1871 and the Criminal Law Amendment Act 1871, which made alterations in the law in favour of trade unions.

3. The second Royal Commission was appointed in 1874 under the Chairmanship of Chief Justice Cockburn following the decision of Brett J. in 1872 in the case of *R. v. Bunn* (12 Cox 316) to the effect that, despite the Trade Union Act 1871 which abolished criminal liability for the act of combining in restraint of trade, it was still a criminal offence at common law to interfere, with improper intent, with an employer's right to conduct his business as he wished. The Commission was directed to inquire into the working of the Master and Servant Act 1867 and of the Criminal Law Amendment Act 1871 and into the law of conspiracy generally and as affecting the relations of masters and servants. The Commission reported in February 1875. There was a dissenting report signed by one Commissioner. Following these reports the Conspiracy and Protection of Property Act 1875 and the Employers and Workmen Act 1875 were passed, and the Master and Servant Act 1867 and the Criminal Law Amendment Act 1871 were repealed.

4. In April 1891 another Royal Commission on Labour was appointed under the Chairmanship of the Duke of Devonshire to inquire *inter alia* into questions affecting the relations between employer and employed. It reported in May 1894. Of its twenty-three members nineteen signed a majority and four a minority report. It was followed by the passing of the Conciliation Act 1896.

5. The next Royal Commission was appointed in June 1903 under the Chairmanship of Lord Dunedin. It was directed to inquire into the subject of trade disputes and trade combinations and the law affecting them, and to report. It did so in January 1906. Of its five members three signed the majority report. Each of the two other members signed his own dissenting report. The Trade Disputes Act 1906 followed these reports. It exempted trade unions altogether from liability to be sued in tort and gave a measure of protection from civil suit for certain acts done in contemplation or furtherance of a trade dispute.

6. In October 1916 a committee (not a Royal Commission) was appointed whose five reports, made in 1917 and 1918, had a far-reaching influence on industrial relations and in particular on the development of voluntary machinery for the negotiation of terms and conditions of employment. This was the Committee on Relations between Employers and Employed under the Chairmanship of the Rt. Hon. J. H. Whitley, M.P. Its report led to the establishment of Joint Industrial Councils in many industries; to the extension of statutory minimum wage legislation, which had first been introduced by the Trade Boards Act 1909; and to the passing of the Industrial Courts Act 1919.

OUR WORK

7. We ourselves were appointed by Royal Warrant dated 8th April 1965, and our terms of reference have already been quoted.

8. As a first step we decided to prepare for our own guidance a survey of the field covered by our terms of reference. This was completed in June 1965 and took the form of a series of 330 questions arising under five heads of inquiry. A printed copy of the survey was sent to all trade unions and all employers' associations. Copies were also sent to a number of Government Departments and to organisations and individuals with special knowledge and experience of industrial relations. The recipients were invited to assist us with written evidence bearing upon the subject matters of our inquiry or upon such of them as the recipients felt were within their competence. We also published in the press a general invitation to the public to submit evidence to us. A copy of the survey is Appendix 1 of this Report.

9. As a result, we received a considerable volume of written evidence. Memoranda were received from Government Departments, the Trades Union Congress, the Confederation of British Industry, numerous trade unions and employers' associations, companies, nationalised industries, organisations connected with industrial relations, individuals having specialist knowledge of the subject, and members of the public. In all some 430 organisations, persons or groups of persons sent us written submissions.

10. A list of all those submitting papers is to be found in Appendix 2. The Commission wishes to tender its grateful thanks to all those who assisted it in this way.

11. A considerable proportion of those who submitted written evidence came before us for oral questioning. It was not possible, nor indeed necessary, to ask all the authors of written memoranda to attend for this purpose, since the same problems were discussed and the same solutions put forward in several such memoranda. We sat on 58 days for the purpose of taking oral evidence, and the names of those who gave it appear in Appendix 3. For this additional help and co-operation the Commission is much indebted. The evidence heard in public has been printed and published by HM Stationery Office.

12. It was clear from the outset that research would be needed into a number of questions, and Dr. W. E. J. McCarthy, a lecturer and tutor in industrial relations at Oxford University, was appointed Research Director to the Commission on 1st August 1965. The Commission was particularly concerned

as part of its programme of research to obtain information about industrial relations at workshop level, and especially about the role played by shop stewards. With this object arrangements were made for the Government Social Survey Department to conduct interviews on the basis of a series of questionnaires with some 1,400 shop stewards, 200 full-time trade union officers, 500 workers belonging to trade unions, 400 non-union workers, 600 foremen, 300 works managers and 120 personnel officers. Research was conducted on behalf of the Commission into many other subjects including the structure and government of trade unions and of employers' associations, trade union recognition, disputes procedures, strikes, productivity bargaining and the contribution of industrial sociology to industrial relations. The main results of the Commission's programme of research have already appeared in a series of Research Papers published for the Commission by HM Stationery Office. A full list is in Appendix 4.

13. Members of the Commission made a number of visits to industrial establishments, in the course of which they were able to hear the views of both managements and shop stewards and attend meetings of joint bodies at that level. Members also attended as observers a number of meetings of national joint negotiating bodies including a Wages Council at which wage claims were under negotiation, and were able to witness voluntary disputes procedures in operation at various levels.

14. In October 1966, seven members of the Commission took part in visits to Sweden and the Federal Republic of Germany to gain first-hand information about the system of industrial relations in those countries. They were very hospitably received, and a great deal of assistance was given to the Commission by Ministers, trade union officers, representatives of employers' associations and individuals with special knowledge of the subject in both countries. This help was very valuable. It was duly acknowledged at the time, but the Commission desires here to repeat its thanks.

15. We held meetings on 128 days in all.

SOCIAL AND ECONOMIC CHANGE SINCE THE LAST ROYAL COMMISSION

16. The impact of two world wars and changes associated with developing technology, increasing scale of industrial organisation, growing wealth and greater Government intervention have contributed to a transformation of the social and economic life of the country since the last Royal Commission reported 62 years ago.

17. Old industries—cotton, coal and railways—have shrunk and new industries—synthetic fibres, oil and motor vehicles—have emerged. In other industries processes of production have been revolutionised, old crafts disappearing and new skills emerging. With increasing mechanisation and rising productivity, manual employment has declined and white-collar employment increased; and service industries have expanded in response to growing wealth. Technical change, increasing affluence and rising standards of education have therefore all been working in the same direction.

18. With a continuing growth in the size of industrial units and the amalga-

4

mation of companies there has developed a managerial society in which ownership has become divorced from control. The running of large businesses is in the hands of professional managers. They are responsible to boards of directors who can be regarded broadly as trustees for the general body of shareholders. While in the long term shareholders, employees and customers all stand to benefit if a concern flourishes, the immediate interests of these groups often conflict. Directors and managers have to balance these conflicting interests, and in practice they generally seek to strike whatever balance will best promote the welfare of the enterprise as such.

19. Meanwhile trade unions have increased their membership from less than 2¼m. in 1906 to over 10m. in 1966, and the membership has been increasingly concentrated in a comparatively small number of large and powerful unions. These accessions of strength have resulted in a widespread extension of collective bargaining. Trade unions are also consulted by the Government of the day in a large range of matters and provide representatives who serve on many official bodies, committees and tribunals. Employers' associations are similarly recognised.

20. The Government's involvement in economic affairs has been extended by the nationalisation of a number of basic industries. The establishment of a separate Ministry of Labour in 1917 was a recognition of the Government's concern with the promotion of good industrial relations.[1] The acceptance of full employment as an objective of Government policy has brought a more detailed and continuous central management of the economy. More recently Governments have accepted the further responsibility of promoting a prices and incomes policy whereby money prices and incomes should be prevented from running too far ahead of increasing productivity.

21. Legislation now provides a whole range of services which not only give greater social security than before, but have also helped to modify the class structure of society. In addition this process has been fostered by the erosion of some of the distinctions between manual and white-collar employment and by successive reforms of the educational system.

22. It is against such far-reaching changes as these that the Commission has had to survey its problems and reach conclusions. Our report covers a very wide field and contains many expressions of view and a large number of recommendations. The disagreement of members on certain points is recorded. We should add that members have not thought it necessary or desirable to make a reservation about every view or recommendation contained in the report which they would not necessarily, if acting on their own, have adopted. It seemed right on occasion to modify or abandon individual opinions and preferences so as to enable a collective view to be expressed. This has of course been possible only where members did not feel that a major point of principle was at stake; on such major points the only proper course is to record the reservations of those concerned.

---

[1] The functions of the Ministry of Labour have now been transferred to a new Department of Employment and Productivity. We have however to refer to the Ministry of Labour in this report so far as concerns its evidence and activities and the information supplied by it.

Chapter II

THE SUBJECT-MATTER OF OUR REPORT

23. Our task requires us to examine the relationships between managements and employees, and the work of trade unions and employers' associations. This inevitably involves us also in an investigation of collective bargaining and of the part played in industrial relations by the State.

MANAGEMENTS

24. Those who settled our terms of reference no doubt chose the term "managements" deliberately, instead of the term "employers". For today most people are employed by a corporation, endowed by law with separate and independent existence. Among these are joint stock companies, local authorities, and the Boards of nationalised industries, whose business is conducted and managed by individuals acting for them. These persons will often be employees themselves; but as "the management" they will settle the terms and conditions of employment within their concerns, by negotiations with the employees affected or with trade union representatives on their behalf. Where we use the term "employer" in this report it is to be understood as being the counterpart of "employee".

EMPLOYEES

25. The total working population of the United Kingdom is almost 26 millions, of whom over 23¾ millions are employees.[1] These people are distributed approximately as follows:

	Million
In manufacturing industries	9
In building and construction	1¾
In transport and communication	1¾
In distributive trades	3
In financial, professional and scientific services	3¼
In national and local government service	1½
In other industries, including, e.g., gas, electricity, coalmining and agriculture	3½

There are about 15 million male employees and 8¾ million female. Over 14 million employees are manual workers, and over 9 million are white-collar workers.

26. There are some 200,000 different establishments in manufacturing alone, at about three-quarters of which there are ten employees or less. On the other hand, the vast majority of employees in manufacturing are employed

---

[1]The figures relate to the latest date for which figures are available, June 1967. They include both full-time and part-time employees and also those unemployed at the time.

in larger establishments, 6½ millions being in factories where 100 people or more work. At the top of the scale there are about 70 establishments at which more than 5,000 people are employed, nearly half of them in the motor manufacturing industry. The number of companies with over 5,000 employees is larger than this, there being many companies which own several establishments.

TRADE UNIONS

27. The statutory definition of a trade union is to be gathered from section 23, Trade Union Act 1871; section 16, Trade Union Act Amendment Act 1876; and sections 1 and 2, Trade Union Act 1913. The combined effect of these provisions is to define a trade union as " any combination, whether temporary or permanent, the principal objects of which are under its constitution statutory objects, namely the regulation of the relations between workmen and masters, or between workmen and workmen, or between masters and masters, or the imposing of restrictive conditions on the conduct of any trade or business, and also the provision of benefits to members ". Thus an association of employers whose principal objects were to regulate relations among masters, or to impose restrictive conditions on the conduct of their trade, would be a trade union in the eye of the law though the man in the street would hardly regard it as such. We have proposals to make about this definition: and in this report we use the term trade union as connoting combinations of employees only.

28. At the beginning of the present century there were 1,323 trade unions of employees with a membership of 2,022,000 workers. The number of unions has steadily decreased since then while the number of members has increased. At the end of 1966 there were 574 trade unions with a total membership of 10,111,000. Unions vary in size from the 24 members of the Jewish Bakers' Union to the 1,482,000 members of the Transport and General Workers' Union. One half of all trade unionists are in the nine largest unions and four-fifths are in the 38 largest unions. By contrast there are 245 unions with under 500 members and over 450 with under 5,000 members. Out of the total of 574 unions 170 are affiliated to a central organisation, the Trades Union Congress, hereinafter called " The TUC ", but these unions between them have a total membership of nearly 9 million employees.

EMPLOYERS' ASSOCIATIONS

29. The Department of Employment and Productivity lists some 1,350 employers' associations. They range in size from the Engineering Employers' Federation, which covers 4,600 separate establishments with over two million employees, to small organisations covering a section of a trade in one locality. Many of these are however local associations subordinate to industry-wide federations of which they are members. There are, for example, some two hundred and fifty local associations affiliated with the National Federation of Building Trades Employers. All of these bodies are concerned directly or indirectly with the negotiation of wages and working conditions, but many of them also concern themselves with such matters as standard forms of trading contracts, standardisation of products and so on, which is the business of a " trade association ". This type of activity is really outside our field of

7

inquiry. Were it otherwise we should have to consider the activities of many organisations which are not employers' associations at all.

30. In 1965 the three main central employers' organisations, the Federation of British Industries, the British Employers' Confederation and the National Association of British Manufacturers formed one new central organisation, the Confederation of British Industry, to take their place. The CBI admits to membership employers' associations, trade associations, individual companies in productive industry and transport (including companies which are not members of employers' associations) and the public corporations administering the nationalised industries. Other companies such as banks and insurance companies may become "commercial associates". The 108 employers' associations in its membership are estimated by the CBI to represent companies whose employees amount to more than three-quarters of all employees in the private sector of industry and transport.

COLLECTIVE BARGAINING

31. The relationship between trade unions and employers' associations arises principally in the process of negotiating and applying collective agreements, and the rules established by these agreements form a considerable part of the framework within which managers and workers deal with each other. "Collective bargain" is a term coined by Beatrice Webb to describe an agreement concerning pay and conditions of work settled between trade unions on the one hand and an employer or association of employers on the other. Thus it covers any negotiations in which employees do not negotiate individually, and on their own behalf, but do so collectively through representatives.

32. The best-known type of collective agreement in this country is the industry-wide agreement (a more precise term than "national agreement"). This is an agreement between an employers' association (or in some instances two or more associations) and a trade union (or, more commonly, two or more unions or a federation of unions) which is intended to operate throughout an industry. Where industry-wide bargaining is practised the resulting agreements can be classified into substantive agreements, which deal with matters such as rates of pay, hours of work, overtime rates and holiday arrangements, and procedural agreements dealing with the procedures for reaching substantive agreements and for dealing with disputes which may arise in the establishments within the industry. Substantive agreements and disputes procedures are almost invariably written down and often printed in a handbook of agreements for the industry. Some industries have agreed formal constitutions for joint bodies at industry level which meet regularly to deal with such matters as negotiating or amending substantive agreements. Where they exist, these constitutions are generally included in the handbooks. Other industries prefer to rely on arranging *ad hoc* meetings for negotiating and revising substantive agreements.

33. Some large corporations which do not belong to employers' associations negotiate their own substantive and procedural agreements with the unions. A few of these agreements, like that of the Ford Motor Company, operate throughout the undertaking and cover more workers than many industry-wide agreements. Some of the major oil companies, on the other hand, negotiate

separate agreements for each of their refineries. In a few instances, including the National Coal Board, an agreement with a single corporation is also an industry-wide agreement.

34. Companies in membership of employers' associations (usually called "federated" companies) may negotiate agreements with unions representing their employees to supplement industry-wide agreements, either substantive or procedural, but such agreements are relatively rare. More commonly bargaining to supplement industry-wide agreements takes place between managers and representatives of particular groups of workers. In a company possessing two or more factories it is normal for managers in each factory to deal separately with representatives of groups of their own workers. This type of bargaining we refer to as "workplace bargaining". In some instances workers are represented by full-time trade union district officials in workplace bargaining. More commonly, however, their spokesmen are representatives chosen from among themselves, usually called "shop stewards", and full-time officials are called in only where managers and shop stewards cannot reach agreement. Many of these agreements affect only one group of workers in a single shop, and may be settled between a shop steward and a foreman or departmental manager. This is "workshop" or "shop floor" bargaining. Most industry-wide disputes procedures give some guidance on the conduct of workplace bargaining, although often in practice this guidance is not strictly observed.

35. Workplace agreements may be written down, but are rarely collected together into a single coherent document. Many of them, especially shop floor agreements, are oral. These oral agreements are difficult to distinguish from "custom and practice". This is the body of customary forms of behaviour among groups of workers which managers have permitted to grow up and are therefore assumed to accept. Examples of matters widely covered by custom and practice are "tea-breaks" and tasks reserved for members of a given craft. These customs play an important part in shop floor industrial relations, and some have their origin in oral agreements.

36. The pay and conditions of an individual employee may therefore be the result of collective bargains struck at one or more (even, conceivably, all) of the foregoing levels. The following is an example of the composition of the wage packet of a skilled engineering time-rated fitter in a factory in north-east England in a particular pay week in December 1967:

£ s. d.	
11 1 8	Time rate for the *industry* negotiated between the Engineering Employers' Federation and the Confederation of Shipbuilding and Engineering Unions (rate for 40 hours' work).
4 8 8	Overtime (8 hours at double time) paid at rates negotiated at *industry* level as above.
3 13 11	Night-shift premium, paid at rates negotiated at *industry* level as above.
11 14 11	Lieu bonus, negotiated between management and shop stewards *in the factory*.
£30 19 2	Total gross pay.

9

37. There is no generally accepted term for an agreement which deals comprehensively with the terms and conditions of employment for all employees at a particular establishment, no doubt because such agreements are rare in Britain today. It is not easy to find a suitable expression, but we have decided in the end to use the term " factory agreement ". It must be understood, however, that we do not here use " factory " in the literal sense but rather as the equivalent of " establishment ". Wherever therefore we speak of a " factory agreement " in this report we have in mind a comprehensive agreement which might apply not only to a factory but, for example, to a construction site, a bus garage or a commercial office.

38. Although trade unions at present represent only a minority of the total number of employees—10 million out of nearly 24 million—the number of workers whose wages and conditions are directly affected by collective bargaining exceeds 15 million. This is partly because the terms reached in collective bargaining are applied to workers who come within the scope of the agreement whether they are trade unionists or not.

THE STATE

39. Until recent times it was a distinctive feature of our system of industrial relations that the State remained aloof from the process of collective bargaining in private industry. It left the parties free to come to their own agreement. It imposed some, but few, restrictions on the right of employees to strike or of employers to resort to a lock-out. The parties to the collective agreement themselves rarely intend that their bargain shall be a legally enforceable contract, but rather that it shall be binding in honour only. The law goes out of its way to provide that such bargains between employers' associations and trade unions shall not be directly enforceable.

40. This abstentionist attitude has reflected a belief that it is better in the long run for the law to interfere as little as possible in the settlement of questions arising between employers and workmen over pay and conditions of work. Parliament has long been committed to the view that the best means of settling such questions is voluntary collective bargaining and has equipped Governments in various ways to support, assist and promote collective bargaining.

41. One example of support for collective agreements is the Fair Wages Resolution of the House of Commons. The first was passed in 1891, and the Resolution at present in force was adopted in 1946. Its basic purpose is to ensure that employers engaged on Government contracts do not give their employees terms and conditions inferior to those established generally. Other examples are the Terms and Conditions of Employment Act 1959, under which an employer may be required under certain conditions to observe terms and conditions not less favourable than those established for his trade or industry by collective bargaining; and the statutory obligation placed on the boards of nationalised industries to seek agreement with trade unions over the establishment of negotiating machinery for settling terms and conditions of work for their employees.

42. Assistance to collective bargaining is provided by the activities of the

Department of Employment and Productivity in the fields of conciliation, arbitration and inquiry under the Conciliation Act 1896 and the Industrial Courts Act 1919.

43. The State has long intervened in certain aspects of the relations between employer and employee where there were evils calling for a remedy, such as protection of safety, health, welfare, and the right of employees to receive their wages in coin of the realm; and for similar reasons it has established statutory machinery for fixing wages in certain industries. The first Trade Boards Act for this purpose was passed in 1909, and the current Act is the Wages Councils Act 1959. This enables the Secretary of State for Employment and Productivity to establish a Wages Council if of the opinion that no adequate machinery exists for the effective regulation of the remuneration of particular workers, and that, having regard to their existing remuneration, it is expedient to establish such a Council. The Councils are thus not intended to override collective bargaining but to provide means of regulation where collective bargaining is ineffective. They are regarded as a method of promoting voluntary machinery in the industries which have not been able to develop such machinery unaided. At the present time there are some 57 Wages Councils in existence covering about 3½ million workers employed in about half a million establishments. Other Acts of Parliament provide for the fixing of minimum wages in agriculture.

44. In addition there are further Acts of Parliament which regulate certain aspects of industrial relations in particular industries whose circumstances make this necessary, as for example the Merchant Shipping Acts.

45. Certain recent Acts of Parliament, however, have made a new departure from the general principle of non-intervention. They include the Contracts of Employment Act 1963, the Industrial Training Act 1964 and the Redundancy Payments Act 1965, all of them bringing statutory regulation into fields previously left to voluntary action. We return to each of them in subsequent chapters. More recently, the Prices and Incomes Acts 1966 and 1967 have enabled employers and trade unions to be compelled to notify pay claims and awards to the Government and have permitted the Government to hold up pay increases, in certain circumstances, for a period of up to seven months. Further legislation on prices and incomes is now under consideration. It may fairly be said therefore that as a Royal Commission we have been sitting at a time when the basic principles of our system of industrial relations are in question. Should they be restored, revised or replaced? In order to set out the reasoning by which we have arrived at our own answers to these questions we now turn to a more detailed examination of the system and its working.

Chapter III

THE SYSTEM OF INDUSTRIAL RELATIONS

46. Britain has two systems of industrial relations. The one is the formal system embodied in the official institutions. The other is the informal system created by the actual behaviour of trade unions and employers' associations, of managers, shop stewards and workers.

47. The foundations of the formal system are described in the conclusions of the Royal Commission on Labour of 1891. In their final report the Commissioners wrote:

"Powerful trades unions on the one side and powerful associations of employers on the other have been the means of bringing together in conference the representatives of both classes enabling each to appreciate the position of the other, and to understand the conditions subject to which their joint undertaking must be conducted. . . . We see reason to believe that in this way the course of events is tending towards a more settled and pacific period. . .".

48. The Whitley Committee of 1917 took up the same theme. It was their "considered opinion that an essential condition of securing a permanent improvement in the relations of employers and employed is that there should be adequate organisation on the part of both employers and workpeople".

49. The informal system is founded on reality, recognising that the organisations on both sides of industry are not strong. Central trade union organisation is weak, and employers' associations are weaker.

50. The keystone of the formal structure is the industry-wide collective agreement, compared by the Royal Commission on Labour to a "regular and well thought out treaty". Each side, so it is assumed, can see that its own members honour the treaty. There may be room for help from outside, but only when the two sides fail to agree. Then the Government may help by conciliation, by arranging for arbitration, or by setting up an inquiry.

51. In this system pay, hours of work and other conditions of employment appropriate to regulation by agreement are all settled by this treaty—except where there is some devolution to districts of the unions and local employers' associations to make agreements supplementing industry-wide decisions. "But there are also", wrote the Whitley Committee, "many questions closely affecting daily life and comfort in, and the success of, the business, and affecting in no small degree efficiency of working, which are peculiar to the individual workshop and factory". They therefore proposed works committees "to establish and maintain a system of co-operation in all these workshop matters", but not to interfere with "questions such as rates of wages and hours of work, which should be settled by District or National agreement". Agreements should be made outside the factory by trade unions and employers' associa-

tions; within the factory managers and workers should consult on other matters.

52. This is the system embodied in our official institutions. Other countries also have both formal systems of industrial relations embodied in official institutions and informal systems created by the behaviour of people and organisations. But in Britain the informal system is often at odds with the formal system. In order to show why this is so it is necessary to describe collective agreements, employers' associations, trade unions, managers and workshop organisation, not as they are meant to be, but as they are.

COLLECTIVE BARGAINING

53. According to the Ministry of Labour's evidence, there are about five hundred separate industry-wide negotiating arrangements in Britain for manual workers alone (statutory wage-fixing bodies being included in the total). This figure necessarily depends on a rather liberal interpretation of the word "industry". At one extreme it treats as a single engineering industry the great majority of undertakings eligible for membership of the Engineering Employers' Federation with their $3\frac{1}{2}$ million employees, and at the other the Hair, Bass and Fibre Wages Council with a few hundred employees also constitutes a separate industry.

54. In many industries there are no industry-wide agreements relating to white-collar workers. Where there are such agreements, the white-collar unions almost invariably negotiate separately from the manual workers' unions. In many industries maintenance workers' unions also negotiate separately from the unions of process or production workers, as in the chemicals industry. The bus industry partitions its negotiations in an unusual fashion. The London Transport Board negotiates separately from the provinces, and outside London the municipal bus undertakings negotiate separately from the so-called " company " undertakings.

55. As we have already said, agreements reached in negotiations can be separated into substantive agreements, which lay down rules governing employment in the industry, and procedural agreements, which set out the ways in which substantive agreements can be amended or interpreted and how disputes within the industry should be handled.

56. Substantive industry-wide agreements lay down the length of the normal working week, regulations for overtime, weekend and shift working, and for statutory and annual holidays. These provisions are usually observed fairly closely in the industries to which they apply. They also regulate pay. In this respect their provisions show a great deal of variety. Some fix only two time rates, one for skilled workers and another for unskilled, leaving individual firms to deal with intermediate and other grades. Others prescribe a list of different rates for a catalogue of different grades, with in addition a series of special additional payments for special duties or conditions of work. In industries in which a substantial number of women are employed, women are usually treated as forming a separate grade with rates of pay lower than those for unskilled men. Some agreements make no provision for payment by results; others do so, but in different degrees of detail. Some describe their rates as minimum rates, others as standard rates.

57. The figures in Tables A-C show that over the last thirty years there has been a decline in the extent to which industry-wide agreements determine actual pay. In 1938 there was only a modest " gap " between the rates which they laid down for a normal working week and the average earnings which men actually received. By 1967 the two sets of figures had moved far apart. Table C reveals the process of divergence, or " drift ", at work over the years 1962-67. Together the tables record a remarkable transfer of authority in collective bargaining in this group of industries. Before the war it was generally assumed that industry-wide agreements could provide almost all the joint regulation that was needed, leaving only minor issues to be settled by individual managers. Today the consequences of bargaining within the factory can be more momentous than those of industry-wide agreements.

TABLE A

Earnings and time rates of men in October 1938

Industry	Time rates for a normal week		Average earnings of adult male manual workers in last pay week October 1938
Engineering	Fitters:	£3. 7. 2½ (average rate in 14 towns)	£3.13. 8 (General engineering and iron and steel founding)
	Labourers:	£2.10. 4 (average rate in 14 towns)	
Shipbuilding and repairing	Platers:	£3. 8. 0 (average rate in 8 towns)	£3.10. 1
	Labourers:	£2. 9. 0 (average rate in 9 towns)	
Building	Bricklayers:	£3.13. 2 (average rate in 38 towns)	£3. 6. 6 (Building and decorating)
	Labourers:	£2.15. 0½ (average rate in 38 towns)	
Civil Engineering	Labourers:	£2. 4. 0 to £3. 2. 0 (according to district)	£3. 2.10 (Public Works Contracting)

Source: Ministry of Labour.

58. The three major elements in the " gap " between agreed rates and average earnings are piecework or incentive earnings, company or factory additions to basic rates, and overtime earnings. Most industry-wide agreements give no more guidance on piecework or incentive earnings than to say that, for the " average " worker, there should be a given minimum level. The actual prices or incentive " values " are usually fixed within the factory and earnings now generally exceed the minimum by a generous margin. Additions to basic rates include " lieu " payments to those on timework to compensate them for not having the opportunity to raise their earnings through piecework, and job-rates which may be settled on some system of job evaluation. Both are usually fixed within the factory or the company. The length of the normal working week and the rate of overtime pay, are both generally

14

settled by industry-wide agreements, but the decision to work overtime is a matter for the factory, and this governs the volume of overtime earnings.

TABLE B

EARNINGS AND TIME RATES OF MEN IN CERTAIN INDUSTRIES IN OCTOBER 1967

Industry	Times rates for normal week of 40 hours (national or provincial rate)	Average weekly earnings of adult male manual workers for industry (Second pay-week in Oct. 67)
Engineering Fitter: Labourer:	£11. 1. 8 £ 9. 7. 4 (Minimum earnings levels: Fitter: £12.17. 8 Labourer: £10.17. 4)	*Engineering and electrical goods* £21. 7. 9 *Vehicles* £24. 8. 5
Building Craftsmen: Labourer:	£14.13. 4 £12.11. 8	*Construction* £21.13. 8
Shipbuilding and repairing Fully skilled: Labourer:	£11. 1. 4 £ 9. 6. 0 (Minimum earnings levels: Skilled: £12.17. 4 Labourer: £11. 3. 6)	*Shipbuilding and marine engineering* £21.17. 8
Dock labourers	(Guaranteed minimum weekly pay) £15. 0. 0	*Dock labour** £22.16. 6
Cocoa, chocolate and sugar confectionery	£10.15. 6	*Cocoa, chocolate and sugar confectionery* £21. 7. 5
Electrical cable making	£11. 8. 4½ to £13. 5. 6	*Insulated wires and cables* £23. 9. 4
Furniture manufacturing	£13. 0. 0 to £14. 3. 4	*Furniture and upholstery* £22. 5. 4
Motor vehicle retail and repairing trade	£11. 0. 0 to £13.10. 0	*Motor repairers, garages, etc.* £18.10. 4
Soap, candle and edible fat manufacturing	£10. 6. 6 to £11. 7. 0	*Vegetable and animal oils, fats, soap and detergents* £23.10. 5
Footwear manufacturing	£11.12. 6	*Footwear* £19.14. 4

Source: Ministry of Labour.

* April 1967 figure.

59. Besides substantive agreements intended to regulate the employment of labour within their jurisdiction, industry-wide negotiators also conclude procedure agreements. These provide means for conciliating or determining disputes which arise between organised workers and their managers. Patterns vary, but normally speaking a worker is expected to raise an issue with his

supervisor. Thereafter a shop steward can take it further. Perhaps it comes before a joint committee within the factory. At some stage the full-time trade union officer and the employers' association are brought in. Finally the industry-wide negotiators may be involved, either by bringing the question before a national joint body, or by sending a joint investigating sub-committee to the factory.

TABLE C

COMPARISONS OF INCREASES IN WAGE RATES WITH INCREASES IN EARNINGS IN THE PERIOD OCTOBER 1962—OCTOBER 1967

Industry groups in which manual workers concerned were employed	Percentage increase, October 1967 compared with October 1962		
	Average weekly wage rates (1)	Average weekly wage earnings (2)	"Earnings drift" (col. (2) minus col. (1)) (3)
Construction	21·7	35·9	14·2
All metal industries	23·1	32·3	9·2
Food, drink, tobacco	23·0	39·5	16·5
Textiles	17·9	37·7	19·8
Paper, printing, publishing ..	22·9	36·5	13·6
Chemicals and allied industries ..	24·8	38·1	13·3
Timber, furniture, etc.	18·4	35·8	17·4
Bricks, pottery, glass, cement, etc.	25·8	36·7	10·9
Clothing and footwear	20·6	33·2	12·6
All industries*	23·1	36·4	13·3

Figures supplied by Ministry of Labour.

* All industries covered by the Ministry of Labour's half-yearly earnings inquiries.

60. Theoretically the disputes which may arise can be divided into differences concerning the interpretation of existing industry-wide substantive agreements, and differences over claims for improvements in terms and conditions of employment within the factory. The first are sometimes classified as "disputes of right", and the second as "disputes of interest". Where industry-wide agreements include a detailed grading system with separate rates of pay for different classes of worker, disputes about the correct grading of a post can occupy much of the attention of a disputes procedure. This is not uncommon among white-collar workers, for example in local government and on the railways. But for most manual workers whose industry-wide agreements prescribe minimum rates of pay, disputes of interest predominate. Moreover, because of the prevalence of "custom and practice" in British industrial relations, a sharp distinction between the two types of dispute is unrealistic. When what is in dispute is some workshop privilege it does not much matter whether the issue is seen as a difference about what is

16

provided by an existing unwritten and ill-defined understanding, whose very existence may be in doubt, or as a claim for a new concession. Another impediment to distinguishing between the two types of dispute is the general practice in this country of allowing agreements to run for an indefinite period. In most other countries agreements run for a stipulated period. Matters of interpretation can be raised during the period, but disputes of interest arise mainly on its expiry.

61. Many of these procedures have been subjected to strain by the transfer of authority in industrial relations to the factory and the workshop. They have responded in one of two ways which can be illustrated from the contrasting experience of our two largest industries, engineering and building.

62. In the procedure covering manual engineering workers, there are three stages for dealing with a dispute that cannot be resolved within the factory: a works conference attended by full-time officers on both sides; a local conference between the district organisations; and a national conference invariably held at York. The number of works conferences rose from 1,564 in 1955 to 3,854 in 1966[1], the number of local conference hearings from 282 to 1,033 and the number of central conference hearings from 113 to 519. This rapid increase records the industry's attempt to keep some control over the mounting volume of matters decided or disputed in the workshop. The kind of control which is exercised is suggested by the record of central conferences in 1966. Thirteen of the 519 cases were withdrawn or "not proceeded with"; in 239 cases "failure to agree" was recorded; and in 55 a settlement was reached. Of the remaining 212 cases, 85 were "referred back" and 127 were retained. Reference back normally implies that some compromise arrangement has been found which will keep the peace in the factory but cannot be recorded as a settlement for fear of the implications for other factories elsewhere; and this is also the ultimate conclusion of many of the cases which are retained. Thus the procedure maintains its function of conciliation largely at the expense of abandoning any notion of common standards for the industry. It is true that most disputes are settled before they reach York, but one of the main factors in their resolution is the expected consequence at York: "failure to agree" or an *ad hoc* arrangement.

63. The building industry has two separate procedures. The normal procedure handles site disputes about industry-wide agreements through local, regional and national joint committees or panels. The second is a streamlined emergency procedure intended to handle issues not covered by the industry-wide agreements, such as demarcation and the closed shop, especially where a stoppage is imminent. Even taking into account the difference in size between the two industries, the joint bodies in building are called upon to perform only a fraction of the work that falls to their counterparts in engineering. In 1967 72 ordinary disputes and 44 emergency disputes reached regional level, and of these 15 and 14 respectively went on to the national joint bodies[2]. Moreover there does not seem to be any marked tendency for the numbers to rise.

---

[1]Research Paper No. 2 (Part 2), A. I. Marsh and W. E. J. McCarthy, *Disputes Procedures in Britain*, pp. 21, 27; HMSO, 1968.
[2]*Op. cit.*, p.58.

64. The explanation for this seems to be that both sides of the industry still act as though their industry-wide agreements set firm standards. They are expressly committed to tolerate no variations except for a rule first introduced in 1947 authorising incentive schemes under which earnings higher than those yielded by the prescribed hourly rates are related to the performance of definite allotted tasks. In fact, however, although properly-constructed incentive schemes are not widely adopted in the industry, payment above the prescribed rate is common, and in many areas general. Site bonuses are paid at 1s., 2s. or more an hour above the rates laid down in the agreement. But these are usually regarded as matters outside the jurisdiction of both procedures. In other words the disputes machinery keeps the volume of its business at a low level by handling a diminishing proportion of the real industrial relations issues of the industry. In addition there is the growing practice of " labour-only sub-contracting " which takes the workers concerned wholly or largely outside the sphere of joint regulation between the two sides of the industry. That is the subject of another inquiry.

65. These are two responses of industry-wide procedures to the growing volume of bargaining which now takes place within the factory or on the site. What can be said about this bargaining itself? In his evidence Mr. Allan Flanders characterised it as " largely informal, largely fragmented and largely autonomous". The evidence put before us and the research conducted on our behalf confirms his analysis. They reveal that the shift in authority from the industry to the factory has been accompanied by decentralisation of authority in industrial relations within the factory itself.

66. Workplace bargaining is largely autonomous because, however the external collective bargaining procedures respond to its growth, their control has continued to diminish, and with it the control of trade unions and employers' associations.

67. Workplace bargaining is fragmented because " it is conducted in such a way that different groups in the works get different concessions at different times ". The consequence is competitive sectional wage adjustments and disorderly pay structures. The engineering industry encourages fragmentation, in two ways. First, it allows individual unions to pursue the claims of their own members through the procedure separately from other unions in the same factory. Secondly, disputes which cannot be resolved in the factory are referred to the local employers' association. A company with branches in two or more areas plays no direct part in the procedure. This hampers any comprehensive control of pay structure throughout a multi-plant firm. If industry-wide procedures established a joint negotiating body covering the factory or the company, and empowered it to deal for the factory or the company as a whole, with all matters of pay and conditions not covered by industry-wide substantive agreements, then fragmentation might be avoided. But few procedures in private industry provide anything of the kind.

68. Workplace bargaining is informal because of the predominance of unwritten understandings and of custom and practice. Informality applies not only to arrangements concerning pay and conditions of work at the factory, but also to the procedure under which these arrangements are

reached. Most industry-wide agreements give only sketchy guidance about the procedure to be followed within the factory. There is, for example, rarely any provision for compensating shop stewards for any loss of earnings due to their work as stewards. Usually nothing is said about stewards holding meetings with their constituents on the employers' premises, inside or outside working hours. Our investigations show that in factories with several shop stewards there is usually a "senior steward" or "convenor of stewards", but no provision is made for this in engineering or in many other procedures. Joint committees of stewards and managers to discuss and settle problems are also normal, but if they are mentioned in industry-wide procedure agreements there may be little guidance on their powers and conduct of business. Some managements draw up their own procedures in agreement with their shop stewards or district union officers, but it is more common to rely on precedent. Even where written procedures are established they often come to be "short-circuited" in the interests of speedy settlements.

69. In addition to these characteristics of workplace bargaining, there is one more important aspect of industrial relations at the place of work to be noted. In many instances the word "bargaining" is an inappropriate term for the way in which some decisions are reached, for the essential ingredients of discussion and agreement may both be absent. This is so when an issue is settled by custom and practice. If the custom is clear there is no discussion and nothing to decide. It is equally so when the decision is taken by workers and accepted by management. If managers acquiesce in a decision to work with non-unionists no longer, or to impose a limit on output, there has been no discussion and nothing that could be called an agreement. It is a matter of unilateral regulation by workers.

70. These characteristics of collective bargaining provide the explanation for the pattern of strikes in this country, which we discuss at greater length in Chapter VII. Although the number of working days lost in strikes in this country has remained relatively low since 1926, the average number of strikes a year in the last decade has been higher than ever before. The number of strikes in mining has dropped, from over two thousand in 1956 to 553 in 1966 and (provisionally) 391 in 1967. Meanwhile strikes in other industries have risen from 572 in 1956 to 1,384 in 1966 and (provisionally) 1,694 in 1967. This second trend now dominates the picture.

71. There is no tendency for official strikes to rise from year to year, and recently they have accounted for only five per cent of the total. The remainder are "unofficial"; they lack the approval of the appropriate trade union authority. Almost invariably they are also "unconstitutional", that is they occur before the various stages of the appropriate procedure for dealing with disputes have been able to deal with the matter, often indeed before any of the stages have been used.

72. The overwhelming majority of these strikes are not concerned with industry-wide issues in any way. They arise from workshop and factory disputes, and are settled within the workshop and the factory. Indeed the incidence of such strikes is a good deal higher than the official statistics suggest. Evidence from figures collected by individual industries and firms show that a good many relatively small strikes escape the net even though

they are large enough to be recorded; and there are also the strikes which are too small to be included. All these must be workshop and factory stoppages.

73. In addition there are other forms of workshop pressure: overtime bans, work-to-rule, go-slows and so on. The evidence is that these too are mainly used in factory and workshop disputes, and that their usage is also rising.

74. The decentralisation of collective bargaining has taken place under the pressure of full employment which has been almost continuous since 1938. Full employment encourages bargaining about pay at the factory and workshop levels. Because they cannot easily be replaced the bargaining power of individuals and groups of workers is increased; and because their employer is anxious to keep them, and perhaps to recruit new workers, he may be willing to "bid up" their pay without much prompting. But most other industrialised countries have also experienced full employment over most of this period. In Britain it has brought special consequences because of the way in which our industrial organisations have reacted to it. Among these reactions has been a decline in the authority of employers' associations.

EMPLOYERS' ASSOCIATIONS

75. The practice of industry-wide bargaining is closely bound up with the existence of employers' associations. Trade unions can and do bargain with individual firms. In the United States this is the standard form of collective bargaining. But except where a single undertaking embraces a whole industry, industry-wide bargaining requires association among employers. Consequently the growing importance in average earnings of payments settled in the factory represents a waning in the direct control over pay exercised by employers' associations.

76. In most public services and nationalised industries agreed rates of pay are regarded as standard, so far as timeworkers are concerned. In the private sector this is true of electrical contracting. However an inquiry into employers' associations conducted on our behalf shows that electrical contracting is exceptional. Of twenty-four industry-wide associations which negotiate wage rates, twenty were described by their officials as negotiating "basic rates" only, allowing management at local level to agree to higher or supplementary rates, whereas four asserted that their associations' rates were "effective rates, with very little freedom to negotiate other rates at local level". On further questioning, however, one of these four officials changed his position, saying that the rates were in fact minima, and another said that his organisation made no effort to prevent its members exceeding the rate if they wished. The other two emphasised that their powers were limited to persuasion.[1]

77. The contribution made by employers' associations to industrial relations has changed greatly since 1914. Up till then they were innovators. In industries such as coal and iron they instituted collective regulation of pay on the employers' side of industry before stable unions were formed; in iron, in hosiery and in other industries it was the employers who took the

---

[1] Research Paper No. 7, *Employers' Associations*, HMSO 1967, pp. 92-93.

initiative in developing collective bargaining with the unions on a district basis; in several of our most important industries, including engineering and building, the employers' associations forced the unions, in some instances through prolonged lock-outs, to accept the first principle of industry-wide bargaining—that local disputes should be submitted to a central conference before a strike or lock-out is begun. By contrast, from 1914 until very recently nearly every important innovation in industrial relations which was not the work of the unions came from the Government or from individual companies. The introduction of the second principle of industry-wide bargaining—the settlement of general movements of pay in industry-wide negotiations—was mainly a consequence of Government intervention in industrial relations during the first world war; and the Government had to call new employers' associations into existence in some industries in order to create Joint Industrial Councils for industry-wide bargaining.

78. Recent years have brought a considerable development in "fringe benefits", but only in public services and the nationalised industries has this been generally accomplished through industry-wide schemes. Elsewhere, the Ministry of Labour said in written evidence, such matters as "arrangements for dealing with possible redundancies, sick pay, pension schemes and the circumstances justifying individual dismissal have not been the subject for collective bargaining generally". Instead they have been settled within firms. This has not been a transfer of authority from employers' associations, but innovation which has largely passed them by.

79. In some instances methods of government and administration of the associations have failed to keep up with the times. The Engineering Employers' Federation still has no formal place in its constitution for the large companies owning many factories which have come to play so important a part in the industry. The Federation's 4,600 members are grouped into 35 local associations. Companies cannot belong to the Federation directly but individual factories belong to local associations. Some large companies have both "federated" and "non-federated" factories. Consequently the General Council of the Federation, elected by the local associations, does not give adequate representation to the major firms. The real business of the Federation, however, is conducted by a Management Board made up of the office-holders, representatives of the local associations, and co-opted members. The latter are "persons who, from their wide industrial experience, can make a valuable contribution to the deliberations and discussions of the Management Board".[1] The majority are senior directors of major firms, but most of them lack specialist knowledge in personnel matters. To meet this deficiency the officers of the Federation have had to devise special means of consultation outside the formal constitution.

80. According to the Confederation of British Industry, "in many major industries federated companies employ 80 per cent of the industry's labour force, and in few industries is the proportion below 50 per cent". Evidence from particular industries shows that the "non-federated" firms are for the most part relatively small. This poses the question: why most medium-sized and large British firms should continue to belong to employers' associations?

[1]Written Evidence of the Engineering Employers' Federation.

21

81. Where an association also deals with commercial matters, the value of its commercial services may be the explanation; but membership is also high in associations which restrict themselves to labour matters. Some associations provide a financial indemnity to firms involved in stoppages, but this is not thought to be an important consideration in retaining membership. Of more general interest is the service rendered by associations in representing their members' views to Government departments on proposed legislation and orders, and in giving their members advice on the meaning and application of Acts and regulations which have come into force. A number of associations have instituted training departments and work study departments to advise and assist their members. Probably, however, the most important benefit for most members is access to a disputes procedure. Especially when there is the prospect of a stoppage, managers find outside support, even moral support, very welcome. The settlement provided by the procedure may not be precisely to their taste, and the stoppage may not be averted, but at least the managers know that, so long as they abide by the advice of their association, their fellow-managers throughout the industry will be committed to approve their actions.

82. Above all, however, membership of employers' associations is a consequence of unquestioning commitment to maintain the formal system of industrial relations. The system provides for industry-wide bargaining; employers' associations are essential for this; therefore companies belong to employers' associations. In practice managers have more and more difficulty in reconciling reality with the formal system, but most of them have not yet questioned the formal system itself. On the contrary, it still seems to offer an alternative to anarchy. It has " stood the test of time ".

MANAGEMENT

83. The readiness of employers to federate does not, however, arise from a desire for strong organisation. On the contrary, the changing status of employers' associations is the consequence of companies allowing matters to be settled in their own factories and workshops instead of holding closely to common regulation.

84. Equally, however, most companies do not have comprehensive and well-ordered agreements for regulating the employment of labour within their factories over and above the minimum conditions laid down in industry-wide agreements. Generally speaking only non-federated concerns negotiate with the unions as companies. Federated companies generally leave negotiations to their factory managers, but comprehensive factory agreements are as rare as comprehensive company agreements. Factory managers may enter into written settlements on some issues to supplement industry-wide agreements, but on other matters there will be oral undertakings and on still others each workshop will have its own practices.

85. Why is this so? One reason is provided by the attachment of British employers to their associations. Even now some associations are reluctant to admit that the rates they negotiate are only minima, and in the past many more would have been unwilling to do so. A board of directors may be willing to pay more than the agreed rates, but to advertise it in a formal

company agreement would be a different matter. Even in recent years several companies have left their associations in order to sign productivity agreements with the unions, one purpose of which has been to introduce orderly company or factory pay structures. Esso, Mobil, Alcan and several major bus undertakings have done so. Other companies have been able to sign such agreements only because they were non-federated and therefore not bound by industry-wide agreements.

86. The situation is now beginning to change. Other companies have been able to negotiate productivity agreements without leaving their associations, and some associations are beginning to offer positive encouragement to productivity agreements.

87. Secondly, methods of wage payment and the ways they are applied have obstructed the development of orderly company and factory pay structures. Most important of these is payment by results. In the nineteenth century employers' associations and trade unions tried where they could to regulate piecework by drawing up " lists " of piecework prices to apply throughout the areas of their jurisdiction. This method was used in printing, shipbuilding, iron and steel, hosiery, lace and clothing, and above all in the great cotton industry of that time. The success of these lists depended, however, on standard methods of production and standard machinery. Otherwise standard prices would have brought very different levels of earnings in different factories. When piecework was introduced into engineering following the development of mass production, standard lists could not be used, for machines were not standardised and methods of production changed again and again. The prices were therefore fixed separately for each job in each factory. This left scope for wide variations in earnings, both within and between factories and the scope grew with the spread of piecework from 5 per cent of the male labour force in engineering in 1886 to about 46 per cent in 1961. The spread of mass production methods to other industries including chemicals, rubber, food manufacture and light metals led to systems of payment by results akin to those in engineering. Meanwhile most of the old price-lists dropped out of use.

88. Within the factory it is possible to achieve a fair degree of consistency in fixing piecework prices by using the techniques of work study. Even so, there is room for error. Of central importance is the accuracy of " effort-rating ", or judging whether the individual under study is a worker of average ability working at a normal piecework speed, and making an adjustment upwards or downwards for any deviation from that standard. Reasonable consistency can be achieved and maintained where time-studies are made by men and women trained by the same method and subject to frequent cross-checking. But such rigorous control is far from general in British industry.

89. Moreover in many factories work study is not in use even to-day and prices are fixed by bargaining methods often described as those of a " Persian market ". In many factories where it is used its results are very considerably modified in negotiation with individual workers and shop stewards. Where jobs change frequently, new prices have to be fixed, with new opportunities to bargain. There may also be negotiations over circumstances where piece-workers are idle through no fault of their own, such as a shortage of parts, or

23

are unable to reach their normal earnings because of faulty machinery or poor materials. The outcome can be erratic and rising piecework earnings, notorious in the car industry, but common enough elsewhere. These in turn promote attempts by workers to stabilise their earnings by such methods as holding back some of the " tickets " recording the completion of jobs in a good week to hand in later during a week in which earnings would otherwise be low, or by imposing " ceilings " on output.

90. Where pieceworkers and timeworkers are employed in the same factory rising piecework earnings lead to demands for increased pay from the time-workers. To meet them all manner of " lieu " payments have been intro-duced, some of them fluctuating with the earnings of pieceworkers or with the output of the factory.

91. Even where timework is the rule, the granting of merit pay, grade rates, extra payments for special conditions or particular jobs can lead to com-peting claims from groups of workers who feel that they have been left behind. Various techniques of " job evaluation " have been devised to determine the relationship between jobs and to establish a systematic struc-ture of wage rates for them, but, although fairly common in white-collar employment, job evaluation has as yet been applied to only a small minority of manual workers in Britain.

92. In addition there is overtime pay. Throughout the fifties and sixties the volume of overtime in Britain has fluctuated about a rising trend. Although the standard working week has in most industries fallen from 47 or 48 hours in 1938 to 40 to-day, the average weekly hours actually worked by men fell by only one and a half between 1938 and 1967. In 1967 their average overtime was then running at more than six hours a week, and in some industries, such as cement and road haulage, it ran at about fifteen hours a week. The notion that labour shortage requires these levels of overtime is refuted by comparison with countries abroad. Among countries for which figures are available, only France comes close to the British level. The others are well below. The only simple explanation which fits the facts is that overtime is widely used in Britain to give adult males levels of pay which they and those who arrange the overtime regard as acceptable. But who does arrange it? In some companies detailed returns are required and overtime is centrally checked and controlled. Commonly, however, it is arranged by the managers and supervisors immediately responsible for production. Consequently levels of overtime may differ from section to section and from department to department within the same firm. It is not unusual for directors and senior managers to have little knowledge concerning the detailed distribution of overtime and the purposes which it actually serves.

93. Effective regulation of overtime has been hindered by the notion of " managerial prerogative ". This holds that matters not settled in collective agreements should be decided by managers, although managers can if they wish consult with their employees, or representatives of their employees, before taking their decisions. Decisions about the working and distribution of overtime have generally been regarded by managers as within their prerogative. Consequently arrangements made with workers and shop

stewards about overtime tend to be informal and tacit. Managerial prerogative has also generally covered the employment and discharge of workers, the manning of machines, the pace of work, the introduction of new machinery and new jobs. These matters have therefore usually been excluded from formal negotiations, and—piecework apart—decisions on pay have been largely divorced from decisions about the work which is to be done for the pay; this being within managerial prerogative. Accordingly, where arrangements have been made with workers and shop stewards on methods of work, they have also tended to be informal.

94. The growth in the size of factories and companies, which has been an important factor in the transfer of power from the associations to managers, has also led to a division of functions within management which has brought specialisation including specialisation in industrial relations. From a tiny band of women factory welfare officers in 1914, personnel managers have multiplied to well over ten thousand to-day, most of them men; and the scope of the job has greatly increased. This poses a further problem. If companies have their own personnel specialists, why have they not introduced effective personnel policies to control methods of negotiation and pay structures within their firms?

95. Many firms have no such policy, and perhaps no conception of it. They employ a personnel officer to be responsible for certain tasks: staff records, selection, training, welfare, negotiation and consultation. Many of the older generation of personnel managers see themselves simply as professional negotiators. Even if a personnel manager has the ability to devise an effective personnel policy, the director responsible for personnel (if there is one), or the board as a whole, may not want to listen to him. Many firms had acquired disorderly pay structures and unco-ordinated personnel practices before they appointed a personnel manager, and the burden of dealing with disputes and problems as they arise has absorbed his whole time and energy.

SHOP STEWARDS AND WORK GROUPS

96. In most factories in which trade unions are strong their members in each workshop choose one of their number to speak for them. If there is more than one union, each usually has its own representative, although in some instances one representative speaks for two or more unions. He or she may go under a number of titles, but the most common is " shop steward ". In some undertakings works committees or councils are elected by all the workers, regardless of union membership. Where this is so, the shop steward may be elected to the committee, or the committee member may be accepted as the steward, as in the railways' Local Departmental Committees. In some unions in which the branch is based on the factory, branch officers carry out the tasks which shop stewards perform elsewhere.

97. These tasks include recruiting new members and seeing that existing members do not lapse. The stewards may be helped in this by an understanding that only union members will be employed. About two out of five of Britain's trade unionists are covered by some such understanding. A small minority of these arrangements are formal closed shop agreements between unions and employers, but the great majority are informally sustained, mainly

25

by the vigilance of shop stewards. In many instances shop stewards are also responsible for collecting union subscriptions. Some unions provide for separate collecting stewards appointed by the branch, but the two offices are frequently held by the same person. In addition shop stewards have a responsibility for communications between unions and members; and with average attendance at branch meetings well below ten per cent, this is the main link between unions and their members.

98. These are important services. Without shop stewards, trade unions would lack for members, for money, and for means of keeping in touch with their members. Even so none of them is the most important of the British shop steward's tasks. That is the service which he performs by helping to regulate workers' pay and working conditions and by representing them in dealings with management.

99. Until a few years ago little was known for certain about this part of the steward's work, but several studies have now appeared and are summarised in our first research paper. Their findings have now been generally confirmed by the inquiry conducted for us by the Social Survey[1]. First of all it must be emphasised that there is no uniformity. A minority of stewards do not negotiate with managers at all, whereas some of them negotiate over a wide range of issues. But over half of them regularly deal with managers over some aspect of pay, and about half of them deal regularly with some question relating to hours of work, the most common being the level and distribution of overtime. About a third of them regularly handle disciplinary issues on behalf of their members, and other matters which some of them settle include the distribution of work, the pace of work, the manning of machines, transfers from one job to another, the introduction of new machinery and new jobs, taking on new labour and redundancy. Since there are probably about 175,000 stewards in the country, compared with perhaps 3,000 full-time trade union officers, this suggests that shop stewards must be handling many times the volume of business conducted by their full-time officers.

100. From where does the shop steward derive his authority to deal with all these items? Where union rule books mention shop stewards, and many of them do not, they generally say something about method of appointment, and the body to whom the steward is nominally responsible. They may mention the duties of recruiting and retaining members, and collecting subscriptions. If the business of representing members is touched on, little is said about it. Most major unions now have *Shop Stewards' Handbooks*, which set out some of these tasks at greater length. But when it comes to telling the steward what issues he is competent to handle and how he should go about raising them, most handbooks refer the steward to the industry-wide agreement in force in his industry. These in their turn are rarely comprehensive. Few say much more than the engineering agreement, which authorises the steward to take up questions which the worker or workers directly concerned have been unable to settle with the foreman. The engineering steward is to raise them with the " Shop Manager " and/or Head Shop Foreman and, if need be, to have them considered by a Works Committee.

---

[1]Research Paper No. 10, W. E. J. McCarthy and S. R. Parker, *Shop Stewards and Workshop Relations*, HMSO 1968.

101. In dealing with pay or overtime or discipline the steward could be dealing with the application of industry-wide agreements, a responsibility mentioned in most of the handbooks. In fact this rarely happens, for two reasons. In the first place most industry-wide agreements on pay lay down minimum rates or minimum levels of piecework earnings which are very generally exceeded. In dealing with such issues, therefore, the steward must be concerned with obtaining or retaining a concession in excess of the terms in the agreement. In the second place most industry-wide agreements say nothing at all about many of the issues with which the steward deals, such as discipline, the pace of work, the introduction of new machinery and the distribution of overtime.

102. In dealing with this second class of issue the steward might merely be entering into consultation at the discretion of management on matters outside the industry-wide agreement but nevertheless of interest to the workers. However, case studies show that this is not so. When a decision is reached it is regarded as an agreement even though it may not be recorded. Managers would not normally alter it without further negotiation, and if they did sanctions might be applied. These are not the procedures of joint consultation. Joint consultation, moreover, has never been as popular with shop stewards as with managers. A wealth of evidence supports the conclusions reached by Dr. McCarthy that shop stewards regard " any committee on which they serve which cannot reach decisions . . . as essentially an inferior or inadequate substitute for proper negotiating machinery ", and that joint consultative committees in the strict sense " cannot survive the development of effective shop floor organisation. Either they must change their character and become essentially negotiating committees carrying out functions which are indistinguishable from the processes of shop floor bargaining, or they are boycotted by shop stewards and, as the influence of the latter grows, fall into disuse."[1]

103. In any case there are many shop floor decisions on these issues in which managers take no part at all. " Ceilings " on piecework earnings and limits imposed by road haulage drivers on the scheduling of their vehicles are examples of the regulation of work by workers themselves. The distribution of overtime is another matter which may be left to the stewards.

104. These instances show the basis of the shop steward's power. He could not of his own volition impose a limit on output or a ban on non-unionists. This can only be done by decision of the group of workers which he represents. " Custom and practice ", which settles so much in British industrial relations, consists of the customs and practices observed by work groups. If workers did not keep to them, the customs would cease to exist.

105. The work group does not derive its power from the union. The printing chapel with its chapel father, the best-organised of all work groups, existed before the printing unions and was subsequently incorporated into their branch structure. Work groups can exert considerable control over

[1]Research Paper No. 1, W. E. J. McCarthy, *The Role of Shop Stewards in Industrial Relations*, p. 33.

their members even where there are no trade unions, or where unions refuse them recognition. Until recently there were no shop stewards in most British docks. Accordingly the " ganger " or " hatch-boss " negotiated for the members of the gang in any dispute with management, although he was paid to be the gang's supervisor and all negotiations were supposed to be reserved for full-time officers. In coalmining " chargemen " performed the same service for facework gangs, although they too were supervisors.

106. Full employment would in any case have increased the influence of the work group, but British managers have augmented it by their preference for keeping many matters out of agreements, by the inadequacy of their methods of control over systems of payments, by their preference for informality and by their tolerance of custom and practice.

107. There is no question but that this is largely the choice of management. Previous inquiries have shown that where managers have a choice of dealing with either full-time officers or shop stewards, three-quarters of them choose shop stewards[1], and our own surveys have confirmed this finding. Their chief reason for this is the " intimate knowledge of the circumstances of the case " possessed by shop stewards, but this is as much a consequence of their preference as a cause of it. If managers choose to deal with shop stewards on an informal basis, full-time officers cannot be expected to acquire a detailed knowledge of the issues which arise in the factory.

108. In an earlier survey[2] conducted by Dr. McCarthy managers were questioned about their preference for informal and unwritten arrangements. Four reasons were generally put forward. If agreements were formalised they would become established *de jure* rights which could not be withdrawn; even if existing stewards would not abuse formal confirmation the next generation might, and managers like to believe that they can vary privileges according to the response they get; once the process of formalising began it would extend indefinitely; and, finally, " some *de facto* concessions could not be written down because management, particularly at board level, would not be prepared to admit publicly that they had been forced to accept such modifications in their managerial prerogatives and formal chains of command ". The more concessions are made the stronger become all these reasons for preferring informality.

109. It does not follow however that shop stewards and work groups exercise effective control where industry-wide agreements and managers fail to do so. In systems of payment by results with no effective work study, each man may settle his own times with the rate fixer, and this may lead to a wide spread of earnings with an uncontrolled upward drift. In other instances the control of shop stewards over the distribution of overtime may be undermined by workers " greedy " for overtime earnings. In such circumstances industrial relations can border on anarchy.

110. Consequently it is often wide of the mark to describe shop stewards as " trouble-makers ". Trouble is thrust upon them. In circumstances of this

---

[1]Clegg, Killick and Adams, *Trade Union Officers*, Blackwell 1961, pp. 174-7.
[2]Research Paper No. 1, W. E. J. McCarthy, *The Role of Shop Stewards in British Industrial Relations*, pp. 26-29.

kind they may be striving to bring some order into a chaotic situation, and management may rely heavily on their efforts to do so. Both case studies and surveys show that this sort of situation is not uncommon. In addition the shop-floor decisions which generally precede unofficial strikes are often taken against the advice of shop stewards. Thus shop stewards are rarely agitators pushing workers towards unconstitutional action. In some instances they may be the mere mouthpieces of their work groups. But quite commonly they are supporters of order exercising a restraining influence on their members in conditions which promote disorder. To quote our survey of shop stewards and workshop relations[1]: "For the most part the steward is viewed by others, and views himself, as an accepted, reasonable and even moderating influence; more of a lubricant than an irritant."

TRADE UNIONS

111. Trade unions have been as guilty as employers' associations and managers of sustaining the facade of industry-wide bargaining with its pretence of dealing with everything of importance for collective agreements. They cannot, however, bear the primary responsibility for the drift of earnings away from wage rates and the growing ineffectiveness of disputes machinery which have weakened industry-wide bargaining. These have been the consequence of the reaction of employers' associations and companies to full employment, a reaction which it was not within the unions' power to control. Moreover there has not been on the unions' side an exact parallel of the decline in authority of employers' associations. Fitfully and haltingly most of the major unions have responded to changing conditions by recognising shop stewards and making some effort to equip them. Thus it is not so much that the unions have lost power as that there has been a shift of authority within them. Certain features of trade union structure and government have however helped to inflate the power of work groups and shop stewards within the factory.

112. The first of these is multi-unionism, the existence of two or more unions, sometimes many more, in most British industries and factories. In this respect British trade union structure is extremely complex. Description is hampered by the inadequacy of the types traditionally employed for classifying trade unions—craft, industrial and general. Most major British unions fit none of them. But some outline must be attempted.

113. In most industries and services it is possible to divide the labour force into groups such as white-collar workers, maintenance workers and process workers. It is common in Britain for each group to have its own union or unions. Further subdivision can separate white-collar employees into clerical workers, supervisors, technicians and administrators; or maintenance workers into members of separate crafts and their mates. It is by no means unusual for each of these sub-groups to have its separate union. It can happen that two or more unions are competing for members in one of these sub-groups. Our surveys suggest that, even if white-collar workers and their unions are left out of account, about four out of every five trade unionists in Britain work in a multi-union establishment, and perhaps one in six of them belongs to a grade of worker in which two or more unions are competing for members.

[1]*Op. cit.*, p. 56.

114.   If this was the whole picture, the British trade union movement would consist of a large number of small unions, and in fact 480 out of Britain's 574 trade unions have less than ten thousand members.   At the other extreme, however, nine trade unions, with over a quarter of a million members each, account for more than half the trade unionists in the country.   The biggest of them have achieved their position by linking together groups and sub-groups of workers from different industries and services in patterns of astounding complexity which can be given historical explanations, but yield to no logical interpretation.

115.   The Transport and General Workers' Union, for example, organises the great majority of all grades of worker in one or two industries, such as the bus industry, process workers in most manufacturing industries and labourers in shipbuilding and building.   In addition it has a thriving section for clerical and supervisory staff.   Its members are to be found in nearly all the country's major industries and services, and in most of them the members of the General and Municipal Workers' Union are to be seen alongside, for its structure is roughly similar.   Both began as "labourers'" unions.   Starting from a very different origin two one-time "craft" societies, the Amalgamated Union of Engineering and Foundry Workers[1] and the Electrical Trades Union, now appear more and more like the general unions in their make-up.   Their members also work in nearly every industry and service in the country.   In many of them they cover the maintenance craftsmen, and perhaps also their mates, but in engineering and elsewhere these two unions compete with the general unions in organising production workers, both men and women.   In addition each of them is developing its own white-collar section.   The coverage of many other large and middle-sized unions is only somewhat less irrational and complex than the coverage of these four.

116.   This strange structure strengthens the position of work groups, and increases their independence, in three ways.   First, many trade union branches consist of small groups of members from a number of different factories or offices.   The branch is therefore divorced from the real business of the union at the place of work, but it nevertheless remains the official means of contact between the union and its members.   Secondly, full-time union officers cannot easily keep in touch with small groups of members scattered over scores of factories.   Thirdly, the several unions within the factory or office have to work together.   Our evidence is that more than two-thirds of shop stewards have at their place of work a committee in which they meet with management to discuss and settle problems, and that two-thirds of these committees are multi-union.   Where that is so, the committees are not easily made responsible to a trade union authority outside the factory.   Perhaps this helps to explain another finding of our surveys, that full-time officers outside the factories seem to find the difficulties arising from multi-unionism more intractable than do

---

[1]The Amalgamated Union of Engineering and Foundry Workers was formed in January 1968 as a result of the amalgamation of the Amalgamated Engineering Union and the Amalgamated Union of Foundry Workers of Great Britain and Ireland.   When we use the name "Amalgamated Engineering Union" in this report we do so because we are referring to evidence or other information which relates either to that union before the amalgamation took place or to that part of the new union which remains governed by the rules of the Amalgamated Engineering Union.

shop stewards inside. Only half the stewards who often dealt with multi-union issues thought that it would help if fewer unions were involved, whereas four out of five full-time officers thought it would help.

117. It is possible, however, to exaggerate the importance of these influences. The overwhelming majority of union members do not attend branch meetings whether the branch is based on the area or the factory. The evidence is that members and stewards follow much the same pattern of behaviour in both types of branch. Equally the fabric of industrial relations seems to be much the same in industries and factories with simple union structures as with complex structures. At one time the contrast between a strike-prone Ford and a strike-free Vauxhall was widely explained by the twenty-odd unions at Ford and the two (subsequently three) at Vauxhall. Since 1962, Ford has radically altered the manner of its industrial relations, reducing the number of its strikes, without a significant change in the number of unions; and in 1967 Vauxhall's record of industrial peace was shattered by a major stoppage.

118. There is also some truth in the complaint that trade union leadership is " out of touch ". In the conferences and committees of our major unions there are in fact several obstacles to the effective expression of the members' opinions on industrial issues. Nearly all unions have an annual or biennial conference to make policy and amend the rules. In the largest unions, and in many smaller unions, the delegates to conference come from a number of different industries and services, so that most of them are necessarily un-informed on any specific industrial issue. Some of the unions therefore exclude resolutions on the affairs of a particular industry from conference business. A partial remedy is provided by the thirteen trade groups of the Transport and General Workers' Union, each of which has its own conference, and some other unions employ similar expedients. Even so, most of the trade groups have to deal with the affairs of several kindred industries, and they must in the end be subject to the overriding authority of the union's executive.

119. The executive committees or councils, responsible for union business between conferences, may also be drawn from a range of different industries, but many of them are now bodies of full-time officers. The members of the executives of the Amalgamated Engineering Union and the Electrical Trades Union are employed full-time as executive members. Half of the ten members of the executive of the General and Municipal Workers' Union are full-time district secretaries. The Mineworkers' executive consists of representatives of its areas, almost all of them leading full-time area officers. These unions have moved a long way from the nineteenth century notion of a trade union executive as a body of men working at their trade, in close touch with the members, and able to see that union business was conducted to the liking of the members.

120. Multi-unionism adds to the problem. In most major industries and services no single union is in a position to determine what the unions as a whole shall do. This has to be settled at a meeting of them all, where full-time officers generally lead the delegations from each union.

121. Finally the process of collective bargaining itself is bound to give further power to the officers who conduct the negotiations and make the crucial com-promises.

31

122. Consequently, it is not surprising if from time to time groups of trade union members protest that industry-wide agreements are not to their liking, and even indulge in mutinous strikes. But such strikes are relatively rare. The great majority of unofficial strikes have nothing to do with industry-wide agreements. It is a mistake therefore to suppose that the shift of power to the work group could have been prevented by a more ready exercise of disciplinary powers by trade union leaders. Even if successful this could do little to halt the transfer of authority from management to the work group. And it is unlikely that it would be successful. Trade union leaders do exercise discipline from time to time, but they cannot be industry's policemen. They are democratic leaders in organisations in which the seat of power has almost always been close to the members. For a brief period between the wars the conjunction of industry-wide bargaining and heavy unemployment gave trade union leaders an unusual ascendancy in their own organisations. Before that, however, power was generally concentrated in the branches and the districts. Since then, workshop organisation has taken their place.

ATTITUDES

123. It might be expected that arrangements such as have been described would be unpopular with large numbers of those who work under them. Employers' associations might be expected to bemoan their loss of power; managers to decry the power of shop stewards; full-time officers to complain of their exclusion from workshop bargaining. It might also be supposed that shop stewards would be hostile to managers and contemptuous of their full-time officers. It is, however, one of the most consistent findings of the surveys carried out for us that such opinions are to be found among only tiny minorities within each group.

124. More than four out of five officials of employers' associations said that they had sufficient influence over their members. Only 2 per cent of managers held that shop stewards were unreasonable, 95 per cent taking the view that they were either very reasonable or fairly reasonable. Four managers out of five thought shop stewards were either very efficient or fairly efficient at their job. Nearly a third of them thought that shop stewards were a lot of help to management, and most of the remainder that shop stewards were of some help. Shop stewards reciprocated. Almost all of them thought that management was either " very reasonable " or " fairly reasonable " in dealings with them. Although some stewards rarely saw their full-time officer, only 6 per cent complained of difficulty in contacting him when they needed him. More than two-thirds of them thought he played " a very important part " in local negotiations. The proportion of full-time officers who thought they had sufficient influence over their members was no less than 87 per cent.

125. Managers were in some ways more critical than the other groups. A quarter of them had complaints about their employers' associations, most commonly on the grounds that they were weak and unable to enforce their decisions. Only 20 per cent of them thought full-time officers were very important in local negotiations. Even among managers, however, the critics are in a minority.

126. These and other findings suggest that the participants in the current arrangements are, generally speaking, well satisfied with them. How can their attitude be reconciled with the preceding analysis? The only possible answer is that these arrangements have some important advantages which impress themselves upon the participants; and they have.

127. The first advantage is that they are comfortable arrangements. They do not demand of the officials of employers' associations that they should take on the thankless task of enforcing decisions upon their members who are also their masters. They can devote their time to more manageable tasks. Busy full-time union officers are not called in to deal with trivial details within the factory. They can leave the shop stewards to carry on with the job, expecting the stewards to call them in when an issue cannot be resolved within the factory and has to " go into procedure ". Managers have considerable freedom to run their own industrial relations affairs without interference from outside. This also means that shop stewards enjoy considerable authority; but, since stewards are for the most part reasonable people, managers can normally come to an arrangement with them.

128. Secondly, the arrangements are flexible. They enable managers and stewards to circumvent rules and procedures which might otherwise get in their way; and when employers' associations and full-time trade union officers are called into a dispute, they can usually resolve it " on its merits ", reaching an *ad hoc* settlement without having to worry too much about the consequences elsewhere.

129. Finally, a very high degree of self-government in industry is provided. Not only do managers and shop stewards have a considerable freedom from outside interference, but above all work groups are given scope to follow their own customs and to take their own decisions.

130. These are important benefits, enough to explain widespread satisfaction with existing arrangements. They can be condemned only because the benefits are outweighed by the shortcomings: the tendency of extreme decentralisation and self-government to degenerate into indecision and anarchy; the propensity to breed inefficiency; and the reluctance to change—all of them characteristics which become more damaging as they develop, as the rate of technical progress increases, and as the need for economic growth becomes more urgent.

THE GOVERNMENT

131. So far we have been concerned almost exclusively with the private sector and with the operation of voluntary agreements and organisations. The Government now plays an important and growing part in the conduct of industrial relations. How does that part fit into the system?

132. The Government is the direct employer of civil servants. It is the paymaster in those public services such as the National Health Service, the educational services, the police and the fire services in which it supplies the bulk of the funds, and in which departmental representatives, directly or indirectly, play a major part in negotiating pay. The nationalised industries have greater formal independence in conducting their industrial relations, but major decisions are generally reviewed by the Government.

33

133. The pay of civil servants is a delicate issue. If it can be argued that they are underpaid the Government can be attacked as miserly and unjust, setting a poor example to other employers. On the other hand any suspicion that civil servants are overpaid would lead to criticisms of wasting the taxpayer's money. Most Governments have tried to avoid these dangers by relating the pay of civil servants as nearly as possible to that of comparable employees in private industry.

134. In Britain, following the reports of the Whitley Committee, the Government of the day was persuaded that if voluntary collective bargaining was the ideal system for private industry, it was also appropriate to the civil service. Accordingly, a series of joint " Whitley Councils " was established to negotiate pay and conditions of employment. Since the civil service could not recognise strikes and lock-outs as appropriate final sanctions, differences were to be settled in the last resort by arbitration.

135. That left over the question of the standards by which pay was to be regulated, but these have been elaborated by successive Royal Commissions on the Civil Service. There is now a Civil Service Pay Research Unit which conducts periodic investigations into the remuneration and work of outside " analogues " for each class of " non-industrial " civil servants, to discover exactly what they are paid and how close their duties are to those of the civil servants. These studies form the basis of negotiations on the Whitley Councils, and if need be of submissions to arbitration. Generally speaking civil servants are well-satisfied with this procedure.

136. Other groups of public employees also have striven to have their pay determined by the method of comparison. Following Report No. 18 of the National Board for Prices and Incomes, each industrial group within the industrial civil service has had its own pay structure based upon " what is paid for a 40-hour week to timeworkers engaged in similar activities in outside employment ". The Pilkington Commission and the Willink Commission suggested methods of comparison for the medical and dental professions, and for the police; and the independent review bodies for the pay of doctors and dentists, of the higher civil service and of the armed forces have all worked on the basis of comparisons.

137. On the other hand some of the nationalised industries have responded to the pressures of full employment in much the same way as private industry. On the railways, work-studied incentives have been generally introduced into the permanent way, goods and other departments. This form of payment is not so suitable for train men and traffic staff, but for them mileage allowances and productivity payments have been introduced or extended. Earnings have also been enhanced by overtime working, and the consequence of the whole system has been to raise railway earnings to much the same level as earnings in outside industry. Similar developments have been experienced in the gas industry. The Prices and Incomes Board found that in October 1966 the earnings of adult male manual workers in the gas industry averaged £20 5s. 2d., made up of £13 5s. 9d. basic pay, £4 10s. 5d. overtime, 5s. service increments, 18s. 3d. shift allowances, 17s. 2d. incentive payments and 8s. 7d. other payments.

138. Apart from the Factory Acts and recent legislation on prices and

incomes, the Government's two main instruments for intervention in industrial relations in the private sector are statutory wage regulation intended to deal with industries in which pay is low or organisation weak, and the Department of Employment and Productivity's powers of conciliation, arbitration and inquiry.

139. We comment in Chapter V on the paucity of earnings statistics in Wages Council industries. However, reports of the Prices and Incomes Board have provided detailed information on road haulage pay and on pay in one important section of retailing—Drapery, Outfitting and Footwear. A survey in September 1967 showed that the average pay of road haulage drivers was £22 7s. 9d., of which £12 13s. 4d. was basic pay, £1 5s. 9d. bonus and other payments, and £8 8s 8d. overtime payments for an average nominal working week of 58.6 hours. As the Board says: " The large amount of overtime represents units of payment rather than hours strictly worked; in other words, the size of the pay packet is determined not so much by the number of hours worked as by the number of hours for which the employer is prepared to pay." Little overtime is worked in retailing, and earnings above the minimum therefore come mainly from higher rates than those prescribed by the Wages Council or from commission on sales. In October 1966 the statutory minimum rates for male shop assistants varied from £9 15s. 0d. to £10 16s. 0d. according to the area of the country; average earnings were £15 16s. 1d. for a working week of 40.3 hours.

140. It appears, therefore, that in some of the Wages Council industries the pressure of full employment has produced a gap between the statutory minimum for men and their actual earnings not unlike that between basic rates and average earnings in better organised industries. The major difference is that payments over the minimum may be even less subject to collective regulation in Wages Council industries than elsewhere.

141. The aim of the Department of Employment and Productivity's conciliation services is to assist the two sides to reach a settlement for themselves or to persuade them to allow the dispute to be referred to arbitration or inquiry. Such studies as have been made of the work of arbitration tribunals suggest that in pay disputes they tend to award settlements at about the same level as that of voluntary pay increases elsewhere. Where arbitration is by consent of both sides this course of action is almost inevitable. If the tribunal diverged markedly from the pattern of settlements elsewhere one side or the other would soon decide not to make use of its services. In the past, Courts of Inquiry and similar bodies have generally been used to provide a procedure which could yield a result similar to that of arbitration in disputes in which the parties were reluctant to make use of the existing tribunals.

142. Generally speaking, therefore, the Government's considerable powers of intervention in industrial relations are used to support the system of industrial relations as it has developed in private industry. The services of conciliation, arbitration and inquiry ensure that, as far as possible, disputes end in the kind of settlement that might have been expected if there had been no dispute. One way or another statutory wage fixation and systems of wage settlement in the public services for the most part yield results not very dissimilar from those achieved by collective bargaining elsewhere.

THE TWO SYSTEMS

143. We can now compare the two systems of industrial relations. The formal system assumes industry-wide organisations capable of imposing their decisions on their members. The informal system rests on the wide autonomy of managers in individual companies and factories, and the power of industrial work groups.

144. The formal system assumes that most if not all matters appropriate to collective bargaining can be covered in industry-wide agreements. In the informal system bargaining in the factory is of equal or greater importance.

145. The formal system restricts collective bargaining to a narrow range of issues. The range in the informal system is far wider, including discipline, recruitment, redundancy and work practices.

146. The formal system assumes that pay is determined by industry-wide agreements. In the informal system many important decisions governing pay are taken within the factory.

147. The formal system assumes that collective bargaining is a matter of reaching written agreements. The informal system consists largely in tacit arrangements and understandings, and in custom and practice.

148. For the formal system the business of industrial relations in the factory is joint consultation and the interpretation of collective agreements. In the informal system the difference between joint consultation and collective bargaining is blurred, as is the distinction between disputes over interpretation and disputes over new concessions; and the business of industrial relations in the factory is as much a matter of collective bargaining as it is at industry level.

149. The formal and informal systems are in conflict. The informal system undermines the regulative effect of industry-wide agreements. The gap between industry-wide agreed rates and actual earnings continues to grow. Procedure agreements fail to cope adequately with disputes arising within factories. Nevertheless, the assumptions of the formal system still exert a powerful influence over men's minds and prevent the informal system from developing into an effective and orderly method of regulation. The assumption that industry-wide agreements control industrial relations leads many companies to neglect their responsibility for their own personnel policies. Factory bargaining remains informal and fragmented, with many issues left to custom and practice. The unreality of industry-wide pay agreements leads to the use of incentive schemes and overtime payments for purposes quite different from those they were designed to serve.

150. Any suggestion that conflict between the two systems can be resolved by forcing the informal system to comply with the assumptions of the formal system should be set aside. Reality cannot be forced to comply with pretences.

151. There is, however, room for argument about the extent to which the informal system we have described applies to British industrial relations, and therefore for argument about the extent to which the formal system has ceased to apply. The informal system has been described mainly in terms of private industry, and not so much in terms of public employment; mainly in terms of manual workers and less in terms of white-collar workers; mainly in terms

of men and not of women; mainly in terms of organised workers and less in terms of the unorganised. In their written evidence to us the TUC divided industries into five classes according to the influence of industry-wide agreements on actual wages and salaries. Five million employees are not covered by agreements on pay and another million are covered mainly by company agreements. Of the remainder, the TUC placed four million in Wages Council industries, seven million in industries in which industry-wide agreements were closely followed at company and local level, and only six million in industries with industry-wide agreements where bargaining within companies has an important influence on actual earnings.

152. There is some validity in these categories but they greatly underestimate the scope of the informal system. As we have shown, the pattern of earnings in many Wages Council industries approximates to that in industries where factory bargaining has an important influence on pay. Those industries in which industry-wide agreements are, according to the TUC, closely followed include all the public services, although pay in many of these follows the same pattern, and private industries in which overtime earnings constitute almost as important an element in the pay packet as basic rates. We set out in Appendix 5 our view of how various industries might be classified according to the influence that industry-wide agreements and statutory wage regulation exercise on actual earnings.

153. The degree to which industry-wide agreements determine pay is not the only criterion of the extent to which the formal system determines behaviour. In those public services such as the civil service in which pay is effectively settled by central negotiations, the rates laid down, being based on comparisons with earnings in the private sector, reflect the influence of the informal system in determining pay in the private sector. Moreover, it would be a grave mistake to suppose that collective bargaining is concerned only with pay. Even when industry-wide agreements on pay are closely followed, bargaining on work practices and other issues can occupy an important place in industrial relations in the factory and may conflict with the assumptions of industry-wide bargaining.

154. The extent to which at the moment industry-wide agreements both on pay and on other issues are effective in the workplace cannot be exactly determined. What is of crucial importance is that the practices of the formal system have become increasingly empty, while the practices of the informal system have come to exert an ever greater influence on the conduct of industrial relations throughout the country; that the two systems conflict; and that the informal system cannot be forced to comply with the formal system.

Chapter IV

THE REFORM OF
COLLECTIVE BARGAINING

INTRODUCTION

155. Having analysed our system of industrial relations and set out what we consider to be its main defects, we turn now to the question of remedies. First we deal in this chapter with our proposals to meet the overriding need for a reconstruction of voluntary collective bargaining. In Chapter V we turn to the related topic of the extension of effective collective bargaining to those areas in which it is weak or non-existent. Chapters VI and VII deal with two specific aspects of industrial relations closely bound up with collective bargaining, the efficient use of manpower and the problems of strikes. They set out the evidence at greater length and show how the reform of collective bargaining can lead to improvements. There then follows, in Chapter VIII, the discussion of a subject closely related to that of strikes, the legal enforcement of collective agreements. Up to this point we are concerned with the collective institutions of industrial relations. The next three chapters deal mainly with the rights of the individual in industry. Chapter IX is concerned with unfair dismissal and makes proposals for dealing with this important source of injustice and conflict in industry by establishing more adequate rights. Chapter X deals with the establishment of labour tribunals to provide improved means for the judicial settlement of disputes between individual employers and employees. Chapter XI makes proposals for the protection of the rights of union members and of applicants for membership of trade unions. Chapters XII and XIII set out the implications of our proposals for trade unions and employers' associations. In Chapter XIV we deal with the law except in so far as it has already been covered, and in Chapter XV we turn to the subject of workers' participation in management. Finally, in Chapter XVI, we summarise our main conclusions and recommendations.

SIGNS OF CHANGE

156. Several developments in recent years suggest a growing dissatisfaction with the system of industrial relations described in the previous chapter, and a growing desire for change.

157. The first of these is the development of incomes policy. Sooner or later full employment leads to incomes policy. Rising or full employment is almost always accompanied by increases in pay which outstrip any rise in productivity, and therefore lead to higher costs and higher prices. At the same time demand for goods and services rises and imports go up. This leads to difficulties at home and, even more, abroad. Not only do we import more goods than we otherwise should, but if our prices rise faster than those of countries with which we compete our earnings from exports suffer; and a

38

balance of payments crisis follows. In Britain we have had a series of incomes policies since 1948, when the post-war Labour Government called for a period of restraint, most of them concerned almost exclusively with restricting the rate of increase of wage and salary rates. Experience over the last three years, however, has demonstrated that restricting rates is not enough. Earnings rise faster than rates, so that the policy-makers have become increasingly concerned with the agreements and methods of payment in the factory.

158. The 1965 White Paper on *Prices and Incomes Policy* permitted increases in pay above the norm laid down for money incomes in four circumstances, one of which was where there was a direct contribution to increasing productivity. This exception was a recognition that higher productivity can contribute to price stability just as much as can restraint in pay. It also acknowledged the development of productivity agreements— a radical departure from traditional methods of collective bargaining. Starting with Esso's refinery in Fawley a number of important undertakings have shown their discontent with the divorce between agreements on pay and the arrangement of work practices, with the distortion of payment systems and with the weakness of management control in industrial relations, by signing new agreements, generally on a company or factory basis, revising work practices in return for concessions on pay, absorbing additional payments into effective pay structures, and providing the basis for more efficient utilisation of labour and plant.

159. These agreements are only the most remarkable among a number of experiments in collective bargaining. Others include attempts to replace disintegrating piecework systems by better managed methods of payment, and a bid by the engineering industry to exercise greater control over pay in the factory by means of an industry-wide agreement known as the " package deal " signed in 1964. The Engineering Employers' Federation has also recently published a research paper[1] advocating productivity bargains and this contains many indications of new thinking in this industry, although not yet adopted as the Federation's policy.

160. With the passage of the Prices and Incomes Act in 1966, Parliament showed its growing willingness to intervene in the system of industrial relations where it judged voluntary action had failed. But this willingness has not been confined to incomes policy, and has been evident under Conservative as well as Labour administrations. In 1963 the Contracts of Employment Act laid down minimum periods of notice and obliged employers to give their workers written particulars of certain terms of their employment, indicating that Parliament felt that voluntary agreements gave inadequate protection in these respects. The Industrial Training Act 1964 and the Redundancy Payments Act 1965 were intended to make good the failure of voluntary arrangements to provide adequate training and sufficient mobility of labour.

161. This legislative trend has been accompanied by a tendency to place a restrictive judicial interpretation upon those provisions of the Trade Disputes Act 1906 which confer protection against civil actions upon trade unions and

---

[1]*Productivity Bargaining and the Engineering Industry*, March 1968.

others acting in contemplation or furtherance of a trade dispute. Both may reflect a swing in public opinion favouring greater legal intervention in industrial relations and the use of sanctions in support.

THE DIRECTION OF REFORM

162. These recent changes offer some guidance as to the direction which a reform of our system of industrial relations might take. Its central defect is the disorder in factory and workshop relations and pay structures promoted by the conflict between the formal and the informal systems. Consequently the remedy must seek to introduce greater order into factory and workshop relations. This cannot be accomplished by employers' associations and trade unions working at industry level, or by means of industry-wide agreements. What is required is effective and orderly collective bargaining over such issues as the control of incentive schemes, the regulation of hours actually worked, the use of job evaluation, work practices and the linking of changes in pay to changes in performance, facilities for shop stewards and disciplinary rules and appeals. In most industries industry-wide agreements cannot deal effectively with these issues because individual companies have not delegated authority to settle them to their associations, and they have no intention of doing so now. Even if they were willing it would make no difference, for variations between firms in size, management structure, management policies, technology and market situations would defeat any attempt to exercise detailed control over most of these issues from outside the firm even before it had begun.

163. A factory-wide agreement, however, can cover matters which industry-wide agreements must omit. It can, for example, deal with methods of production in the factory, and with the distribution of overtime. A factory agreement can regulate where an industry-wide agreement can only specify minimum conditions. It can, for instance, specify in detail the method of timing jobs for systems of payment by results and determine a realistic conversion factor from time to money. A factory agreement, moreover, can settle differential rates of pay which apply to jobs as they are actually performed in that factory, and lay down rates of merit pay together with the means of deciding merit. For all these reasons a factory agreement can regulate actual pay where many industry-wide agreements can deal only with minimum payments, and can therefore be the means of settling an effective and coherent pay structure.

164. A factory agreement can set out a procedure for dealing with grievances within the factory which suits the organisation and managerial structure of the factory, and one that it is therefore reasonable to expect managers, shop stewards and workers to follow. It can also include the constitution for a factory negotiating committee. If this committee covers all the unions in the factory then it can help to put an end to fragmented bargaining. It can be empowered to deal with work practices within the factory, so that it can negotiate changes in work practices to suit existing or proposed production methods.

165. A factory agreement can deal with subjects commonly excluded from industry-wide negotiations, such as redundancy and discipline. The steps to be taken when a redundancy is proposed can be set out in the agreement,

along with the method of selecting those to go. The agreement can include a disciplinary code, and prescribe a method of appeal for workers who feel aggrieved by disciplinary decisions.

166. A factory agreement can cover the rights and obligations of shop stewards within the factory. Within the limits of union rules it can set out the stewards' constituencies and the method of their election. The facilities for stewards to meet with each other and their chief steward can be covered, along with arrangements for meeting their constituents, access to a telephone and an office, and entitlement to pay while performing their jobs as stewards.

167. A factory agreement, however, does not accomplish any of these things automatically. It can make provision for them, but equally it may not. Even if it does, its provisions may not be observed. By itself no agreement can prevent increases being disguised as merit payments, or the abuse of a system of payment by results by both management and workers. The stages of a procedure agreement can be by-passed, telescoped or ignored. Fragmented bargaining and informal workshop understandings can flourish under a factory agreement as they can in its absence. All that is claimed for a factory agreement is that it is a means for the effective regulation of industrial relations within the factory where managers and workers choose to use it for that purpose. By contrast, even if the will is present, most industry-wide agreements cannot provide effective regulation of industrial relations, and could not be made to do so. No agreement can do a manager's job for him. A factory agreement, however, can assist competent managers. Many current industry-wide agreements have become a hindrance to them.

168. Who is in a position to make factory agreements the basis of industrial relations in Britain? Trade unions cannot do so by themselves. They can negotiate with employers or managers only at the level at which the latter are willing to meet them. Employers' associations cannot do so. They lack the authority and their members would not wish them to have it. Factory managers can do so only if authorised by their boards of directors. If Britain is to shift to factory agreements therefore the change must be accomplished by boards of directors.

169. If the change is made, boards of directors will lose the protection provided by the existing system against their being held fully responsible for their own personnel policies. At present boards can leave industry-wide agreements to their employers' associations, and the task of dealing with workers within those agreements to their subordinate managers. Removing this protection will direct the attention of companies to the need to develop their own personnel policies.

170. Boards of multi-plant companies may, however, prefer to negotiate company agreements rather than allow each factory manager to negotiate separately on his own. A company agreement will be more effective than a series of factory agreements in ensuring that the company's collective arrangements with the unions square with its personnel policies. The agreement will have to permit some scope to subordinate negotiating committees in each factory, especially since work practices are to be a subject of negotiation; but there is no reason why this delegation of authority cannot be accomplished successfully. There is a fundamental difference between factory negotiations

within the scope of present industry-wide agreements, and factory negotiations within a company agreement. The factory manager is a subordinate of the board of the company, but not of the employers' association. There is thus a greater possibility of controlling factory relations by means of a company agreement than by means of an industry-wide agreement. The basis of reform must therefore be a combination of company and factory agreements.

171. Boards of directors, and their managers, however, cannot accomplish the reform by themselves. They need the co-operation of the trade unions, which must sign the agreements and take their share of responsibility under them. This will demand reform within the unions. Most of them will need to appoint additional officers to negotiate and service the agreements along with the shop stewards. The constitution of the company and factory negotiating committees will require the presence of full-time officers, at least for certain decisions and the ratification of proceedings by the unions. Such a degree of contact between full-time officers and shop stewards may involve changes in union constitutions. Above all, in multi-union factories and companies the unions must be prepared to co-operate and to sign a common agreement.

172. These things are difficult but not impossible. Already trade unions have to negotiate with non-federated firms and in some instances the agreements they sign have some of these features. The experience of productivity agreements is especially relevant. In negotiating some of these agreements trade unions have been willing to work together as never before, and the process of negotiation has developed unusually close co-operation between full-time officers and shop stewards.

173. It is important to emphasise that these changes have been brought about by the process of negotiation. They did not precede negotiations, and if negotiations had had to wait until the trade unions had put their house in order, they would probably never have started. The significance of this can be illustrated by reference to a feature of the British trade union movement which many managers consider to be one of the greatest obstacles to reform in industrial relations, the powers exercised by district committees of the Amalgamated Engineering Union. These powers come from two sources: the tradition of regulating work practices on a district basis; and the constitution of the district committee, which tends to make it a coalition of representatives of the most powerful groups of stewards in the district. Accordingly the committee's writ runs through the district without the leave of the employers, and it is admirably placed to resist change. There is little hope that this situation can be changed by amending the union's rules, for district representatives are firmly entrenched in the rule-making body and also in the union's Final Appeal Court. However, the unusual powers of the district committee are largely due to its ability to operate outside collective bargaining, or on its margins. Once involved in negotiating comprehensive agreements factory by factory, a committee would be discussing and settling the very issues it now determines unilaterally, and it would become party to procedures for revising settlements by joint decisions. Of course the transformation would not take place if the committees refused to have anything to do with comprehensive factory agreements, but the experience of produc-

tivity bargaining suggests that most of them will not do so. The benefits are too persuasive. Some may try to hold out, but they could not indefinitely resist the example of success elsewhere and pressure from their members and from other unions.

174. If an initiative from large companies and a response from the unions was all that was needed, the shift from industry-wide to company and factory agreements could be accomplished without reference to employers' associations. Companies could dissociate themselves from industry-wide agreements as they signed their own agreements, and employers' associations would remain to negotiate on behalf of companies which had not made the change. This however will not happen, and if it did would be at the cost of overlooking the useful part employers' associations can play. Many large companies still feel so committed to their associations and to industry-wide agreements that the reform can be carried through within a reasonable period only if the associations lend it their support. Moreover many smaller companies are not as yet equipped to negotiate their own agreements with the unions, and they may wish to continue to rely on negotiation through their associations at least for some time to come.

175. Employers' associations can continue to have a most important role in a system of factory and company agreements. Apart from commercial matters they could still represent their members to the Government and Government departments, and provide work study and training services and circulate information. In addition they could provide advice to members on the negotiation of their own agreements. This advice would be essential, since many boards, even of sizeable companies, are at the moment poorly equipped to enter into negotiation with trade unions on their own. But what part would industry-wide agreements then play?

176. The overriding need is to put an end to the conflict between the pretence of industry-wide agreements and the realities of industrial relations. Industry-wide agreements are capable of dealing with the length of the standard working week and the length of the annual holidays. There are also instances where industry-wide bargaining can and does establish effective pay structures. Electrical contracting seems to be one of them, although examples are more common among white-collar employees, especially in public employment. Most industry-wide agreements on pay, however, cannot effectively settle more than minimum rates and their periodic adjustment. What they can all do is to set out what matters companies are expected to settle for themselves, and provide guidance on how it should be done.

177. An agreement on these lines was recently signed between the Chemical Industries Association and associated trade unions (including both process workers' unions and craftsmen's unions which have previously negotiated separately). This *Joint Agreement on Principles and Procedures of Productivity Bargaining* makes clear that existing agreements settle standard conditions of work but only minimum rates of pay, which companies are free to exceed. It acknowledges that industry-wide negotiators are not capable of dealing with work practices. These must be settled within the plant. It points out the merits of productivity agreements and recommends them to the industry, setting out guide-lines for successful productivity bargaining and establishing

43

a joint standing committee to review and advise on proposed productivity agreements. This committee is empowered to release undertakings which negotiate productivity agreements from the obligation to apply certain standard conditions.

178. This last provision is capable of extension. Many employers' associations include companies of very varied size. Generally speaking the larger companies are those to which existing industry-wide agreements are least fitted and which could draw most benefit from signing their own company agreements; whereas the smaller companies tend to conform more closely to existing agreements and might find less advantage in their own individual agreements.

179. Over recent years growth in the size of companies has emphasised the unsuitability of the existing institutions of industrial relations to large companies. Most of them have factories in various parts of the country which do not fit into the regional or district structure of many employers' associations and collective bargaining procedures. This structure therefore fails to recognise the prime responsibility of boards of directors for industrial relations throughout their companies, and it thwarts attempts to design company personnel policies. Even greater obstacles are placed in the way of the growing number of companies which operate in more than one industry. Large companies maintain, or should maintain, competently-staffed and adequately-equipped personnel departments. Most large companies are innovators and therefore in special need of negotiating arrangements linking improvements in pay with improvements in methods of operation. Many of them are pacemakers in pay, and the problems which arise from the gap between agreed industry-wide rates and actual earnings are therefore especially acute for them. Moreover competition for higher earnings between different factories within the company can be effectively controlled only by negotiating pay structures on a company basis, making agreed allowances for any appropriate regional differences. Present methods of industry-wide bargaining offer no encouragement to the negotiation of company pay structures and in some industries they obstruct it.

180. Accordingly there would be advantage in an agreement between the association and the unions which set out guide-lines for acceptable company or factory agreements and exempted such agreements from the obligation to uphold all the terms of the existing industry-wide agreement. This might be especially important where industry-wide bargaining arrangements are fragmented between different unions and groups of unions.

181. With the spread of productivity bargaining more and more companies are beginning to object to increases in pay which bring no return in increasing efficiency through modifying work practices and adopting new methods. Most industry-wide pay settlements do not and cannot provide such a return. Agreements to raise minimum rates of pay are no more to be preferred than others, for the general practice is that, each time the minimum is raised, the pay of all workers covered by the agreement is raised by the same amount regardless of whether existing pay exceeds the minimum and by how much. This objection to industry-wide pay agreements can be removed by negotiating minimum earnings levels for a standard working week. Companies within

the association can then negotiate productivity agreements confident that, so long as their employees' earnings for the standard week are in excess of the prescribed minimum level set out in any subsequent industry-wide agreement, they would not be obliged to raise their pay again. It would also enable industry-wide agreements to set more realistic levels of minimum pay without causing all-round inflation in costs.

182. In order to promote the orderly and effective regulation of industrial relations within companies and factories we recommend that the boards of companies review industrial relations within their undertakings. In doing so, they should have the following objectives in mind:

(1) to develop, together with trade unions representative of their employees, comprehensive and authoritative collective bargaining machinery to deal at company and/or factory level with the terms and conditions of employment which are settled at these levels;

(2) to develop, together with unions representative of their employees, joint procedures for the rapid and equitable settlement of grievances in a manner consistent with the relevant collective agreements;

(3) to conclude with unions representative of their employees agreements regulating the position of shop stewards in matters such as: facilities for holding elections; numbers and constituencies; recognition of credentials; facilities to consult and report back to their members; facilities to meet with other stewards; the responsibilities of the chief shop steward (if any); pay while functioning as steward in working hours; day release with pay for training;

(4) to conclude agreements covering the handling of redundancy;

(5) to adopt effective rules and procedures governing disciplinary matters, including dismissal, with provision for appeals;

(6) to ensure regular joint discussion of measures to promote safety at work.

183. We believe that machinery of this kind should assist companies to work towards the negotiation of pay structures which are comprehensive, fair and conducive to efficiency; the linking of improvements in terms and conditions of employment with improvements in methods of operation; and the use of overtime for such purposes as emergencies and fluctuations in work and not as a means of providing an acceptable pay packet.

184. In pursuit of the objectives set out in paragraph 182 companies should welcome the exercise by employees of their right to join trade unions as a prerequisite of orderly and representative joint institutions. They will need to develop positive management policies on such matters as recruitment, promotion, training and re-training. They will have to collect systematic information on which to base action in all these matters, and to make available to workers' representatives such information as they may reasonably require.

185. We consider that action by companies on these lines is as much in the interests of trade unions and their members as of the companies themselves. We therefore recommend that unions should be ready to respond positively to initiatives resulting from these reviews, and should be prepared to revise their procedures and practices where necessary.

186. Employers' associations should support and assist companies in con-

ducting their reviews. They should join with trade unions to consider what amendments may be needed in industry-wide agreements to facilitate effective collective bargaining in the company and the factory, confining industry-wide agreements to matters which they are capable of regulating, providing guide-lines for satisfactory company and factory agreements, and where appropriate granting to agreements which follow these guide-lines exemption from clauses of the industry-wide agreements. Reform on these lines will not diminish the authority of industry-wide agreements or employers' associations. On the contrary, it will give them greater influence in the actual conduct of industrial relations in the factory than they have been able to exert for many years.

187. Employers' associations which act in accordance with the recommenda-tions in the last paragraph will greatly strengthen their position because they will retain the support of their more progressive members, who may at present feel themselves hampered by the attitude of their association.

AN INDUSTRIAL RELATIONS ACT AND AN INDUSTRIAL RELATIONS COMMISSION

188. If this is the instrument of reform, can companies, trade unions and employers' associations be relied upon to make their contributions towards shaping it?

189. Recent developments show that some companies and some employers' associations are moving in this direction, and that trade unions are for the most part willing to move with them, but the pace of change is by no means sufficient to meet the country's needs. If the analysis and recommendations of this report are accepted by the Government, the Confederation of British Industry and the Trades Union Congress, the pace should quicken. Even so, given the need and the magnitude of the change, it is impossible to be confi-dent that voluntary action alone will achieve what is required in time. It is therefore necessary to inquire whether legislation could assist the change.

190. In the United States employers are under an obligation to bargain in good faith with trade unions where a majority of their employees signify that they wish to be represented by a union. In several continental countries, includ-ing the Federal Republic of Germany, establishments of a certain size are obliged by law to set up Works Councils in which elected representatives of the workers discuss and settle a range of issues laid down by statute. Neither of these measures, however, is wholly relevant to the purpose in hand. Both of them were intended to strengthen the power of workers to influence the running of industry, in the United States by encouraging collective bargaining where it did not exist, and on the Continent by supplementing industry-wide bargaining with machinery for workers to influence decisions within the factory. In addition the United States legislation has led to a great deal of litigation about the determination of the representative organisation and over what constitutes bargaining in good faith. In Britain collective bargaining is already widely accepted, and where organisation is strong workers and their representatives usually wield considerable influence over decisions in the factory. What is needed first of all is a change in the nature of British collective bargaining, and a more orderly method for workers and their representatives to exercise their influence in the factory; and for this to be accomplished, if possible,

without destroying the British tradition of keeping industrial relations out of the courts.

191. As a first step to accomplish this, a statute, which might be called the Industrial Relations Act, should lay an obligation on companies of a certain size to register collective agreements with the Department of Employment and Productivity. Initially the limit should be set high, say at 5,000 employees, in order to keep the administrative burden within bounds. The objective would be two-fold; to impress upon the boards of companies, and upon the public, that the primary responsibility for the conduct of industrial relations within a concern, and for the framework of collective agreements within which those relations are conducted, lies with the board; and, secondly, to draw attention to the aspects of industrial relations such as those set out in paragraph 182 which the public interest requires should be covered wherever possible by clear and firm company and factory agreements.

192. It is reasonable to start with the larger companies (in which we include groups of companies under common ownership or control). On the whole, they are better equipped than others to develop personnel policies and reconstruct their collective bargaining arrangements and pay structures, or they are better placed to equip themselves for the task. In several respects they have even more to gain than other companies. Fragmented bargaining, for example, hits them most of all. Moreover, they are in a position to exercise a crucial influence on developments throughout British industrial relations. Preliminary figures derived from the 1963 Board of Trade Census of Production show that out of over $8\frac{1}{2}$ million employees in the private sector of industry covered by the census (that is in mining, manufacturing and construction), nearly $3\frac{1}{2}$ million—or about 39 per cent—were working for the 221 companies, or groups of companies under common ownership or control, which employed 5,000 or more people. In 1935 there were only 88 companies or groups with 5,000 or more employees and the number of employees in them totalled less than a million. Concentration of employment in large units has increased since 1963 as the continuing spate of mergers shows. The census of production does not cover such industries as agriculture, transport, distribution, banking and insurance; but in some of these also, particularly the two last named, individual companies employing very large numbers of employees are found.

193. Initially many companies will register the industry-wide agreements to which they are parties, but it is evident that most industry-wide agreements fail to deal with many of the subjects listed in paragraph 182 and deal with others only inadequately. Neither the engineering nor the building agreement, for example, deals with redundancy, or specifically with discipline, and their provisions on disputes procedures within the plant, on shop steward facilities and on payment by results are extremely sketchy. Consequently it will be evident that concerns which register only industry-wide agreements like these do not adequately cover the subjects in question. To do so, they will either have to negotiate and register their own agreements on these matters, whether outside or supplementary to the industry-wide agreements, or persuade the employers' association to which they belong to negotiate, if it can, an industry-wide agreement which deals with these issues and deals with them adequately.

194. Other companies may prefer to register separate agreements for each

47

of their factories. There is no reason why factory agreements should not deal satisfactorily with all the items on the list. The obligation upon the company to register them, however, will emphasise the final responsibility of the board for the conduct of industrial relations throughout the undertaking.

195. A company may be unable to register an agreement on a particular matter because, despite its efforts to negotiate, the union or unions are unwilling to settle, perhaps because of inter-union disagreements. If so the facts should be reported. Similarly a company may report different agreements with two or more groups of unions, when it would prefer to negotiate comprehensive agreements covering all its manual workers, or both manual and white-collar employees.

196. If a company does not recognise trade unions, it will have no agreements to register, and this will have to be reported to the Department of Employment and Productivity with reasons. In this event the company will be failing in its public duty unless it can show that its employees are unwilling to join trade unions and to be represented by them.

197. The Act should apply to nationalised industries and to public services other than the civil service. The obligation to register agreements will rest upon the employing authority. In fact its requirements could be met by most public authorities and boards with less changes than in private industry.

198. In addition to the obligations it places upon companies and employing authorities, the Act should establish an Industrial Relations Commission, with a full-time chairman and other full-time and part-time members, who should include persons with practical experience in industrial relations, and power to appoint its own administrative and research staff. Among its duties the Commission will be expected, on a reference from the Secretary of State for Employment and Productivity, to investigate and report upon cases and problems arising out of the registration of agreements. These may include instances in which companies do not recognise trade unions, especially if one or more unions make representations to the Department that they have in membership substantial numbers of the firm's employees. Equally, the Secretary of State may decide that there is a case for investigation where a company recognises trade unions for only some sections of its employees and a union or unions claim substantial membership among other sections. The Secretary of State may also refer cases in which companies report failure to negotiate satisfactory agreements because of union opposition or of disagreement between unions; and cases where a company's agreements appear to fall short of a reasonable standard for some other reason. The Secretary of State may also refer general questions affecting a number of companies, deficiencies in factory disputes procedures for instance, or in disciplinary procedures, or problems concerning the recognition of white-collar unions. In dealing with such references the Commission may choose to issue specimen agreements to give companies guidance on what is expected of them.

199. Agreements will be registered with the Department of Employment and Productivity, not the Commission, and the Department's industrial relations service will handle queries and problems up to the point at which a reference to the Commission is thought advisable. Over the last two years the industrial

relations service has been dealing with notifications of pay increases from concerns under the " early warning" machinery of the prices and incomes policy. Its conduct of this task has been one of the policy's successes, and this new responsibility should therefore fit in with its present work. As the administrative machinery and procedures become established the minimum size of company to which they apply should be progressively reduced.

200. Our recommendations and the operation of the Act should lead to an early review by smaller companies of their industrial relations. In any case it will not be possible to prevent difficulties and disputes arising in such companies about issues which fall within the scope of the Commission's responsibility, which is the proper functioning of the machinery of collective bargaining. It must therefore be possible for the Secretary of State to refer such difficulties and disputes, if they are urgent, to the Commission. To this end it will be important to distinguish the kind of dispute which is appropriate to the Commission and the kind of dispute which is and will continue to be referable to arbitration. The basis of the distinction is the division between substantive agreements—those that lay down the terms on which workers are employed—and procedural agreements which lay down the machinery through which substantive agreements are reached and interpreted. Disputes concerning substantive agreements and their interpretation are referable to arbitration; disputes concerning procedural agreements, including disputes about whether such agreements should be concluded and with whom, will fall within the province of the Commission.

201. This does not mean that the Industrial Relations Commission's investigation should be confined to procedural agreements. In practice procedural and substantive agreements are closely intermeshed in the working of industrial relations. The effectiveness of a pay structure depends in large measure on the method of reviewing claims for pay adjustments; the method of fixing piecework prices is crucial to the successful operation of a system of piecework payment. The Industrial Relations Commission should be the body to carry out inquiries into the general state of industrial relations in a factory or an industry such as have previously been entrusted to *ad hoc* committees, for example the Devlin Committee on the docks or the Pearson Court of Inquiry into the shipping industry. These involved investigation of the whole range of agreements in those industries, and the Industrial Relations Commission's inquiries should be given equal scope. But if it was required to arbitrate on particular disputes about terms and conditions of employment its attention would be diverted from the proper functioning of the machinery of collective bargaining to finding acceptable settlements, and from long-term objectives to short-term compromises.

202. We have considered whether industry-wide agreements as such should be registered with the Department of Employment and Productivity. It could be argued that their registration is essential to providing the information which the Commission will need for its work. On the other hand such agreements have effect only insofar as they regulate industrial relations within companies and factories. Therefore so long as an industry-wide agreement is applied within any company which is required to register, that agreement itself will be registered. To place the obligation on the company emphasises

that the primary responsibility for the conduct of industrial relations within the company rests on the board, and that industry-wide agreements are to be judged first of all by their effect on relationships within companies and factories.

203. It would be wrong to attempt to lay down a detailed set of rules to which the Commission will be expected to work. It will be entrusted with a novel task and will therefore have to develop its own rules and methods in the course of its work. Equally, however, it will be important that the principles which guide the Commission's work should be known and understood. We suggest that they might be these:

(1) that collective bargaining is the best method of conducting industrial relations. There is therefore wide scope in Britain for extending both the subject matter of collective bargaining and the number of workers covered by collective agreements;

(2) that, since collective bargaining depends upon the existence, strength and recognition of trade unions, the test in dealing with any dispute over recognition—other than a dispute between unions over recognition—should be whether the union or unions in question can reasonably be expected to develop and sustain adequate representation for the purpose of collective bargaining among workers in the company or factory concerned, or among a distinct section of those workers. A ballot may be useful in applying the test, but could rarely determine the issue by itself;

(3) that a system of industrial relations must be judged principally by its effects in the company, the factory and the workshop. Industry-wide procedures and agreements should be confined to those issues which they can effectively regulate;

(4) that wherever possible, collective agreements should be written and precise;

(5) that pay agreements should provide intelligible and coherent pay structures;

(6) that it is desirable for agreements whenever it is possible to link improvements in terms and conditions of employment with improvements in methods of operation;

(7) that procedure agreements should be comprehensive in scope and should provide for the rapid and equitable settlement of disputes, whether they refer to the interpretation of existing or the making of new agreements;

(8) that it is desirable for each company or factory to be covered by a single set of comprehensive agreements applying to all the unions representing its employees; if this is unattainable, that separate sets of agreements covering distinct groups of employees should be accepted by all the unions representing workers within each group. This principle should guide the solution to any dispute between unions concerning recognition.

204. Failure on the part of a company to register its agreements, or to report that it has no agreements and why, will render it liable to a monetary penalty.

Subject to what we say in the next paragraph we propose no other penalties for failure to carry out the recommendations of the Commission, whether the fault lies with the company or with the union (or unions). Equally we propose no penalties on companies which refuse to recognise trade unions. (Lord Tangley and Mr. Shonfield however have reservations on this point which they express in separate notes at the end of our report.) The intention of the Act is to promote the reform of industrial relations by establishing a system of registration which will enable society's expectations in the field of industrial relations to be brought home clearly and unambiguously to the boards of companies and to trade unions; and which will make sure that they are given adequate assistance in meeting those expectations. We do not think the shortcomings of our existing industrial relations are due to malice or moral weakness on the part of employers, managers or trade unionists. They are primarily due to widespread ignorance about the most sensible and effective methods of conducting industrial relations, and to the very considerable obstacles to the use of sensible and effective methods contained in our present system of industrial relations.

205. If the reform was largely successful, so that relations in most companies of any size were carried on within the framework of clear and effective agreements, and yet stoppages in breach of those agreements remained a common occurrence, it would be possible to consider enacting some penalty against trade unions or workers responsible for such stoppages (and, of course, against managers and employers where they were responsible). The question of penalties for refusal to carry out the recommendations of the Commission on questions of recognition will also have to be reviewed in the light of experience. We refer to these questions again in Chapter V when we discuss problems of trade union recognition and in Chapter VIII when we discuss the enforcement of collective agreements.

206. The legislation we propose should have an appeal to companies, employers' associations, trade unions, shop stewards, managers and supervisors. Many companies are now casting about for a method to bring about a radical improvement in their industrial relations. The Act could show them the method and assist them to use it. Employers' associations would be given a positive task within their compass instead of a responsibility which they manifestly no longer fulfil. Trade unions would be able to close the gap between head office and shop stewards, and between full-time officers and members, by concentrating on the negotiation of agreements at a level meaningful to them all. Shop stewards would be assured a constitutional position, with recognised authority to deal with workshop and factory issues, and the full support of their unions in doing so. Both stewards and managers would be able to deal openly through a recognised and effective procedure with many issues that must now be arranged covertly or left unsettled. In the short run, however, the change would demand a great deal from them all. Time-honoured assumptions would have to be abandoned; there would have to be a great deal of hard thinking and tough negotiating, and no doubt there would be disputes. But the consequences of failing to reform our system of industrial relations are far more alarming than these consequences of the Act.

207. We have not thought it necessary to describe at length the details of the various attempts at incomes policy in this country during the post-war period or to set out the many developments in the present incomes policy inaugurated in 1964; nor have we thought it wise to enter into discussion of the merits of particular policies. We are, however, convinced that incomes policy can make a contribution of outstanding importance to the economic growth of this country and a more ordered system of industrial relations, and that any proposals which we make for the reform of industrial relations should assist an incomes policy to work effectively. The proposals we have made in this chapter will do so.

208. The functions of the Industrial Relations Commission will differ from those of the Prices and Incomes Board. The Industrial Relations Act will be concerned with the long-term reconstruction of British industrial relations, whereas incomes policy is concerned with the short-run improvement of the country's economic position, and has been revised at fairly frequent intervals. Experience at home and abroad suggests that, in incomes policies, periods of tight control are followed by periods of relaxation. The reconstruction of industrial relations must be continuous. It is true that the Prices and Incomes Board has from time to time included proposals for the reform of industrial relations in its reports on particular references; but this is a subsidiary function and the Board can proceed only in a piecemeal fashion; whereas what is needed is a general reconstruction. The Industrial Relations Commission will have that as its only function, and will not be directly concerned with incomes policy. Its success will be imperilled if it becomes the agent of short-run policies.

209. Nevertheless the results of the Industrial Relations Commission's work will assist the working of incomes policy. The registration of company and factory agreements will provide far more information about the decisions which affect pay than is at present available. It is a valid criticism of past incomes policies that they have been too closely limited to dealing with industry-wide decisions. The institution of an early warning system and the growth of productivity bargaining has started to change this state of affairs, but the registration of company and factory agreements would expose the whole process of pay settlement to the influence of policy.

210. In their evidence the Confederation of British Industry stated that plant bargaining " if widely resorted to, makes impossible any national planning with regard to incomes; that in conditions of full employment it cannot be other than inflationary; that it encourages instability in the labour force (through the ' bidding-up ' for labour to which it gives rise); that it increases the scope for unofficial strikes and other forms of industrial action; and that it is calculated to weaken the organisation of trade unions and employers' organisations, to the ultimate detriment of both workers and managements and of the economy ". While intended as a description of things to be avoided this in fact describes the consequences of collective bargaining as it is now practised, with the continuous shift from industry-

wide decision-making to workshop arrangements, understandings and practices. That state of affairs weakens unions and employers' associations, promotes unofficial strikes and " bidding-up ", is inflationary and undermines incomes policy. Properly negotiated factory and company agreements as here proposed, however, would " if widely resorted to " permit all these tendencies to be brought under control. They would strengthen trade union organisation and confine employers' associations to tasks within their power. By encouraging regulated factory pay structures and substituting agreements for understandings and practices they would remove many of the causes of unofficial strikes. They would bring " bidding-up " for labour into the open, and thus render it susceptible to control. Finally they would assist the planning of incomes. Incomes policy must continue a lame and halting exercise so long as it consists in the planning of industry-wide agreements most of which exercise an inadequate control over pay. So long as workplace bargaining remains informal, autonomous and fragmented the drift of earnings away from rates of pay cannot be brought under control. Well-regulated company and factory agreements would enable companies to exercise effective control over their own wage—and salary—bills, and that in turn would make the control of drift a possibility.

211. Our proposals for the reform of collective bargaining cannot of themselves put an end to " bidding-up " of pay by employers, or to " leap-frogging " tactics by trade unions in which they attempt to push first one company and then another into the lead in levels of pay. Our view is that the present system of bargaining permits both " bidding-up " and " leap-frogging " at workshop and factory level, without any possibility of national control because companies themselves cannot exercise control. Our proposals are designed to provide effective control of industrial relations, including pay, at the level of the factory and company by means of properly constructed agreements between companies and trade unions. If the decisions companies and trade unions take accord with incomes policy, then incomes policy will work.

Chapter V

THE EXTENSION OF
COLLECTIVE BARGAINING

INTRODUCTION

212. Properly conducted, collective bargaining is the most effective means of giving workers the right to representation in decisions affecting their working lives, a right which is or should be the prerogative of every worker in a democratic society. While therefore the first task in the reform of British industrial relations is to bring greater order into collective bargaining in the company and plant, the second is to extend the coverage of collective bargaining and the organisation of workers on which it depends. In this chapter we first describe the general situation and then say how we think it can be improved. Freedom of association and trade union recognition, Wages Councils and compulsory arbitration all have a bearing on the question and we deal with these subjects in turn. In a final section we deal with the relationship between incomes policy and the work of Wages Councils and of arbitrators.

THE GENERAL SITUATION

Freedom of Association and Trade Union Recognition

213. The State has taken little positive action in the past to encourage workers to join unions or to protect them from retaliatory action by their employers should they do so or induce others to do so. The Government, it is true, encourages its own employees to belong to appropriate trade unions; and Government contractors are obliged to recognise the freedom of their workpeople to be members of trade unions. In industry at large however employers are still legally free to stipulate that an employee shall not join a trade union, on pain of dismissal if he does.

214. We have had various instances drawn to our attention where employers discourage employees from joining trade unions. Thus in one case an employer asks new employees to sign a document which includes a clause in the following terms:

> " The employee agrees to give one month's notice in writing of any request he/she may have for a meeting with the Management on any matter concerning a trade union; the employee also agrees that failure to do so will constitute a breach of agreement with this Company and will entitle the Company to terminate their employment ".

In another case which came to our knowledge an employee joined a trade union, and recruited other employees at first secretly and later at a meeting held outside the works. Subsequently employees were asked individually by the employer to sign a document declaring that they were not members of any trade union. Those who refused to sign or admitted that they were union members were dismissed. The employer has ignored invitations to put his case to us.

215. The report of the TUC's General Council to Congress for 1967 sets out the results of a survey which confirmed that these and similar practices are still adopted by some employers to hinder the exercise of freedom of association.

216. The State has taken a more positive attitude to trade union recognition. This is a pre-requisite of collective bargaining and it has been Government policy generally to support collective bargaining at least since the last decade of the 19th century. In furtherance of this policy the Department of Employment and Productivity's conciliation and arbitration services, and the good offices of its industrial relations officers, are used to encourage and support collective bargaining arrangements. Governments have operated a system of statutory minimum wage regulation one of whose objects is to stimulate collective bargaining. Under the Terms and Conditions of Employment Act 1959 an employer may be obliged to accord terms and conditions of employment no less favourable than those established in a relevant collective agreement. Under the Fair Wages Resolution an obligation of this kind is put on Government contractors. The nationalised industries have a statutory duty to seek agreement with organisations representative of their employees for the purpose of joint negotiations. The terms and conditions of employment of the Government's own employees are settled by collective bargaining.

217. Nevertheless many problems of trade union recognition still arise. For example the Amalgamated Engineering Union was reported to have been refused recognition by 72 firms in the course of 1965, almost all of which employed less than 200 workers and many less than 100. The Transport and General Workers' Union has reported that it has difficulty in obtaining recognition in industries where there are considerable numbers of medium and small sized firms. Serious difficulties have arisen in banking and in insurance.

218. A certain number of strikes take place each year over the issue. In the years 1964-1966 there was an annual average of 23 strikes for recognition, of which 18 were unofficial. The figures have shown a tendency to increase: in 1958-1960 the annual average was 5 and in 1961-1963 it was 12. The figures may understate the importance of the problem since some strikes which are essentially for recognition may be recorded as stoppages arising out of wage claims. About 30 per cent of the differences in which industrial relations officers conciliate concern recognition.

219. It is impossible in practice to separate problems of freedom of association from those of trade union recognition. Unless employees join a union, there will be no union for the employer to recognise. Moreover if an employer is known to be "anti-union" employees may be deterred from joining for fear of dismissal or of incurring other disadvantages, and the consequent failure of the union to recruit many employees can be used by the employer as a reason justifying non-recognition. Conversely, if an employer recognises a trade union it is much easier for the union to persuade employees that it is worth their while to join. The attitude of employers towards trade unions

55

c

is especially important for the organisation of white-collar workers, since most groups of white-collar workers are traditionally reluctant to strike or otherwise coerce their employers into granting recognition.

220. Employment trends show that the strength of trade unionism will depend more and more on the organisation of white-collar workers. Just over a half of all British manual workers are trade union members, but only 30 per cent of white-collar workers. Over the last fifty years however the proportion of white-collar employees in the labour force has doubled and is now about 40 per cent. Within the next twenty years the majority of employees will be white-collar workers. These figures suggest that a continued shift from relatively well-organised manual employment to relatively ill-organised white-collar employment will, other things being equal, lead to a decline in trade unionism. Other considerations point in the same direction. Among manual workers some of the most highly-organised groups are to be found in industries where manpower is falling such as coal-mining, railways, cotton and shipbuilding, whereas in the rapidly growing construction industry trade union membership is relatively low and declining. White-collar membership is at its highest in national and local government (over 80 per cent), relatively low in insurance, banking and finance (31 per cent), and very low in distribution (13 per cent) and manufacturing industry (12 per cent). Employment in these last three groups, however, is expanding far faster than in local government and still faster than in national government. With all these factors working against trade unionism it is not surprising that the proportion of British employees in trade unions has declined gently from a peak of about 45 per cent in 1948 to about 42 per cent today. Without vigorous expansion in some fields the decline would have been faster. Much of the expansion has however been in the public services and nationalised industries, where saturation point has been reached. White-collar employment in manufacturing industry is a field of great potential, but here the proportion of employees in trade unions has risen only slightly in the post-war period and is still only 12 per cent.

221. Some employers hold that there is a special relationship between the employer and white-collar staff which is incompatible with their representation by a trade union. This view is becoming increasingly unrealistic and out of date. It fails to recognise the growth of large bodies of white-collar workers in no way involved in management whose hours and conditions of employment cannot be settled by discussion with each individual. Even among managers trade unionism is not necessarily inappropriate, as the experience of the nationalised industries and the civil service show. Though in private industry such persons at present normally prefer to negotiate their own terms and conditions, they nevertheless frequently combine to protect their interests in professional matters.

222. The importance of employers' attitudes is borne out by the development of collective bargaining for white-collar workers in the past. There are many instances where unions were recognised long before they could possibly have forced their employers to grant recognition against their will. This is true for example of the recognition of the National Union of Journalists by such bodies as the Newspaper Proprietors Association in 1917 and the years following.

Sometimes the employers' motive has been to encourage a trade union with which they would prefer to deal rather than its rivals.

223. Of no less importance however have been the influence of Government policies. Thus following the decision of the House of Lords in *National Association of Local Government Officers v. Bolton Corporation* [1943] the union was able to use the compulsory arbitration machinery set up by the Government in 1940 to secure awards against local authorities which would not deal with it. The duty to grant recognition placed upon the boards of nationalised industries led to a rapid expansion of trade union membership among their white-collar employees after vesting day. In private manufacturing industry compulsory arbitration enabled several white-collar unions to compel employers to deal with them, and there have been several instances in which recognition has been the consequence of Government intervention. Early in 1943, for example, Sir Stafford Cripps as Minister of Aircraft Production gave considerable assistance to the Association of Supervisory Staffs, Executives and Technicians in gaining recognition from the Engineering Employers' Federation.[1]

224. Consequently, there is now a dilemma for public policy. Collective bargaining is recognised as the best way of conducting industrial relations and as depending on strong trade union organisation. The proportion of employees who are organised has however been declining. Employment is increasing in areas which have proved difficult to organise, so that the effect of obstacles to the development and recognition of unions in these areas is assuming greater importance for the future of collective bargaining. The evidence is that if these obstacles are to be surmounted more effective means of dealing with problems of trade union recognition are needed.

Wages Councils

225. Statutory minimum wage regulation was introduced by the Trade Boards Act 1909 as a means of dealing with the evils of " sweated labour ", and it has ever since been one of its purposes to protect the low paid. The Trade Boards Act of 1918, passed under the influence of the Whitley Committee, added a second purpose, that of providing wage-fixing machinery where collective bargaining does not exist. It was hoped that the statutory machinery would foster the growth of voluntary organisation and would in time be replaced by voluntary collective bargaining.

226. Wages Councils now operate under the Wages Councils Act 1959. They consist of equal numbers of persons representing workers and employers, together with up to three independent members, one of whom is chairman. There are at present 57 Wages Councils covering about 3½ million workers in about half a million establishments. Nearly 2½ million of the workers covered are in catering, retail distribution and hairdressing.

227. In agriculture there are somewhat similar statutory bodies, the Agricultural Wages Board for England and Wales and the Scottish Agricultural Wages Board operating respectively under the Agricultural Wages Act 1948 and the Agricultural Wages (Scotland) Act 1949. However, these Boards make their own statutory Orders and Ministers play no part in the process, though

[1] The details of this and several other instances are given in our Research Paper No. 6, *Trade Union Growth and Recognition*, by G. S. Bain, HMSO 1967.

agricultural wages inspection is the responsibility of the Departments concerned with agriculture. About 430,000 workers are employed in agriculture and horticulture in Great Britain. Altogether, therefore, arrangements for the statutory fixing of minimum wages and conditions cover nearly 4 million workers and form an important element in the British system of industrial relations.

228. The Ministry of Labour supplied us with information about the distribution of trade union members by industry and the following table is based upon it:

Number of Employees and Estimated Number and Percentage of Employees in Trade Unions in Certain Industry Groups

Industry Group	Number of Employees[1] (000s)	Estimated Number of Trade Unionists[2] (000s)	Percentage of Employees in Trade Unions
Agriculture, forestry, fishing ..	551	167	30
Clothing, other than footwear ..	453	123	27
"Other manufacturing industries"[3]	326	86	26
Distributive trades	3,026	386	13
Catering and hotels	633	25	4
All employment	23,616	9,743	41

Figures supplied by Ministry of Labour.

[1] Number of employees (employed and unemployed) in June 1964.
[2] Number of trade unionists at end 1964.
[3] " Other manufacturing industries " is a residual category which includes about 50,000 workers covered by Wages Councils.

The employment figures in this table include many part-time and family workers whom it would be difficult or impossible to organise, so that the full extent to which unions have succeeded in persuading potential recruits to join, for example in agriculture, is not apparent. It is clear nevertheless how little progress has been made in trade union organisation in distribution and catering, which are in terms of employment the two main sectors where Wages Councils operate.

229. Agriculture is a relatively well-organised industry whose circumstances are exceptional, as we show later in paragraph 261. In the Wages Council field, however, a number of the trade unions with a major interest have told us that the statutory arrangements are a hindrance to trade union organisation. Thus the Transport and General Workers' Union commented, with reference to Wages Councils:

" Unfortunately, however, the existence of even this inadequate form of wage-fixing machinery often acts as an encouragement to non-unionism, since it tends to establish the idea that a system of fixing wages does exist without the necessity for membership of a trade union. The incentive to the trade union movement itself to set up voluntary machinery is weakened."

Similar views were expressed by the Union of Shop, Distributive and Allied Workers and the General and Municipal Workers' Union. The National

Union of Tailors and Garment Workers pointed out that " where there are substantial numbers of anti-trade union employers the abolition of a Council would demand more vigorous trade union activity but this might stimulate local agreements ".

230. The extent of voluntary machinery for collective bargaining in Wages Council industries is generally related to trade union membership. In catering there is very little voluntary machinery, and in retail distribution not much outside the co-operatives and some of the multiple shops and large departmental stores. On the other hand voluntary bargaining arrangements are more general in such industries as clothing, baking, paper bag and paper box. Indeed there are some Wages Councils which usually adopt as they stand agreements reached in voluntary negotiations and thus do no more than give force as statutory minima, within their jurisdiction, to the rates of pay laid down in the agreements. In such instances it is reasonable to question whether statutory enforcement of minimum rates of pay is really necessary and whether therefore the continued existence of the Councils is justified.

231. The Wages Councils Act 1959 lays down the procedure for abolishing Wages Councils. Action can be taken on the Secretary of State's own initiative or in response to a joint application from representative bodies on both sides, but if any objection of substance is raised the Secretary of State must refer the matter to a Commission of Inquiry and cannot proceed without the backing of the Commission. A Council cannot be abolished unless certain conditions are met. These are that adequate machinery for the effective regulation of pay and conditions of work exists; and that the machinery is substantially representative of both sides of industry. The machinery must be adequate both in that it produces agreements and in that the agreements are observed in practice.

232. The Ministry of Labour pointed out in its evidence that whereas statutory machinery has been viewed as a temporary expedient for industries not yet able to set up their own voluntary arrangements, in practice progress in the replacement of Wages Councils by voluntary machinery has been disappointingly slow. Between 1953 and 1963 ten Wages Councils were abolished, including some covering fairly large industries such as rubber and furniture manufacturing. None have been abolished since, although in a few cases action with a view to abolition is in train.

233. The Ministry of Labour also pointed out that in recent years suggestions for the abolition of Councils have tended to meet opposition from employers, although the unions would welcome abolition. It seems that, at any rate in some cases, so long as they can rely on statutory machinery the employers are disinclined or are unable to strengthen their organisation sufficiently to secure the voluntary observance of minimum rates. So long as this is so, it may well not be possible to meet the statutory conditions for the abolition of a Wages Council.

234. Whatever may have been the case in the past, therefore, to-day many Wages Councils are doing little to fulfil the aim of extending voluntary collective bargaining. In the main areas of employment covered by Wages Councils voluntary organisation remains too weak to support extensive

59

machinery for voluntary negotiation, and in some of the remaining Councils the continued existence of statutory machinery seems to be a barrier to fully independent machinery. Here, too, new measures are necessary.

Compulsory Arbitration

235. We have already referred briefly to the contribution which the compulsory arbitration arrangements introduced in 1940 have made to the extension of collective bargaining. Compulsory arbitration may take various forms. Under the form which existed in this country from 1940 to 1959, at the request of either party to a dispute the matter could be referred by the Minister of Labour for arbitration without the consent of the other party, and the resulting award became an implied term of the contracts of employment of the workers concerned. When the restoration of compulsory arbitration is proposed, it is an arrangement of this kind which the proposers generally have in mind. It will avoid confusion if we refer to it as " unilateral arbitration ".

236. When unilateral arbitration was instituted in 1940, it was the result of agreement by employers and unions that in order to avoid impeding the war effort strikes and lock-outs should, with virtually no exceptions, be made illegal, and that disputes should be resolved by arbitration instead. This arrangement was embodied in the Conditions of Employment and National Arbitration Order 1940 (S.R. & O. 1940, No. 1305) which set up a National Arbitration Tribunal.

237. In 1951 it was decided that, since the prohibition could not be effectively enforced, strikes and lock-outs should no longer be illegal and that arrangements for unilateral arbitration must be revised. The Industrial Disputes Order 1951 (S.I. 1951, No. 1376) took the place of the previous Order. It provided for an Industrial Disputes Tribunal. Access to this Tribunal was confined, on the trade union side, to unions which habitually took part in the settlement of terms and conditions of employment in the industry, section of industry or undertaking concerned; or which, in the absence of negotiating machinery, represented a substantial proportion of the workers concerned in the relevant industry or section of industry. This restriction was designed to protect established voluntary machinery by preventing breakaway unions and other unrecognised bodies from making use of the statutory machinery. Another important limitation was continued, namely that no reference should be made to the Industrial Disputes Tribunal of a case which could be dealt with by existing voluntary arrangements for the settlement of disputes. Thus recourse to the Tribunal was possible only where no agreed arbitration arrangements existed, or where any other voluntary arrangements had been used and had failed. Nor was recourse allowed as a form of appeal against awards by the Industrial Court or any other arbitration body.

238. Not all trade unions made use of the Industrial Disputes Tribunal, some being parties to arrangements for voluntary arbitration and others preferring to rely on their industrial strength. Among those which did make use of it were to be found both powerful and weak organisations. However, some powerful organisations like the general workers' unions operate in many poorly organised industries and trades, and the great majority of references seem to have concerned comparatively weak groups of workers. The Tribunal's

awards were by and large in line with settlements being reached by other means.[1]

239.   Unilateral arbitration was based on temporary legislation; and throughout its life it was understood that it should continue only so long as it had the support of both sides of industry.   A feeling developed among employers that the Industrial Disputes Tribunal procedure worked in a one-sided way and that, while its awards could be effectively enforced by employees, it was difficult in practice for employers to benefit from awards in their favour. The knowledge that arbitration was available which in practice worked this way tended, in the employers' view, to undermine negotiation.   When therefore in 1957 the Government decided to abolish the Defence Regulation on which the 1951 Order was based, and consulted industry about what, if anything, should replace the Order, the employers decided that they wished to support unilateral arbitration no longer.   As a result the Tribunal was wound up in 1959.   During its existence of some 7½ years the Tribunal made over 1,270 awards.

240.   All that is now preserved of the former arrangements for unilateral arbitration is embodied in section 8 of the Terms and Conditions of Employment Act 1959.   Under this section representative trade unions or employers' organisations are enabled to secure adjudication by the Industrial Court in cases where they think that an employer is failing to observe terms and conditions of employment not less favourable than those established by agreement or award for his industry or section of industry.   If the Industrial Court finds that this is so, it makes an award requiring the employer to observe the terms and conditions concerned.   This has effect as an implied term of the contracts of employment of the workers concerned, and also of other workers of the same description employed from time to time by the employer.

241.   While therefore section 8 of the 1959 Act provides support for collective bargaining its contribution is limited.   Moreover the fact that in most industries workers in practice commonly enjoy levels of pay considerably above those laid down at industry level inevitably diminishes the importance of a procedure for securing terms and conditions not less favourable than those in the agreement.   Here too it is evident that existing measures do not provide a fully effective means of extending the scope of collective bargaining.

WHAT NEEDS TO BE DONE

Freedom of Association
242.   The United Kingdom has ratified two International Labour Conventions—Nos. 87 and 98—dealing with freedom of association and the right to organise and bargain collectively, as well as the European Social Charter and the Council of Europe Convention for the Protection of Human Rights and Fundamental Freedoms, both of which contain relevant Articles. Article 1 of International Labour Convention No. 98 reads as follows:

" *Article 1*
   1.   Workers shall enjoy adequate protection against acts of anti-union discrimination in respect of their employment.

---

[1]See Research Paper No. 8, *Three Studies in Collective Bargaining*, HMSO 1968, p. 39, para. 25.

2. Such protection shall apply more particularly in respect of acts calculated to—

    (a) make the employment of a worker subject to the condition that he shall not join a union or shall relinquish trade union membership;

    (b) cause the dismissal of or otherwise prejudice a worker by reason of union membership or because of participation in union activities outside working hours or, with the consent of the employer, within working hours."

243. Ratification does not of itself make observance of an International Labour Convention obligatory, but the Government undertakes that the country's law and practice will conform with it. Neither Convention No. 87 nor Convention No. 98 is drafted in terms which make legislation mandatory; and successive British Governments have taken the view that the trade union movement here is sufficiently strong to make legislation on these matters unnecessary. The TUC has not so far pressed for legislation.

244. Accordingly there is nothing in the law, outside the nationalised industries, to prevent employers from deliberately obstructing freedom of association, and, as we have shown, some in fact do so. This has the further result that the extension of collective bargaining, which it is Government policy to encourage, is also impeded.

245. We consider that it is contrary to the public interest that an employer should stipulate in a contract of employment that an employee is not to belong to a trade union: and that any such stipulation should in law be void and of no effect. We except from the scope of this recommendation employment in the police and in the armed forces of the Crown.

246. Such a change in the law will not end all discrimination by employers against employees who join trade unions. This may take various forms which are not amenable to legislation. For example, an employer may conclude no contract at all with a prospective employee whom he suspects will join a union. Nevertheless our recommendation, if implemented, will give a useful measure of protection to employees who wish to join trade unions, especially if coupled with a remedy against unfair dismissal which we later propose. It will also encourage employers who are at present disposed to obstruct the development of trade union organisation among their employees to reconsider their attitudes.

247. This recommendation will not meet a major specific complaint of some trade unions in relation to freedom of association which must now be examined. This concerns the Foremen and Staff Mutual Benefit Society. This Society is registered under the Friendly Societies Acts, and provides pensions, sickness insurance and benefits to foremen and similar grades of staff in the engineering and shipbuilding industries. It has over 61,000 members. The Society has two kinds of member: contributory members, who are employers and who make contributions towards the provision of benefits; and ordinary members, the foremen and other staff referred to, who both contribute towards and draw the benefits. The employers, that is the " contributory members ", pay at least half, and sometimes more, of the total

contribution in respect of each ordinary member. There are at present over 2,600 employers who are contributory members.

248. So far there is nothing about the Society to which trade unions would object. They complain, however, of rule 7 of the Society's Rules which provides as follows:

> " An ordinary member who at the date of his admission to the Society is a member of a trade union, registered or unregistered, shall forthwith resign from such trade union. If he fails to do so he shall immediately resign from the Society. An ordinary member who, after admission to the Society, joins any such trade union shall immediately resign from the Society. . . ."

The Association of Supervisory Staffs, Executives and Technicians in particular alleged in evidence that the Society is a type of employer-sponsored organisation which is openly ranged against *bona fide* union organisation. The Association said that " the main reason for the continued support given to the Society by many large firms is its anti-trade union rule " and that its existence " offends against the spirit and intention of ILO Conventions which have been ratified by Britain ".

249. The Society answers that its benefits are an alternative, not an addition, to those of a trade union; that many foremen and staff do not want to join a union " because of the possibility of a division of loyalty in times of dissension between the management they represent and the unions "; and that they should not be denied the right of free and exclusive association in a society which exists only for benefit purposes. The only possible objection, it is said, is that employers pay contributions to the Society, but it is denied that undue influence is brought to bear on employees to make them join or stay in the Society. The few allegations to this effect which it has received have not, says the Society, stood up to investigation. In summing up its case the Society contends that " employers are fully justified in contributing through the Society to an employee who freely decides to resign from or not to join a trade union. Such an employee identifies his interests with those of management and, in the process, may well relinquish accrued trade union benefits."

250. We have already examined and rejected the view that trade unionism is inappropriate for white-collar workers, whether managers or not. Where managerial staff are organised at present, appropriate arrangements can be made—as is done in the civil service and nationalised industries—to prevent any conflict of loyalties. Where supervisors are concerned a new procedure agreement for the shipbuilding industry which came into force in August 1967 points one way out of the difficulty: it provides that supervisors below head foremen should be encouraged to retain membership of their original trade union, so long as they are not subject to the jurisdiction of shop stewards or any local committee or officials of the union, whether at district or branch level.

251. This does not however inevitably lead to the conclusion that the trade unions' complaint must be upheld. Trade unions claim the right to draw up their rules in full freedom; are they justified in complaining when the Society claims the same right? The unions' answer is that the real reason

behind the Society's rule is discrimination against them, and that managements prefer, for reasons which they will not openly allow, to have foremen and staffs who do not belong to trade unions and who are deterred from joining (or remaining) in them because of the considerable financial loss which will follow; to that extent therefore their freedom of association has been bought by the employer and this is something which should not be permitted.

252. In our view it is quite foreign to the purposes of a Friendly Society that it should prescribe in its rules that no one can be a member and draw benefits if he is a trade unionist. If the State's policy is to encourage collective bargaining through the medium of representative trade unions, since this is in the public interest, then such a rule as rule 7 is contrary to the public interest. The contract between the Society and its members is not, of course, a contract of employment; and it would go far beyond what is necessary to deal with this particular problem if the law were to enact that such stipulations in *all* contracts were void. It should be sufficient in our view to provide that no Friendly Society should have such a rule, and we so recommend.

Trade Union Recognition

253. Many witnesses have made suggestions to us for new machinery to deal with disputed claims by trade unions for recognition. Thus Professor Wedderburn proposed that it should be made a condition of incorporation with limited liability that companies (apart perhaps from the smallest companies) should be obliged to engage in responsible collective bargaining, and a number of trade unions supported him. This proposal is in our view unworkable and wrong in principle. For example it would not affect recognition by unincorporated employers or by employers' associations, and use of the sanction envisaged for continued non-compliance—to strike the company off the register or wind it up—would be a strange way of promoting the interests of its employees.

254. Other proposals envisage that a right to recognition should arise if a certain percentage of workers—usually 50 per cent—is organised in a trade union. The fixing of a figure in this way might set up an impassable barrier to a union which would if only it were granted recognition organise a majority and represent them successfully. Conversely it could in some cases act as a target for mushroom organisations whose activities do not conduce to sound industrial relations. Moreover the crucial problem of how to define the unit within which this degree of organisation is to be obtained would at times present great difficulty.

255. Mr. Allan Flanders proposed to us that an independent tribunal be established to which recognition disputes might be referred by the Minister of Labour. He argued as follows:

"What is needed if the institution of collective bargaining is to be given more practical support is a permanent public authority empowered to hear recognition disputes and to make recommendations for their settlement. Although one does not wish at this time to multiply the separate pieces of machinery for public intervention in industrial relations, I would favour the creation of a special Tribunal for this purpose rather than extending the powers of the existing Industrial

Court. One important reason is that a body dealing with disputes of this character would not be acting as an arbitrator but more like a permanent Court of Inquiry. It could not possibly rely, for example, only on the parties' submissions for evidence. It would probably have to employ its own investigating officers to discover relevant facts, such as the degree of support for the union and whether other unions were involved. It should certainly be empowered to arrange a secret ballot, if this was thought to be desirable, although equally it should not be compelled to do so. Contrary to the usual practice in arbitration, it would also be necessary for such a Tribunal to give reasons for its decisions and ensure that they were reasonably consistent with each other. It would in fact have gradually to evolve a set of working principles."

Mr. Flanders went on to point out that the tribunal could deal with disputes between rival unions for the right to represent particular workers (a factor which often complicates recognition disputes) and would thus supplement the TUC's machinery for dealing with inter-union disputes.

256. We agree with Mr. Flanders on the essentials of his proposals. They offer a method of encouraging the development of collective bargaining on sound lines. Moreover they avoid the difficulty of detailed intervention by the courts in the processes of industrial relations which appears to us to be a consequence of enforcing recognition by law as in the USA. We envisage that problems of trade union recognition should be dealt with by the Industrial Relations Commission whose establishment we propose in the previous chapter, and that it will be able to approach its task in the spirit of the tribunal recommended by Mr. Flanders. The Commission will provide a powerful new instrument for encouraging the extension of collective bargaining and its guidance will help to ensure that new machinery is developed on sound lines. Mr. Flanders did not propose that initially at any rate there should be any penalties for refusing to carry out recommendations about recognition, and (with the exception of Mr. Shonfield, who expresses a different view in his note at the end of our report) we agree. But this question will need to be reviewed in the light of experience.

Wages Councils

257. What role Wages Councils might play for the future must be assessed in the light of their contribution not only to extending collective bargaining but to the protection of low paid workers. There is however a regrettable lack of information about earnings of workers in Wages Council industries. There are, for example, no official figures at all relating to catering, where there are four Wages Councils covering about a million workers, and those relating to other sectors, especially retailing, are patchy and difficult or impossible to relate to the coverage of individual Councils. Moreover there are no recent figures for the distribution of earnings in industry generally. It has however been possible to make some use of a survey of distribution of earnings carried out in 1960 so as to determine where groups of low paid workers are to be found. Satisfactory figures are available for agriculture and special *ad hoc* inquiries into pay have been carried out by the National Board for Prices and Incomes in such industries as road haulage and retail drapery.

258. In the great majority of industries for which information is available earnings are below the national average. Thus in October 1966 the average weekly earnings of adult males nationally were £20 6s. 1d. Of the 22 Wages Council industries for which we have sufficiently relevant figures, only four had higher earnings—cutlery, paper bag, paper box and road haulage. In 17 of these industries average weekly earnings for adult males were below £19 and in 11 they were below £18. However there are, it must be noted, other industries not covered by Wages Councils which have low earnings levels and there are pockets of low paid workers in many industries which enjoy relatively high average earnings.

259. By and large it may be inferred that statutory protection is accorded to industries where many workers are low paid. There is, however, a good deal of evidence that statutory protection does not result in raising the pay of lower paid workers in relation to other workers. Increases settled by Wages Councils are in general treated as "across-the-board" settlements and given to workers throughout the industry. Nor does pay in Wages Council industries seem to have improved significantly in relation to that in other industries. Just as voluntary industry-wide settlements keep broadly in step with each other, so also increases in statutory minimum rates follow the general pattern set by those settlements.

260. Wages Councils are even less capable than most voluntary industry-wide collective bargaining bodies of exercising effective control over actual pay and conditions of work. Since their task is to settle minimum standards this is almost inevitable. Such control could be provided only by voluntary machinery concerned with standard arrangements over the whole industry, or with the promotion of effective company or plant agreements; but in most Wages Councils such machinery is lacking or weak.

261. Agriculture is an exception. Organisation is relatively strong on both sides of the industry and the representative bodies negotiate with considerable authority. Because employment is spread over a very large number of small and scattered units, however, statutory regulation is needed to secure adequate enforcement. In these circumstances the minimum standards laid down by the Agricultural Wages Boards come far closer to exercising control over earnings than do those of most Wages Councils. The gap between actual pay and conditions and those laid down in agricultural wages orders is considerably less than the gap between earnings and statutory minima in those Wages Council industries for which information is available and indeed than the gap between earnings and nationally agreed rates in many other industries. There may be Wages Councils in which all these circumstances are also present, but we have not been able to find evidence of it.

262. The first step required as a contribution to extending voluntary machinery is that the Wages Councils Act 1959 should be amended to empower the Secretary of State for Employment and Productivity to abolish any Wages Council where satisfied, on the application of a trade union which is representative of a substantial proportion of the workers concerned, that the wages and conditions of the workpeople would not be adversely affected if the Council ceased to exist. This possibility is referred to by the Ministry of Labour in its written evidence (Fifth Memorandum, page 117, para-

graph 16) and it should lead to the early abolition of a number of Wages Councils.

263. The Act should also be amended so as to enable the Secretary of State to exclude from the scope of a Wages Council any undertaking in which he is of the opinion that there are satisfactory arrangements for voluntary collective bargaining covering a substantial majority of its employees. The application for exclusion might be made jointly or by either party to the collective bargaining arrangements in question. This recommendation is of some importance in view of the widespread need for improved company and plant bargaining arrangements. There are numbers of large undertakings at present covered by Wages Councils, for example in distribution and catering, where it should be possible to develop satisfactory collective bargaining arrangements; and where this is done it is unnecessary and undesirable that they should be obliged also to observe statutory requirements in all their detail.

264. Next, it would ease the transition from statutory to voluntary wage-fixing if the Act were also amended to enable the Secretary of State to continue to use the inspectorate for a limited period after the abolition of a Council for enforcement of the statutory rates in force at the time of abolition. This is another possibility referred to by the Ministry of Labour (Fifth Memorandum, page 117, paragraph 17).

265. The move towards voluntary machinery would also be encouraged by amending section 8 of the Terms and Conditions of Employment Act 1959 so as to remove the provisos to subsection (1) which prevent a claim that " recognised terms or conditions " are not being observed from being reported as respects workers in Wages Council industries. It would then be possible for the Industrial Court, on the application of a representative union or employers' association, to make an award obliging an employer to observe a voluntary agreement covering his section of an industry, as for example the section of retail distribution covered by multiple shops. Wider effect would thus be given to voluntarily agreed standards. The experience gained in the application of the section 8 procedure would be valuable when the time came to abolish statutory machinery and rely on voluntary means only.

266. Finally, it is a defect of Wages Council machinery that it has no means of encouraging the development of collective dealings between managers and shop stewards or other workers' representatives in individual factories. The structure of the Councils was established at a time when attention was centred on collective bargaining at the level of the industry, and is inappropriate to a period in which the importance of workplace bargaining must be recognised and its procedures must be ordered. Wages Councils would be able to make a greater contribution to the development of effective organisation if they could handle grievances raised by the unions about matters not covered by minimum wage regulations and not therefore dealt with by the Wages Inspectorate. We therefore propose that Wages Councils should be empowered to establish disputes procedures for handling grievances raised by individual workers and groups of workers through their representatives. Observance of the disputes procedure will not be enforceable at law, and it may be that some employers will disregard them, but others will not and the opportunity to obtain a hearing for grievances should encourage organisation

and may lead on to the development of voluntary machinery. The Agricultural Wages Boards should also be empowered to establish disputes machinery of this kind. Rather than deal with all grievances themselves, both Wages Councils and Agricultural Wages Boards may find it desirable to give this task to specially appointed committees, if necessary operating on a regional basis.

Compulsory Arbitration

267. Many trade unions have represented to us that unilateral arbitration of disputes should be restored. They include large unions such as the Transport and General Workers' Union, the Amalgamated Engineering Union (as it then was) and the General and Municipal Workers' Union. Many smaller unions made a similar request. The unions' general view is that unilateral arbitration would enable them to seek redress in sections of employment where they are sometimes not recognised, and where the strike weapon is not used, and that it would also provide a means of obtaining a decision in a case where negotiation has failed, and where the employer is unwilling to treat further. The TUC in particular suggested that the restoration of unilateral arbitration " would to some extent provide a substitute for imposing a legal duty on employers to bargain and would in many cases promote collective bargaining ".

268. Employers are opposed to the restoration of unilateral arbitration. The CBI's view is that unilateral arbitration tends to undermine the effective operation of voluntary negotiating machinery; and that the absence of it has led to the parties acting with more responsibility in collective bargaining and to increased willingness to settle differences without recourse to a third party. They also feel that the greater complexity of present-day agreements, not all the items of which may be arbitrable, has tended to diminish the usefulness of conventional arbitration.

269. On its own, unilateral arbitration would not in our view make a major contribution to the extension of collective bargaining. It is true that if an employer can be compelled by a union to submit to the award of a third party on its claim, his motive for refusing recognition will be weakened, and if the union can obtain a favourable arbitration award its ability to recruit new members is likely to be strengthened. However, the criteria which determine whether a trade union is to have the right of access to arbitration are of crucial importance; they are themselves in a sense a " recognition " test.

270. Under the Industrial Disputes Order the criteria were that the union habitually took part in settling terms and conditions of employment in the trade or industry, section of trade or industry or undertaking concerned, where voluntary machinery existed; or, where it did not, that the union represented a substantial proportion of the workers in the trade or industry or section of trade or industry concerned. These criteria are such as to favour well-established unions and are not helpful to the others. Thus a union represented on the National Joint Council for the Building Industry would have been able to take to arbitration a claim against a building employer, whether or not the employer belonged to the building employers'

federation, and irrespective of whether the union had more than a handful of members employed by the employer in question. On the other hand, a white-collar union not previously active in the industry which succeeded in organising all the white-collar employees of a large building contractor would probably not have had access to arbitration, because of the difficulty of showing that it represented a "substantial proportion" of workers " in the trade or industry or section of trade or industry concerned". Its degree of representation with the particular employer would have been irrelevant.

271.   It would hardly be possible satisfactorily to widen access to this kind of arbitration. The terms of the Order were deliberately drawn up in the way they were (and on much more restrictive lines than those of the preceding Conditions of Employment and National Arbitration Order 1940) in order to avoid giving splinter and breakaway unions the opportunity to establish themselves by way of the statutory machinery. Thus, whatever its other merits, where recognition was concerned the Industrial Disputes Order gave least help to those most in need of it. It is hardly a coincidence therefore that no major concessions in the field of recognition were made as a result of the existence of the Industrial Disputes Tribunal (see Research Paper No. 6, paragraphs 138-150 and 261). Given the extent to which the capacity of a union to organise is affected by the extent it is recognised, the restitution of the Industrial Disputes Tribunal would of itself hardly be likely to provide much impetus to the development of collective bargaining.

272.   The restoration of unilateral arbitration must in any case be considered in the context of the future development of our industrial relations system as a whole. Many matters will come within the scope of company and plant bargaining, for example working practices and the flexible use of man-power, which unilateral arbitration is unlikely to deal with effectively. Moreover, where voluntary machinery is relatively well developed, the provi-sion of unilateral arbitration must tend to have a distorting effect. It is already open to the parties to agree upon arrangements for arbitration, and if they have not done so it is because one party or the other, or perhaps both, do not consider it in their interests. They may have valid reasons for not putting into the hands of a third party responsibility for decisions of great importance to them.

273.   We do, however, see a useful role for unilateral arbitration to support the work of the Industrial Relations Commission, in three different sets of circumstances. First, where the employer rejects a recommendation of the Commission to grant recognition, the Commission should be empowered to recommend that the union or unions should have the right of unilateral arbitration. This will give them at least a foothold and may encourage the employer to change his mind. Secondly, even where the employer accepts a recommendation to grant recognition he may still be able to evade effective bargaining, for where workers are traditionally reluctant to strike or scattered in small units so that it is difficult to bring their collective strength to bear he may be able to exploit the position to reduce bargaining to a mockery. In these circumstances the Commission should also be

empowered to recommend unilateral arbitration as a means of imposing a fair settlement of the union's claims and a means to strengthen its organisation. Thirdly, the Commission's investigations may reveal circumstances of this kind even in industries in which unions are already formally recognised. Here again it should be empowered to recommend unilateral arbitration.

274. We recommend therefore that unilateral arbitration should be available for use on a selective basis. Its use should be confined to circumstances where it can contribute to the growth or maintenance of sound collective bargaining machinery. It should therefore be available only in industries, sections of industry, or undertakings in which the Secretary of State for Employment and Productivity has certified that such circumstances exist, after the Industrial Relations Commission has so advised following an inquiry in which both sides have had an opportunity to put their point of view. The Secretary of State would at the same time define or specify in the light of the Commission's recommendations the parties who are to have access to the arbitration machinery. We envisage that the Industrial Court would be the arbitration body.

275. Section 8 of the Terms and Conditions of Employment Act continues to serve a useful purpose and should be retained, but certain amendments are desirable. We recommend earlier (in paragraph 265) the removal of the provisos which prevent its application to workers in Wages Council industries. It will also be necessary to ensure that its use does not hamper the development of company and plant bargaining. This could happen if an employer were compelled to comply with a particular term or condition laid down in an industry-wide agreement, although a company or plant agreement had varied that particular term or condition in return for other advantages granted to employees. Section 8 should therefore be amended to make clear that in considering a claim made under it the Industrial Court should take into account not only the particular term or condition to which the claim relates but the terms and conditions laid down by collective agreement as a whole.

INCOMES POLICY AND THE WORK OF WAGES COUNCILS AND ARBITRATORS

276. In setting out our conclusions so far about the part which Wages Councils and arbitration can play in promoting the extension of collective bargaining we have not touched on the implications of incomes policy for these institutions. We now turn to this question.

Wages Councils

277. Wages Councils have no power to determine rates of pay other than minimum rates for each designation of worker which they cover. After inquiries undertaken on our behalf the Ministry of Labour informed us that the prevalent view among chairmen of Wages Councils was that it was the primary duty of a Wages Council to fix reasonable minimum standards of remuneration and that it should not be influenced by considerations of probable repercussions on workers with higher rates of pay. The trade unions took the same view. The employers generally disagreed, holding

70

that such matters as average earnings (including overtime) should be considered.

278. Wages Council chairmen were reported generally to hold that Councils were not debarred from taking the prices and incomes policy into account and to assert that they commonly did so. It is evident however that chairmen meant by this that they would consider whether proposals to increase minimum rates could be justified in the light of incomes policy and not that they had the duty (or the power) to consider their effect on pay in the industry as a whole in the light of the incomes policy. This is of course a very important distinction. Low pay has from the beginning been one of the criteria under which exceptional pay increases have been permitted under the incomes policy, and many workers on statutory minimum rates of pay may reasonably be considered low paid. The evidence we have received makes it clear, however, that increases settled by Wages Councils are generally treated as " across-the-board " increases for workers throughout the industry, and this may be quite contrary to incomes policy. The trade unions for their part in the main considered that Wages Councils should not be required to base their proposals on incomes policy considerations. The employers generally took the opposite view, though they felt that sometimes Wages Councils were in fact prevented from taking incomes policy into account by the attitude of trade union and independent members.

279. It is evident that incomes policy raises very difficult problems in relation to Wages Councils. If their role is restricted, as a majority of their members believe it to be, to the narrow issue of setting reasonable minimum rates, then it is impossible for them to give adequate consideration to the implications of incomes policy for their decisions. However, even if Wages Councils were able to take a wider view of their function, they would still be faced with the fact that they do not and were never designed to exercise effective control over actual earnings and conditions in the industries with which they are concerned and are therefore in no position to secure the observance of incomes policy.

280. The only adequate long-run solution to the problem is the extension to Wages Council industries of voluntary collective bargaining which can exercise control over actual earnings. In the short run some improvement might be achieved by more precise guidance on the interpretation and application of any provision contained in the relevant White Papers concerning special treatment for the low paid. What is required in particular is a clear indication of the means to be adopted to ensure that exceptional increases granted on grounds of low pay are not extended to other workers so as to defeat the object of exceptional treatment. Guidance is not required for Wages Councils only. Some of the lowest-paid workers are not covered by Wages Councils, either because it has not been found possible so far to set up Councils to cover them (as in the case of employees in unlicensed residential establishments) or because they are in industries where organisation and general levels of pay are such that they are not needed. Alternative methods of protecting the lowest-paid therefore need to be examined, including the possibility of a national minimum wage or of fixing statutory minimum earnings for broad groups of industries. These are complex and difficult problems

to which it is not for us to provide answers. In our view it is for the Government, having carried out a review of all the associated problems, to formulate and state in clear terms what its policy is in relation to the lowest-paid workers and how it is to be pursued.

Arbitration

281. The criteria by which successive incomes policies require pay claims and settlements to be judged have been set out in a series of White Papers "intended to be applied by all concerned with the determination of employment incomes in the private and public sectors whether at industry, company or plant level and including arbitrators, independent review bodies and statutory wage fixing bodies".

282. The President of the Industrial Court, Sir Roy Wilson, Q.C., told us in evidence that incomes policy was one of the matters taken into account by the Industrial Court but that the Industrial Court felt no overriding obligation to make awards complying with it.[1] Other arbitrators adopt the same view.

283. Where arbitration is agreed upon privately between the parties there is at present nothing to prevent the parties from expressly excluding consideration of the policy, or of the national interest generally, from the arbitrator's terms of reference. Probably a more practical danger is that the arbitrator may be limited by his terms of reference to making an award in an area bounded on the one hand by the claim of the trade union and on the other by the highest offer of the employer, whereas the application of the prices and incomes policy might indicate an award lower than the employer is prepared to give.

284. The application of incomes policy will be frustrated if arbitrators make, and may even feel themselves compelled by their terms of reference to make, awards which do not conform with the incomes policy. It is open to the Government to refer any arbitration award to the National Board for Prices and Incomes; but the number of references it is possible for the Board to deal with is limited and if references of arbitration awards became at all frequent they would inevitably undermine the authority of arbitration.

285. It is desirable therefore that effect should be given to incomes policy in the making of the arbitration awards. To this end we recommend legislation placing on all arbitrators an obligation to take incomes policy into account when making their awards.

286. Even so, in view of the general terms in which policy has so far been formulated, it may not always be possible to tell from awards whether arbitrators have in fact had regard for incomes policy. It is the tradition in Britain for arbitrators to give no reasons for their awards. This practice has a great deal to recommend it so long as the only object of arbitration is to resolve disputes. One or both parties to a dispute might cavil at the reasoning when they would be willing to accept the award. Nevertheless the practice is incompatible with any attempt to develop a rational incomes policy. If the policy were a simple matter of restricting all increases in wage rates to *x* per cent a year, it would be evident whether or not an arbitration decision

[1]Minutes of Evidence 45, pp. 1936-7, paras. 9-10.

was in accordance with the policy, but policies never are so simple. There are the exceptions, there are the effects on earnings, and there may be consequences for other groups of workers. The successful evolution of a policy depends on a growing understanding of how to recognise and handle exceptional cases and how to foresee and provide for the consequences of decisions on pay. This cannot be done unless decisions are reasoned.

287. There are disputes in which no reason can be given. Where the parties can see no right answer to some vexed question but want a verdict to put an end to their squabbling, the arbitrators may have to plump for an answer without other justification than that it will end the squabble. In other instances the arbitrators may agree on the decision but not on their reasons. But arbitrators should be encouraged to give reasons whenever they can, especially in major decisions on pay which are likely to be significant for the development of incomes policy, and in those cases where they do not feel able to give reasons to state so plainly. There is no need for a change in their terms of reference to enable this to be done. Arbitrators are free to give reasons if they choose. A statement from the Government, backed by the TUC and the CBI, should be enough to put an end to the old tradition.

Chapter VI

THE EFFICIENT USE OF MANPOWER

288.   In the previous two chapters we have applied our analysis of the system of industrial relations to develop proposals for the reform of collective bargaining as a whole and for its strengthening and extension.   We now turn to consider particular aspects of industrial relations also in the light of our general analysis of the system.   The first of these is the efficient use of manpower.   We divide our discussion of it into two parts: restrictive labour practices and training.

(1) RESTRICTIVE LABOUR PRACTICES

HOW EFFICIENTLY IS MANPOWER USED NOW?

289.   It is necessary first to consider how efficiently manpower is used at present.   One obvious line of inquiry is to compare our situation with that in other countries.   Dr. Angus Maddison, of the Organisation for European Co-operation and Development, has submitted to us in evidence a paper (which we are publishing) in which he sets out tables in which levels of output in relation to numbers employed and also in relation to man hours worked in 1965 in twelve industrialised countries are compared.   The main basis for Dr. Maddison's figures was provided by a comparative study by the Organisation for European Economic Co-operation of the gross national product of various countries in 1955 and by series published by the Organisation for European Co-operation and Development showing the rates at which these have been increasing in the period 1955-1965, together with OECD statistics of employment.   The figures in the following table are reproduced from Tables 10 and 12 of Dr. Maddison's evidence:

International Comparisons of Levels of Output per Person Employed and of Output per Man Hour in 1965
Index UK=100

Country	Adjusted Comparative Level of Real Output per Person Employed in 1965	Adjusted Comparative Level of Real Output per Man Hour in 1965
USA	184·1	188·0
Canada	137·1	140·8
Germany (Federal Republic) ..	130·6	129·6
Norway	119·7	120·9
Belgium	118·1	119·4
France	116·0	110·7
Netherlands	114·8	106·3
Denmark	101·8	104·2
UK	100·0	100·0
Italy	87·9	88·5
USSR	82·8	89·5
Japan	74·0	74·2

Source: Evidence of Dr. Angus Maddison.

The table shows that the USA has a long lead over any European country in terms of real output per person employed, with Canada next. Of Western European countries included in the table, only Italy ranks lower than the United Kingdom. The figures comparing output per man hour do not show a very different picture, though the lead of France and the Netherlands over the United Kingdom is less pronounced.

290. It is possible to argue about the choice of date and about the most accurate methods to use in making these international comparisons, but there is no reason to think that the selection of another year would have made a significant difference or to doubt the validity of the general picture the figures quoted give. It is a disturbing picture. It has resulted from the relatively slow growth rate of the British economy in recent years as compared with most other industrialised countries. But to what extent is it due to poor use of manpower? It is known for example that the rate of investment in new machinery and equipment in this country lags behind that of many of our competitors, and this is clearly a factor of outstanding importance. A man may be working efficiently with the tools at his disposal, but still be producing far less than a man backed by more modern equipment.

291. We have studied the available information about comparative manning standards in different countries. Only tentative conclusions are possible because of the limited amount of work done in this field. Among the most useful studies has been that carried out by the Chemical Economic Development Committee. Studies such as this suggest that more men are usually needed to produce the same output in the United Kingdom than in the USA. In some cases such factors as economies of scale which are possible in the USA but not in this country are very important; but even allowing for these it appears that manpower tends to be used more efficiently in the USA. There is little evidence that the pace of work is faster in the USA, but it is said that workers in American plants are in some cases willing to accept greater responsibility than is usual here; and that this saves manpower, especially where supervision and maintenance are concerned. Differences in union structure or attitudes do not seem to be a major factor. It is generally considered, however, that American management is more effective, with objectives more clearly defined, more delegation of responsibility and a simpler managerial structure. American managements are also said to be more cost-conscious where the use of labour is concerned; and if this is so a major contributory cause is, undoubtedly, that labour costs are far higher there than here.

292. One of the conclusions reached by those who studied the British chemical industry was that changes in attitudes and practices could, on their own and without other changes, produce a manpower saving in the industry in this country which " could well be as much as 20 per cent of the present numbers employed; alternatively it could take the form of a 25 per cent increase in output from the existing employee force ". The report went on to say that " the changes required to achieve this greater efficiency are entirely within the control of the people involved in the British chemical industry, and could all be effected within a relatively short time ".

293. Studies made and results achieved in this country confirm that there is

75

substantial room for improvement in the efficiency with which labour is used. Management consultants to whom we have talked asserted that industry in this country could, with existing capital, raise its output very considerably, and they have given examples. Some of the best evidence available concerns productivity bargaining.

294. It was estimated by Mr. Allan Flanders that following the first productivity agreements at the Fawley refinery of the Esso Petroleum Co. productivity per man hour rose by about 50 per cent in two years. The study of productivity agreements carried out by the National Board for Prices and Incomes (Report No. 36, Cmnd. 3311) shows that the undertakings concerned have been enabled thereby to secure considerably more efficient use of manpower. Thus in electricity supply between April 1964 and April 1966 Area Boards' business expanded substantially, although average weekly hours worked fell from 49 to 43, while manpower increased by only 1.7 per cent. British Oxygen calculated that, as a result of a productivity agreement representing only a first phase in improving manpower use, they could reduce the average hours worked at each depot by 15 per cent while maintaining output, and without increasing the labour force. These are examples only. They are supplemented by evidence collected by ourselves about productivity bargaining.[1] For example, the Steel Company of Wales negotiated a productivity agreement enabling them to reduce the number of mates employed at their Port Talbot works from 1,500 to 500, the labour force as a whole being reduced by that figure without any adverse effect on output.

295. Productivity bargaining has largely been pioneered by progressive undertakings, and this leads us to infer that in industry as a whole the room for the better use of manpower is at least as great, and very probably greater. The National Board for Prices and Incomes has said, in reporting on the reference concerning productivity agreements (Report No. 36, paragraph 134):

" Outside the industries covered by this reference, we have encountered wide scope for increasing the pace of economic growth by the more effective utilisation of manpower and existing capital equipment. There are examples in the printing industry, in road haulage, in railways, in buses, in the industrial Civil Service and in local authority services and hospitals."

The Board has produced reports on each of these industries which suggest that there is ample scope for improving labour productivity. In the docks, the Committee of Inquiry under Lord Devlin (Cmnd. 2734, August 1965) revealed much inefficiency and great scope for improved working practices. A number of reports have thrown light on the disturbing lack of efficiency with which manpower is used in the newspaper and printing industries; these include the report of the Royal Commission on the Press under the chairmanship of Lord Shawcross published in 1962 (Cmnd. 1811) and the report of a Court of Inquiry into the printing industry under the chairmanship of Lord Cameron published in January 1967 (Cmnd. 3184). The reasonable conclusion is that there is great scope for improvement; and that this represents not only a challenge, but a major opportunity.

---

[1]Research Paper No. 4, *Productivity Bargaining*, HMSO 1967.

WHAT ARE RESTRICTIVE LABOUR PRACTICES?

296. Restrictive labour practices may be defined as " rules or customs which unduly hinder the efficient use of labour ". It is necessary to limit the definition to cases where efficiency is " unduly " hindered, because there are many provisions in safety legislation and in collective agreements, for example, which limit employers' freedom in the use of manpower but which can unhesitatingly be accepted as justified. Indeed all restrictive labour practices have or once had some justification. The justifications should not be ignored, but judged against the loss which the practices entail.

297. Most of the practices which result in serious waste of manpower can be understood only in relation to particular circumstances in particular undertakings or plants. For example, there is no standard practice as regards the use of craftsmen's mates. Practice varies from company to company, and even within companies from plant to plant. The use of mates may not be inefficient at all; on the other hand the high priority given in many productivity agreements to the redeployment of mates, and the improvements in productivity gained as a result, show that they are often seriously under-employed. Again, each company has its own levels of overtime; and although the use of habitual overtime may be very extensive the problems it presents are complex and vary a great deal from one factory or workshop to the next.

298. Where practices of this kind exist, insistence on retaining them usually comes from workers themselves, acting as groups which have certain interests in common which they try as best they can to further, rather than from trade unions as such. For example, if an employer wishes to reduce overtime he will find himself having to confront opposition from work groups who see the removal of overtime as a threat to their earnings. If a management decides to get rid of craftsmen's mates, the mates, as a group, will feel their interests to be threatened. Will they be sacked? If not, what other jobs will they be asked to do? Will their earnings suffer? Likewise the craftsmen as a group will want to know if they are going to lose status. Are they going to be expected to do mates' work in future? How convenient will the new working arrangements be? The fears associated with change are reasonable fears. For change may face people—and their families too—with urgent practical problems. Technological change, the expansion of new industries and the decay of old, and the need for mobility of labour mean that men are obliged to change jobs, and perhaps to move to completely new areas to live and work. They may find the skills they possess are no longer in demand. They may face a severe cut in pay, and so on. These are substantial problems and so long as they go unsolved the introduction of change itself will be held up.

299. Most restrictive labour practices are not enforced by the unions as such. Most responsible trade union leaders deplore the habitual use of overtime. If time-keeping is bad, it is because management has been slack, not because trade unions have encouraged it. It is not trade union policy that mates should be under-employed.

300. However, this is not to gainsay that trade unions have an important influence. If a union is generally resistant to change, then resistance on the shop floor will be reinforced. If it is favourable to change, then proposals designed to improve efficiency may be helped. There have also been occasions when trade unions have set their faces so obdurately against change as to justify the conclusion that they see little connection between the efficiency of industry and the living standards of their members. This attitude has in the past been found in unions operating in the shipbuilding and ship-repairing industry, though there have recently been encouraging signs of changed attitudes on their part. Some trade unions in the printing and newspaper industries still maintain an unreasonably negative attitude to the need for change. We invited the Printing and Kindred Trades Federation, the Society of Graphical and Allied Trades, the National Graphical Association and the Society of Lithographic Artists, Designers and Engravers to submit their views on comments about restrictive labour practices made by employers and we regard it both as significant and as a matter for regret that none of them saw fit to accept our invitation.

301. Sometimes proposals affecting craft demarcations in industries like shipbuilding and printing may run up against deep-rooted trade union resistance because they appear to threaten the whole basis on which a craft union exists. Since this is inextricably bound up with the system of training through apprenticeship as it now works, we return to it in the second part of this chapter.

302. Whereas the desire of work groups for security frequently explains resistance to the removal of restrictive labour practices, many such practices came into existence for quite different reasons. Thus in the past the general use of craftsmen's mates almost certainly made more sense than it does today, because mates were used to perform a wider range of tasks, the content of jobs being such as to make greater demands on the specialised skills of craftsmen. Many practices which managements have sought to change through productivity bargaining are simply practices which have been accepted as normal in the past, but which have in time become a clear hindrance to efficiency. For example, the need to carry out maintenance in the evenings and at the week-ends so that power stations can operate at full capacity when demand for electricity is at its highest meant that the traditional "normal hours of work" could not be observed without inefficiency in the electricity generating industry; staggering of hours was therefore necessary. Many inefficient labour practices are simply the result of changing circumstances and technological advance. What was once appropriate, or at any rate tolerable, becomes in time inefficient and wasteful.

303. It would however be totally misleading to suggest that the primary responsibility for the wasteful use of manpower in this country rested either upon workers or upon trade unions. Even where restrictive labour practices exist, their removal is only one element in securing the efficient use of resources, which is the task of management. To emphasise the importance of getting rid of restrictive labour practices is to distort the problem. It results in stating what is essentially a positive task in negative terms. Those who regard productivity agreements as no more than a means of "buying out"

78

certain practices have a wholly inadequate idea of their purpose. This point was emphasised by the National Board for Prices and Incomes when they said (Report No. 36, paragraph 9):

" We must, however, emphasise that the starting-point of most agreements has not been a list of proposed changes in working practices and in pay, but the preparation by management of plans for new and more effective methods of operation for the whole plant or company. Only when these have been drawn up and explored can a company know what particular changes in practice are most needed and what alterations in pay are feasible."

304. There are indeed industries in which restrictive labour practices in the commonly accepted sense of the term hardly exist, but in which manpower is nevertheless used inefficiently, either because managements are unaware that it is being wasted, or because they are so preoccupied with other matters that the problem is never tackled. Thus the National Board for Prices and Incomes has said, as regards local authorities, that while it was frequently asserted that the low capacity among many of their manual employees accounted for any lack of efficiency, " the more important reason . . . is the acceptance by management of low standards of performance as normal, and a failure to take steps to realise the full potential of the labour force " (Report No. 29, Cmnd. 3230, paragraph 61). The Board said in the same report that in the National Health Service much improvement in the use of the manual workforce was possible, and " the main deficiencies would seem to be in organisation and the use of modern labour management techniques " (paragraph 70); and as regards water supply that " supervision and job organisation is inadequate in many cases " (paragraph 74).

RESTRICTIVE PRACTICES AND THE BRITISH SYSTEM OF INDUSTRIAL RELATIONS

305. This account of restrictive labour practices makes it evident that the formal system of industrial relations in Britain is especially ill-fitted to accomplish improvements in the use of manpower. Where restrictions are enforced on the workers' side of industry, this usually rests with work groups rather than with their unions. The formal system provides for negotiation between unions and employers at industry level, but these negotiations can rarely exercise effective control over the methods of work employed in individual factories. In the factory the assumption of the formal system is that managers have the final decision on methods of work, although they may wish first to consult. In practice this leads to informal and fragmented bargaining and fosters " custom and practice ". This is an environment in which work group restrictive labour practices are likely to thrive, and yet any attempt to negotiate relaxation runs counter to the formal assumptions of the system.

306. In paragraphs 92 and 93 we have drawn attention to the increasing use of overtime working in post-war Britain, and to the methods used by workers whose standard of living depends on overtime pay to ensure that overtime work will be available and that they will control its distribution. These are practices which can bring about a situation in which decisions on the volume

and distribution of overtime bear little relation to the production needs of the undertaking, and in which men cannot be expected to show much interest in the efficiency of the undertaking because they know that they must waste time to safeguard their earnings and that managers are conniving at the practice, despite the disregard for the value both of a man's labour and of his leisure which this implies. Nevertheless it is clear that no remedy can be found so long as it is assumed that pay is settled in industry-wide negotiations and that overtime is a matter of managerial prerogative.

307. Overmanning provides another example of the way in which the practical situation in the factory and workshop is at variance with the formal assumptions. Printing employers have particularly complained of it, and we have learned of its existence in many other industries, including shipbuilding, the docks and engineering.

308. There are instances in which work groups are able to use their power to bring about a gradual increase in manning standards akin to the upward drift in overtime working. More commonly, however, work groups obstruct any reductions in manning below the existing level, whatever that may be. This demonstrates that " managerial prerogative " cannot be as effective as the formal system assumes. If it were managers would eliminate overmanning wherever they found it.

309. Usually resistance to reduction in manning reflects a desire by workers to protect their jobs. In the docks, for example, insistence on retaining existing gang sizes despite changes in working methods has offered some safeguard to workers in what has hitherto been the most casual of employments. At times the use of overmanning goes beyond this to serve as a device for raising earnings. In printing, for instance, where manning complements are excessive it can happen that a smaller number of men actually performs the job and they share between themselves the pay of the full complement.

310. These instances of overmanning show that it is used in the rational pursuit of the interests of workers, narrow and shortsighted though these interests may sometimes be. Managers are not likely to achieve efficient standards of manning unless they take this into account. And yet the formal system of industrial relations provides no means whereby they can be taken into account; it postulates that manning is a matter for managers to decide and that work practices are not subject to negotiation.

311. While the formal system of industrial relations offers no means for negotiating the relaxation of restrictive practices enforced by work groups, it also fails to encourage the improved use of manpower in industries where agreements have not been undermined by workshop practices to the extent that is common in manufacturing and where the main reason for inefficiency can only be the acceptance of low standards by management. The local authorities and the National Health Service provide examples. Their pay statistics bear witness to the unusual importance of their industry-wide agreements in determining earnings. In October 1966, for example, the average basic pay of male manual workers employed by the local authorities stood at £12 13s. 0d. and their average earnings were £15 18s. 10d., most of this relatively small difference being made up by overtime pay. The comparable figures for the Health Service were £12 19s. 11d. and £16 13s. 6d. with shift

allowances and overtime pay accounting for almost all of the modest gap between them.[1] Nevertheless the National Board for Prices and Incomes held that the " root cause " of low pay in these services was " low productivity ". The proper remedy was " for individual local authorities and employers in the National Health Service to introduce properly worked out and controlled schemes that will directly relate pay to improvements in productivity ". Because of the time involved in developing such schemes the Board suggested an interim arrangement for a productivity increment to be paid to manual workers where an equivalent saving in manpower had been achieved. It was proposed that " local joint committees could be established and start working out schemes for saving manpower and putting them into effect ". In other words efficiency in these services as elsewhere could be achieved only by recognising the limitations of industry-wide agreements and by introducing negotiations within the undertaking to link pay and performance. These negotiations were not, however, to be autonomous, informal and fragmented. They were to be within the framework of a revised industry-wide agreement, they were to be recognised as leading to formally negotiated agreements, and they were to cover all the manual workers employed by a given authority.

A RESTRICTIVE LABOUR PRACTICES TRIBUNAL?

312. It has been suggested to us that it may be desirable to deal with restrictive labour practices by means of a tribunal, and we now consider this. (Mr. Shonfield's view, which differs from that of the remainder of us, is set out in his separate note.) The suggestion was developed by the Engineering Employers' Federation in its evidence. The Federation drew attention to a number of restrictive practices, and went on to say:

> " Efforts have been made to remove these practices by discussion and negotiation but not always with success. It is hoped that informal discussions currently taking place will be more successful, but if experience shows that no significant improvement can be achieved, then the Federation suggests that such practices should be examined publicly by an independent tribunal. Publicity is in itself some deterrent but it is doubted whether this alone would be enough. It is suggested for consideration that the tribunal which investigates such restrictive practices should have power to issue an order requiring those insisting on or supporting a restrictive practice to desist therefrom. Thereafter, any breach of such an order might be attended by penalties or treated as a contempt of court."

313. The Restrictive Trade Practices Act 1956 is sometimes quoted as a parallel. This Act lays down that certain trading practices are *prima facie* against the public interest, and the Restrictive Practices Court's task is to judge whether particular practices satisfy conditions justifying the making of an exception. It would however be out of the question to list all restrictions on the use of labour and say that these were to be assumed to be against the public interest, unless the contrary were proved. Only those which " unduly hinder " the efficient use of manpower could be included. But it would be

---

[1]National Board for Prices and Incomes, Report No. 29, p.13.

impracticable to list them, since the same practice may be efficient in one set of circumstances while inefficient in another. It is in any case mistaken to think that it is possible to deal with practices which are part of a worker's way of life in the same way as specific and clearly identifiable trading practices.

314. It might still be argued that a tribunal could deal with specific complaints that particular restrictive practices were being unilaterally imposed; it might be said that it would be easy to show that these were unreasonable and restrictive, and that a tribunal should be able to order union officials supporting them to desist. The matter is not however so simple. One is often dealing with what is essentially a bargaining situation. The real question at issue may be the rates to be paid for new jobs or the proper safeguards or compensation to accompany change. Often the difficulty runs deeper. Craftsmen may be firmly convinced that it is their duty to guard and uphold the " rights " of their craft. This is essentially a situation in which only educative processes and reasoning can lead people to revise their attitudes, and become willing to bargain.

315. In situations of these kinds it would not be useful or desirable to have a procedure under which a tribunal could order those insisting on or indulging in a restrictive practice to desist from doing so. Nor would it conduce to good industrial relations to enforce such an order by committing to prison for contempt of court those who refused to obey it. As regards the workers themselves such enforcement would be impracticable. Enforcement of the tribunal's order by punishment of their trade union officials (as envisaged by the Federation) would also be unlikely to promote efficiency, quite apart from considerations of justice. If employers are seeking increased co-operation from their employees, resort to legal sanctions is not likely to produce it.

316. It could be argued alternatively that what is needed is not a tribunal which will order people to desist from restrictive labour practices, but one which will promote collective bargaining by hearing complaints of failure to negotiate in good faith. Where it found that trade union officials were not negotiating in good faith because they were not making a reasonable attempt to reach a settlement providing for improved working practices, then the tribunal might order them to do so; and if they did not do so, a monetary penalty might in the last resort be inflicted on the union.

317. We do not propose in this report as a solution to problems of trade union recognition that an obligation to bargain in good faith should be placed upon employers. Neither do we think that such an obligation should be placed upon trade unions as a solution to the problem of restrictive labour practices. Trade union negotiators have the skill to parry almost indefinitely allegations that they are not acting in good faith. In any case the major difficulty is not a lack of good faith but disagreement as to what would constitute a reasonable bargain. The tribunal would in effect be asked to define an area marking out the limits of reasonable negotiation; and the danger is that the area so marked out would either be so large that the tribunal's judgment would have little or no effect on the situation or so narrow that it would amount to an attempt to impose an arbitration decision. The former would be valueless, the latter impracticable.

318. Although preceded by some famous examples overseas, like the East Coast agreement in the American docks, the Fawley agreements covering Esso's main refinery, first drew British attention to productivity bargaining. Fawley was followed by other refineries, by the oil companies' distribution undertakings, by ICI and other chemical firms, by the " status " agreement in the electricity supply industry, by the Steel Company of Wales, and by many others.

319. These agreements were based on plans for more efficient methods of working. To achieve these new methods, work practices had to be modified. First, workers agreed to perform tasks they had previously regarded as outside their jobs, and to allow others to perform part of their work, so that labour might be used more effectively. This new " flexibility " affected not only craftsmen, but also their mates, process workers, semi-skilled production workers in manufacturing, drivers and their mates, loaders and other workers as well. Secondly, limitations on output were terminated or modified. Thirdly, tea breaks and other interruptions of work were ended. Fourthly, manning scales were revised, in some instances on the basis of work study. Fifthly, all these changes released labour from some jobs and put an end to others, like that of the craftsman's mate, and workers agreed to be redeployed to new jobs, which might require training. In some cases where the surplus men could not be absorbed there were special redundancy arrangements.

320. Many of these changes were consciously aimed at putting an end to overtime, or to reducing it to the level required for emergencies and fluctuations in work and to bring it under the control of managers. To meet demands for services at unusual times, and to secure fuller use of expensive equipment, shift systems were introduced in several of the agreements.

321. At the same time, arrangements for pay were revised. The most common form of revision was a substantial increase in basic rates, sufficient to compensate for the loss in overtime and perhaps a little more, together with a simplification in the number of grades and rates of pay in order to facilitate flexibility. In some instances a number of special payments were terminated and incentive bonus schemes " bought out ", compensation again being given in the basic rate. As a consequence workers gained in security. Their weekly pay was stable, instead of dependent on overtime or incentive earnings, and pensions, holiday pay and sick pay were based on a realistic figure.

322. In some cases the opportunity was taken to eliminate or reduce distinctions between manual and white-collar workers. Manual workers were given an annual salary, and such things as holiday entitlements, sick pay schemes and rights to notice were improved to bring them into line with, or at any rate nearer to, those enjoyed by white-collar workers. Distinctions between manual and white-collar workers in industry, whose origins lie far in the past and which have now become artificial, manifest themselves in many ways besides formal fringe benefit arrangements, but changes such as these have helped to reduce them and so to create an atmosphere more conducive to good industrial relations.

323. Agreements of this kind involve radical departures from traditional collective bargaining. There is formal negotiation about work practices. There is no separation of negotiable issues and issues suitable only for consultation. Matters previously covered by " custom and practice " are for the first time made the subject of formal collective bargaining. Most of the agreements are comprehensive in the sense of applying to all manual workers in the factory or undertaking, and the pay of white-collar workers is indirectly affected too.

324. Perhaps most important of all, these agreements mean changes in management attitudes and organisation. Planning them induces new attitudes to costs, to measurement of performance and to control over performance. Because more managers are brought into these negotiations than into conventional negotiations, many of them are " made closely aware for the first time of the consequences for industrial relations of technical and financial decisions " and " the experience of applying the agreements . . . has brought about nothing less than a revolution in managerial control over working hours and practices in many of the undertakings affected "[1].

325. With productivity as one of the main grounds for pay increases under incomes policy, there has been great pressure to develop productivity bargaining. Not all the agreements made under such pressure will necessarily be satisfactory. " Partial " productivity agreements affecting only one group of workers in an undertaking may distort a complex pay structure still further. Concessions to powerful groups may be dressed up as productivity bargains for the sake of appearances. But a genuine productivity agreement offers solutions to many of the typical problems of industrial relations. It raises standards of supervision and of managerial planning and control. It closes the gap between rates of pay and actual earnings. It permits negotiations on performance. It enables demarcation difficulties to be eliminated or reduced. It concentrates decisions at the level of the company or factory. It formalises and regulates the position of the shop steward.

326. Productivity bargaining is not however a unique way of solving problems of the efficient use of manpower. It is a current fashion to emphasise the dramatic increase in productivity which can sometimes be achieved by negotiating changes in methods of production. However, a number of organisations including the National Coal Board and certain motor and engineering factories have reshaped their wage structures by agreements intended to get rid of payment by results or to bring it firmly under control. Work has started in new factories on the basis of agreements designed to allow controlled pay structures from the start. These are not productivity agreements in the accepted sense, but like productivity agreements they not only promote orderly industrial relations but also make a long-run contribution to efficiency. What they have in common with productivity agreements is that they too are concluded at the level of the company and factory and that they too cut across the traditional methods of conducting industrial relations at that level.

---

[1]National Board for Prices and Incomes, Report No. 36, *Productivity Agreements* (Cmnd. 3311).

327. It is one of the features of our traditional approach to collective bargaining that negotiations about pay are largely separated from considerations of efficiency. This approach contrasts with that of such countries as the USA and Canada where company collective contracts lasting for a fixed period, usually up to two or three years, are negotiated in the light of the prosperity of the individual company and where therefore during the currency of the contract employees have the incentive to accept change derived from the knowledge that the more efficient the company becomes the higher the wages it will be able to afford when a new contract comes to be negotiated. In this country the system does not provide any formal method of linking levels of pay with the efficiency of companies, with the result that workers are encouraged to wrest what increases they can piecemeal as opportunities arise. The introduction of new methods or machines offers such opportunities. Thus change itself becomes the subject of dispute and controversy, and is too often as a result delayed or even not attempted.

328. Our traditional system means also that in conditions of full employment substantial increases are periodically conceded by employers at industry level without any gain in return. It is a one-sided affair. It propagates the notion that higher wages happen automatically rather than having to be earned. And the individual employer is placed in a cleft stick: he needs to organise work more efficiently to meet the higher wages bills thrust upon him, but can do so only by negotiation; and his scope for negotiation is drastically narrowed because so much has already been given away at industry level.

329. Our proposals for the reform of the collective bargaining system are therefore fundamental to the improved use of manpower. They will get rid of assumptions and attitudes to collective bargaining which have allowed restrictive labour practices to grow and efficiency to languish. They will put in management's hand an instrument—the factory agreement—which, properly used, can contribute to much higher productivity. The work of the Industrial Relations Commission can give an impetus to change and progress which has been signally lacking hitherto. The direct benefits will be felt not only by employers but also by their employees, and indirectly the community as a whole will gain. That this is so underlines the urgency of the need for reform.

(2) TRAINING
INTRODUCTION

330. Training is an area in which restrictive traditions have especially deep roots in British industry and where the pressure of technological advance makes the need for a radical change in outlook particularly urgent. The general criticism can also be levelled at British industry that there has been too much apathy about training for all kinds of jobs at all levels. Only in recent years have steps begun to be taken to remedy the inadequacy of the effort put into training, and in particular to make good the comparative neglect of training outside apprenticeships.

331. Since the last war many trade unions and employers' associations have entered into joint recruitment and training agreements. These have usually

dealt only with apprenticeships or learnerships for young people and not with adult training or re-training. They have covered such matters as the age of recruitment, length of apprenticeship (varying between 3 and 5 years) and day-release of employees with pay for further education. According to the evidence of the Ministry of Labour the parties to these agreements have tended to lay greater emphasis on apprenticeship as a condition of employment than as a form of training.

332. There has been a constant shortage of skilled manpower in the post-war period. Previous attempts to remedy the situation entirely by voluntary methods having failed, the Industrial Training Act 1964 was enacted. The Act has three main objectives:

(i) to ensure an adequate supply of properly trained men and women at all levels in industry;

(ii) to secure an improvement in the quality and efficiency of industrial training;

(iii) to share the cost of training more evenly between firms.

The Act empowers the Secretary of State for Employment and Productivity to set up industrial training boards for such "activities of industry or commerce" as he thinks appropriate, and these boards have the responsibility of securing the provision of adequate training in the areas they cover. The boards have an equal number of employer and trade union members, as well as a number of educational members. The boards are required to make a levy on employers, and have power to make grants to employers who provide training of an approved standard, so that in this way the cost of training can be evened out. By the end of 1967 twenty-one boards had been set up covering some 11 million workers in all.

333. The main responsibility for training adult workers no less than apprentices lies and must continue to lie with industry. However, the Department of Employment and Productivity in addition runs government training centres which enable workers displaced from contracting industries to be re-trained for new jobs. Intensive full-time courses, usually of six months' duration are given in a variety of trades. Syllabuses are worked out by specialist staff of the Department in consultation with both sides of industry. This training has until recently been provided on a very limited scale, but the position is being improved. Four years ago there were only 13 centres in operation. By the end of 1967 there were 38, and some 10,600 persons were trained in them in that year. Seventeen more centres are now planned or under construction, and when completed the 55 centres will be able to train about 23,000 people a year. This expansion is being carried out with the full co-operation of employers' representatives and leaders of the unions concerned.

334. The best test of the usefulness of the courses given at government training centres is their success in securing appropriate employment for the trainee. The evidence we have is that normally over 90 per cent of trainees successfully completing their courses secure appropriate employment at the end of their courses, or within a short time afterwards. Higher levels of unemployment led to a somewhat slower rate of placing in 1967.

335. The craft system is deeply rooted in much of British industry. The broad assumptions underlying its observance are that ranges of skilled work can be identified, the right to perform which should belong exclusively to a particular kind of craftsman; and that the normal way of becoming a craftsman should be the serving of an apprenticeship of a specified length of time before the age of 20 or 21.

336. In its origins the craft system reflects the need for specialisation in any but the most rudimentary economy. Workers can be trained in the special skills necessary for the performance of identifiable types of task. The craft conception has fostered pride in skill and high standards of workmanship. It is true that a craft union pursues a sectional interest, as do all trade unions and employers' associations; but a craft union also stands as a witness to its members' pride in their special skill, which they believe makes a valuable contribution to the well-being of society.

337. Against the merits must be set the disadvantages. In practice precise and rigid boundaries between crafts or between a craft and semi-skilled grades of labour can be settled only on an arbitrary basis. The boundaries are therefore a fruitful source of dispute especially where new work is introduced which does not conform to established limits. Yet the knowledge that they have virtually committed themselves to a craft for life makes men alert to guard what they consider to be their own preserve, and to oppose relaxations in practices which, however desirable and even essential for efficiency, may seem to constitute a threat to their whole way of life. The most highly skilled are less endangered because the difficulty of acquiring their expertise protects them. Where the craft is less skilled its boundaries must be fixed on largely artificial lines which may nevertheless be stubbornly defended. Moreover, because the definition of work practices is in Britain often a matter for the work group, the boundaries of a craft vary widely from factory to factory and from area to area, and are not amenable to regulation by the formal processes of industry-wide bargaining. All this is comprehensible from the point of view of the craftsman; but it can be very prejudicial to efficiency and to the needs and aspirations of workers outside the craft.

338. In the context of technological change the drawbacks of the craft system become even more marked. It is unreal to assume that the demand for any particular range of skill will be constant. If the only normal method of entry into the craft is via an apprenticeship, supply will respond slowly and inadequately to demand. Where expansion is required it will be delayed. Where technological innovation reduces the demand for a given craft then there will be waste and suffering among the men whose livelihoods and expectations for the future are bound up with its continuing existence.

339. An apprenticeship served in the trade concerned is the normal badge of a craftsman. Whether the apprenticeship course was a good course is of secondary importance. Those run by the best industrial concerns are very good. On the other hand in very many cases training plays only a secondary part in an apprenticeship. What happens in practice is that those engaged

D

as apprentices are put on to "skilled" work after a few weeks' elementary training, and from then on they are doing "skilled" work just as much as any other skilled worker. In such cases apprenticeship is a farce and provides less training than a properly constructed course lasting only a few months. There are cases also where a reasonably diligent apprentice could learn the skills involved in a few months but is prevented from actually performing skilled work while an apprentice, with the result that he is compelled, at this most formative period of his life, to spend up to five years under-employed and under-occupied in order to comply with the formal requirements of an apprenticeship.

340. The fact that a man has completed an apprenticeship does not therefore of itself guarantee that he has acquired any particular level of skill, or that he has passed any form of test of ability. It is perhaps because of the emphasis on the period of apprenticeship as the qualifying factor that there has so far been a failure to develop objective standards; and as a result there is no accepted way of judging the claims of a person who has not been apprenticed but who says that he is capable of skilled work.

341. The gathering speed of technological change will make still more obsolete the craft system organised on its present lines. As some industries decline and others expand, workers have to change jobs. They must be free to acquire new skills. There would be neither social justice nor economic sense in denying them training simply because the jobs for which they had originally been trained had disappeared and they were now past the age of apprenticeship. Indeed for the future it will be less and less reasonable to regard an apprenticeship as equipping a worker with a skill for life. It must be accepted as normal for men and women to undergo re-training and further training at intervals during their working lives so as to adapt their capabilities to new techniques.

342. It has not in fact been possible to maintain the craft system in all its exclusiveness everywhere. In the building industry there are many thousands of bricklayers, carpenters and other so-called "skilled workers" who have picked up their knowledge on the job, especially in the South of England. In the engineering industry "dilution" agreements have been in force since early in the last war, under which if skilled men are not available and production is prejudiced "an alternative class of workers may be employed on jobs hitherto done by skilled men". Under these agreements employers maintain registers showing the type of work done by dilutees together with their names and various other details: and it is stipulated that as and when skilled labour becomes available practices in force previously are to be restored. Similar agreements apply in railway workshops, government industrial establishments, shipbuilding and other industries. In practice in some trades in some parts of the country no register of dilutees is kept and employees are freely upgraded to do skilled work.

343. In addition there has been the training of adults in government training centres referred to above. The centres are training workers in skills used in such industries as engineering and construction, where there has been a

88

continuing shortage of skilled manpower, and the number of apprentices being trained is not sufficient to overcome it.

344.   It would be a delusion to think that only craftsmen or other workers doing work normally reserved for craftsmen are engaged on skilled work in British industry.   In process industries for example there are process workers who are ahead of most craftsmen both in the degree of their skill and the scope of their training.   In such cases age constitutes no artificial barrier to access to skilled work and workers are promoted according to their capabilities.   On the other hand strict lines of demarcation often separate the work which process workers are permitted to perform from that proper to the maintenance craftsman.   These have no more relevance to modern industry than most inter-craft demarcations, though no less costly.

OBSTACLES IN THE WAY OF ACCESS TO SKILLED WORK

345.   We have had evidence from a number of sources of obstacles being placed in the way of the employment as skilled workers of persons trained at government training centres.   The Engineering Employers' Federation said, for example, that in the Manchester area officials of the Amalgamated Engineering Union refused to allow such persons to be employed as skilled men even if registered as dilutees; and that the union's Tyne district committee adopted the same attitude.   Trade union opposition to placing of such persons in skilled work was alleged to exist also in Scotland.   The Ministry of Labour's evidence confirmed that government training centres met difficulties of this kind.

346.   We find it deplorable that such difficulties should be encountered. Their existence contrasts with the positive attitude which many trade union leaders have taken to the expansion of adult training.   In the long term the cure for such difficulties lies in a fundamentally different approach to training.   In the shorter term it is for trade union leaders to do all in their power to secure the loyal implementation of the policies of their unions, and agreements into which they have entered, at district as at other levels.   We are referring here to the application of dilution agreements, but in our view these agreements are themselves not satisfactory.

347.   The dilution agreements do not provide for dilutees to become skilled workers.   Indeed they make it clear that a dilutee is not to be regarded as a skilled worker, but as someone else temporarily allowed to do skilled work. In the event of a recession, dilutees stand to lose the right to do skilled work in favour of those regarded as skilled workers, that is, by and large, ex-apprentices.   This arrangement neglects the skills and experience which can make a dilutee as valuable an employee as the worker who has served an apprenticeship, perhaps even more valuable than one who has not yet acquired a wide range of experience.   We think it wrong that dilutees should be regarded as a class whose status, work and pay can at any time be drastically reduced if this should be necessary to protect the interests of those who have served apprenticeships.

348.   After performing skilled work for a specified period dilutees should if they have reached the required standards be regarded for all purposes as

skilled workers—both by their unions and their employers. It is also unsatisfactory that dilution agreements make no mention of the training to be given to dilutees to enable them to do skilled work. In other words, it should now be accepted explicitly, as it has been widely accepted implicitly, that in order to remedy shortages of skilled manpower it is necessary to enable adults to undertake skilled work; and consequently that proper standards should be laid down for their training; and that once trained they should be fully accepted by all concerned as skilled workers. We recommend that where dilution agreements are in force they should be revised with these considerations in mind. We also recommend that when revised agreements come into force, all existing dilutees should be regarded as skilled workers for all purposes after a specified period of time spent on skilled work.

WOMEN'S ACCESS TO SKILLED WORK

349. One other restriction hindering free access to skilled work is that related to the training of, or rather the failure to train, women. From the point of view of improving the position of women in industry this is a problem whose solution is in the long run even more important than that of equal pay. The facts are so disturbing, and the implications—both social and economic—so important, that they must be singled out for discussion. In our consideration of it we have been greatly assisted by the paper on " The Position of Women in Industry " written for us by Miss Nancy Seear.[1]

350. The following table enables the distribution of employment of women in different industries and services to be compared with that of men:

Number of employees in the United Kingdom, June 1967 (thousands)

Industry Group	Males	Females	Total
Agriculture, forestry and fishing	377	80	457
Manufacturing industries, mining, quarrying, construction, gas, electricity and water ..	8,719	3,000	11,719
Transport and communications	1,388	274	1,662
Distributive trades	1,325	1,589	2,914
Insurance, banking and finance	356	311	667
Professional and scientific services (including teachers, nurses, etc.)	890	1,805	2,695
Miscellaneous services (entertainment, sport, catering, laundries, hairdressing, garages, domestic service)	961	1,242	2,203
Public administration	1,013	439	1,451

Source: Ministry of Labour.

Nearly three million women were at this date employed in manufacturing, etc., but they were greatly outnumbered by men. On the other hand, women outnumber men in a number of service sectors—the distributive trades; financial, professional and scientific services; and the group of miscellaneous services which includes catering, laundries and hairdressing—and it is here that their employment is mainly concentrated.

[1]Research Paper No. 11 (to be published shortly).

351. The following table shows the distribution of apprenticeships amongst young men and women in various occupations in May 1966:

Numbers of Males and Females in Apprenticeships, May 1966.

Apprenticeships for:						Males	Females
Scientists and technologists	..	..	..	..	..	9,630	110
Draughtsmen	..	..	..	..	..	17,450	350
Other technicians	..	..	..	..	..	12,150	160
Clerical and office staff	..	..	..	..	..	3,150	1,410
Other administrative staff	..	..	..	..	..	3,300	620
Skilled craft workers	..	..	..	..	..	271,650	5,430

Source: Ministry of Labour Gazette, January 1967.

352. The table shows how extraordinarily limited is the access to apprenticeships accorded to girls in the occupations covered. At school, girls have as good a performance at " O " level standards as boys. And yet when they come to leave school only some 7 per cent of girls enter apprenticeships (hairdressing predominantly) compared with 43 per cent of boys. Some 49 per cent of male manual workers in industry are classified as skilled, but only 29 per cent of females—19 per cent if the clothing and textile industries are excluded. In engineering and electrical goods manufacture nearly 580,000 skilled men are employed but only 13,200 skilled women (out of a female labour force of nearly 340,000); and yet during the last war women were without difficulty trained to do many kinds of work traditionally performed by men.

353. Women have limited opportunities where other types of training are concerned. In 1966 some 538,000 men in employment were released by their employers during working hours to take part-time day courses at grant-aided establishments, but the corresponding figure for women was only 87,000. Not surprisingly, therefore, women's access to the better-paid jobs is restricted. The Ministry of Labour's occupational analysis for retail distribution in May 1967 covered a labour force of over a quarter of a million; women outnumbered men by 3 to 1, but male managers outnumbered women managers by nearly 2 to 1. Only one of the 319 works managers interviewed in our workshop relations survey was a woman, and only 10 of the 121 personnel officers. Of the 183 full-time trade union officers interviewed from six trade unions, only one was a woman. In industry generally, women comprise only 5 per cent of managers and 2.5 per cent of scientists and technologists. In some fields there are much better opportunities for women, notably teaching, the non-industrial civil service and some professions, including of course nursing; but these do not compensate for the comparative lack of opportunity over much of the employment field.

354. There are some obvious practical reasons why opportunities for women are restricted. Managements are reluctant to give expensive training to women when the likelihood is so high that they will shortly marry and leave their service. A married woman returning to the employment field after a dozen years' absence will not have the same chance of promotion as other employees who have not been absent at all. Married women with family responsibilities often cannot work the full normal hours of a factory or office. However,

these practical obstacles cannot by themselves account for the present state of affairs. They are reinforced by conservatism and prejudice among men, both employers and trade unionists, which foster the unwarranted assumption that nothing can be done. This assumption is sometimes accepted by women themselves. Young women first entering employment are often reluctant to commit themselves to lengthy training when they can get higher pay in undemanding work, because they see employment as a brief period preceding marriage and bringing up a family. However, employment figures show that this short-term view is increasingly unrealistic; employment of women and girls has gone up by some 14 per cent in the last decade (compared with less than 6 per cent for men), and much of it is accounted for by a remarkable increase in the number of married women taking up jobs when their families become less dependent.

355. The existing situation if prolonged will give rise to increasingly acute social problems. Many more mixed schools are being established. Girls who do as well as boys at school will want the opportunities for training available to boys. More and more able girls are going to universities. Many married women who return to full-time or part-time employment have, through lack of training, to take jobs which are below their capacity.

356. In economic terms, there is a still more important problem. Lack of skilled labour has constantly applied a brake to our economic expansion since the war, and yet the capacity of women to do skilled work has been neglected. This becomes more serious as the proportion of women in the labour force increases; and the failure to train sufficient girl school-leavers now will continue to have ill effects a long time ahead. Forecasts of the size of the working population indicate that there will be a very limited increase between now and 1981. Women provide the only substantial new source from which extra labour, and especially skilled labour, can be drawn during this period. It is essential that in the development of training over the next few years all those with responsibility in the field—education authorities, the Youth Employment Service, industrial training boards, the Department of Employment and Productivity, employers and trade unions—should grasp the opportunity to bring about a revolution in attitudes and in practical performance so far as the training of women is concerned.

THE FUTURE DEVELOPMENT OF TRAINING

357. Responsibility for the future rests largely in the hands of the industrial training boards. Some of the longest established boards are now examining far-reaching proposals for the future. In the engineering industry for example training will be transformed if a scheme now under consideration is put into practice whereby trainees will undergo a series of separate programmes of training termed " modules " which can be combined in different ways to qualify a worker in a variety of skills and to which further " modules " can be added later as required. However, even the first boards have been in operation for only three years, and it is too early to assess their success and their prospects. There can however be no doubt that an urgent need exists to secure the rapid and general adoption of systems of training which accord with the social and economic needs of a modern industrial society: and that any

such system should incorporate the following as basic features:

(i) objective standards to be laid down by which qualifications may be judged;

(ii) a person who has attained such standards to be universally accepted, on proving that fact, as qualified and eligible to do the work in question;

(iii) apart from introductory training and further education for young people, the content and duration of training courses to be determined by what is required to enable trainees to reach the set standards;

(iv) no artificially restrictive barriers to be placed against access to training or re-training, for example on grounds of age, sex, colour, etc.

358.   Once objective standards have been laid down by which qualification for skilled work can be judged, trade unions should review their rule books and make any revision of the rules necessary to ensure that no qualified worker will be arbitrarily denied either the right of admission to the union or the right to use the skills which he has acquired.   Failing this, any worker who alleges that he or she is qualified to do skilled work but has nevertheless been refused membership of the union (or of the skilled section of the union) should have the right of appeal to the independent review body whose establishment we recommend in Chapter XI.

359.   We recognise that there is a long way to go before principles and practice in training will have been transformed in the way they ought to be. Many of the attitudes which support the present system of craft training and discrimination against women are common to both employers and trade unionists and deeply ingrained in the life of the country.   Prejudice against women is manifest at all levels of management as well as on the shop floor.   Among the professions there are to be found demarcation rules and rules for qualifying to practise which are no less strict and no less open to question than those practised in many crafts.   There are, however, some encouraging signs that the need for a transformation in our system is gaining wider recognition.   The trade unions' co-operation in the rapid expansion of the government training centres is greatly to be welcomed.   The levy and grant system under the 1964 Act has stimulated employers to devote greater attention to industrial training in all its aspects.   The imaginative proposals currently being examined by several training boards promise to lead to radical reform of training courses and methods of training.   We doubt, however, whether the urgency and scale of the problem have yet been appreciated.   What is required is a sustained attack on outworn ideas and groundless preconceptions at all levels.   Aided by the other departments concerned, the Department of Employment and Productivity will have to take the major responsibility for rousing the country to the gravity of the issues and for carrying through the required reforms in time.

Chapter VII

STRIKES AND
OTHER INDUSTRIAL ACTION

360. We have already indicated in Chapter IV that the pattern of strikes and other forms of industrial action in Britain is a consequence of the British system of industrial relations working under the pressures of full employment. In this chapter we pursue the same theme in greater detail and consider a number of suggestions intended to diminish the volume of stoppages and disruptions to production.

361. First we must indicate the role which we think that industrial action fills in a system of industrial relations. Trade unions enable the collective strength of workers to be brought to bear in a systematic way. Striking is the most dramatic form of collective action; so much so that many people suppose that the strike is the ultimate sanction which gives reality to collective bargaining in a free society. There is some truth in this but it is not the whole truth. The first, and less important, qualification is that there are other forms of industrial action which under full employment can be as effective or almost as effective as the strike. They include the work-to-rule; the go-slow; the banning of overtime; and the " blacking " of goods. Secondly, and more important, there are many unions which have considerable bargaining power but which would not normally contemplate action of these kinds at all. Their strength lies in the operation of subtler forms of pressure. In the public sector many unions can make use of the degree of compulsion upon public authorities to show themselves to be " good employers " and to be willing in normal circumstances to submit disputes to arbitration. In private industry also companies may set considerable store by their reputation as " good employers " and on the maintenance of good relations with their employees.

INCIDENCE OF STRIKES AND OTHER INDUSTRIAL ACTION

362. A country's strike pattern may take many different forms. In order to delineate our own and to see how it compares with those of other countries, we begin with an international comparison of statistics of stoppages of work due to industrial disputes. The table on the following page sets out statistics relating to the years 1964-66.

363. Figures of working days lost in relation to numbers employed give the best available measure—though a far from precise measure—by which to compare economic loss directly due to strikes and lock-outs in different countries. Judged by this measure, the United Kingdom's recent record has been about average compared with other countries. We lost on average 190 working days each year for each thousand employees. A group of five

countries did considerably better: Finland, Norway, the Federal Republic of Germany, the Netherlands and Sweden. The United Kingdom formed a second group together with Belgium, Denmark, France, New Zealand and Japan; the members in this group lost between 150 and 240 working days per 1,000 employees annually. The five remaining countries—Australia, Canada, Republic of Ireland, Italy, USA—fared worse, all except Australia very much worse.

INTERNATIONAL COMPARISONS OF STATISTICS RELATING TO STOPPAGES DUE TO INDUSTRIAL DISPUTES IN MINING, MANUFACTURING, CONSTRUCTION AND TRANSPORT

Average Annual Figures for the three years 1964-1966 inclusive[1]

Name of Country	No. of Stoppages per 100,000 employees	Average No. of persons involved per stoppage	Average duration of each stoppage in working days	No. of working days lost per 1,000 employees
United Kingdom	16·8	340	3·4	190
Australia	63·8[2]	350[2]	1·8[2]	400[2]
Belgium	7·0	680	9·2	200
Canada	15·8	430	14·0	970
Denmark	5·5[3]	370[3]	7·3[3]	160[3]
Finland	10·8	360	2·1	80
France	21·8	1,090	0·8	200
Federal Republic of Germany	[4]	[4]	3·6	—[5]
Republic of Ireland	25·6	450	15·2	1,620
Italy	32·9	720	5·3	1,170
Japan	7·6	1,040	2·9	240
Netherlands	2·2	370	2·4	20
New Zealand	26·8	250	2·1	150
Norway	0·6	100	26·0	—[5]
Sweden	0·5[6]	570[6]	15·4[6]	40[6]
United States	13·2[7]	470[7]	14·2[7]	870[7]

Based on information supplied by the International Labour Office.

[1]Because countries adopt different statistical practices, the figures are not strictly comparable in every respect. The most important variation is in the level below which strikes are regarded as too small to be included; some other countries adopt levels lower than the United Kingdom, notably Australia, Canada, Japan, Norway and the United States. Some countries, unlike the United Kingdom, exclude from their statistics workers laid off as a result of stoppages at their place of work. The footnotes which follow record the more important other variations.
[2]Including electricity and gas.
[3]Manufacturing only.
[4]Figures not available.
[5]Fewer than 10 working days lost.
[6]All industries.
[7]Including electricity, gas, water, sanitary services.

364. The table shows that the United Kingdom had, over the period in question, a comparatively large number of strikes for the size of the workforce, though five other countries listed had more—Australia very many more. The figures give a broadly accurate picture, but the difficulty which always exists in making strict international comparisons is greater than usual in this case because different countries adopt different criteria in deciding whether a strike is too small to be included in the statistics.

365.   Different overall patterns of industrial disputes emerge from a study of the table.   While this country has a comparatively large number of stoppages, they are of fairly short duration and do not usually involve very large numbers of people.   The pattern in Australia and New Zealand is similar, though both have more stoppages than ourselves in proportion to the workforce. Stoppages in Canada and the USA are less frequent than ours in proportion to the workforce, and involve comparable numbers of workers, but each one lasts more than four times as long as our own.   Of the remaining countries, it may be remarked that France has a comparatively large number of stoppages involving many people but of very short duration, indicating the frequent use of " token " strikes.   Some countries are fortunate in having so few stoppages that no established strike pattern can be said to exist: this applies to the Netherlands, Norway, Sweden and the Federal Republic of Germany.

366.   The impression which these international statistics give of the general pattern in this country is confirmed by a closer examination of our own figures. From time to time this country still experiences big strikes.   Out of a little more than 38 million working days lost in strikes between 1957 and 1966, more than sixteen millions were lost in eight strikes, each accounting for over half a million days, all of them concerned with industry-wide disputes about pay or hours of work or both.   Three were in engineering, two in the bus industry and one each in shipbuilding, shipping and printing.   But the typical stoppage involves small numbers of workers and is quickly over—though such stoppages occur comparatively frequently. How frequently is indicated by the following table, which shows the trend in numbers of stoppages over the period 1957-1967:

**UNITED KINGDOM: NUMBER OF STOPPAGES DUE TO
INDUSTRIAL DISPUTES, 1957-1967**

| Year | Number of stoppages: | | |
	Coalmining	In the rest of the economy	Altogether
1957	2,224	635	2,859
1958	1,963	666	2,629
1959	1,307	786	2,093
1960	1,666	1,166	2,832
1961	1,458	1,228	2,686
1962	1,203	1,246	2,449
1963	987	1,081	2,068
1964	1,058	1,466	2,524
1965	740	1,614	2,354
1966	553	1,384	1,937
1967 (Provisional figures) ..	391	1,694	2,085

Source: Ministry of Labour.

The total number of stoppages fluctuated between 1,937 and 2,859, no clear trend up or down being discernible.   However, once stoppages in coalmining are separated from the rest very clear trends do emerge.   In coalmining the number of stoppages has been decreasing rapidly, and in 1967 there were little

96

more than a sixth of the number of stoppages there were ten years previously. At the same time the number of stoppages in all other industries was on the increase, the 1967 level being over two and a half times as high as that ten years before. This increase has been fairly general throughout industry, though many industries remain largely strike-free.

367. At this point it is useful to draw a distinction between official and unofficial strikes. We mean by an official strike one which has been sanctioned or ratified by the union or unions whose members are on strike, all others being unofficial. Unofficial strikes are also in practice usually, though not always, " unconstitutional " in the sense that they take place in disregard of an existing agreement laying down a procedure for the attempted settlement of a dispute before strike action is taken. In 1960 the Ministry of Labour began to keep records separating official and unofficial strikes but did not publish them because for various reasons—including the fact that a strike might be made official by a union at a date later than when it was recorded by the Ministry—they are liable to a margin of error. The Ministry nevertheless told us that it considered the figures broadly accurate; and our view is that, even if they fall short of perfection, the figures throw very valuable light on the nature of strikes in this country. The following table shows the pattern for the years 1964-66:

OFFICIAL, UNOFFICIAL AND OTHER STOPPAGES OF WORK DUE TO INDUSTRIAL DISPUTES

Average annual figures for stoppages in the period 1964-1966[1]

Type of Stoppage	Number of Stoppages	Number of workers involved[2]	Number of working days lost
Official strikes	74	101,100	733,000
Partly-official strikes[3]	2	600	7,000
Unofficial strikes	2,171	653,400	1,697,000
Others, e.g. lock-outs or strikes by un-organised workers, unclassified ..	25	2,700	15,000
ALL	2,272	757,800	2,452,000

Source: Ministry of Labour.

[1]The figures relate to stoppages *beginning* in the years covered and the total number of working days lost due to them.

[2]Including workers thrown out of work at establishments where stoppages occurred, although not themselves parties to the dispute.

[3]I.e., a strike involving more than one union and recognised as official by at least one but not all the unions concerned.

368. These figures show that the overwhelming majority of stoppages—some 95 per cent—are due to unofficial strikes. Over these three years each unofficial strike involved on average about 300 workers and lasted a little over 2½ days. By contrast each official strike involved on average approximately 1,370 workers, lasted nearly three times as long, and caused the loss of over twelve times as many working days.

97

369. Official strikes have not shown any consistent tendency to grow in number in recent years. The figures since 1960 are as follows:

Number of official strikes, 1960-1966[(1)]

1960	...	...	...	...	...	...	68
1961	...	...	...	...	...	...	60
1962	...	...	...	...	...	...	78
1963	...	...	...	...	...	...	49
1964	...	...	...	...	...	...	70
1965	...	...	...	...	...	...	97
1966	...	...	...	...	...	...	60

[(1)]The figures include "partly-official" strikes, i.e. strikes involving more than one union and recognised as official by at least one but not all the unions concerned.

370. By contrast, unofficial strikes have shown a strong general upward trend in numbers in recent years. We have already pointed out that some 95 per cent of strikes are unofficial. The general increase in the number of strikes in industries other than coalmining is attributable almost wholly to an increase in the number of unofficial strikes. The increase has been spread widely over the industrial field, but the records of different industries are naturally varied, and some industries remain immune or nearly so. The following table shows the industry groups most affected by unofficial strikes in the period 1964-66:

AVERAGE ANNUAL FIGURES RELATING TO INDUSTRIES IN WHICH MOST UNOFFICIAL STRIKES TOOK PLACE IN RELATION TO NUMBERS EMPLOYED, 1964-1966

Industry	Number of unofficial strikes per 100,000 employees	Number of days lost in unofficial strikes per 1,000 employees
Coalmining	138·7	466
Docks (port and inland water transport)	62·1	850
Shipbuilding, ship-repairing and marine engineering	43·7	379
Motor vehicle manufacturing	30·9	798
All industries	9·2	72

Source: Ministry of Labour Statistics.

371. The four industries in this table have consistently had the poorest strike records in recent years in relation to the size of the workforce, both in terms of numbers of stoppages and in terms of days lost.

372. Outside the four worst-affected industries the picture is brighter, but here too unofficial strikes are becoming more common. In 1965 and 1966 they reached a total of 1,159 and 1,004 respectively, whereas for much the same area of industry the figure in 1960 was 756. In 1953, for *all* stoppages both official and unofficial, it was 326.

373. The statistics for this country quoted so far have been based mainly on figures supplied by the Ministry of Labour. However, the Department's

statistics of stoppages are not complete. They do not include all stoppages, since any stoppage which is very small, i.e. involving fewer than 10 workers or lasting less than one day, is omitted from the records unless it causes a loss of over 100 working days. Moreover, whereas the statistics relating to stoppages in coalmining are extremely accurate, in the private sector of industry there are undoubtedly many strikes which escape inclusion in the figures (as the Ministry of Labour pointed out in its written evidence—see footnote to paragraph 129 on page 38). However information gathered in the course of our workshop relations survey[1] throws some further light on the situation. It also throws light on other forms of industrial action, on which no official statistics are kept since they do not readily lend themselves to statistical recording.

374. The shop stewards covered in our survey had on average held their present posts as stewards for six years. They were asked whether there had been a strike at their place of work since they became stewards, and 40 per cent replied that there had—16 per cent saying that a strike had taken place once since they took office, 20 per cent that strikes had taken place "seldom" and 4 per cent that they had taken place "frequently". Further answers from stewards with experience of strikes in their present posts indicated that, while a few had in mind a "national" strike called officially by their union, in nearly seven cases out of ten the latest (or only) strike of which the steward had experience took place without permission having first been obtained from the union. Almost 90 per cent of the stewards worked in plants with an agreed procedure for the settlement of disputes. Over 74 per cent of them said that the procedure had not been exhausted before a strike occurred, as compared with 16 per cent who said that it had and 10 per cent who did not know, or who had in mind a national strike not governed by such disputes procedure. Over half the strikes referred to lasted one day only or less, and some 84 per cent were over in a week or less.

375. The shop stewards covered in our survey were also asked about other forms of pressure used in disputes with management since they had been shop stewards; threats to strike were said by 30 per cent to have been used, bans on overtime by 42 per cent, working to rule by 28 per cent and going slow by 12 per cent. It appears from this that overtime bans may be as frequent as strikes—a reflection of the extensive use of overtime in this country; and working to rule is not much less commonly used. Altogether 68 per cent of the shop stewards covered by our survey said that one form of pressure or another—strike, threat of a strike, overtime ban, etc.—had been used since they took office.

376. The general picture revealed by the shop stewards' answers was confirmed by the replies given by other groups covered by our workshop relations survey. Of ordinary trade union members, some 34 per cent said that there had been a strike since they joined their present firm, and about the same proportion that other forms of pressure had been used. On the management side—works managers, personnel managers and foremen—roughly three out of ten said that they had had experience of strikes since taking up their present jobs.

[1]Research Paper No. 10, *Shop Stewards and Workshop Relations*, HMSO 1968.

377. The conclusion is that industrial disharmony manifests itself in overt action on the shop floor more frequently than the official statistics imply. Presumably the larger a stoppage is the more likely it is to be reported and included in the official statistics; and the survey indicates that small stoppages, and the use of the various other forms of industrial pressure, occur a good deal more frequently than one might otherwise suppose.

CAUSES

378. Official statistics are published relating to causes of disputes. They have to be used with caution. As is inevitable, they relate to the immediate issue which gave rise to a stoppage and this may not be the fundamental underlying cause. Even the immediately apparent causes may be mixed, and it may not be easy to decide which of them preponderates. Nevertheless if these limitations are kept in mind the figures can be of considerable value.

379. So far as official strikes are concerned, no elaborate analysis of cause is necessary. Most major strikes, though not all, are official and result from a breakdown of negotiations at industry level about a claim tabled by the trade union or unions concerned for improved terms and conditions of employment. As regards unofficial strikes, which it will be remembered form some 95 per cent of all strikes, we have had further analyses of the causes carried out for the period 1964-66, and these have enabled the table on page 101 to be prepared.

380. The table shows that about half of all unofficial strikes—1,052 a year—concern wages; and that this pattern is general throughout industry. It is unfortunately not possible to tell what proportion of these stoppages is due to disputes about piece-workers' pay. The table further shows that, after wages, the next most prolific immediate causes of dispute are " working arrangements, rules and discipline " (646 or 29 per cent of the total) and " redundancy, dismissal, suspension, etc." (326 or 15 per cent of the total). These are matters which are usually dealt with at the workplace and not at industry level; the prevalence of stoppages due to these causes is a reflection on the adequacy of the procedures available to settle them. Stoppages arising out of disciplinary issues are included under both these headings; if they are separated from the others it emerges that an annual average of 223 unofficial strikes, or 10 per cent of all unofficial strikes, took place over disciplinary issues. It may also be noted that an annual average of 276 unofficial strikes resulted from disputes about whether individuals should or should not be employed, suspended or dismissed (whether on disciplinary grounds or not)—about 13 per cent of all unofficial strikes.

381. As to the remaining immediate causes, demarcation gave rise to an average of 57 stoppages a year in the period under consideration—2.6 per cent of the total. It was a more significant cause in shipbuilding and ship-repairing than elsewhere, being responsible for 12 per cent of the unofficial strikes in this industry. Hours of work gave rise to 30 stoppages a year. The closed shop gave rise each year to 29 unofficial strikes on average, most of these arising out of unionists' objections to working with non-unionists. (By contrast, there was an average of only three *official* strikes each year concerning the closed

100

AVERAGE ANNUAL FIGURES* OF UNOFFICIAL STRIKES IN THE PERIOD 1964-66 ANALYSED BY CERTAIN INDUSTRY GROUPS AND BY CAUSE

PRINCIPAL CAUSE	INDUSTRY GROUPS							
	Coal-mining	Motor Vehicles	Docks	Shipbuilding, ship-repairing and marine engineering	Engineering (other)	Construction	Other Industries	All Industries
Wages	365	77	45	58	149	111	245	1,052
Hours of Work	—	6	1	5	5	—	14	30
Demarcation	3	4	7	12	7	9	13	57
Redundancy, dismissal, suspension etc.	26	24	5	13	56	81	118	326
Working arrangements, rules and discipline	384	35	27	10	43	26	119	646
Trade Union recognition	—	1	—	1	4	1	11	18
Closed shop	—	2	‡	‡	6	3	16	29
Alleged victimisation for trade union membership, and other disputes about trade union status	—	1	1	1	1	3	7	16
Sympathetic strikes	4	‡	‡	1	2	2	7	18
All causes	783	154	87	98	277	242	553	2,196

A further analysis has been made of two of the above principal causes, as follows:—

Redundancy, dismissal, suspension etc

	Coal-mining	Motor Vehicles	Docks	Shipbuilding, ship-repairing and marine engineering	Engineering (other)	Construction	Other Industries	All Industries
(i) for increased security against redundancy	1	6	1	2	10	12	14	48
(ii) individual cases†								
(a) disciplinary	5	11	‡	5	28	42	57	150
(b) non-disciplinary	19	6	3	4	14	18	37	103
(c) not clearly defined	1	—	‡	‡	4	8	9	23

Working arrangements, rules and discipline:

	Coal-mining	Motor Vehicles	Docks	Shipbuilding, ship-repairing and marine engineering	Engineering (other)	Construction	Other Industries	All Industries
(i) for a change in arrangements	51	16	11	7	16	15	48	166
(ii) against a change	274	7	10	1	11	3	34	341
(iii) disciplinary issues	27	6	3	1	10	3	22	73
(iv) others (inc. not clearly defined)	31	5	2	1	5	5	14	65

Source: Ministry of Labour Statistics.

*The figures have been taken as the nearest whole number; the sums of the constituent items may not, therefore, agree with the totals shown.

†Strikes for and against the employment, dismissal, suspensions, etc., of individuals.

‡Less than one strike a year on average.

shop.) Trade union recognition was the immediate cause of an average of 18 unofficial strikes. Only five *official* strikes were caused by this each year. It is a reasonable inference from the statistics relating both to the closed shop and to trade union recognition that members of unions, rather than the unions as such, tend to make the running on these issues.

382. In order better to understand the causes of strikes, and their nature generally, we decided to investigate more fully the causes of unofficial strikes in the motor vehicle manufacturing industry. We chose this industry as of particular interest because its strike-proneness in this country contrasts with general experience in other car-manufacturing countries. Coalmining and docks on the other hand are industries in which strikes give rise to problems in many countries. We had the advantage of written and oral evidence from the motor industry employers and the Engineering Employers' Federation and from many of the trade unions concerned. We also took evidence in private from academic witnesses with special knowledge of the industry; also from Sir Jack Scamp, the independent chairman of the Motor Industry Joint Labour Council; from the motor industry sub-committee of the Confederation of Shipbuilding and Engineering Unions; and from members of management, local full-time trade union officials and shop stewards concerned with five different plants in the motor industry. Many of those concerned also prepared memoranda specially for our consideration. We are most grateful for the ready help we received. We have also profited from a study of reports of inquiries carried out by or on behalf of the Motor Industry Joint Labour Council and of the book on " Labour Relations in the Motor Industry " by Professor H. A. Turner, Mr. G. Clack and Mr. G. Roberts.[1] We had talked to the authors earlier, but their book was published after our hearings were complete.

383. It may be as well at the outset to refer to certain explanations of the motor industry's strike record which are sometimes suggested, but which in our view do not survive close examination. One such explanation is that un-official strikes are fomented by shop stewards bent on disruption. Our clear impression, reinforced by the results of our surveys of workshop relations, is that shop stewards in the motor industry, like shop stewards elsewhere, are in general hard-working and responsible people who are making a sincere attempt to do a difficult job. Often, in fact, the stewards are cast in the role of mediators trying to prevent stoppages taking place while grievances can be examined. Not all shop stewards in the industry would fulfil the foregoing description, and it would be surprising if they did. We have talked to some shop stewards whom we can believe to be over-ready to exploit trouble, and to be reckless of the interests of the companies on whose prosperity the liveli-hoods of those whom they represent depend. We can also believe that there exist some shop stewards who have political motives for stirring up trouble. However, such people are very much in the minority. In their book Professor Turner and his colleagues say that there is no evidence to ascribe a generally inflammatory role to shop stewards as such. They say: " Strikes have been as common in plants where the stewards' organisation is weak and divided as where it is strong: and there is more to suggest that senior stewards attempt

---

[1]George Allen & Unwin Ltd., 1967.

to control the development of disputes and are pushed into stoppages from behind than that they lead workers into such crises."[1]

384. It is also sometimes suggested that the dull and repetitive character of the work in the industry contributes to its strike-proneness. Of this, Sir Jack Scamp said in his report in November 1966 on the activities of the Motor Industry Joint Labour Council (in paragraph 25):

"One recognises, of course, that some of the work is repetitive and may induce feelings of frustration or boredom. It is uncertain, however, how far such considerations are of material importance in determining the incidence of industrial disputes. There may be scope for research here, but it is interesting, and possibly significant, that no complaints or representations on this score have been made by the men's representatives at any of the inquiries conducted by the Council."

It is possible that boredom may be an indirect cause of disputes by affecting workers' attitudes without their being aware of it, but if so, one would expect it to operate in other countries also, and as we have pointed out motor manufacture is not remarkable for strike-proneness in other countries.

385. We doubt also the importance of another factor which it has been suggested may contribute to the industry's strike-proneness, namely that it has been obliged to engage a good deal of "green labour" without previous experience of work of the type it is called upon to perform in car factories. Professor Turner and his colleagues point out that labour turnover in the industry is lower than that for either engineering or manufacturing generally, and that the periods of most rapid general expansion of employment in the industry since the war have not been related to periods of increased readiness to strike. Although particular difficulties may have been encountered when new plants have been opened, sometimes in areas where the motor industry has not before operated, we cannot ascribe the strike-proneness of the industry to any significant extent to the rawness of the labour it recruits.

386. Unofficial strikes almost invariably involve a breach by each striker of his contract of employment in that due notice to stop working is not given. The question therefore arises whether managements exercise enough discipline in the face of such breaches of contract, even granted that the sack has lost some of its potency as a disciplinary weapon. Sir Jack Scamp points out that motor car manufacturing companies have not always had a high enough standard in this respect, but at the same time underlines the difficulties which the imposition of stricter discipline involves (in paragraph 27 of his report of November 1966):

"The Council has indeed encountered examples of failure to impose discipline when it clearly should have been imposed. Is it always wise, for instance, to permit men who have walked out without warning to resume work again at their pleasure? But the problem is not so simple as that. If a company suspends or dismisses a group of men for refusing to carry out the work of their section while any grievance they may have, real or imagined, is being dealt with by their own representatives and those of the company, who is then to perform their work? One cannot

---

[1]Op. cit., p.330.

103

simply bring in other men on to the disputed job. The result of suspension or dismissal is thus all too probably the bringing of the whole or large parts of the plant to a standstill and the sending home of hundreds of other workers."

In the motor manufacturing industry great power lies in the hands of relatively small groups of workers because of the close interdependence of the various processes of production; and this makes the imposition of discipline even more of a problem.

387. Trade unions themselves have disciplinary powers over their members; and this being so the question arises to what extent the unions concerned bear responsibility for this industry's strike record. There is no doubt, in our view, that the unions have not had sufficient influence on the workplace situation. There are a number of reasons for this, one of which is the readiness of management to deal directly with shop stewards to the exclusion of full-time union officials. Another is the multiplicity of unions active in individual factories. Among production workers large numbers are members of the Amalgamated Union of Engineering and Foundry Workers, the Transport and General Workers' Union, and the National Union of Vehicle Builders. Many others are members of the General and Municipal Workers' Union; others again of smaller unions. This situation inevitably handicaps the development of firm and coherent policies by the unions in matters of industrial relations. It has also led to inter-union jealousies and rivalries, producing on occasions jurisdictional and demarcation disputes. Union structure is therefore a factor which may play some part in the industry's propensity to strike, but we do not believe that it can be one of the major factors. The Ford Motor Company has been able to achieve a considerable reduction in its strike-rate without a significant diminution in the number of unions with which it negotiates.

388. We attach more importance to the industry's wage structure as a cause of strikes. It is plain that employees' actual earnings are not determined by the negotiations conducted at industry level in the engineering industry. Two major motor manufacturers (Ford and Vauxhall) are not in any case in the Engineering Employers' Federation, which is one of the parties to such negotiations. In the remaining companies earnings are a long way in advance of the rates so settled at industry level, and a crucial part is therefore played by workplace negotiations. In most of these " federated " establishments systems of payment-by-results are employed, and it is apparent that considerable difficulties are encountered both in maintaining fair relativities between different groups of workers and in keeping a reasonable amount of control over wage levels. In addition it is clear that workers' pay is subject to considerable fluctuations as a result of variations in the flow of work due to factors beyond their control. Professor Turner shows that working hours in vehicle manufacturing from 1956-1964 varied within a range twice that of engineering as a whole, and he quotes a typical assembly worker's earnings which ranged from £13 to £31 per week during 1962-1963.[1] In these circumstances the seeds of dispute in matters of pay are present in abundance.

[1] *Op. cit.*, pp. 160, 162.

If groups of workers see that other groups with whom they have hitherto enjoyed equality are able to improve their position because of the vagaries of the pay system, it is not surprising if they feel indignation and seek to recover a position of parity. That is one side of the coin. The other side is that if workers know that much of their pay packet depends on rates of pay settled at the workplace they will rightly judge that their prospects of higher pay depend mainly on securing concessions in workplace bargaining; and inequalities arising out of the system give obvious opportunities for claims for improvement.

389. We fully endorse the following conclusions reached by Sir Jack Scamp about wage structures in the industry (paragraph 30 of the same report):

"There is no doubt that the present complex structure with, in most cases, the additional complications which derive from piecework systems, leaves much to be desired and there is need for most of the companies to take a serious look at their methods of payment. In particular, any review of the wage structure demands a careful and comprehensive approach rather than the continued application of the present piecemeal and often inflationary solutions."

In our view the failure to devise adequate wage structures, and to agree upon them in comprehensive negotiations with representatives of all the workers concerned, is responsible to a large extent for the industry's industrial relations difficulties.

390. Most of the unofficial strikes which are not over wages in the motor industry arise from disputes over "working arrangements, rules and discipline" or "redundancy, dismissal, suspension, etc.". Disputes from such causes reflect in part the insecurity of the industry. They also reflect the increased power and readiness of workers, in conditions of full employment, to resist unwelcome disciplinary or other managerial decisions by their employers. There is no standard by which to measure whether the decisions taken by management are or are not justified in such cases, nor whether it is reasonable or not of the workers concerned to reject or resist them. A number of points are however clear. First, these are workplace issues, not issues regulated at industry level. Secondly, one is concerned here with an area in which it is for the most part nominally within management's prerogative to reach decisions unilaterally, but in which workers can and do dispute the decisions so arrived at. Thirdly, in modern circumstances—the most significant of which is full employment—workers are more ready to insist on what they regard as fair and reasonable treatment. Management is less able to wield its traditional disciplinary sanction—the sack—than in the past and workers' organisation at the workplace is now highly developed. Workers expect their interests, and such rights as they have acquired by custom, to be increasingly respected by management. Finally, in matters of this kind the disputes procedure cannot always work satisfactorily because it does not offer an effective means of redressing grievances about decisions which, once implemented, can no longer be effectively challenged. Altogether the number of unofficial disputes which arise over "working arrangements, rules and discipline" and "redundancy, dismissal, suspension, etc." in the motor industry (59 a year according to the Ministry's statistics in the period 1964-66)

indicates that there is considerable confusion as to what management does and does not have the right to do; or, where it is conceded to have the right, whether it is or is not making reasonable use of it.

391. The need to deal with the many problems arising at workplace level means that a considerable strain is thrown on negotiating arrangements, and the attempt to handle them by means of disputes procedures has not always been successful. Indeed in some plants things have reached such a pitch that strikes frequently take place before the dispute reaches even the first stage in the agreed procedure. Thus Sir Jack Scamp states in paragraph 24 of the report already quoted above:

" At Morris Motors Ltd., Cowley, for instance, the Council found that in 1965, 256 out of 297 stoppages of work had occurred before the senior shop steward had even had a chance to put the grievance into procedure. In the first half of 1966, again 128 stoppages out of 142 took place before the senior shop steward had had time to act on them, in spite of special efforts made by the company to provide facilities for the bringing in of senior shop stewards as soon as a problem was known to exist."

392. The general picture described in paragraphs 18-19 of Sir Jack Scamp's latest report, which covers the period ending December 1967, is as follows:

" During 1967 less than 2 per cent of disputes that led to stoppages had been taken right through procedure. 22 per cent were not dealt with in procedure at all, while 20 per cent went no further than the first stage . . . before a stoppage occurred. Some 50 per cent went to the second stage . . . but no further. Only one in a hundred stoppages was made official by endorsement by the union concerned.

" Regard for the procedures tends to vary according to the question at issue. Not one of the disputes over discipline, trade union matters, manning scales, mobility of labour and transfers was taken to the final stage of procedure. Dismissals and other disciplinary matters tend of course to be associated with precipitate action and nearly 40 per cent of stoppages for such reasons took place without any regard for the procedure."

393. The engineering industry's disputes procedure must bear a large share of the responsibility for the failure of federated undertakings to devise adequate wage structures and for their inability to solve disputes over other issues in a constitutional manner. The procedure functions slowly. It hampers the development of well-designed pay structures by allowing sectional claims to be pursued right through to " central conference " regardless of their implications for other workers in the same factory. It discourages effective company personnel policies because companies have no place in the agreed procedure, unresolved disputes in individual factories being referred to local conference and not to the company. It provides no general guidance on dealing with issues of discipline, redundancy and work practices and it is not well equipped to handle individual disputes on these topics, which, it implies, fall within the prerogative of employers " to manage their own establishments ", despite the obvious impossibility of fixing clear and immutable limits for such a prerogative. Those companies which are not " federated " have been obliged to devise procedures suitable to their own

circumstances, a situation which, so far as we are aware, has brought no disadvantages in its train.

394. The charge can justly be made against trade unions that they have failed to respond adequately to the challenge inherent in the growth of workplace bargaining. Their leaders have remained pre-occupied with collective bargaining at industry level, while shop stewards have been left largely on their own to set the pace in negotiations at plant level. The disputes procedure in the engineering industry indeed offers no formal part to full-time trade union officials at an earlier stage than a " works conference "; that is until all the stages of negotiation within the plant have been observed without success. Union leaders however have made no sustained efforts to improve the procedure. Communications between the rank-and-file and the leadership have been left in a very poor state. The defect is made good only to a very limited extent by meetings between union officials and shop stewards at district committee and other meetings. The multiplicity of unions operating within plants has hindered the development of an organic link between negotiators at plant level and those higher up in the hierarchies of trade unions.

395. The shop steward system has developed its strength in an informal and piecemeal way. Thus it is that, despite the great importance of shop stewards to the maintenance of good industrial relations in the industry, they still do not have the facilities or the status which are desirable. It is the exception, not the rule, for a chief shop steward to have a room put at his disposal as an office, although in practice he may rarely or never work at the machine to which he is nominally allotted. This is not invariably the company's fault. We heard of one case where the company would be willing to afford the chief shop steward an office, but where he is reluctant to accept the offer for fear that he might be regarded as having " sold out " to the management.

396. To summarise, it is apparent that the causes of unofficial strikes in the motor manufacturing industry are complex, and that employers and unions both bear a considerable responsibility for them. Insofar as fluctuations in demand have been caused by fiscal measures which fall with particular force on the motor industry, Governments too must take some responsibility, since these fluctuations have led to insecurity of employment and of earnings. Employers have failed to develop adequate management policies, and in particular have not tackled effectively the problem of devising rational wage structures. Trade unions have been handicapped by their multiplicity and consequent rivalry, and have failed to bring an effective influence to bear at workplace level.

397. Above all, employers and trade unions have failed to develop adequate institutions in changing circumstances. The conclusions of Professor Turner and his colleagues are worth quoting here. They say that an inadequacy of institutions is the factor of broadest practical significance which has induced the strike-proneness of the industry.[1] They say that " the traditional collective organisation of the old mechanical engineering trades has proven incapable of adapting itself either to the actual development and specialisation of the

[1]*Op. cit.*, p.350. The quotations which follow are from pp. 342-3.

107

metalworking sector . . . or to the new popular standards created by the achievement of full employment and a steady advance in real incomes ". They criticise the outdated structure of the trade unions and of the Engineering Employers' Federation and the failure of the engineering disputes procedure " to embody either the actual development of workplace labour organisation and relationships of the past generation, or the national integration of separate engineering establishments into giant combines " or " to provide for either a speedy or definitive settlement " of disputes. In our view they are right.

398. The further we have pursued our inquiries, the stronger has become our belief that the motor industry's difficulties over strikes arise in the main not so much from special factors peculiar to the industry as from factors which are present in many other industries, although to a less marked degree. The analysis in Chapter III of the shortcomings of the industrial relations system emphasises how important and how general a failure there has been to devise institutions in keeping with changing needs. Unofficial strikes and other types of unofficial action are above all a symptom of this failure.

399. This conviction is borne out by consideration of circumstances in all four industries which suffer most from unofficial strikes—coalmining, docks, ship-building and ship-repairing and motors. In all these industries work group organisation is exceptionally strong, fragmented bargaining has been the rule, and wage structures have been notoriously anarchic. The experience of the iron and steel industry is also significant. Changing technology has altered the importance of different groups of workers in the production process, and as a result maintenance craftsmen, whose pay is settled separately from that of process workers, have become increasingly dissatisfied with the wages structure. The industry's once good strike record has deteriorated and, in a list of industries which in recent years have most suffered from unofficial strikes, iron and steel comes next after the main four.

THE NATURE AND IMPORTANCE OF THE STRIKE PROBLEM

Trade Unions and Unofficial Strikes

400. It is sometimes assumed that unofficial strikes are demonstrations against the official policies of trade unions. This is so in some cases. Thus the unofficial strike in the London docks in connection with the introduction of decasualisation in September 1967 took place when dockers and their unofficial leaders refused to put into effect the terms of an agreement nego-tiated by union leaders on their behalf. However unofficial strikes for reasons of this kind are exceptional. Most of them concern issues arising at plant level which are not dealt with at all in agreements negotiated by union leaders, such as rates of pay or piece-rates settled at workplace level, dismissals or working arrangements.

401. In most cases trade unions adopt no official attitude to individual un-official strikes, since the question seldom arises whether they should be treated as official or not. They commonly take place before any full-time union official at district level, let alone at headquarters, is aware that the problem exists; and indeed we have pointed out that even senior shop stewards may have no forewarning. The question whether these strikes should be authorised by the union has generally never been considered before they take place.

402. In many trade unions there is no rule under which members are expressly forbidden to go on strike without prior authorisation. What the official attitude of the union should be to a strike begun without prior authorisation is a question which has to be considered only if the strike lasts long enough to make intervention by full-time officials necessary or if there is a question of paying dispute benefit (i.e. strike pay). The majority of unofficial strikes are however over too quickly for either eventuality to arise. Thus in the period 1964-66 according to the Ministry of Labour's records a majority of unofficial strikes were over in two days or less, and over 80 per cent were over in a week or less. In some unions, such as the Amalgamated Engineering Union, the General and Municipal Workers' Union and, until recently, the Electrical Trades Union, dispute benefit is paid only if a stoppage lasts three days or more.

403. Nevertheless when an unofficial strike does last long enough for the strikers to apply for strike benefit, the trade union's attitude towards the strike has to be made clear retrospectively; since the authorisation of dispute benefit appears in all unions which pay such benefit to be a matter for decision by the executive. Most of them permit the executive to decide to pay benefit in respect of strikes which did not have prior authorisation by the union. We examined the position in the fourteen largest unions in the country, organising between them some $6\frac{1}{4}$ million workers. We found that in 1965 the payment of dispute benefit was authorised in respect of nearly 200 strikes which did not have prior approval; and that the corresponding figure for 1966 probably exceeded 150. Virtually all these cases were confined to five out of the fourteen unions.

404. It is important to consider why unions authorise benefit in these circumstances. In the case of one union, the Electrical Trades Union, the rules make it clear that members are entitled to strike first and to seek to have the strike made official afterwards. In many other cases the union executive concerned took the decision to pay strike benefit because the strike involved other unions with more members involved; so that its own members had little choice but to join in, or alternatively were laid off in circumstances which disqualified them from receiving unemployment benefit. In yet other cases action without prior authorisation was regarded as justified because of " provocation " by the employer, or because the union's vital interests were thought to be involved, for example by the dismissal of a shop steward, or by the actions of a breakaway union. Finally unions occasionally regard the retrospective payment of benefit as justified in a case where a claim at workplace level has initially been refused more or less out of hand by an employer, and then conceded as soon as the strike takes place.

405. It may be concluded therefore that in the majority of unofficial strikes the unions do not officially declare an attitude: and that in a substantial proportion of the remainder they are prepared to pay dispute benefit after the event.

406. Since a very high proportion of unofficial strikes are also unconstitutional, it might be inferred that union leaders view breaches of procedure with indifference. This is not so. Many trade union leaders have gone on record unequivocally as being opposed to such breaches, and we have no

doubt of their sincerity in the matter. On occasions when their active intervention in an unconstitutional dispute has become necessary they have almost invariably sought to persuade strikers to go back to work so that the dispute can be settled by constitutional means. They have been no less anxious than employers' associations to exclude intervention by the Ministry of Labour in unconstitutional stoppages, for fear that this might undermine the working of established procedures.

407. How then are these apparently contradictory attitudes to be understood? The explanation lies largely in the inadequacy of both procedural and substantive agreements in many of our industries. Industry-wide procedures leave a great deal to be settled in the plant, but the disputes procedures, which commonly provide the only formal negotiating machinery available at plant level, were not designed to provide machinery for the settlement of complex wage structures. Trade union leaders feel themselves committed to support procedures to which their unions are party, but at the same time they are bound to sympathise with the frustrations of workers on the shop floor who suffer from their inadequacies. This conclusion is supported by the results of our workshop relations survey. District officials, shop stewards and trade union members were asked to say whether they thought that workers were justified in withdrawing their labour, or using other forms of pressure in disregard of procedure, in a number of different situations. In each case only a minority supported such action by workers " in any situation where they think that by acting in this way they can get what they want ". There was little difference between the attitudes of ordinary trade unionists and shop stewards (27 per cent of ordinary trade unionists and 23 per cent of shop stewards), but only 11 per cent of full-time trade union officials thought such action justifiable. On the other hand there was majority support in all three groups for the view that unconstitutional action was justified:

(a) " if management has broken an agreement ";

(b) " if it (i.e. management) appears to be resorting to unreasonable delay in dealing with grievances "; and

(c) " if there is no other way of preventing management from discharging workmates unfairly ".

408. A further explanation of the apparent contradictions is to be found in the extent to which trade union leaders have been content to accept the situation in which workplace bargaining is conducted by shop stewards. This has not happened as a result of defiance by shop stewards of their unions. Our survey of district officers showed that 87 per cent thought that they had sufficient influence over the activities of shop stewards and members in the industries for which they were responsible. Virtually all district officers regarded the work done by stewards very highly. On average each district officer had 172 shop stewards and 102 different plants within his field of responsibility; and it is obvious therefore that district officers have to place great reliance on shop stewards. In these circumstances trade union leaders would weaken still further their influence over their members if, having accepted that the brunt of workplace bargaining falls on shop stewards, they

110

created the impression that their main anxiety was not to support the stewards but to exercise discipline over them.

The Importance of Strikes

409. It is now possible to make some estimate of the importance of strikes and other industrial action in economic terms. Official strikes tend to be much more serious individually in terms of working days lost, and individual official strikes may have particularly serious economic effects. Thus the national seamen's strike which took place in the summer of 1966 had serious consequences for our export trade and for the economy as a whole. Strikes in service industries can do grave damage because their effects may rapidly be felt over a wide range of industry. Nevertheless official strikes are relatively infrequent and their number shows no consistent tendency to grow. Since the end of the war there have been only three years when major official strikes have resulted in raising the number of working days lost above the 4 million mark; these were 1957, 1959 and 1962 when the numbers lost were 8.4m., 5.3m. and 5.8m. respectively.

410. So far as unofficial strikes are concerned, the immediate effect in terms of working days lost might seem to indicate that in economic terms no very serious problem is involved. After all, international comparisons of working days lost through stoppages show the United Kingdom better off than several other countries. In fact, however, it would be seriously misleading to base one's assessment of the economic significance of these stoppages merely on the tally of working days lost on their account.

411. That tally gives a very imperfect measure of the economic consequences of a strike. It records days lost at the place of work, whether by the strikers or by other workers laid off in consequence of the strike. Days lost at other establishments because of the indirect effects of a stoppage are not included in the statistics, though they may nevertheless be substantial, especially in any industry where a strike by a handful of workers may make idle hundreds or even thousands of workers at other establishments (as is borne out by the experience of motor manufacture, for which special estimates are made). Similarly a railway or a bus strike may prevent other workers from getting to work. On the other hand it is possible for some of the loss of working days to be made good after a strike, either by overtime or by greater effort under incentive schemes.

412. It is also necessary to take account of the effects on management of fear of the possibility of strikes even if they do not take place. If an employer forestalls a strike by making concessions in the face of threats which it might have been better to resist, or by refraining from introducing changes which he believes to be necessary in the interests of efficiency, then the economic consequences of his doing so may be more serious than those to which a strike would have given rise. Naturally, however, it is impossible to measure such consequences statistically.

413. It is in fact only when the impact on managements of unofficial strikes and other forms of unofficial action is taken into account that their gravity becomes apparent. Such action may face a manager with a sudden and acute dilemma. He may be under severe pressure from customers to produce

111

goods or materials by a particular deadline, and in a competitive market such pressure is not easy to resist. No doubt it should be resisted if the alternative is to surrender to blackmail exerted by unofficial strikers. But it is not surprising if managers sometimes make unwise concessions which secure peace for the time being at the cost of storing up trouble for the future.

414. Moreover it is characteristic of unofficial action that it is unpredictable. For the most part it concerns issues which are not regulated by written collective agreements. The formal rules which are supposed to govern workplace bargaining—those contained in disputes procedures—are frequently ineffective and cannot be relied on. The informal network of rules and undertakings built up by managements and shop stewards in their day-to-day dealings with each other lack precision and stability. The upshot is that some managements lack confidence that the plans they make and the decisions they reach can be implemented rapidly and effectively or, in extreme cases, at all.

415. This situation is found in its most acute form in the small number of establishments where there is what might be termed an " endemic " strike situation. In 1965 thirty-one establishments experienced five or more officially-recorded strikes, and in 1966 the number was twenty-seven, several of them appearing in both lists. In many of them the number of unrecorded strikes was probably much higher. In these establishments managers and supervisors are in a constant state of anxiety lest they do something which might inadvertently lead to a strike. There are also a growing number of establishments where occasional strikes and other forms of industrial action take place, and here managements tend to be worried lest the situation deteriorate. The economic implications are obvious and serious; the country can ill afford the crippling effect which such managerial attitudes are liable to have on the pace of innovation and technological advance in industry. We have no hesitation therefore in saying that the prevalence of unofficial strikes, and their tendency (outside coalmining) to increase, have such serious economic implications that measures to deal with them are urgently necessary.

TACKLING THE STRIKE PROBLEM

416. Any consideration of measures designed to reduce strikes must take into account whether the law has a part to play, in the circumstances of today, in ameliorating the situation. This question is considered in detail in the next chapter of our report, and also in Chapter XIV. In this present chapter we deal with other possible remedies.

Official Strikes: Breakdowns in Negotiations at Industry Level

417. Despite the infrequency of major official strikes resulting from the breakdown of negotiations at industry level, because these strikes can have serious consequences when they do occur we have thought it right to consider several proposals intended to reduce their number still further.

418. *National emergencies.* The Emergency Powers Acts of 1920 and 1964 enable a state of emergency to be declared by royal proclamation if the community, or a substantial part of it, appears likely to be deprived of the essentials of life because of interference with the supply of food, water, fuel

or light, or with transport. Emergency regulations may then be made to secure the essentials of life to the community, though it cannot be made an offence to take part in a strike. The powers under the Acts can be used if a strike or threatened strike leads to the proclamation of a state of emergency.

419. It was urged by the Society of Conservative Lawyers and by others that it should be open to the Minister of Labour, acting on behalf of the Government, to apply for an injunction compelling continuance of work and the cessation of any lock-out or strike for some period, say 60 days, on the ground that the stoppage is "creating grave national loss or widespread hindrance to public health or safety". The 60-day period would enable negotiations to continue, but if they were not successful the stoppage could be resumed at the end.

420. This suggestion was based on the powers which the President of the USA has had since 1947 under the Taft-Hartley Act in relation to industrial disputes which imperil the national health or safety. The President may appoint a board of inquiry to investigate and report (though not to make recommendations). On receiving the report he may seek an injunction against the strike or lock-out as likely to imperil national safety or health. If granted, the disputing parties must during the next 60 days try to settle their differences with the help of the Federal Mediation and Conciliation Service; and the board of inquiry must make a further report by the end of the 60 days, unless a settlement has been reached meanwhile, including in that report a statement of the employer's latest offer. During the following 15 days the National Labor Relations Board must hold a ballot of the workers concerned on whether to accept this offer, and five further days are allowed to certify the result. When this has been done, and if a settlement still eludes the parties, the injunction is discharged and the stoppage can proceed.

421. The record as regards the use of the Taft-Hartley procedure is as follows. In all but one of 24 cases in which injunctions were granted, a stand-still period was successfully imposed. In sixteen cases a settlement was reached during or shortly after the stand-still period, but in seven cases stoppages did take place or were resumed after it. There has not been a single case in which a vote has gone in favour of acceptance of the employer's latest offer.

422. In the United Kingdom when a major strike occurs or appears imminent the Government has a wide range of action which it can take if it feels it desirable to intervene. It can set in motion the conciliation machinery of the Department of Employment and Productivity, or appoint conciliators, or arrange arbitration, or order an inquiry, which may take any of several forms. The Government also has great freedom as to the timing of its intervention, which is often very important.

423. The record under the Taft-Hartley Act in the United States has been worse than the record in our country. We have been singularly free from strikes in recent years which would have come within the scope of a "Taft-Hartley" kind of procedure.

424. The proposal of the Conservative Lawyers would however cover a wider field than the American legislation since it would cover strikes "creating grave national loss". It is possible of course to argue that in the case of any par-

113

ticular strike the proposed procedure would have helped. However, account must also be taken of the occasions when strikes have been imminent but have been averted through our existing flexible procedures. If the more rigid arrangements of the fixed cooling-off period had been used in their place, strikes might have taken place which were in fact avoided. The 60-day period may be taken into account in advance by the parties and in any case fits more easily into a system where collective agreements expire on fixed dates, unlike the system here, where the timing of negotiations is less hard and fast.

425. On the whole therefore we do not think that the introduction of a procedure such as is proposed by the Society of Conservative Lawyers would be beneficial. We think it preferable that the Government's present freedom of action should be preserved, and we do not think that it has been shown that its powers need to be increased.

426. *Compulsory strike ballots.* A number of witnesses have suggested to us that a secret ballot should be required before a strike can lawfully take place. This proposal is based on the belief that workers are likely to be less militant than their leaders and that, given the opportunity of such a ballot, they would often be likely to vote against strike action.

427. It is clear that the scope of any legislation to this end, if it were to be effective, would have to be confined to major official strikes. A law forbidding strike action before the holding of a secret ballot could not be enforced in the case of small-scale unofficial stoppages, which make up the overwhelming majority of the total number of strikes.

428. There is little justification in the available evidence for the view that workers are less likely to vote for strike action than their leaders; and findings from our workshop relations survey, already cited, confirm this. Experience in the USA has been that strike ballots are overwhelmingly likely to go in favour of strike action. This is also the experience of Canada, where strike ballots are compulsory in the provinces of Alberta and British Columbia. Two instances of ballots held in recent years in this country where the vote went against strike action are sometimes quoted in support of the case for compulsory secret ballots. One was held in connection with an industry-wide wage claim in engineering in 1962, and one in connection with action to secure the reinstatement of certain employees dismissed by the Ford Motor Company in 1963. But these ballots were held on the initiative of the unions concerned. They do not provide reliable evidence of what the outcome would be if ballots were held in quite different circumstances, and under the compulsion of the law.

429. There are other objections to such ballots. Once a vote has been taken and has gone in favour of strike action, the resulting stoppage may delay a settlement by restricting union leaders' freedom of action. Moreover, how is the question on which the vote is to be taken to be framed? If the vote is, for instance, about whether to accept the employer's latest offer, its result can be stultified if the employer subsequently makes a slightly improved offer.

430. We do not recommend that it should be compulsory by law, either generally or in certain defined cases, to hold a ballot of the employees affected upon the question whether strike action should be taken. We think it prefer-

114

able that trade union leaders should bear, and be seen to bear, the responsibility of deciding when to call a strike and when to call it off. Occasions may of course arise when union leaders would themselves wish to hold such a ballot or are required to do so by their rules. The decision on such a matter should continue to rest with the unions.

431. *Improving existing services.* A few negotiating bodies at industry level have independent chairmen, as for example the newly formed Joint Industrial Board for the Electrical Contracting Industry, and the National Joint Council for Local Authorities' Administrative, Professional, Technical and Clerical Services. Recently, following the report of a Court of Inquiry under the chairmanship of Lord Pearson, the National Maritime Board—the negotiating body for the shipping industry—also decided to appoint an independent chairman. Moreover, in certain industries, especially in the public sector of the economy, provision is made for matters which cannot be resolved by negotiation to go to arbitration. In some cases arbitration is to be by a permanent tribunal set up specially for the industry, as in the civil service, the railways and coalmining. In other cases, such as building, the identity of the arbitrator or arbitrators is to be settled on each occasion when the need arises. An agreement may mention arbitration without committing the parties. Thus in the coalmining industry disputes are to be referred for decision by the industry's " National Reference Tribunal " but only if neither side objects; and the awards of the Railway Staff National Tribunal are not regarded by the parties as binding.

432. Even if nothing is said about it in a procedure agreement, those concerned can always enlist the aid of some third party. They can for example seek the help of the Department of Employment and Productivity's conciliation service or agree to arbitration by the Industrial Court.

433. Ever since it was established in 1917 it was an important part of the Ministry of Labour's work to promote good industrial relations; and the continuing policy of successive Governments has been to support the growth of effective voluntary negotiating machinery in industry. It has been regarded as a corollary to this that conciliation and other services provided by the Government should supplement procedures for the settlement of disputes which industries have devised for themselves, and not provide an alternative or a substitute for them.

434. The Ministry of Labour's evidence gives a full description of the services which it used to provide and which are now provided by the Department of Employment and Productivity to help resolve differences and disputes. We here give a brief summary only. First, the Department of Employment and Productivity provides a conciliation service staffed by officials which operates throughout its regional network as well as at headquarters. The Department's staff have close contacts with representatives of employers and trade unions at all levels and keep in touch with negotiations. It is estimated that the Department's officers conciliate in some 300 or 400 differences a year, the trend being upward. In most cases their help is first requested by one or both of the parties, though occasionally it is volunteered. In our opinion this service makes a very considerable contribution to good industrial relations.

435. Secondly, the Department can arrange arbitration with the consent of the parties to a dispute, provided that any agreed negotiating machinery has first been exhausted. Arbitration can be by the Industrial Court, or by one or more people specially appointed, or by a board of arbitration consisting of nominees of the parties under an independent chairman nominated by the Secretary of State. The Industrial Court is a permanent arbitration tribunal whose members are appointed by the Secretary of State. In practice the Court consists of an independent chairman, who is normally the Court's President, and an employers' and a workers' representative. Arbitration awards are not legally binding, but where parties freely consent to the arbitration there is always a moral obligation on them to accept the award, and this they almost invariably do.

436. Finally, the Secretary of State can appoint inquiries into industrial disputes under the Conciliation Act 1896 or the Industrial Courts Act 1919, and can do so without the consent of the parties. An inquiry can also be set up under the Secretary of State's general powers. This can be given somewhat wider terms of reference than a statutory inquiry. Thus the Committee of Inquiry under Lord Devlin which inquired into the long-term labour problems of the docks as well as a dispute was appointed under the Minister of Labour's general powers. This inquiry was an example of a welcome tendency in recent years to set up inquiries which have wide terms of reference and are able to examine long-term problems and implications as well as the immediate causes of dispute. Such inquiries can lead to changes of fundamental importance both to the community and to an industry.

437. This tendency should continue, but its growth will require a considerable increase in the resources made available to those conducting such inquiries. The Department has need of its own industrial relations research section. This could help to keep it abreast of the growing volume of research conducted in universities and elsewhere as well as enabling it to conduct its own surveys and investigations into particular problems of industrial relations. The section could be especially helpful in assisting the Department's regional industrial relations service with its growing functions. But it could also provide a research service to supplement the secretarial assistance already given to special inquiry bodies appointed by the Secretary of State. The work of such a body would be greatly facilitated if one of its first tasks was to discuss with its research officer the special investigations which needed to be put in hand to enable it to carry out its job.

438. For the future, we believe that the proposed Industrial Relations Commission should be well equipped to carry out inquiries into long-term problems. We envisage that its staff also will include research workers of adequate experience and suitable qualifications to carry out investigations in depth into those problems which call for this treatment.

439. While we would expect the Industrial Relations Commission normally to be given responsibility for carrying out inquiries of this kind, we think it desirable that the Secretary of State should still have open the existing range of choice of inquiry agencies so that if in any particular case an *ad hoc* inquiry seems preferable this can be arranged. It is desirable, however,

116

that inquiries into long-term problems should be statutory inquiries. They should have the status and powers which an Act of Parliament can give, but which a Minister acting simply under his general powers may not be able to give. The powers at present contained in the Conciliation Act and the Industrial Courts Act should be extended so that statutory inquiries may be conducted under terms of reference wide enough to enable them to investigate long-term problems, irrespective of whether a dispute or difference exists or is threatened; and may be appointed by other Ministers in conjunction with the Secretary of State for Employment and Productivity.

Unofficial Strikes

440. We now turn to the aspect of strikes which seems to us more serious than the occasional official strike—the rapidly growing number of unofficial and unconstitutional strikes in this country (outside coalmining). We have kept constantly in mind that measures aimed at reducing the number of unofficial strikes which merely lead trade unions to make those strikes official would not improve industrial relations.

441. In its written evidence to us the Ministry of Labour remarked that it was sometimes criticised for not intervening more frequently in strikes. It pointed out, however, that most strikes are unofficial, and that conciliation was inhibited by the desire not to take action which might appear to condone or even encourage breaches of agreements. Employers normally expect trade union officials to get their members back to work so that discussions according to agreed procedures can take place; and union officials usually try to do this. Intervention by the Ministry might therefore also undermine union authority. The Ministry continued (page 98, Third Memorandum, paragraph 22):

> " Exceptionally, however, conciliation action is taken while such strikes are still in progress, although the Ministry of Labour never deals with unofficial strike leaders but only with authorised officers of the trade unions concerned. This action is generally justified on the grounds that the continuation of a particular stoppage would have a seriously damaging effect on the economy. As far as possible such discussions are limited to finding a basis on which work can be resumed and the original matters in dispute are left for subsequent negotiation in procedure. The question arises as to whether the Ministry of Labour should intervene more frequently in circumstances of this kind."

442. The Ministry told us that it had been attempting to find ways of bringing more influence than in the past to bear on unofficial and unconstitutional strikes. It is already possible to appoint formal inquiries into major unofficial strikes under the powers referred to in paragraph 436 above, but the Ministry suggested to us that a less formal procedure was needed where unofficial strikes in general were concerned. The Ministry discussed a proposal for such a procedure with the British Employers' Confederation and the TUC in 1964. It was suggested that there might be value in fact-finding teams consisting of a Ministry chairman together with an employer and a trade unionist which could investigate at short notice and report urgently on the circumstances of selected stoppages—whether official or unofficial—in order to elicit the facts and bring the force of informed public opinion to bear on those

117

involved. However, the British Employers' Confederation and the TUC were unwilling to agree to this, fearing that it would enhance the status of unofficial leaders and undermine the authority of the unions and established procedures. They nevertheless decided to carry out a joint study of their own with certain selected disputes which had already occurred.

443. Relevant experience has been gained since that time through the working of the Motor Industry Joint Labour Council set up in 1965 by employers and unions in the industry, of which Sir Jack Scamp was appointed independent chairman by the Minister of Labour. The Council's functions include the following:

(i) to keep the general state of industrial relations in the industry under review and to examine matters of general significance for relations in the industry;

(ii) to review the state of industrial relations in individual firms;

(iii) to inquire into particular disputes leading to serious unofficial strikes or lock-outs in breach of procedure.

However, no inquiries into unofficial strikes have in fact been carried out by the Council. In his report to the Minister in November 1966, Sir Jack Scamp said (paragraph 4):

" It is implicit in [the above] terms of reference that the Council was not authorised to act in respect of official strikes, but was expected to investigate serious unofficial strikes. It was, however, necessary from the outset to avoid situations in which intervention by the Council might come to be regarded as an alternative to the full use of the normal procedure for the resolution of disputes. In the event, there has been no unofficial strike of long enough duration to warrant the intervention of the Council."

On the other hand the Council has conducted inquiries into several official strikes over matters not settled by the agreed procedure, and these have been very largely successful in settling the issues in dispute.

444. The Ministry suggested to us that there were three types of inquiry of which use might be made in the future in connection with unofficial strikes:

(i) inquiries carried out in particular industries by bodies constituted on lines similar to those of the Motor Industry Joint Labour Council under an independent chairman;

(ii) inquiries conducted by an independent chairman, together with representatives of employers and workers, on the lines suggested to the British Employers' Confederation and the TUC in 1964— these would not be confined to a particular industry;

(iii) investigations carried out by an industrial relations officer of the Ministry of Labour.

445. We have doubts as to the value of the first two types of inquiry. It is difficult to draw any firm conclusions from the experience of the Motor Industry Joint Labour Council as to the possible value of the establishment of similar bodies in other industries and circumstances. This Council itself

does not seem to have had any significant effect on the incidence of unofficial strikes in the motor industry. Nor does it seem to us very likely that the second type of inquiry mentioned would be much more profitable. Both kinds of inquiry could take place only some time after a particular strike had been settled, and their fairly formal nature would make them unsuited to the detailed investigation in depth which is needed to unravel the facts underlying an unofficial strike. The mere setting up of a formal inquiry makes each party react by getting up its case and establishing the position it proposes to defend.

446. It is important to distinguish between action designed to resolve a particular dispute, and action designed to obtain more information with a view to future avoidance of disputes. In our view there is no case justifying the establishment of inquiry agencies whose primary purpose would be to conduct rapid investigations with a view to influencing the course of unofficial and unconstitutional strikes. Unofficial strikes in breach of procedure agreements are usually very quickly over, and there is neither time nor need for an inquiry to secure their termination. It is one of the specific functions of the Motor Industry Joint Labour Council to investigate such strikes, and yet it has never in fact done this, even though operating in one of the most strike-prone parts of industry. When elsewhere major unofficial stoppages have occurred, and investigation has become desirable, the need to set up a separate formal inquiry does not appear to have been a handicap.

447. We conclude that the most useful of the three types of inquiry suggested by the Ministry is the third, namely an investigation carried out by one of the Ministry's own staff of industrial relations officers. These officers are already in close daily contact with employers and trade union officials at all levels and they are well placed to discover and evaluate the details of events and attitudes that make up the complex relationships at the workplace. They receive many confidences and they give much useful advice which often avoids strikes without any formal conciliation at all.

448. We therefore suggest that the Secretary of State for Employment and Productivity should, in appropriate cases, place on an industrial relations officer or officers the duty of obtaining the full facts about unofficial and unconstitutional stoppages in any industry, region or undertaking where they are causing particular difficulties. Such facts might occasionally be obtained during the course of disputes, but in most cases the inquiry would be after the event since such strikes are usually of short duration. The principal object would be to build up a much clearer and more comprehensive picture of the circumstances of these unofficial stoppages than the Department is able to obtain in the ordinary way. Normally an inquiry should take place in private, but the industrial relations officer should be given powers to oblige people to appear before him (although we do not think he will often have to use such powers). He would normally need to interview not only employers' association officials and full-time trade union officials but also representatives of management and shop stewards and even on occasion unofficial strikers. Whether the parties should be given copies of his reports would depend on the circumstances.

119

E

449. The proposed Industrial Relations Commission would also be available to investigate the problems of unofficial strikes in particular companies or particular sections of industry. The information obtained by industrial relations officers would be useful in indicating whether a full-dress inquiry by the Commission was desirable and, if so, what the major questions needing investigation were.

450. The anxiety that outside intervention in unofficial and unconstitutional action will undermine procedures and enhance the status of unofficial leaders is understandable but can be exaggerated. Where authority in practice resides with unofficial leaders, it is questionable how useful it is to pretend otherwise. Whether the discovery and publication of the facts will enhance the status of unofficial leaders depends on what the facts are. If they are discreditable they will have the opposite effect. If on the other hand the facts reveal that full-time trade union officials have little influence, or that managements have acted unwisely, this is all the more reason for publishing the facts. The possibility that a strike may lead to an inquiry by an industrial relations officer could conceivably be a contributory motive for calling a strike, but invariably more immediate and substantial reasons would also exist. On the other hand the possibility of an inquiry may spur managements and trade union officials into being more assiduous in seeking solutions. We hope that in future those concerned, while properly mindful of the need not to undermine agreed procedures or trade union authority, will nevertheless adopt a bolder and more realistic approach when endeavouring to ascertain causes and seek solutions.

451. We recommend that the powers at present contained in the Conciliation Act and the Industrial Courts Act should be widened as necessary to enable inquiries on the lines indicated in paragraph 448 (as well as earlier in paragraph 439) to be conducted. It would be appropriate for the Government at the same time to consider whether the powers which may be conferred on Courts of Inquiry by virtue of s.4(4) of the Industrial Courts Act need to be brought up to date.

452. *Remedying the underlying causes.* Investigations on these lines will assist towards an understanding of the causes of unofficial strikes, but they will do little of themselves to remove these causes.

453. We make elsewhere a number of recommendations which should have an important effect on certain specific causes of strikes, including disputed claims to recognition and dismissals alleged to be unfair.

454. By far the most important part in remedying the problem of unofficial strikes and other forms of unofficial action will however be played by reforming the institutions of whose defects they are a symptom. Unofficial strikes are above all the result of the inadequate conduct of industrial relations at company and plant level. They will persist so long as companies pay inadequate attention to their pay structures and personnel policies and the methods of negotiation adopted at the workplace remain in their present chaotic state. They will also persist so long as neither employers nor trade unions are willing adequately to recognise, define and control the part played by shop stewards in our collective bargaining system. They will continue

until the confusion which so often surrounds the exercise by management of its " rights " has been resolved by the settlement of clear rules and procedures which are accepted as fair and reasonable by all concerned. Our proposals for reforming the collective bargaining system are therefore fundamental to the solving of this problem also.

455. *Arbitration as an aid to effective procedures.* In this country arbitration is commonly used when the parties have failed to reach agreement on a proposal for changing terms and conditions of employment. It is sometimes suggested that its more widespread use to interpret agreements might help to avoid unofficial strikes.

456. The introduction of this kind of arbitration into the existing unsatisfactory procedures of most industries would solve nothing. In other countries a distinction is drawn between " disputes of right " (that is, disputes about the application of an existing collective agreement) and " disputes of interest " (disputes arising out of the negotiation of a new collective agreement or the renewal of an agreement made for a fixed term which has expired). The distinction is not at present important in Britain because most collective agreements lay down minimum standards which are improved and elaborated on by further negotiation at subsidiary levels. Moreover shopfloor agreements are closely linked with customs and practices which are not set down in any agreement, so that at this level no clear distinction exists between disputes of right and disputes of interest.

457. When collective bargaining has been reformed, however, and companies negotiate comprehensive and effective agreements, the parties may conclude that their arrangements would be strengthened by providing for arbitration on all unresolved differences relating to the application of the agreement during its currency (which might have to be for a fixed term), with voluntary acceptance of the resulting awards as binding. Disputes over the application of the terms of company agreements would go through the company procedure only before submission, if unresolved, to arbitration. Provision on these lines, which would mean that a " peace obligation " would be accepted during the currency of an agreement, could be of great importance. It could be introduced now in companies which make their own agreements. Where it is introduced it will be necessary to provide machinery for arbitration which can work speedily and on the spot.

Chapter VIII

THE ENFORCEMENT
OF COLLECTIVE AGREEMENTS

THE NATURE OF THE PROBLEM

458. The central problem of legislation which we have to solve can be summarised in one question: "What can the law do to help to improve our
industrial relations?" Most of the proposals for legislation which have been
made to us must stand or fall by this test: would their acceptance help or
would it hinder the reform of our system of industrial relations which it is
our main concern to promote?

459. In Chapter IV we recommend that an Industrial Relations Act should
be passed under which certain collective agreements would be registered with
the Department of Employment and Productivity. To this extent, therefore,
we have already accepted the view that legislative measures are required for
the purpose of the reform we have in mind.

460. The specific feature of our present industrial relations, however, which
is uppermost in the minds of those who recommend increased legal intervention in those relations is the frequency of unofficial, and especially of
"unconstitutional", strikes. It is urged that in comparable countries, such
as the Federal Republic of Germany, Sweden, or the United States, the law
plays a significant role in regulating the exercise of the freedom to strike, and
—this is the most important point—that it seeks to prevent and to some
extent succeeds in preventing strikes in breach of obligations imposed by
collective agreements. The hope is expressed that if the law intervened on
a larger scale in our industrial relations, and especially if those organising and
participating in strikes of this character were threatened with legal penalties
of some sort, the incidence of these strikes might be reduced. A number of
legislative techniques have been proposed with a view to reducing the
number of strikes, and some of these have been discussed in the previous
chapter. Much the most important of these techniques however is the
transformation of either collective agreements in general or of procedure
agreements in particular into legally binding contracts which (in one form
or another) can be enforced in a court of law. Our evidence shows that this
is a problem which is being actively and anxiously considered in many
quarters. Many people expect measures of this nature to help to reduce the
number of unofficial strikes to a considerable extent. If this expectation were
justified, the law might indeed be able to make a most significant contribution
to the improvement of our industrial relations. It might make it worth while
to reverse the entire trend of our industrial history and to give to the law
a function it has never had in the past. This is therefore a question of
the utmost gravity and significance.

461. To answer this question it is necessary to see it in the perspective of

122

our industrial relations and in the perspective of the law. When dealing with the impact which the law may have on strikes, one must consider the nature of those strikes, and when considering a reform of the law governing collective bargaining and agreements, one must bear in mind the nature of the bargaining process and of the agreements which are its result. This is important if one seeks to draw lessons from the legal experience of other countries. It is sometimes possible to transplant from one country to another legal institutions or principles which have stood the test of time. But to do so may be useless or even harmful if the social conditions of the country which seeks to adopt them differ from those which have given rise to their growth in their country of origin.

462. As pointed out in the last chapter, 95 per cent of all strikes in this country are unofficial. Unofficial strikes account for more than two-thirds of the days lost through stoppages. The number of unofficial strikes is growing, that of official strikes is not. Official strikes in breach of a collective agreement are very rare, and offer no urgent problem of legislation or otherwise. Unofficial strikes in breach of a procedure agreement are common in a small number of important industries. That is: procedure agreements are broken, and broken all too frequently. But they are not, or they are hardly ever, broken by trade unions. They are broken by trade union members. This is a fact of fundamental importance, and a feature of our industrial relations peculiar to this country. During the years 1964-1966 each unofficial strike lasted on average $2\frac{1}{2}$ days. Our problem is the short spontaneous outburst, not the planned protracted industrial action of long duration which is the main problem, for example, in the United States and in Canada.

463. Most of those participating in these strikes are, under the present law, liable to court proceedings. This is because notice of the strike is hardly ever given to the employer. The employer however has a right to notice in most cases, either by express agreement, or by custom, or through the operation of the Contracts of Employment Act 1963. Hence, as the law stands, the employer can sue the large majority of strikers in the county court or, under the Employers and Workmen Act 1875, summon them before a magistrates' court, so as to obtain damages for breach of contract. In this sense no legislation is needed to make unofficial strikes " illegal ". The law can intervene—at the employer's option. The point is that hardly any employer exercises that option. As the CBI stated in its evidence (paragraph 170) this is " not so much because the measure of damages against one man might be very small compared with the cost and inconvenience of litigation and because the chance of recovering the damages was doubtful, but because the main interest of the employer is in a resumption of work and preservation of good will ". It cannot be in the employer's interest to exacerbate his relations with his own men by summoning them before a court, and to do so at a time when, in the large majority of cases, the strike will be over. Whatever deterrent effect such court proceedings may have will be outweighed by the harm they are liable to do to future relations on the shop floor, on the building site, in the office. The same would in our opinion also apply if an employer deducted from wages any amount awarded to him by way of damages, a possibility referred to by the CBI in its supplementary oral evidence.

464. When considering proposals for the legal enforcement of procedure agreements and other proposals for the enforcement of industrial peace through legal sanctions we have had to take into account that, as long as industrial relations are what they are now, employers do not and cannot be expected to proceed against those who cause a stoppage or to participate in any proceedings against them. Unless and until our system of industrial relations itself has been reformed, no proposal to impose legal sanctions is practicable if it assumes that the employer takes an active part in their enforcement.

COLLECTIVE AGREEMENTS AND THE LAW

465. With these facts in mind, that is the prevalence and the shortness of unconstitutional strikes, and the reluctance of employers to make use of such remedies as the law places at their disposal against unconstitutional strikers, we now examine the various legislative techniques which have been proposed with a view to reducing the injurious impact of such strikes on our economy.

466. It has been pointed out that in many, if not in most, comparable countries, collective agreements are contracts enforceable by and against those who are parties to them. Of the obligations thus imposed upon the parties the most important is the " peace " or " no strike, no lock-out " obligation which means that the unions or employers or employers' associations parties to the agreement may not use industrial sanctions during the currency of the agreement, not at any rate with a view to changing to their advantage or to the advantage of their members the terms laid down in the agreement. If they violate this obligation, they may be liable to heavy damages, and injunctions or their equivalent may be issued to prevent them from taking such action or to compel them to stop it.

467. The " peace " obligation is imposed upon both sides, but it is more important in practice as a remedy to assist the employers than as a remedy to assist the unions; strikes are everywhere a more significant feature of industrial relations than lock-outs. This aspect of the legal enforcement of collective agreements is therefore of special importance to protect the interest of management in the continuous flow of production. Where this interest is thus legally protected, a corresponding legal protection usually exists for the interest of the unions in the maintenance of the standards laid down in the agreement. Under such a system employers who are themselves parties to collective agreements, or members of associations which are parties, are by operation of statute prevented from contracting out of the terms of the agreement to the detriment of their employees. This means that any contract of employment within the scope of the collective agreement which is concluded by an employer bound by its terms is automatically void insofar as it purports to be less favourable to the employee than the terms of the agreement; and that the corresponding terms of the agreement compulsorily become terms of the contract of employment in the place of those which, by operation of the statute, are void. The terms of the agreement thus become a compulsory code for all employers parties to the agreement or members of associations which are parties, and the agreement may by special administrative acts be extended to non-federated employers as well. These two matters, the agreement as a compulsory contract and the agreement as

a compulsory code, are closely connected: the legal restriction of the freedom to strike is so to speak the consideration for the legal guarantee of the agreed minimum. The obligation to refrain from strike or other "hostile" action is generally understood to be co-extensive with the scope of the substantive agreement: strikes are prohibited only in so far as they are intended to compel employers to consent to a change of the matters regulated in the agreement itself while that agreement is in operation, and industrial sanctions are permitted if their application is unrelated to matters dealt with in the collective agreement.

468. No one has raised before us the issue of the legally guaranteed minimum. This is not surprising in view of the present structure of our industrial relations, which is discussed in Chapter III. In so far as there is any legal obligation upon employers to observe the terms of collective agreements, it is provided by section 8 of the Terms and Conditions of Employment Act under which the Industrial Court can, upon a reference by the Secretary of State, impose upon individual employers the obligation to apply recognised terms and conditions or conditions not less favourable to the employee. We have no general law to impose such obligation: it can only be imposed *ad hoc*, as the need arises. Experience has shown that the need does not arise very frequently, and yet the provision has proved its use and should (with modifications discussed in Chapter V) be maintained. It is however totally different from the legal provisions existing in foreign systems of law under which employers are generally and by operation of law obliged to apply the standard terms or terms not less favourable to the employee, and the unions are generally and by operation of law obliged to refrain from industrial sanctions in violation of the agreement.

469. Legislation giving contractual force to collective agreements may conceivably be passed without any corresponding step being taken towards giving to the terms and conditions laid down in agreements the force of a compulsory code. But, whilst conceivable, such legislation would in its character and impact on industrial relations be different from legal systems in which the obligation to keep the peace is intertwined and co-extensive with the compulsion to apply the terms of the agreement. It is because and in so far as the law guarantees those terms that the unions are made to guarantee the peace. To enact the peace obligation as a legal obligation without the corresponding legal guarantee for the enforcement of the substantive terms of the agreement would be an unusual step in labour legislation which only very exceptional circumstances could justify.

470. In this country collective agreements are not legally binding contracts. This is not because the law says that they are not contracts or that the parties to them may not give them the force of contracts. There is in fact nothing in the law to prevent employers or their associations and trade unions from giving legal force to their agreements. It is true that under a statutory provision—section 4 of the Trade Union Act 1871 (which is separately considered in Chapter XIV)—agreements between one trade union and another cannot be "directly" enforced in a court of law and damages cannot be recovered for their breach. An employers' association may be a trade union in the eyes of the law, and therefore a trade union and such an employers'

association could not, if they wished, make their collective agreement enforceable " directly " or through an action for damages. They could however, were they so minded, make it " indirectly " enforceable, and for example obtain from a court a declaration concerning the meaning of the agreement. Nor would anything in this statute stand in the way of a union and an individual employer giving their agreement the full effect of a contract and making it enforceable even " directly " and through actions for damages in the event of breach. The fact is that nothing of this nature normally happens. That it does not happen is not, as we have already said, due to the law. It is due to the intention of the parties themselves. They do not intend to make a legally binding contract, and without both parties intending to be legally bound there can be no contract in the legal sense.

471. This lack of intention to make legally binding collective agreements, or, better perhaps, this intention and policy that collective bargaining and collective agreements should remain outside the law, is one of the characteristic features of our system of industrial relations which distinguishes it from other comparable systems. It is deeply rooted in its structure. As we point out in Chapter III collective bargaining is not in this country a series of easily distinguishable transactions comparable to the making of a number of contracts by two commercial firms. It is in fact a continuous process in which differences concerning the interpretation of an agreement merge imperceptibly into differences concerning claims to change its effect. Moreover, even at industry level, a great deal of collective bargaining takes place through standing bodies, such as joint industrial councils and national or regional negotiating boards, and the agreement appears as a " resolution " or " decision " of that body, variable at its will, and variable in particular in the light of such difficulties of interpretation as may arise. Such " bargaining " does not fit into the categories of the law of contract.

472. As is also pointed out in Chapter III collective bargaining takes place at a number of levels simultaneously, and, in so far as it takes place at workshop or plant level, it is fragmented and it is informal. That it is fragmented means, from the legal point of view, that it is difficult and perhaps often impossible to identify the " party " who made it on the workers' side, and that it is informal means that it would sometimes and probably very often be impossible for a court to receive evidence enabling it to ascertain the content of the " agreement " in a way required for its legal enforcement. In fact most of these " agreements " would probably, in the legal sense, be " void for uncertainty ". Industry-wide bargaining and workshop or plant bargaining are however closely intertwined. To enforce one without the other would be to distort the effect of our collective bargaining system. That system is today a patchwork of formal agreements, informal agreements and " custom and practice ". No court, asked to " enforce " a collective agreement, could disentangle the " agreement " from the inarticulate practices which are its background.

473. It may be alleged that none of these considerations applies to procedure agreements. Nevertheless it is a generally admitted fact that even procedure agreements are not contracts, and this again for the reason that the parties to them do not intend to create legal obligations. This lack of intent is manifest

126

from the style in which the agreements are expressed. To make them enforceable would in the first place require their redrafting, a task which could only be undertaken by or with the assistance of professional lawyers. And with procedure agreements as with substantive agreements the choice of the parties not to be legally bound is far from being arbitrary. Our analysis in paragraphs 61-64 of the procedure agreements of two of our most important industries—engineering and building—shows that neither of these agreements necessarily produces a final settlement of disputes. In the engineering industry the central conference at York often fails to secure a settlement of the issue and in the building industry the existing code of procedure does not apply to a large number of disputes, namely all those arising from matters not covered by industry-wide bargaining or by the " emergency procedure ". To spell anything comparable to the legal " peace " or " no strike, no lock-out " obligation known abroad out of a disputes procedure which is " open-ended " (as in engineering) or fragmentary (as in building) would have been plainly impossible. In engineering the extent of the obligation would have been indefinite in time (in view of the unforeseeability of the duration and the nature of the termination of the procedure). In building it would have been indefinite in scope (because in each case a dispute within a dispute might have arisen as to whether or not the case was within one or the other or neither of the two procedures). Clearly there are good reasons why the parties never intended these procedure agreements to operate as legal " peace clauses ".

474. If therefore our existing collective agreements or if our existing procedure agreements were to be made into legal contracts this would have to be done by a statute attaching the force of law to the terms of a bargain contrary to the wishes of the parties. This would be an unprecedented step, and a step wholly at variance with the principles of the common law which apply to the law of contract. Since the law of contract exists to give effect to the wishes of the parties some strong justification must be sought at the outset for a law designed to set those wishes aside and to impose on the parties a relationship which they do not desire. This measure would be tantamount to a new departure in the law of contract and also to a breach with a long tradition of our industrial relations. The case for such a change might be argued if it could be shown to promise a decisive turn for the better in our industrial relations and in particular a substantial reduction in the number of unofficial strikes. The question whether such expectations are justified must be examined in the light of what we know of the causes of the frequency of unofficial strikes in a number of industries.

THE ROOT OF THE EVIL

475. If these causes were to be found, or mainly to be found, in the irresponsibility of those taking such action or participating in it, then the threat of sanctions for the breach of agreements never intended to be legally binding might create a counter-motive. It might thus reduce the number of strikes and improve our industrial relations. Such, however, is not the case. No doubt the desire on the part of a minority to make trouble and the irresponsibility or weakness of others are factors which contribute to the frequency of unofficial

127

strikes. But this is not the root of the evil. As we found when seeking to identify the underlying causes of unofficial strikes, the root of the evil is in our present methods of collective bargaining and especially our methods of workshop bargaining, and it is in the absence of speedy, clear and effective disputes procedures. Until this defect is remedied, all attempts to make procedure agreements legally binding are bound to defeat themselves. One of the principal objects of the factory and company agreements which, according to our recommendations, should be concluded in the near future will be to develop " joint procedures for the rapid and equitable settlement of grievances ". This is what is lacking at present, and this is the indispensable condition for reducing the number of unofficial and unconstitutional strikes. To make the present procedure agreements legally enforceable would be at variance both with our analysis of the causes of the evil and with our proposals for a remedy. It would divert attention from the underlying causes to the symptoms of the disease and might indeed delay or even frustrate the cure we recommend. It might perpetuate the existing procedures instead of replacing them by clear and effective methods of dispute settlement which at present do not exist.

476. Any attempt to deal with unofficial and unconstitutional strikes in isolation must be deprecated. This applies to the legal enforcement of procedure agreements as much as to the proposal to eradicate these strikes by imposing an overall obligation to give notice before resorting to a stoppage or to similar action such as go-slow, work to rule or overtime bans. None of these measures promises any success in the sense of improving our industrial relations as long as the underlying causes of these strikes have not been removed. We expect the reform of the collective bargaining system to lead to a very considerable reduction in unofficial strikes. This expectation may not be entirely fulfilled. If so, it may then be necessary to reconsider the desirability and practicability of giving some legal support to procedure agreements.

THE PROBLEM OF SANCTIONS

(a) Sanctions against Trade Unions

477. To gauge the legal effect of a possible transformation into contracts of collective agreements in general and procedure agreements in particular one must face the question who would be the parties to such contracts. Collective agreements are, on the employees' side, concluded by trade unions. This is true in any event of industry-wide agreements, including those procedure agreements which are most important in the present context. Whether a shop steward or shop stewards' committee bargaining at plant or workshop level could, in the legal sense, be regarded as acting for the union or unions concerned, or for the individual workers, is a difficult question which we need not pursue. At industry level it would be wholly unrealistic to consider a union concluding a collective agreement as anything but a principal to the transaction. True, it acts in the interest of its members, but it does not act as their agent. Any other view would lead to insoluble difficulties as regards members who (in the event of a ballot or other vote) voted against the agreement and as regards members who joined the union after the agreement had

been concluded. Thus, on the employees' side the union (or unions) is (or are) the party or parties and no one else. The same is likely to be true of the employers' association on the employers' side, though it is more arguable here that the association acts as an " agent " for its members.

478. If procedure agreements gave rise to legally enforceable " peace " obligations, these would therefore be obligations imposed upon the unions and not obligations imposed upon their members. This is well understood in those countries in which " no strike, no lock-out " or " peace " obligations are considered as implied in collective contracts. In those countries the legal " peace " obligation was and is intended to ensure that trade unions which are parties to collective agreements do not take what in this country is called " unconstitutional " action, that is action at variance with a concluded agreement. This is a policy which can be well understood against a background of a situation in which trade unions do not invariably apply the policy of carrying out the agreements they have made. We have already pointed out that unconstitutional action by trade unions is not a live issue in this country at present nor expected to be in the future.

479. Our problem is the strike which is both unofficial and unconstitutional, and from a purely legal point of view the transformation of collective procedure agreements into contracts cannot make any contribution to the solution of this problem at all: those who would be bound by the agreements do not break them in any event, and those who are in the habit of breaking them would not be bound.

480. The law might however go one step beyond merely transforming procedure agreements into contracts: it might impose upon trade unions parties to such contracts a mandatory obligation to guarantee the " good behaviour " of, that is the loyal execution of the agreement by, their members. Alternatively it might go less far and, as the Confederation of British Industry recommended in its evidence (paragraphs 179 ff.), require the union to do all in its power to prevent its members from taking unconstitutional action. Such a measure could, it is sometimes said, be coupled with a threat of deregistration in the event of non-compliance by the union with its obligations and a consequential threat of the loss of immunity from tort liability. It could also be linked with the formulation of a set of " model ", i.e. compulsory, trade union rules containing wide powers of disciplinary action (including expulsion) against members in breach of procedure, powers which, as a result of the agreement, the union would, under the threatened penalty of deregistration, have to exercise.

481. We have given careful consideration to these and similar proposals. They are designed to overcome the legal dilemma referred to at the end of paragraph 479. The proposal made by the CBI is in essence that the " peace " obligation imposed upon a trade union or an employers' association should be given a wide interpretation and that it should include (as it does in some foreign countries, for example in Sweden) a duty, as the Swedish Collective Agreements Act puts it, to " endeavour to prevent its members from committing unlawful offensive actions ", or, where they have occurred, " to endeavour to cause such members to cease committing such action ". An obligation of this kind could be imposed by law without being linked

129

with the threat of deregistration and the consequential loss of immunity for tort action envisaged by the CBI. Its effect would then be a liability to pay damages, possibly to be subjected to injunctions. This could be supplemented by a provision to the effect that, once the union has given its credentials to a shop steward, the steward would be deemed to be its agent.

482.   Such a measure could be contemplated only if it was likely to result in a rapid diminution in the number of unofficial strikes. This however is not the case. The problem with which we have to deal is the readiness of work groups to take action without regard to the procedures of collective bargaining. This stems from causes which we have set out in Chapter III. Among them any failures on the part of the unions to exercise discipline plays a very secondary part. The causes lie in the structure of our system of collective bargaining and the economic conditions under which it has operated since the war. The principal defect of the proposal made to us for forcing the unions to discipline unofficial strikers is that it fails to deal with these causes. It is the method of collective bargaining and the role which unions and work groups play in the bargaining process which has to be reformed in the first instance, and it is for that reason that we have set out our proposals for the reform of collective bargaining in Chapter IV. If, when this reform has been accomplished, unofficial strikes continue to be a serious problem, it will then be time to see what the law can do; but not until then. As things now stand proposals such as those made by the CBI are more likely to lead to internal disruption in the unions than to a reduction in unofficial strikes. The house of the law collapses if it is not built on a solid foundation of fact.

(b) Sanctions against Trade Union Members

483.   Although the members of the union are not bound by agreements and would not, on the general principles of the law of contract, be bound by them if they were legal contracts, it is of course open to Parliament to lay down by statute that they should be so bound. Such steps are not unheard of. The best known example is the Swedish Collective Agreements Law of 1928 which lays down that collective agreements entered into by an association are binding on its members and that employers and employees so bound may not during the period of the validity of the agreement take part in strikes, lock-outs and other " offensive action " for a number of stated purposes, including that of bringing about an alteration of the agreement. Contravention entails liability to pay damages which, however, in the case of an individual employee may not in any case exceed the amount of 200 kronor (about £15).

484.   If the mutual promises of employers and employees were—as they are in Sweden—clearly spelled out in agreements concluded between employers and trade unions, and if an effective procedure for the settlement of disputes was laid down in such agreements, that is if the recommendations in Chapter IV were carried into effect, it might be more practicable in this country to envisage visiting spontaneous action undermining the application of such agreements with legal disadvantages. The agreements to which the Swedish law applies must be drawn up in writing—a provision existing in many countries—to ensure that those who may be made liable for the breach of an agreement are not in ignorance of their obligations and these obligations are articulated and clear.

These conditions are not fulfilled in this country at the moment. They might be if the recommendations in Chapter IV were accepted. Unless and until this is done the enactment of legislation on the Swedish pattern would mean that sanctions were attached to uncertain norms—by general consent the worst legislative policy any lawgiver can adopt.

485. There is, moreover, the very real difficulty caused by the reluctance of employers to enforce legal sanctions against their employees, a reluctance demonstrated by their failure to enforce their claims to damages under the existing law of contract, to which reference is made in paragraph 463 above. There is no reason to think that the liability of unofficial strikers to pay damages for breach of a procedure agreement would be more likely to be enforced than is their present liability to pay damages for breach of their contracts of employment. This too, however, may be different if the employer could expect that a real improvement of the strike situation might be the result of such enforcement—as he might after the reform of the collective bargaining system to which we have made reference.

486. The difficulty to which we have referred in the preceding paragraph could—in theory—be overcome if those acting in contravention of a procedure agreement were to be made liable to pay a fine to the State in criminal proceedings initiated by a public authority, such as the Secretary of State for Employment and Productivity. This was the method of enforcement employed during the Second World War under the Conditions of Employment and National Arbitration Order 1940 (SR&O 1305). The evidence which we have received shows that it was not effective: it did not succeed in reducing the incidence of unofficial strikes at that time. Indeed from 1941 until the Order was revoked in 1951 strikes were considerably more frequent than in any of the preceding twenty years. In December 1941 an attempt was made to enforce penalties against a number of miners who had struck work in the Kent coalfield. This attempt did not succeed. The evidence which we have received from Sir Harold Emmerson, which is reproduced in Appendix 6, shows the fruitlessness of the use of penal sanctions for the purpose of enforcing industrial peace.

487. Moreover—and quite apart from all intrinsic objections to the use of the criminal law for the purpose of enforcing industrial peace—one has to consider that most of the strikes are over in a few days, and some in a few hours, and such criminal proceedings would often have to be instituted after the resumption of work. The trial itself would in the large majority of cases occur at the time when the strike was already a matter of the more or less distant past. Many employers would rightly object to this reopening of the conflict and to creating an acute risk of a renewed stoppage. It is true that under the Prices and Incomes Act 1966, s. 16 (as amended by the Prices and Incomes Act 1967, s. 4(1)) it is a criminal offence for " any trade union or other person " to take or to threaten action, particularly strike action, with a view to compel, induce or influence an employer to implement an award or settlement in contravention of the statute. No occasion has as yet arisen for the application of this provision, but whatever its effect may be in the limited field of its application, it cannot yield any lesson for the larger problem we have to consider. Prosecution under the Prices and Incomes Act would be for a clearly defined offence,

committed against a statute passed in the public interest. The protection of the prices and incomes policy is assumed to be of sufficient importance in the national interest to justify the possibility of creating additional industrial friction through the institution of criminal proceedings—proceedings which (s. 22) can in England be instituted only by or with the consent of the Attorney General. It is a unique situation without parallel in industrial relations.

488.   Another proposal for sanctions is that those who participate in unofficial action should be deprived of the immunities provided by the Trade Disputes Acts 1906 and 1965 for those who commit certain torts in contemplation or furtherance of a trade dispute. This would mean that the strikers could be made civilly liable for conspiracy, for inducing a breach of contract, and for intimidation. Such proceedings for damages or for injunctions would be open either to the employer himself or to third parties. Thus, the employer might, in certain circumstances, have a cause of action for conspiracy, and also for inducing breaches of contract, for example, against one workman who induced another to participate in a strike. There is however no reason to believe that normally employers would be more inclined to sue their own men in tort than they are inclined to sue them for breach of contract. Third parties too may, however, also have rights of action in tort. Thus where an unconstitutional strike has the object of inducing the employer to discharge an employee, e.g. a non-unionist (that is in a situation resembling that in *Rookes v. Barnard* [1964] AC 1129), if the protection of the Trade Disputes Act 1965 were removed, an employee dismissed as a result of an unconstitutional strike or a threat of an unconstitutional strike might indeed claim damages against the strikers. Whether such a claim would ever be made, one cannot say, but it is perhaps not very likely. In a number of recent cases the courts have held that the provisions of the Trade Disputes Act 1906 did not afford a defence to those engaged in industrial action. But cases such as *Rookes v. Barnard* [1964] AC 1129, *Stratford v. Lindley* [1965] AC 269, *Emerald v. Lowthian* [1966] 1 WLR 691, *Morgan v. Fry* [1967] 3 WLR 65, originated in official trade union action, and the trade union concerned could be expected to pay any damages awarded by the court. It does not follow that such proceedings would be instituted against unofficial strikers, and that the change in the law here contemplated would act as an effective deterrent and thus lead to a reduction in the number of these stoppages. A majority of us think it proper that the protection of the first limb of section 3 of the 1906 Act and the corresponding provision in the 1965 Act should be limited to those acting on behalf of a trade union, and make a recommendation to this effect in Chapter XIV. But none of us sees this as the primary means of securing a reduction in the incidence of unofficial strikes, though a majority of us think that there might be occasions when employers would sue unofficial strike leaders.

(c) *An " Automatic " Sanction?*

489.   To overcome the difficulties to which we have referred in the last four paragraphs it has been suggested that an " automatic " sanction should be used against those who participate in strikes or use other forms of industrial sanction in breach of procedure agreements: the strikers should suffer a detriment which will arise irrespective of the wish of some person to bring

legal proceedings. Under the Contracts of Employment Act 1963 employees are entitled, if they been employed for twenty-six weeks or more, to a minimum notice of termination of their employment which varies from one week to four weeks according to the length of continuous service with an employer. Under the Redundancy Payments Act 1965 employees who are dismissed by reason of redundancy or are laid off or kept on short time to the extent specified in the Act are entitled to receive money payments which also vary according to the length of continuous service. Under section 37 of the Redundancy Payments Act 1965 strikes do not break continuity of service either for the purposes of that Act or for those of the Contracts of Employment Act 1963. The proposal is that where a strike, a " go-slow ", " work to rule " or overtime ban was in breach of procedure, the seniority of service which had accrued for purposes of the two statutes should be automatically forfeited, and those participating in such action should for the purposes of these Acts be treated as if their employment with the employer had begun at the moment of the resumption or the full resumption of work. An employee who had reasonable grounds for alleging that his breach of procedure was due to some provocative act by the employer, or was for some other reason excusable, or that the penalty was in the circumstances excessive, should, it has been suggested, have a right to appeal to some independent body such as the Industrial Court. This could order that no loss of seniority should occur or that it should be mitigated as it thought just.

490. At first sight this sanction seems to have the advantage that no one, whether the employer or a public authority, would have to take any action in order to impose it. It would, so it appears, impose itself, and it would be for the employee himself to invoke an independent body to ask for its mitigation.

491. This impression is however erroneous. The sanction would not be automatic. In the first place the Department of Employment and Productivity would have to be notified of the unconstitutional strike or other action and of the names of those who had participated in it. This would be necessary so that, if at a later date any of the strikers became redundant and the employer made redundancy payments to them and claimed a rebate from the redundancy fund administered by the Department of Employment and Productivity, the Department would be able to take into account the effect of the strike in calculating what refunds were due. This notification to the Department would have to be made by the employer, who would thus be immediately involved in imposing the sanction.

492. The employer would also have to notify the employees concerned if only so as to enable them to appeal against the forfeiture of their seniority. Alternatively, the notification could be left to the Department of Employment and Productivity, but if it was it might come a considerable time after the strike was over and might then cause a renewed outbreak of trouble.

493. Many of the employees concerned could be expected to appeal against the forfeiture of seniority. The body hearing the appeal would have to examine each case separately, because the degree to which an individual had participated in the action in breach of procedure and also the hardship suffered in each individual case would be relevant to the decision. The

133

employer or his representative would inevitably have to give evidence. Indeed the employer would have to bear the burden of proving that, and to what extent, the employee concerned was involved in the strike or other action. He would in fact if not in name be a party to the proceedings no less than if he sued for damages.

494. All the reasons which induce employers not to sue for damages for breach of contract would also induce them, if possible, to keep the matter quiet and not to take those steps which would be required to make the sanction effective. They would do all in their power to escape from the deleterious effect on their relations with their workers which the proceedings before the independent body would inevitably produce. For this reason alone, that is for the reason that the sanction would be automatic in appearance only, we cannot recommend its use as a contribution to an improvement of our industrial relations.

495. There are other reasons why such a measure would not have the effect it is intended to have. As we point out in Chapter VII unofficial strikes are most frequent in four industries. One of these is the docks, to which the Redundancy Payments Act does not apply. Another one, shipbuilding and ship-repairing, has a very high rate of labour turnover with the result that only a small minority of workers would be affected by the envisaged forfeiture of seniority rights. Moreover, in the "trouble spots" where unconstitutional strikes are particularly frequent the potency of the sanction would soon evaporate. Once a worker has, through participation in an unofficial strike, lost his "seniority", he will cease to be interested in the threatened penalty. Nothing much can happen to him, at least for some considerable time, and whatever deterrent effect the sanction may have had is now lost. This however means that where it is most urgently necessary to reduce the number of unofficial strikes, this penalty will be subject to a very fast-working "law of diminishing returns". After a short time it will lose its effect as a deterrent, and only the bitterness will remain. It is a penalty which, as it were, can effectively be imposed only for the first offence.

496. The sanction is intended to operate by way of delayed action: it would be felt years, possibly many years, after the event, and only by those employees who happened to be given notice or made redundant. One must envisage the situation at the time of the termination of the employment which, but for the strike, would have given rise to a claim for notice under the Act of 1963 and to a claim for a redundancy payment under the Act of 1965. By that time the unofficial strike for which the employee is now to suffer the penalty may be and is indeed likely to be forgotten. The employer will often have an interest in letting sleeping dogs lie and in not stirring up new trouble by reviving the memory of ancient battles. He may find it, at that moment, invidious to discriminate between those about to lose their jobs. He is likely to "condone" the "offence", to waive the penalty and to treat the employees to be discharged as if the strike had never occurred. This is what many employers can be expected to do and what many people, including strikers, will expect them to do—in so far as in the heat of the moment the thought of the amount of their notice and redundancy

pay enters their consciousness at all, For this reason too the deterrent effect of this sanction is likely to be illusory.

497. There is of course nothing in the law to prevent an employer from " condoning" the offence by giving to the employee the full notice and the full redundancy pay to which he would have been entitled but for the strike. He will not, however, be able to recover the " rebate" payable to him out of the Redundancy Fund for more than an amount calculated on the basis of a seniority shortened by the strike: the Department of Employment and Productivity has no power to pay a rebate for more than what the employer owes as a matter of law. In such a situation it is the employer and not the striker who is penalised: instead of recovering the larger amount of the redundancy pay from the Fund he pays it all out of his own pocket.

498. Since both employers and employees can be expected to foresee this situation, it is all too probable that they will agree, if they can, not to allow the news of the strike to become too widely known and above all not to come to the notice of those administering the Redundancy Fund.

499. For the older workers, and especially the most steady workers with long records of employment, that is for the most responsible workers who are least in need of a " deterrent", the threat would be drastic indeed—far more drastic than the payment of damages or of a fine. To gauge its magnitude one must see the offence and the penalty in perspective. The offence would be participation in a strike, or a go-slow, or a work to rule, or an overtime ban. This may be action taken on the spur and in the heat of the moment, and it may last only for a short time—many unofficial strikes are over in a few hours. It may and often will be action taken by a group of men under some real or imagined provocation, and action in which only a person of unusual strength of character can refuse to participate. It is true—and this is claimed as one of the merits of the proposal—that it would enlist the interest of the older and more thoughtful men who may succeed in persuading their younger colleagues from taking rash and sudden action. But the burden it imposes on these men is perhaps more than an ordinary individual of no more than average strength of personality can be expected to bear. For the risk involved to the older men may be almost intolerable: it may be the risk of losing an expectation to payments amounting to up to £1,200 and acquired through decades of work for an employer, and losing it through inability to dissuade one's fellows from ill-considered action and inability to dissociate oneself from it. The fruits of a life-time's work may thus be lost in five minutes and through participation in an action which may be over in an hour. The history of our law—especially of our criminal law—shows that where the penalty is too harsh it will not be imposed. Those making this proposal suggest that an appellate body should have jurisdiction to mitigate the penalty. It would soon do so in a radical way and to the extent of making the threat completely unreal. There must be some proportion between means and ends. This is out of proportion.

OUR CONCLUSIONS

500. It is imperative that the number of unofficial and especially of unconstitutional strikes should be reduced and should be reduced speedily. This is not

135

only a serious, it is also an urgent problem, and our recommendations are designed to deal with it. Such differences of opinion as exist among us refer not to the end to be achieved, but to the means of achieving it.

501. The problem is peculiar to this country. It has been created by a number of factors which are analysed in Chapter III. The most important among these is the inadequacy of our collective bargaining system, and especially the lack of clear, speedy, comprehensive and effective procedures for the settlement of grievances and other disputes such as exist in other countries. The first and the most important step to be taken in order to get rid of unconstitutional strikes is the reform of our collective bargaining system. This is our central recommendation. We cannot recommend anything that may jeopardise its success.

502. We are not in principle opposed to the use of legal sanctions for the enforcement of agreed procedures. No such sanctions can however be enforced without the active participation of the employer. There is no such thing as an " automatic " sanction. It follows that sanctions will remain unworkable until a fundamental change in our system of industrial relations has led to a situation in which employers may be able and willing to use such rights as the law gives them. At the present time legislation making procedure agreements legally enforceable would not in fact be enforced, and like all legislation that is not enforced would bring the law into disrepute.

503. It would, moreover, be unjust to ask men to abide by procedures which, as everyone knows, cannot deal with some of the most important grievances, and which more often than not yield no result at all. It would be futile to expect men to be deterred from using the strike weapon if they know that its speedy use is the only means at their disposal to get speedy redress for their grievances.

504. Those resorting to unconstitutional action should not be threatened with any disadvantages imposed by law until new procedures have been put into operation, procedures which are clear where the present procedures are vague, comprehensive where the present procedures are fragmentary, speedy where the present procedures are protracted, and effective where the present procedures are fruitless.

505. Until this has been done it would be as futile and as unjust to require men to observe a waiting period of (say) a week as it would be to expect them to refrain from using their own sanctions until the present procedures are exhausted. The employer could not enforce a statute imposing a week's strike notice any more than he can now enforce his contractual right to notice, and as long as there is no adequate system of settlement a measure imposing an obligation to observe a period of notice would be as unfair as an attempt to enforce the procedure agreement itself. As long as no effective method for the settlement of grievances exists no one can expect a threat of legal sanctions to restrain men from using the advantage they feel able to derive from sudden action in order to obtain a remedy for grievances which cannot be dealt with in an orderly fashion. Self-help has always been the response to the absence of " law and order ". In industrial relations, " law and order " can be created only by adequate collective bargaining arrangements.

136

506. We thus reject the proposal to make collective agreements—whether substantive or procedural—enforceable at the present time. We do so, not because we think that the law could not in any circumstances assist in the reduction of the number of unofficial strikes. It cannot do so in this country today—this is the point. To take steps in this direction today would be not only useless but harmful, and they would undo a great deal of the good we hope to see done through the reform of the collective bargaining system which we recommend.

507. The prime condition, then, for imposing any legal sanctions is the reform, mainly through factory and company agreements, of the existing procedures. We emphasise the need for agreements. A disputes procedure must be operated by the two sides of industry working together. They work together if they have accepted the procedure. They cannot be expected to make the procedure work unless they have freely agreed to do so. If either or both sides reject it, it is likely to remain a dead letter. It has been suggested that in certain circumstances the Secretary of State should have the power to promulgate a Statutory Instrument imposing a disputes procedure on which the two sides have failed to agree. This would be tantamount to using a kind of compulsory arbitration in order to compel the parties to co-operate in the settlement of grievances, and to do so through the force of law. But this is one of the things no law can do: it cannot make people co-operate if they do not want to do so. Such imposed procedures are almost certain not to be used. Nevertheless it has been suggested that those participating in a strike in breach of such an imposed procedure should undergo very heavy penalties. Men who walk out because they have or think they have some grievance would, it has been suggested, forfeit their redundancy pay or undergo some other penalty because they did not, instead of walking out, refer their grievance to some committee which (not having been agreed upon by the two sides of industry) does not in fact function at all. This we cannot accept.

508. Once the reforms we recommend have had their effect, there will be a new situation. It will then be possible to distinguish the cases in which unconstitutional strikes have been the result of inadequate procedures from those in which strike-proneness is due to irresponsibility or to agitation by eccentrics or by subversives. Moreover, if the majority of the workers in a factory accept the procedure and have confidence in its effectiveness, those who defy the procedure may be isolated from that majority. It may then be possible for the employer to do what at the moment he cannot do: to take such action as the law allows him to take against this minority. That action may in the first place consist in the use of the most obvious remedy which the law puts at his disposal, that is to dismiss those who foment strike or similar action in defiance of the procedure agreement. It is impossible at the present time to say whether in this situation any further sanctions will be required.

509. We are confident therefore that the size of the problem will be greatly reduced once our recommendations for the reform of the collective bargaining system have been implemented, but we cannot be certain that the problem will disappear altogether. It will then however be possible to identify the situations in which it would be neither unjust nor futile to apply legal sanctions. It would not be unjust to do so because unconstitutional action will have been taken

although constitutional action would have promised a speedy remedy for justified grievances. Nor would it be futile because where irresponsibility or ill-will is the root cause of the evil, the threat of legal penalties can create a counter-motive that may influence men's minds and acts, and the use of such penalties may command the support of many of the other workers.

510. As we say in paragraph 508 it is impossible at this moment to predict whether the problem will arise at all and, if it arises, what will be its magnitude or its nature. It is therefore premature to discuss the details of such measures as may have to be taken. All we can do is to indicate how in our opinion the legal enforcement of procedure agreements may, if the need arises, be made to fit into a system of collective bargaining reformed in accordance with our recommendations.

511. If legal sanctions have to be applied this will have to be done *ad hoc.* Our attitude to the use of legal sanctions for the enforcement of procedure agreements is identical with that which we have adopted towards the problem of the recognition of trade unions by employers. In both cases we hope and expect that the work of the Industrial Relations Commission will make the use of legal sanctions unnecessary, that is, that the persuasive influence of the Industrial Relations Commission will suffice to produce the necessary improvements. In both cases we envisage the use of legal enforcement machinery only as an emergency device, to be used from case to case and in exceptional situations in which it is inescapable, and that it should remain operative only for a limited period. This " case by case " or *ad hoc* approach would also be analogous to that adopted in the Terms and Conditions of Employment Act 1959, section 8. Under that provision the substantive terms of collective agreements can be given legally binding force only for such enterprises in which a need for doing so has arisen and has been proved. In the same way procedure agreements would be given legal effect only in concerns or factories where the strike situation makes it necessary.

512. We are of the opinion that it should be for the Secretary of State for Employment and Productivity to initiate the proceedings for making a procedure agreement legally binding in an enterprise or establishment. The decision to institute these proceedings should be in the discretion of the Secretary of State, who should be responsible to Parliament for its exercise. It should however be for an independent body to make the order giving legal force to an agreement. This jurisdiction should therefore be vested in the Industrial Court.

513. Before applying to the Industrial Court for an order the Secretary of State would have to consult both sides of the industry concerned and the Industrial Relations Commission.

514. To proceed further, the Secretary of State would, on the basis of this consultation, have to be satisfied:

(*a*) that the disputes procedure has been agreed between the employer and the union or unions concerned;

(*b*) that it complies with the standards we have set out in paragraph 182(2) of Chapter IV;

(c) that in the enterprise or establishment unconstitutional strikes continue to be a serious problem;

(d) that the employer considers the situation sufficiently serious to be willing to enforce such sanctions as may be put at his disposal; and

(e) that the threat or the enforcement of legal sanctions can be expected to lead to a reduction in the number or in the magnitude of unconstitutional stoppages in the enterprise or establishment.

515.   The Industrial Court would have to hear the two sides of industry, the employer and the shop stewards or other representatives of those employed in the enterprise or establishment.   If it found that the conditions listed in the previous paragraph were fulfilled, it would, by order, declare the procedure agreement to be legally binding on the employer and on all those employed by him in the enterprise or establishment to which the order applies.   The order would be in force for a limited period of, say, one year, but it could be extended by the Industrial Court for further periods if the Court, on application by the Secretary of State and after hearing those concerned, was satisfied that this step was necessary.

516.   Only the parties themselves could enforce an agreement which has been declared binding.   As we point out above, there is no such thing as an " automatic " sanction, and penal sanctions have, during and after the Second World War, proved to be fruitless.   The only way to enforce an agreement is through civil actions for damages.   If, in breach of an agreement declared to be binding, employees in an enterprise or establishment went on strike or applied other industrial sanctions, such as go-slow, work to rule, or overtime bans, they would be liable to pay damages to the employer.   If, on the other hand, in breach of the agreement, the employer resorted to a lock-out, he would have to indemnify the employees concerned.   In both cases the loss suffered by the plaintiff would be the measure of the damages payable by the defendant. They would not, as are damages for breach of the contract of employment, be restricted to the amount of the wages payable for the period of notice.

517.   Such in outline might be the nature of the legal sanctions which might be used to reduce the number of unconstitutional stoppages if and so far as the need for such measures is still deemed to exist after the reform of collective bargaining procedures which we recommend.   In view of the impossibility of predicting whether that need will arise at all and, if it does, what its nature will be, such consideration of administrative, procedural and other details as is required for the purpose of legislation would at the present moment be premature, and must be left to the future.

518.   The possibility of the need for future legislative action should not however be left out of sight, and the Industrial Relations Commission should, by statute, be instructed to keep the matter under review in the light of progress being made with the reform of industrial relations in general and disputes procedures in particular.   This should be done with the view to advising the Secretary of State whether legislation for the enforcement of procedure agreements such as is outlined above has become imperative and, if and when such legislation is enacted, to make to the Secretary of State from time to time such

proposal for its application in exceptional cases as the Industrial Relations Commission thinks fit.

Note of Dissent

519. The following dissent from this chapter in so far as it relates to procedure agreements is expressed by Lord Robens and Sir George Pollock. They take the view that where parties cannot agree on the terms of a procedure, the Industrial Relations Commission after due consultation should draft a procedure agreement for them and the Secretary of State should have power by order to put it into operation. They also take the view that procedure agreements such as they envisage are not likely to survive or to be effective unless they are enforceable. They are therefore of opinion that employees who despite procedural agreements for the settlement of grievances take part in an " unofficial dispute " by stopping work without giving the requisite notice, and thus ignoring the agreed procedures for the settlement of disputes, should be regarded as automatically having broken their contract of service, and upon resumption of work should be re-engaged as new employees, thus automatically losing all title to benefits that would have accrued by reason of previous service.

Chapter IX

SAFEGUARDS FOR EMPLOYEES AGAINST UNFAIR DISMISSAL

520. Previous chapters of our report are concerned essentially with the collective institutions of industrial relations. We now examine safeguards enjoyed by individuals, dealing in this chapter with the protection of the employee against unfair dismissal by his employer, in the next with labour tribunals and in Chapter XI with individuals and their relations with trade unions.

521. In the eye of the law employer and employee are free and equal parties to the contract of employment. Hence, either employer or employee has the right to bring the contract to an end in accordance with its terms. Thus, an employer is legally entitled to dismiss an employee whenever he wishes and for whatever reason, provided only that he gives due notice. At common law he does not even have to reveal his reason, much less to justify it.

522. An employee has protection at common law against "wrongful" dismissal, but this protection is strictly limited; it means that if an employee is dismissed without due notice he can claim the payment of wages he would have earned for the period of notice. From this payment will be deducted any amount which he earned (or through his fault failed to earn) during the period of notice. Beyond this, the employee has no legal claim at common law, whatever hardship he suffers as a result of his dismissal. Even if the way in which he is dismissed constitutes an imputation on his honesty and his ability to get another job is correspondingly reduced he cannot— except through an action for defamation—obtain any redress (see the decision of the House of Lords in *Addis v. Gramophone Co.* [1909] AC 486).

523. Recent legislation has put the employee in a better legal position in some respects. The Contracts of Employment Act 1963 for the first time fixed statutory minimum periods of notice, and gave an employee a right to at least one week's notice after 26 weeks' continuous employment, increasing to two weeks after two years and four weeks after five years. The employer's common law right to dismiss without notice for misconduct was expressly preserved. The Redundancy Payments Act 1965 went further still, giving an employee an entitlement to a redundancy payment from the employer if dismissed through redundancy. The payments vary according to the employee's length of service, the maximum amount—payable to a man over the age of 61 with 20 years' service—being the equivalent of 30 weeks' pay. The Act does not deal with dismissal for other reasons, for example alleged incapacity or misconduct. However the Act does put indirect pressure on the employer to say why he has dismissed an employee because, under section 9(2)(b), "an employee who has been dismissed by his employer shall, unless the contrary is proved, be presumed to have been

so dismissed by reason of redundancy", and will thus become entitled to a redundancy payment from the employer.

524. In practice of course many employees enjoy much greater security against dismissal than is implied in the law. Many employers dislike having to dismiss employees and do so only with reluctance when they feel that there is no alternative. Some employers have introduced formal procedures designed to ensure that employees are not dismissed without an opportunity to get their case reconsidered at a higher level, and in many well-organised industries trade unions can take up a dismissal which they think unjust through an agreed disputes procedure. Sometimes additional factors may have some influence, such as an acute shortage of labour or the possibility that action which seemed arbitrary would provoke a strike.

525. There is nevertheless a very general feeling, shared by employers as well as trade unions, that the present situation is unsatisfactory, and it was reflected in the submissions of many who gave evidence to us. In 1964 the Government announced that they accepted Recommendation No. 119 on Termination of Employment adopted by the International Labour Organisation in 1963 and would discuss the provision of procedures to give effective safeguards against arbitrary dismissal with representatives of employers and trade unions. The Minister of Labour's National Joint Advisory Council subsequently set up a committee to examine dismissals and dismissal procedures. The committee's report was published in 1967, and the committee drew particular attention to a number of points about procedures in Great Britain as compared with the position in some other countries (see paragraph 121 of *Dismissal Procedures* published by HMSO 1967). They pointed out that in law employees are in general protected only against dismissal without due notice, there being no legal protection against being dismissed unfairly or without good reason. Provision by employers of a formal procedure for the handling of dismissals is not very common and is usually found only in large concerns, and this is particularly serious because the great majority of grievances about dismissals are bound to be matters dealt with within the individual concern. Disputes procedures laid down by industry-wide agreement have limitations; for example the delays in their operation may mean that a dismissed worker often takes another job and the case lapses without his grievance having been properly thrashed out. In less highly organised sectors of employment there may be no disputes procedure and an employee may have no effective redress against dismissal. Finally, with rare exceptions employees have no right of appeal to an independent person or body.

526. We share in full the belief that the present situation is unsatisfactory. In practice there is usually no comparison between the consequences for an employer if an employee terminates the contract of employment and those which will ensue for an employee if he is dismissed. In reality people build much of their lives around their jobs. Their incomes and prospects for the future are inevitably founded in the expectation that their jobs will continue. For workers in many situations dismissal is a disaster. For some workers it may make inevitable the breaking up of a community and the uprooting of homes and families. Others, and particularly older

workers, may be faced with the greatest difficulty in getting work at all. The statutory provision for redundancy goes some way to recognise what is really at stake for an employee when his job is involved, but it is no less at stake if he is being dismissed for alleged incompetence or for misconduct than if he is being dismissed for redundancy. To this it is no answer that good employers will dismiss employees only if they have no alternative. Not all employers are good employers. Even if the employer's intentions are good, is it certain that his subordinates' intentions are always also good? And even when all concerned in management act in good faith, are they always necessarily right? Should their view of the case automatically prevail over the employee's?

527. The passage we refer to above in the report of the committee on dismissals draws attention to the unsatisfactory situation in less highly organised sectors of employment. Elsewhere in this report we recommend measures to promote the growth of collective bargaining machinery on sound lines and in particular that any stipulation in a contract of employment that an employee should not belong to a trade union should by law be made void and of no effect. Clearly however the protection given by this enactment will be far from complete so long as it is open to an employer to dismiss an employee because he exercises his right to join a trade union or because, having joined, he takes a part in legitimate trade union activities. It is just where organisation is weak that the danger that this could happen is greatest.

528. From the point of view of industrial peace, it is plain also that the present situation leaves much to be desired. In the period 1964-1966 some 276 unofficial strikes took place each year on average as a result of disputes about whether individuals should or should not be employed, suspended or dismissed. The committee on dismissals analysed stoppages—whether official or unofficial—arising out of dismissals *other than redundancies* over this period and found that there were on average 203 a year. It can be argued that the right to secure a speedy and impartial decision on the justification for a dismissal might have averted many of these stoppages, though some cases would no doubt still have occurred where workers were taking spontaneous action to try to prevent a dismissal being given effect.

529. For all these reasons we believe it urgently necessary for workers to be given better protection against unfair dismissal. We turn now to considering how this should be done.

MEANS OF IMPROVING PROTECTION AGAINST UNFAIR DISMISSAL

530. The committee on dismissals recommended that " the immediate programme should be to encourage the development and extension of satisfactory voluntary procedures ". They strongly recommended that the development of satisfactory internal procedures, and the improvement of those already existing, should be encouraged. They also wished the development or improvement of external procedures capable of dealing with dismissals of all kinds to be encouraged, and felt that industries should re-examine their procedures to see whether changes were required and whether there was not a need for special arrangements under which dismissal cases could be investi-

gated quickly and informally on the spot. The committee saw force in the arguments for the establishment of statutory machinery, especially where workers in less highly organised sectors are concerned, but did not favour early legislation. However, they recognised that progress by voluntary means might well be slow and that changes resulting from our report might lessen some of the difficulties they saw in statutory machinery, and suggested that the Minister of Labour should review the position in due course.

531. The National Joint Advisory Council subsequently supported the committee's recommendations concerning the improvement and development of voluntary procedures. On the question of statutory machinery however the TUC, while agreeing that such machinery must be flexible and complementary to voluntary procedures, considered that there should be legislation to give a right of appeal against dismissal with provision for exemption for satisfactory voluntary procedures. The CBI were against this.

532. We for our part fully share the view of the National Joint Advisory Council that voluntary procedures should be improved and extended. We have given the most careful consideration to the question whether the establishment of statutory machinery is also desirable. This has led a majority of us to the views set out in paragraphs 533-544 following. From these Sir George Pollock and Mr. John Thomson dissent for reasons explained at the end of this chapter.

533. It is necessary first to examine the drawbacks to legislation which the committee on dismissals envisaged. The main argument against legislation, in the committee's view, was that it would lessen the incentive to develop satisfactory voluntary procedures where they do not already exist. We cannot readily accept this argument. It is certainly highly desirable that employers should develop clear-cut procedures for handling dismissals, but if employers know that employees have the right to challenge dismissal in a statutory tribunal then there is a clear incentive for them to see that dismissals are carried out under a proper and orderly procedure, so as to ensure both that as many cases as possible are settled satisfactorily without recourse to an outside appeal and that in those cases where appeal is made it can be shown that the dismissal was fair and justified.

534. So far as procedures provided in industry-wide agreements are concerned, voluntary arrangements have an advantage which statutory machinery cannot match. The possibility of an employee's obtaining reinstatement (as opposed to compensation) when his appeal is upheld is far greater under a properly organised voluntary procedure—a point which is confirmed by the experience of other countries. Moreover employers and trade unions will be more inclined to set up an adequate procedure if they can by so doing avoid the merits of issues which arise in their industries being settled by an outside body. While there may be industries which would have developed or improved voluntary procedures and which might be deterred from doing so by the availability of statutory machinery, others could well find this a spur to establishing voluntary procedures which will be exempted from the coverage of legislation.

535. Another point to which the committee on dismissals attached importance was that statutory machinery might have the effect of importing a legalistic element into relations in the place of work; employers might feel obliged to

144

keep " black books " of workers' misdeeds or shortcomings. We have had no evidence that there has been a significant problem on this score in those foreign countries in which statutory procedures exist. Some employers might feel it necessary to keep rather better records if statutory machinery were established, but this is a desirable improvement.

536. Allied to the previous point, in the committee's eyes, was the possibility that industrial discipline might be undermined. Here again foreign experience has thrown up no evidence of a significant problem. The availability of a statutory procedure which is fair, and known to be fair, could do much to clarify the situation and so to enable discipline to be improved.

537. The committee also referred to the question whether, once statutory machinery for complaining against unfair dismissal was provided, workers should retain unimpaired their freedom to strike in protest against a dismissal or against the decision of a tribunal that a dismissal was not unfair. There is certainly a problem to be faced here, but in our view no more than a marginal problem. We examine fully elsewhere in this report all the practical difficulties attendant upon the use of legal sanctions to prevent or discourage strikes. The efficacy of a statutory dismissal procedure in contributing to the reduction of strikes must stand or fall by the extent that it provides, and is known to provide, employees with adequate safeguards against unfair dismissal.

538. Finally the committee mentioned three other points. The first was that the opportunity to obtain compensation from a tribunal might make workers press for existing voluntary procedures to be abandoned in favour of the statutory machinery. Any risk of this happening is in our view due to a major defect in existing voluntary procedures—the absence of provision for compensation as an alternative to reinstatement for unfair dismissal—which must be remedied if voluntary procedures are to be brought up to a satisfactory standard. We return to the matter shortly. The other two points to which the committee drew attention were the cost of statutory machinery and the possibility of a flood of appeals; but, as they also pointed out, against the cost must be set the possible savings to industry and the country from the improvement in industrial relations which ought to follow, and measures could be taken to discourage frivolous or vexatious cases.

539. Having reviewed the possible drawbacks to legislation we now consider what advantages it would have which voluntary action on its own would not. First, legislation has the advantage of making possible an immediate raising of standards to a much more satisfactory level. In view of the inadequacies of existing voluntary provision, even in well organised areas of industry, which were brought out by the committee on dismissals in the passage referred to in paragraph 525 above, this is an advantage which must weigh heavily.

540. Secondly, statutory machinery can afford increased protection for the exercise of freedom of association which will, as we say in paragraph 246 in Chapter V, reinforce the effect of our other recommendations on that subject, and will therefore assist the growth of collective bargaining on sound lines. Without such growth, the circumstances in which effective

voluntary dismissal procedures can be developed will in some areas of employment not exist.

541. Thirdly, there are many areas of industry where voluntary methods are most unlikely to be effective within the measurable future. We have in mind those which are poorly organised and will be difficult to organise in the future and where there are many small undertakings. Several million workers are concerned and until statutory provision is made they will be without effective protection.

542. Finally, the nature of the remedy for unfair dismissal offered by existing voluntary procedures is not wholly satisfactory. Employers' procedures with rare exceptions leave the final decision in the hands of management, and this cannot be accepted as sufficient to ensure that an employee both has fair treatment and is seen to have it. Most procedures laid down by industry-wide agreement are in essence conciliation procedures and do not enable an adequate fact-finding inquiry to be carried out into dismissals or a quasi-judicial decision on the merits of the case to be reached. Moreover, at present the outcome of an appeal through a voluntary procedure is either reinstatement (or re-engagement) or the confirmation of the dismissal. Often however reinstatement does not offer a satisfactory solution when an employee is found to have been unfairly dismissed, because the circumstances of the dismissal have opened a permanent rift between employer and employee. In such cases monetary compensation affords the only proper remedy. Compensation can be provided under statutory machinery, but without the stimulus of legislation it is unlikely to find a place in many voluntary procedures.

543. There is the further consideration that the Government are already committed to legislation against discrimination on grounds of race or colour which will include the employment field within its scope. If statutory protection is to be afforded against arbitrary dismissal when the reason for it happens to be race or colour, then protection should be afforded against dismissal for other no less arbitrary reasons.

544. When all these considerations are weighed we believe that the balance of advantage greatly favours the establishment of statutory machinery. Accordingly we recommend early legislation to this end. We now turn to consideration of the lines on which statutory machinery might be set up.

STATUTORY MACHINERY

Definition of Unfair Dismissal

545. It will be necessary for legislation to give guidance as to what is meant by unfair dismissal. Here the terms of the International Labour Recommendation (No. 119) on Termination of Employment give a lead. The Recommendation lays down the general principle that " termination of employment should not take place unless there is a valid reason . . . connected with the capacity or conduct of the worker or based on the operational requirements of the undertaking, establishment or service ". It should be possible to state that dismissal is justified only if there is a valid reason for it connected with the capacity or conduct of the worker or based on the

146

operational requirements of the undertaking, establishment or service; and that in the absence of such valid reason it is unfair. It is obviously impossible to give an exhaustive list of reasons for dismissal which are not to be considered "valid", but the example of the ILO Recommendation might be followed in listing certain specific reasons which are not valid. We suggest that it might be laid down that dismissal by reason of trade union membership or activity or by reason of race, colour, sex, marital status, religious or political opinion, national extraction or social origin should be deemed to be unfair. If this approach were followed, the employer would be obliged to explain and if necessary prove the grounds on which he had dismissed an employee, while it would be for the employee to prove any special grounds on which a dismissal would be deemed unfair.

The Right of Complaint Against Unfair Dismissal

546. It is a necessary part of a satisfactory procedure that it should operate speedily. We think that an employee who wishes to lodge a complaint against his dismissal on the ground that it is unfair should be obliged to do so within five working days of dismissal, failing which he should be deemed to have forfeited his right of complaint. Any term of the contract of employment by which an employee purports to waive his right of complaint should be void, and the statute should so provide. Nor should the right of complaint be excluded by any agreement made between employer and employee at or after the time of dismissal, although any amount which the employer has paid or agreed to pay by way of compensation for loss of job will of course have to be taken into account in the assessment of statutory compensation.

547. While a claim by a dismissed employee is pending, what is his position to be? It has been suggested that until the matter is decided the effect of the dismissal should be suspended, since the carrying out of the dismissal before then would amount to allowing " punishment " to precede " trial ". We see the force of this argument, but in our view it would be highly undesirable and indeed impossible to deprive the employer of the power to dismiss without notice for misconduct and it follows that termination on due notice must also be allowed. If the claim is decided in favour of the employee it should be open to the tribunal to award him such wages in respect of the period between the dismissal and the decision as it considers just in the circumstances or to increase the amount of compensation accordingly. Our objections to providing by law that only suspension should be possible while a claim is pending do not apply to any undertaking concerning exercise of the right of dismissal to which an employer may assent in a collective agreement. Indeed it is one of the merits of the voluntary approach that undertakings of this kind can be made (and also that a tribunal can be given power to order that a dismissal be treated as a suspension) if those concerned see fit.

The Tribunal

548. In the next chapter we recommend that the industrial tribunals (which already deal with cases arising out of the Redundancy Payments Act 1965) should be reconstituted as labour tribunals and empowered to settle a variety

147

of cases arising out of individual contracts of employment, including for example wrongful dismissal. These labour tribunals will be very well suited to the work of settling complaints against unfair dismissal. Since we envisage that they will be operating in all major industrial centres and thus easily accessible, the speedy hearing of complaints can be organised; it may however still be necessary to give priority to the hearing of dismissal cases in view of their special urgency.

549. As in all cases concerning employer/employee relationships coming before labour tribunals, it should be the first duty of the chairman and other members to try to conciliate between the parties. Before any claim is heard formally, there should, we suggest, be an informal meeting in private at which an amicable settlement of the dispute should be sought. Even if this fails, it may be possible to resume attempts at conciliation in the course of further proceedings.

550. The formal hearing of a claim should in our opinion normally take place in public. Cases will however arise in which either employer or employee or both have legitimate reasons for wishing the hearing to be in private. The employer may be reluctant to discuss publicly the behaviour of his subordinates; the employee may not wish allegations against him of discreditable conduct ventilated in public. We recommend that it should be in the discretion of the labour tribunal (or possibly its chairman) to sit in private and that this should always be done if both parties so desire or if one party requests it and the other does not object. On the other hand we consider it essential that decisions, together with the reasons for them, should always be announced in public.

Legal Remedies

551. Ideally, the remedy available to an employee who is found to have been unfairly dismissed is reinstatement in his old job. However, there are strong arguments against laying down reinstatement as the only remedy. The courts have always refused to grant decrees for the specific performance of contracts of employment, whether sought by employer or employee. In foreign countries such obligations to reinstate as are laid upon the employer are generally, though not invariably, coupled with an option to pay compensation as an alternative; moreover in France, where the law prohibits the dismissal of a statutory works councillor without the consent of the works council or a Ministry of Labour representative, the courts have laid down that the only remedy available to an employee dismissed in defiance of this prohibition is an action for damages (see *Sortais c. Cie Industrielle des Téléphones*, Cass. Soc. 27.11.1952, D.1953, 239). An employee may have the most compelling reasons for not wishing to work any longer for an employer who has dismissed him unfairly. Difficult cases could also arise where an employee had obtained another job while his claim was pending. The experience of other countries indicates that reinstatement is more likely to be brought about under a voluntary procedure, and that the remedy usually preferred in practice under a statutory procedure is compensation.

552. It is therefore our view that reinstatement and compensation should both be envisaged as remedies. It would be possible to provide that an order

148

for reinstatement should be the primary relief, but that at the option of either employer or employee compensation should be granted instead. However it would be more in accord with reality, and in our view therefore preferable, to lay down an order for compensation as the primary relief, with the order lapsing only in the event of both parties exercising the option of reinstatement within a brief time limit. (Where voluntary procedures are concerned reinstatement may appropriately be provided for as the primary remedy, with or without payment of wages for the period between the dismissal and the reinstatement.)

553. We do not consider it feasible to fix a scale of compensation analogous to that laid down in the Redundancy Payments Act. The labour tribunal must, in our view, be free to take into account such circumstances as the nature of the employer's business, the employee's age, seniority and opportunities for alternative employment, the circumstances and manner of the dismissal, the extent to which the employee's actions were blameworthy and the effect of the dismissal on future pension rights and any other relevant considerations. Account should also be taken of any sums actually earned or which should have been earned since the dismissal took place; and if an employee is dismissed ostensibly for redundancy and receives a redundancy payment, but it is subsequently held that he was unfairly dismissed, the payment he has already received should be taken into account in assessing the compensation due to him for unfair dismissal. The labour tribunal should normally be concerned to compensate the employee for the damage he has suffered in the loss of his employment and legitimate expectations for the future in that employment, in injured feelings and reputation and in the prejudicing of further employment opportunities. "Punitive" considerations should not enter into its assessment except where discrimination is clearly proved.

554. While we do not favour a scale of compensation, we think it desirable for practical reasons to fix a ceiling to the amount of compensation which can be awarded. This will make it easier for employers to insure against the risk of being obliged to pay compensation. It would in our view be reasonable to provide that the maximum should be an amount equal to the employee's wages or salary for two years; and that, as in the case of compensation under the Redundancy Payments Act, in the computation of this amount there should be ignored wages or salary in excess of £40 a week—a limit the Secretary of State should have power to raise.

Scope of Statutory Procedure

555. We think it right to indicate our view as to where the line should be drawn between inclusion and exclusion in certain cases. Employees with less than two years' service are not eligible for redundancy payments under the Redundancy Payments Act. We see no justification however for limiting protection from unfair dismissal to those with at least two years' service, since the fact that he has been dismissed after a short period of employment could in some circumstances have a serious effect on an employee's future prospects. When the terms under which an employee was engaged provide for a probationary period of service this is a factor of which due account must be taken.

We see no justification for setting any upper age limit. Nor in our view should there be a lower age limit since an unfair dismissal may deal a blow to a young person's self-respect or injure his career in a way which means he is hit particularly hard.

556. We do not think it necessary to exclude very small undertakings from the scope of the procedure. It should be possible for the labour tribunal to take adequate account in reaching its decisions of the personal factors which inevitably play a larger part in very small undertakings. However, it would be reasonable to exclude domestic employment in private households from the scope of legislation. It would also be right to exclude cases where the employer is the husband or wife of the employee. The Redundancy Payments Act does not apply to share fishermen paid solely by a share of the catch, and in view of their special position it would not be appropriate to bring them within the procedure.

557. The Redundancy Payments Act also does not apply to registered dock workers engaged on dock work. Under the docks decasualisation scheme dock workers already have statutory protection which gives a very high standard of security against unfair dismissal and so long as they continue to enjoy this they do not need further statutory safeguards. Crown Servants and National Health Service employees are excluded from the Redundancy Payments Act, but we see no reason for excluding them from the scope of the legislation we are proposing, though it will of course be possible for voluntary schemes applying to these employees to be negotiated of a standard sufficient to be exempted from the statutory scheme. We do not think it appropriate to set any upper salary limit to inclusion within the scope of protection, partly because in principle it is desirable that legislation in this field should apply to employees irrespective of their status but partly also because there are many employees in receipt of fairly high salaries who do not have great security against dismissal but for whom an unfair or arbitrary dismissal can cause very considerable hardship. We think that they should have access to the statutory machinery, but the amount they can receive will be restricted, at any rate initially, by the limit of £40 a week to the amount of salary which can be taken into account in assessing compensation.

558. Most employees have contracts of employment for an indefinite period. However the need for protection against unfair deprivation of employment may also arise when the contract of employment has been entered into for a fixed period or for a particular purpose and its renewal is refused by the employer. The Contracts of Employment Act 1963 (s.1(4)) and the Redundancy Payments Act 1965 (s.3(1)(b)) both enable refusal to renew a contract made for a fixed period to be treated in the same way as terminating a contract for an indefinite period, and we suggest that the same should apply to protection against unfair dismissal. The 1965 Act also applies (s.3(1)(c)) where the employee terminates the contract without notice in circumstances (other than a lock-out) in which the employer's conduct entitles him so to do. It will be advisable similarly to extend protection against unfair dismissal to cases in which the employer's conduct has compelled or induced the employee to give up the employment, even though it may not have been such as to justify the employee in quitting without notice.

559. We have already emphasised the importance we attach to the development of satisfactory voluntary dismissal procedures, and it is an essential part of the statutory machinery we are proposing that the Secretary of State should have power, on the recommendation of the Industrial Relations Commission, to exempt from its operation industries or undertakings which apply an agreed voluntary procedure, provided that this reaches satisfactory standards. It is necessary here to draw a distinction between the normal run of internal procedures which enable an employee to appeal against dismissal to higher ranks of management and those procedures, mainly external, which provide for an appeal to be decided jointly or by an impartial adjudicator. The first type of procedure is very valuable and its widespread introduction is most desirable, but it would not be right to exempt a procedure which leaves the ultimate decision in the hands of management alone. As we have said, we consider that the fact that an employee will have a right of appeal to a statutory tribunal will be a stimulus to employers to devise clear-cut dismissal procedures.

560. On the other hand, it is essential that it should be possible for procedures providing for joint or independent decisions on dismissal cases to be exempted from the statutory procedure. Procedures of this kind would be undermined if matters decided under them could be re-opened on further appeal in the labour tribunal. But no procedure should be exempted unless:

(i) it is provided for by collective agreement between parties to collective bargaining arrangements and enables joint or independent decisions on dismissals to be reached; and

(ii) it either enables such decisions to be reached before dismissal takes effect (thus effectively safeguarding the employee against the risk of unfair dismissal) or provides for compensation on conditions no less favourable than those laid down in the statute as an alternative to reinstatement in the event of a dismissal which has taken place being found to be unfair. On the other hand, the parties to a collective agreement should have a wide measure of discretion in determining the composition and procedure of any body they set up to deal with dismissals, so long as it enables a clear-cut decision to be reached.

561. We know of no voluntary procedures at present which envisage compensation in the event of unfair dismissal, but as we have said once dismissal has taken place it may be impossible for the employment relationship to be resumed on a satisfactory basis and in these circumstances the only adequate remedy is the payment of compensation. It is a possible obstacle to the development of voluntary procedures providing for compensation that employers or officials of an employers' association would find it embarrassing to be given the responsibility of assessing the compensation to be paid by an employer and would also not wish to have the task of ensuring that he complied with an award. In order to overcome this obstacle we suggest that it should be possible for an exempted voluntary procedure to provide that, when a dismissal has been found unfair, if the resumption of the employment relationship is impracticable the question of deciding what compensation should be paid

151

F

should be referred for decision by the labour tribunal and the tribunal's award should be enforceable in the same way as its other awards. In this event it would not be possible for the case to be re-opened before the labour tribunal; the decision that the dismissal was unfair, and the facts as found under the voluntary procedure, must stand. While the parties would appear before the labour tribunal their submissions would concern only the question of the amount of compensation which would be appropriate.

562. All employers on whose behalf a voluntary procedure has been negotiated by an employers' association should be bound by that procedure, but it should not apply to other employers who do not belong to the association even though they operate in the same industry. As regards employees, the question arises whether non-members of trade unions should be covered by an exempted voluntary procedure or whether they should have access to the statutory machinery. In our view, it would be wrong to give them access to the statutory machinery. This would weaken collective institutions, for it would mean that any trade union member who was dismissed could in practice exercise an option since he could by resigning from union membership gain access to the statutory procedure, and this seems to us undesirable. Non-members must not however be deprived of a right of appeal and it should be open to them to appeal through the voluntary procedure. There is a possibility that non-members will be put at a disadvantage as a result, since they will often not be able to secure the assistance of a union in using the complaints procedure, but that is a consequence of the decision they have themselves taken not to join a trade union in the first place.

The Closed Shop

563. Occasions will arise when an employer decides to dismiss an employee because he is a non-unionist. This and the following paragraph set out the views of a majority of us on the ensuing situation, the dissent of certain of our number being recorded at the end of the chapter. It may be the case that a closed shop is formally laid down by collective agreement and the employee either resigns from or is expelled by his union. It will be open to an employee discharged in these circumstances to complain on the grounds of unfair dismissal. Where the employee claims that he has been wrongfully or unfairly expelled from his union, the correct course will be for him to lodge a complaint against this under the procedures we recommend elsewhere and the labour tribunal should postpone consideration of a claim on the grounds of unfair dismissal by the employer until the complaint against the union has been decided. Where the employee has resigned from the union knowing that a closed shop exists we do not envisage that the labour tribunal will normally find that dismissal by the employer is unfair. A rather more difficult case arises when an employer dismisses an existing employee who refuses to join a trade union following the introduction of the closed shop. Our view is that the employee should be able to succeed against the employer so long as he can show that he has reasonable grounds for refusing to join the union. It is the responsibility of the employer in concluding a closed shop agreement to bear in mind the interests of existing employees who are not in the union and ensure that they are adequately safeguarded.

564. As things now stand, however, dismissal of a non-unionist is more likely to result from pressure on the shop-floor by workmates who refuse to work, or to go on working, with a non-unionist. If a claim arises, we envisage that the labour tribunal will take into account the dismissed worker's reason for refusing to join a union, and whether he has in some way provoked the action of his fellow-workers, but we do not rule out the possibility of compensation being awarded against the employer. It might be argued that this is unjust, since it is the union, not the employer, which stands to gain from an insistence on an employee's being in the union. But the decision to dismiss is the employer's, taken ultimately because he considers it to the advantage of his business. One important consideration for the tribunal will be the extent to which the employer has previously acquiesced in the development of an informal closed shop, and one of the advantages of our proposals is that they are likely to lead to a regularisation of such situations by formal agreements which can make proper provision for the non-conformist. Without such an agreement the responsibility of the union as such cannot easily be established. The union cannot be expected to be in full control of an arrangement which has been imposed by the action of its members without its knowledge, and accepted by the employer without official reference to it.

Dismissal for Disciplinary Reasons

565. Certain difficulties may also arise out of dismissals for disciplinary reasons. Where an employee is dismissed for breach of rule made by the employer, the labour tribunal should in reaching its decision be able to consider not only the seriousness of the breach but also the reasonableness of the rule. It is the general practice at present for works rules to be laid down unilaterally by managements, and in our view the labour tribunal would be unjustifiably handicapped if it were obliged to accept without question the reasonableness of all such rules—apart from any required for compliance with statutory obligations under the Factories Act or other legislation—whatever their terms may be. However, in any case where the employer can show that the works rules were drawn up with the agreement of the trade union or unions concerned the labour tribunal will not lightly set them aside.

566. An employee who is dismissed for misconduct, and admits that he committed the act alleged, may nevertheless complain that the employer has acted in a discriminatory way since similar acts are normally condoned. We think that in such a case it must be open to the labour tribunal to decide that the dismissal is unfair if the employee establishes his contention, since it would otherwise be possible for an employer to find an opportunity to dismiss an employee of whom he wished to be rid for some quite different reason.

. . . . .

Note of Dissent

567. Sir George Pollock and Mr. John Thomson are opposed to the early establishment of statutory machinery to deal with unfair dismissals. While they agree that this course has some attractions they believe that these are outweighed by the disadvantages. In particular they take the view that there is no evidence that abuse by employers of their right to dismiss exists

on such a scale as to warrant legislation, and that a statutory procedure might damage relationships between employer and employee where there is a comparatively small labour force. They also wish to record that, should legislation nevertheless be proceeded with, they consider that it would be wrong for an employer to be regarded as having acted unfairly and for damages to be awarded against him if he has been compelled against his will to dismiss an employee in the circumstances described in paragraphs 563 and 564 because of pressure from a trade union or from other employees. Lord Donovan and Lord Tangley desire to record their dissent also on this point. In the circumstances envisaged they think that any compensation should have to be paid by the trade union concerned.

Mr. Shonfield also takes the view that a union should be obliged to pay damages in certain circumstances, i.e. where an employer is able to show that he had tried to negotiate an arrangement with the union on reasonable terms which, while conceding the requirements of a closed shop in the future, would have safeguarded the interests of existing employees at the time of its intro- duction, and the union nevertheless insisted on their dismissal. In his view the employer should, in the same way as other persons with complaints about the oppressive use of trade union power, have the right of recourse to the independent review body (recommended in Chapter XI) where he would be able to claim damages from the union up to the amount of compensation which he was ordered to pay the dismissed employees by the labour tribunal.

Chapter X

LABOUR TRIBUNALS

568. We consider it to be of importance that employers and employees should be given improved facilities for the speedy and informal settlement of such disputes as may arise between them. The best way of achieving this end is to stimulate the growth of collective bargaining. With this aspect of the matter we deal in earlier chapters of this report. There are however very large numbers of employees (especially in the white-collar sector) to whom no voluntary machinery applies. Moreover, certain types of dispute, especially those arising from the enforcement of statutory or contractual rights, do not easily lend themselves to settlement through voluntary machinery or at any rate are not usually dealt with that way. It is therefore desirable that provision should be made by statute so as to improve the present machinery for the judicial determination of disputes between employers and employees arising from and in connection with contracts of employment and statutory claims arising between employers and employees.

569. Under the present law the jurisdiction to hear and to determine disputes arising between individual employers and employees is divided between a number of courts. The industrial tribunals which were created under the Industrial Training Act 1964 handle all disputes arising under the Redundancy Payments Act 1965 and certain matters under the Contracts of Employment Act 1963, as well as a number of other issues. The county courts (or, in cases exceeding the jurisdictional limits of the county courts, the High Court) deal with other matters arising out of the contract of employment, but, in so far as manual workers are concerned and the sum involved does not exceed £10, the case may, under the provisions of the Employers and Workmen Act 1875, go to the magistrates' courts.

570. This multiplicity of jurisdictions is apt to lead to waste, to frustration and to delay. Thus, if an employee wishes to claim a redundancy payment, but at the same time alleges that the employer has given him insufficient notice of dismissal, or perhaps that there are still outstanding claims for holiday pay or for overtime pay, he has to go before one tribunal for one part of his claims and to another for the other part. The industrial tribunal can give him no damages for wrongful dismissal, and the county court can give him no redundancy payment. We understand that two or three complaints a week on the grounds of wrongful dismissal are addressed to the industrial tribunals at present even though every opportunity is taken to make it known that they cannot deal with them.

571. The disadvantages inherent in the present system of divided jurisdictions would be aggravated if our proposals relating to compensation for unfair dismissal were adopted by Parliament. Compensation for unfair dismissal would be awarded by the industrial tribunals, but damages for wrongful dismissal would continue to be awarded by the county courts, although in a given case both claims may arise on the same facts.

572. In its evidence the Ministry of Labour invited us to consider whether

the jurisdiction of the existing industrial tribunals should be enlarged so as to comprise " all disputes between the individual worker and his employer ". Having considered the matter, we have come to the conclusion that, subject to certain limitations, this should be done, and that, to signify the change, the industrial tribunals should be renamed " labour tribunals ". The object we have in mind in making this recommendation is not only to overcome the present multiplicity of jurisdictions. It is also, and primarily, to make available to employers and employees, for all disputes arising from their contracts of employment, a procedure which is easily accessible, informal, speedy and inexpensive, and which gives them the best possible opportunities of arriving at an amicable settlement of their differences.

573. We propose therefore that the jurisdiction of the labour tribunals should be defined so as to comprise all disputes arising between employers and employees from their contracts of employment or from any statutory claims they may have against each other in their capacity as employer and employee. This includes the employee's claim for wages, holiday pay etc., for breach of contract, e.g. by wrongful dismissal, and for statutory payments such as those arising under the Redundancy Payments Act. It further includes all such claims for damages for breach of contract as the employer may have against the employee.

574. Actions for damages arising from accidents at work should in our opinion continue to go to the ordinary courts (no matter whether they are made by reason of breach of contract or by reason of negligence or breach of statutory duty) and we recommend that they should be expressly excluded from the jurisdiction of the labour tribunals.

575. We propose that the jurisdiction of the tribunals should cover all contracts of employment, irrespective of the nature of the work done by the employee and irrespective of his place in the hierarchy of employment or the amount of his salary, and that it should extend to persons in public as well as to persons in private employment. The coverage of the jurisdiction should thus continue to be broadly co-extensive with that of the Redundancy Payments Act, and the definition in that statute of an employee should be used for the purpose of defining the jurisdiction of the tribunals. The jurisdiction would therefore cover claims made by or against:

> " an individual who has entered into or works under (or, in the case of an employment which has been terminated, worked under) a contract with an employer, whether the contract is for manual labour, clerical work or otherwise, is express or implied, oral or in writing, and whether it is a contract of service or of apprenticeship."

576. In a number of fundamental respects our recommendation differs from some of the proposals for the creation of " labour courts " or " industrial courts " which have been placed before us. We do not propose that they should be given the job of resolving industrial disputes or differences arising between employers or employers' associations and trade unions or groups of workers, since these are matters which must be settled by procedures of, or agreed through, collective bargaining. Nor do we envisage that any matters arising between trade unions and their members or applicants for membership

should be within the jurisdiction of the labour tribunals: we elsewhere recommend the setting up of a review body for the handling of such cases. Nor do we propose that the tribunals should deal with actions for damages arising from strikes or other labour disputes, except in so far as damages for breach of the contract of employment are claimed by either party to it against the other. In particular all claims for damages by reason of torts alleged to have been committed in connection with strikes would continue to go to the ordinary courts.

577. The labour tribunals are not intended to handle any issues connected with the negotiation of collective agreements or even with their interpretation in so far as this arises between trade unions and employers or employers' associations. In as much as the terms of a collective agreement are incorporated in the individual contract of employment, the tribunals may be called upon to interpret them, but, in order to ensure that nothing in our proposals encroaches upon the operation of voluntarily agreed procedures for the settlement of disputes, we recommend that the tribunals should be authorised to admit as evidence of the intention of the parties to a collective agreement an award or other decision concerning its interpretation rendered by a tribunal, committee or other similar body established by the parties to the agreement.

578. As we have already said, it is one of our principal purposes to provide for the parties an easily accessible, speedy, informal and inexpensive procedure for the settlement of their disputes, and for this purpose to remove the present multiplicity of jurisdictions. This makes it desirable to concentrate in one tribunal all cases arising from the contract of employment and from statutory rights arising from the employment relationship. As far as statutory rights are concerned, such as claims to redundancy payments under the Redundancy Payments Act 1965, or, if our recommendation in Chapter IX is accepted, claims by reason of unfair dismissal, the jurisdiction of the labour tribunals should exclude that of any other courts, subject to an exception referred to in paragraph 580.

579. We have seriously considered whether their jurisdiction in other matters such as claims for wrongful dismissal, accrued wages or holiday pay and other claims arising from the contract of employment should not also be exclusive. The arguments in favour of such exclusive jurisdiction are strong: if, for example, an employee claimed damages for wrongful dismissal in the county court and at the same time compensation for unfair dismissal or a redundancy payment before the labour tribunal, two courts would have to hear and to determine simultaneously two cases on virtually the same facts. Such and similar situations are likely to lead to confusion. They would be avoided if the labour tribunals exercised jurisdiction over all claims arising from the employment relationship to the exclusion of all other courts. There are however some cogent objections to granting exclusive jurisdiction to the labour tribunals. Some employees and some employers might strongly object to being deprived of their access to the ordinary courts, nor is there any reason why, in the absence of proceedings pending or being instituted in a labour tribunal, they should not seek their redress there. Moreover, a party who is charged with fraud has, under the Administration of Justice (Miscellaneous Provisions) Act 1933, the right to ask for a trial by jury and this right should not be curtailed. In addition, some claims for damages for breach

of a contract of employment may raise complicated issues: for example questions arising out of a stipulation that any inventions made by an employee as a consequence of his work shall be the property of the employer; questions arising upon the reasonableness of a covenant not to compete with the employer after the employment ceases; and allegations of dereliction of duty against persons holding high positions of trust. Such cases may take many days to try, and are not really suitable for a tribunal which may not be full-time and is predominantly lay. We therefore recommend that, while the jurisdiction of the labour tribunals should (with an exception referred to in the following paragraph) be exclusive in regard to statutory claims for redundancy pay or by reason of unfair dismissal, it should in all other matters arising from the employment relationship be at the plaintiff's option whether the proceedings are to be instituted in the labour tribunal or in the ordinary courts.

580. If however proceedings between the same parties arising from the employment relationship are pending or are instituted in the labour tribunal it should be incumbent on the county court or on the High Court, on a motion to this effect made by either party, to remit the case to the labour tribunal for consolidation with the case pending there. This should not however be done if either party has made use of his right to ask for trial by jury. Moreover it should be open to either the plaintiff or the defendant in proceedings arising out of a contract of employment instituted before a labour tribunal to ask the High Court for an order that, on the grounds of complexity or probable length, the case should be heard in the High Court (or in the county court if within its jurisdictional limits). If the application is granted, the High Court or county court should have jurisdiction to dispose, if it thinks fit, of any related claim, e.g. for damages for unfair dismissal, which would otherwise have to be tried by the labour tribunal.

581. If our recommendation in paragraph 578 is accepted, most of the provisions of the Employers and Workmen Act 1875 could be repealed.

582. Like the present industrial tribunals, the labour tribunals would be established in all the larger industrial centres. They would consist of a legally qualified chairman and of two lay judges, one taken from a panel presented by the trade unions and one from a panel presented by the employers' associations, so however that the lay judges sitting in a case are, if possible, not connected with the industry in which the dispute has arisen. It would be for the chairman to conduct the proceedings but in deciding the case the three judges would be on a footing of equality. In theory this could lead to the possibility of the chairman being outvoted by the two lay members on a point of law, but the likelihood of this happening is exceedingly small, and any error of law could be rectified through the appellate procedure which we recommend below. It might however be considered whether decisions on points of law should be left to the exclusive jurisdiction of the chairman. The judgment to be pronounced and published would always be that of the tribunal without any indication of dissenting or concurring opinions.

583. If our recommendation is adopted it may be necessary to appoint a number of additional chairmen. The creation of the labour tribunals will

inevitably focus the attention of the legal profession to an increasing extent on questions of labour law. It is desirable that facilities should be provided by the Bar Senate, the Law Society and the universities for the training of lawyers in this subject and for making available to them at least an elementary knowledge of industrial relations.

584. In all proceedings between employers and employees it should be a primary duty of the tribunal to bring about an amicable settlement, and the procedure should be designed so as to make this as easy as possible. Each hearing should be preceded by a " round table " meeting in private between the parties and the tribunal, or one or two of its members, in order to settle the case. If this fails, further attempts at a settlement should be made in the course of the further proceedings. Experience abroad has shown that labour tribunals can settle a very large proportion of all cases before them. There is no reason to believe that a similar result would not follow here. Such conciliation proceedings would not however be appropriate in cases concerning the payment by employers of industrial training levies or the payment to employers of monies due under the Selective Employment Payments Act 1966.

585. The preliminary proceedings as well as the hearing should be informal and expeditious: adjournments should if possible be avoided. To this end, it may be necessary to insist on an exchange of documents before the hearing and to dispense with the application of some of the rules of the law of evidence. The parties will presumably often be represented by officials of their union or employers' association. Where this is not the case, and where the employer is represented by solicitor or counsel, it may be necessary to make legal aid available for the employee. We envisage that the hearing of the cases (as distinct from the preliminary conciliation meeting) would normally be in public, except in certain kinds of dismissal cases to which reference was made above in Chapter IX. Costs should be awarded only against a party who has acted frivolously or vexatiously.

586. The decisions of the tribunal should be enforceable like those of a county court. An appeal should lie on a point of law to the Queen's Bench Division of the High Court.

Chapter XI

SAFEGUARDS FOR INDIVIDUALS IN RELATION TO TRADE UNIONS

INTRODUCTION

587. In this further chapter concerning safeguards for individual workers we turn to consider their relationship with trade unions. We have had a good deal of evidence on the subject. In part this is because a small number of legal and other cases where the rights of individuals have been abused have attracted public attention. A more general reason is that, whereas the individual's statutory safeguards remain broadly as they have been since the passing of the Trade Union Act 1871, trade unions have meanwhile increased immensely in power. We propose in this report many measures calculated to assist and strengthen trade unions for the future. For all these reasons it is necessary to review the adequacy of safeguards against the abuse of trade union power or the misconduct of their internal affairs.

THE CLOSED SHOP

588. We consider first the operation of the closed shop. This is a term with varying meanings. We use it in the sense in which it is used in Dr. McCarthy's book on the subject,[1] namely " a situation in which employees come to realise that a particular job is only to be obtained and retained if they become and remain members of one of a specified number of trade unions ". Dr. McCarthy shows that in 1964 about $3\frac{3}{4}$ million members of trade unions, that is about 2 out of every 5, worked in a closed shop. In some cases a person may have to be a member of a trade union before he can obtain the job he seeks. This is a " pre-entry " closed shop. In other cases he may be obliged to join a trade union within a short time of beginning the job he has secured. This is the " post-entry " closed shop. The pre-entry is less common than the post-entry closed shop, but at the time of Dr. McCarthy's study it included about $\frac{3}{4}$ million workers. The diagram on the following page shows the extent of both types of closed shop on the basis of these estimates.

589. Since 1964 the numbers employed in some industries where the closed shop is common have gone down, but there is evidence that it has spread in other industries. The total extent of the closed shop therefore probably remains about the same today as when Dr. McCarthy studied it.

590. A justification for the closed shop commonly put forward by trade unionists is that the benefits of agreements negotiated with employers apply to employees irrespective of whether they are union members or not. Consequently non-members, who pay no trade union subscriptions, are receiving benefits at the union's expense; they should therefore be obliged to contribute.

---

[1] W. E. J. McCarthy, *The Closed Shop in Britain*, Blackwell, 1964.

However, as Dr. McCarthy has shown, this is not the main reason for its existence. Admittedly some unions insist upon the closed shop wherever they have the strength to enforce it, but there are others which tolerate a minority of non-members even where they could take action to force them to join the union or lose their jobs.

Extent of the Closed Shop in 1964

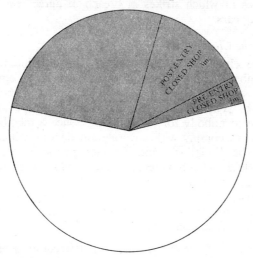

Total number of full-time employees in Great Britain, approximately 22¼ million.
Shaded portion: trade unionists (approximately 10 million).
Unshaded portion: non-trade unionists.

591. Whether a closed shop will be imposed or not depends on the particular circumstances of the industry, and of the undertaking. If it seems probable that a closed shop will add considerably to the bargaining strength of the union or of a group of workers, then the closed shop is likely to be imposed. On the other hand, if non-unionists are not a serious source of weakness, then their presence will be tolerated.

The Case for the Closed Shop

592. The two most convincing arguments for the closed shop refer only to the first group of employments, and depend upon the close link between effective collective bargaining and strong trade unions. The first is that in some industries it is impossible or difficult for a union to establish effective and stable organisation without the help of the closed shop; the second is that even where membership can be recruited and retained without its assistance there are instances where it is needed to deploy the workers' bargaining strength to the full.

593. There are, however, other arguments which can apply even where these two lack force. London Transport told us that they saw advantage in the closed shop, since, as they put it, it ensured that in dealings with the union they were meeting an organisation " which does represent all your people ".

A similar argument is that the closed shop helps to secure the observance of agreements, since it adds to the power of the union to discipline those who ignore them.

594. It must not be supposed, however, that good industrial relations are the invariable accompaniment of the closed shop. On the contrary the closed shop is widespread in motor manufacturing, shipbuilding, coal-mining and the docks, the four industries in which strikes in breach of agreement have been most common in recent years.

The Case against the Closed Shop

595. Against the closed shop, it is argued that it reduces the individual's freedom in a number of ways. If he is to obtain or retain employment where there is a closed shop, he has no choice but to join the trade union and to pay a subscription. The trade union may refuse to accept him as a member, and is answerable to nobody for its decision. Once a member of the union, the individual has to comply with any relevant decisions it may make; if he does not he may be disciplined, and if things go too far he may eventually be expelled and lose his job in consequence. So far as he is concerned, therefore, the trade union is no longer a " voluntary " organisation, at least in the normal sense, and he cannot register his disagreement with the union in the normal way open to members of voluntary organisations—by resignation—unless he is prepared also to face losing his job.

596. The importance of the loss of individual freedom is reinforced by the extent to which, as we show elsewhere, power in trade unions rests with work groups. Where matters are left to work groups to settle, they may need to support their decisions with some authority. Unions' disciplinary procedures designed with the needs of the branch in mind sometimes appear irrelevant to the work group when shop floor questions are at issue. As a result informal disciplinary measures, such as ostracism, may be used. Occasionally, trade union authority is wholly usurped; for example, there have been cases where the closed shop has been used to hound a man out of his job even when he had not formally been expelled, as in the case which reached the courts as *Huntley v. Thornton* [1957] 1 All ER 234.

597. The second principal objection advanced against the closed shop concerns its economic effects. Essentially, what is at issue here is entry to the skilled trades. It is argued that the craft unions use the closed shop to restrict to their own members, or certain classes of their own members, the right to do skilled work; and because they limit the number of entrants they will allow to be trained in the requisite skills, or refuse to recognise as eligible to do skilled work members who have not served apprenticeships, they cause shortages of skilled labour which are economically damaging.

Should the Closed Shop be Prohibited?

598. In our view the closed shop as it operates at present is not always in the best interests either of workers or of the community as a whole. It is liable from time to time to cause substantial injustice to individuals from which they have no effective means of redress. It also contributes to the maintenance

162

of a system of training which is out of date and inadequate to the country's needs.

599. It might be argued on these grounds that the closed shop should be prohibited. As part of the argument for prohibition it might be said that since we suggest elsewhere that any condition in a contract of employment that the employee shall not join a union is to be void in law, it would be right to treat in the same way a condition that a worker *shall* join a union. However, the two are not truly comparable. The former condition is designed to frustrate the development of collective bargaining, which it is public policy to promote, whereas no such objection applies to the latter.

600. In any case, however, a prohibition could not be made effective. Express stipulations in written agreements for the imposition or maintenance of a closed shop would no doubt disappear in the face of a legal prohibition but this would affect less than a fifth of the workers covered by the closed shop. Since moreover some employers as well as trade unionists support the closed shop, there could be no guarantee that formal agreements would not be replaced by informal and tacit understandings of the kind which are much more commonly found. The law would presumably declare such things to be void, but this of itself would not necessarily deprive them of practical effect.

601. Some difficult problems could then arise. For example, if all the employees in a particular plant or enterprise at present subject to the closed shop agreed informally among themselves that they would try to maintain it, would this itself be an offence? If so, what punishment would be imposed, assuming the offence could be proved? The matter would no doubt come into the open when some employee refused to join the union, or resigned and refused to rejoin. If the remaining employees then threatened to withdraw their labour unless the non-unionist was dismissed, how would the law meet this situation? By prosecution of the strikers for conspiracy or for some other offence? If for conspiracy, much of the present law ousting such a charge in the circumstances of a trade dispute, or alternatively the present legal definition of a trade dispute, would have to be re-written. By yielding to the threat of a strike, and dismissing the non-unionist, would the employer be regarded as aiding and abetting the strikers? As regards the dismissed employee himself, what rights or remedies would be given to him? Compulsory reinstatement in his job where he would have to work alongside his hostile fellows would hardly be practicable. The alternative would presumably be damages for the loss of his job to be paid either by the union or by the strikers, with perhaps some contribution by the employer according to the degree of responsibility which each bore. But this would mean that the closed shop remained, and that the law had been defeated, albeit at a price. It is no doubt because of such difficulties as these that no reasoned case has been put to us in evidence for prohibiting the closed shop, even by those who strongly object to it.

602. In our view prohibition of the closed shop must be rejected. It is better to recognise that under proper safeguards a closed shop can serve a useful purpose and to devise alternative means of overcoming the disadvantages which accompany it. We have also borne in mind that throughout this report we advance a number of proposals to assist trade unions to organise

163

effectively and to reduce the incidence of strikes. The effect of our proposals should be to extend to more industries the conditions which now permit many trade unions to organise and bargain without need for the closed shop, and we believe therefore that in many cases unions should in time feel able to dispense with its aid.

Protection for the Individual: What Cases Require Safeguards?

603. It is necessary first to identify cases in which safeguards are needed. In its written evidence the Ministry of Labour drew attention to four instances in which the closed shop might interfere unduly with the freedom of the individual:

(1) where workers have conscientious reasons for not belonging to trade unions;

(2) where workers, though willing to belong to a trade union, are refused admission or expelled unreasonably;

(3) where there are irregularities in the conduct of the affairs of a union operating a closed shop and individual members are adversely affected;

(4) where a closed shop is introduced in an establishment where 100 per cent membership does not already exist.[1]

604. The need for safeguarding workers who do not wish to join unions on conscientious grounds was also urged upon us by several other persons, and in particular by Mr. E. C. Burr and Mr. A. J. E. Welch, who in their written evidence specified grounds on which certain Christians have conscientious objections to joining trade unions, or indeed employers' associations or professional associations. These are that believers are enjoined " be not unequally yoked with unbelievers " (2 Corinthians 6: 14). They sought legislation providing that a person should not be deprived of his employment, or of the opportunity for an employment of his choice, merely because of his objection to joining a union or kindred association. They were ready to accept that such objections should be tested by a tribunal, and that non-members should be made to contribute to public funds or to acceptable charities on a scale at least equal to the appropriate union subscription. While no witness suggested that conscientious objections to trade union membership should be totally disregarded there were several who urged a close scrutiny of such objections, lest they were no more than a device to avoid paying a trade union subscription.

605. Our impression from the evidence we have heard is that trade unions in the main respect genuine conscientious objections, and are usually content if the objectors agree to pay to some charitable body the equivalent of the union dues. Where unions are not prepared to accept an offer of this kind, a majority of us think that some redress is called for in circumstances where the objector loses his job because of the introduction of the closed shop— see paragraph 614 below.

606. We take the same view regarding employees unjustifiably expelled from a union or arbitrarily refused admission to a union operating a closed shop.

---

[1]Ministry of Labour's Written Evidence, HMSO 1965, p.88.

If they are unable to follow their occupations because of an act of this kind they are entitled to redress against the union.

607. Where members object to irregularities in the conduct of a union's affairs their situation may be said to be more difficult if there is a closed shop because it is not open to them to resign without losing their jobs. We accept the force of this, but feel that there is a need to provide some form of redress against irregularities in any case, whether there is a closed shop or not. We therefore deal with the problems later in this chapter.

608. As regards the position of non-unionists in a concern where a closed shop is introduced for the first time, a concrete case brought to our notice was that of Mr. James Watson, an employee of the Glasgow Corporation working in its Lighting Department. He was dismissed in February 1964 following his refusal to join a trade union. Mr. Watson had started work with the Corporation in June 1959, when there was no closed shop, but a resolution was passed by the City Council in December 1962 that membership of a trade union should henceforth be a condition of employment. A majority of us think that in such situations there should be redress for any employee who has reasonable grounds for refusing to join the trade union (see paragraph 614).

Safeguards for the Individual: Our Proposals

609. As things are, nobody applying for trade union membership has any right to become a member, whether or not his prospects of employment depend upon membership. Acceptance of his application is entirely at the union's discretion: and in those cases where admissions are dealt with by union branches, entirely at the discretion of a branch, acting through a branch committee.

610. There is little evidence that applications for membership are dealt with unfairly, or that membership is capriciously refused. After all unions exist on membership. But it may well be thought to be unacceptable that a citizen's livelihood should depend upon the will of a few other citizens being members of a trade union committee or branch committee. If such a would-be member of the trade union concerned, eligible under its rules, is qualified to follow the occupation in question and is of good character, then he is entitled to an assurance that his application will be fairly considered. The significance of this question will be reduced insofar as trade union rules are clarified as we recommend in paragraphs 618 and 650, but even so trade unions must retain ultimate discretion in decisions about whom to admit and whom not to admit, and we think that an unsuccessful applicant for admission to a trade union, or to the skilled section of a trade union, should be able to lodge a complaint that that discretion has been arbitrarily exercised.

611. The complaint should in the first instance lie to the executive committee of the trade union concerned. It is desirable that trade union rules should be revised so as to make provision to this effect, where this is not already done. Trade union rules should also provide for applicants to be informed of their right of complaint to the executive committee at the time they are notified that their applications have been turned down; and for the executive committee to have the power to admit applicants where a complaint is upheld.

612. We think that provision to this effect will be sufficient to enable most cases which arise in practice to be disposed of fairly and satisfactorily. However in view of the importance of the matter to the individuals concerned, we think that a rejected applicant who still considers that his application has been arbitrarily rejected, and who considers also that the rejection is causing him substantial injustice, for example by unduly handicapping him in earning his living, should have a further right of complaint to a new and independent review body. He should be entitled to ask that body for a declaration that, upon his undertaking to abide by the rules of the union affecting existing members, he should, notwithstanding any absolute discretion vested in the union or in any committee of the union, become and remain a member. It would be open to the union to defend its decision by establishing that in refusing the application it was not dealing with the matter in an arbitrary fashion, but was acting impartially and fairly and in furtherance of the legitimate interests of the union. If the union's evidence satisfied the review body that this was so, no order would be made. Otherwise it should grant the declaration requested by the rejected applicant.

613. If despite the terms of such a declaration the union sought to withhold any of the rights of membership from such an individual he would be in the same position under the general law as any other member as regards redress, and would therefore be able to bring an action as for breach of contract against the union. If the union took some other retaliatory action against him designed to secure that he would be unable to continue in any employment dependent upon continued membership of the union, and such action succeeded, then the individual should have the right to receive compensation from the union, the right to be enforced, and the compensation to be measured, as hereafter proposed. This would not involve the discontinuance of the particular closed shop. It would in effect mean that the union regarded full control over it as worth preserving at the cost involved.

614. At the time at which a trade union secures a closed shop, some non-members may decline to join and lose their jobs in consequence. Alternatively a non-member may be dismissed as a result of shop-floor pressure. In either case an employee may have conscientious or other reasonable grounds for refusing to join the union in these circumstances, and a majority of us take the view that he should have a right of complaint to the labour tribunal on the grounds of unfair dismissal. We go into the matter more fully in paragraphs 563 and 564 of Chapter IX.

615. Where members have fallen out with their union or with its officers and have been expelled, this again could lead to the loss of employment by the individual concerned, or make it more difficult for him to obtain suitable employment in the future. If it should do so, the question whether some compensation should be given is one which could not be determined except after investigation of the facts. It would be unreal to suppose that right is always on the side of such members. Trade unions normally seek to act in a fair and responsible way. So long as they do so, no ground for compensation exists. But a trade union can be in the wrong. Some members of the Electrical Trades Union in the recent past, before its change of leadership, faced

expulsion and possible loss of their jobs for protesting against union malpractices. We think that in the kind of case we are considering the individual who has been expelled, and who claims that he has suffered damage in consequence, should be given the right to put his case before the independent review body; the trade union concerned having the right to appear and be heard in opposition. If the review body finds that the individual was unjustifiably expelled, and that he has suffered damage in consequence of no longer being a member of the union, it should award him compensation. If the review body finds that the expulsion was justifiable, then no compensation would be awarded. In any case of divided blame the compensation should be reduced to allow for the individual's proportion of the blame. It should also be reduced by such amount as the review body thought fit (which might be the whole) to allow for the mitigating effect of any new employment which the individual has secured or should have secured in the meantime.

616. Where a member has resigned in a closed shop situation, he must be presumed to have done so with his eyes open. It is not in doubt that a member might have excellent reasons for resigning but it is also open to him to remain within the union and take every opportunity of securing the reversal of policies repugnant to him. We recognise that individuals can be faced with difficult decisions, but our view is that it would not be a satisfactory solution of these difficulties to give individuals the right to claim compensation for any loss they suffer as a result of the decisions they take.

617. We also think that it would be right to ensure that if a person is through an oversight admitted to a union although ineligible under the rules his admission should not be open to question after (say) two years have elapsed on any ground other than fraud on his part when applying for membership. The desirability of provision to this effect is suggested by the case of *Faramus v. Film Artistes' Association* [1964] AC 925. While such cases are bound to be rare, when one does occur it may imperil a person's livelihood through no fault of his own.

The Economic Effects of the Closed Shop

618. The safeguards proposed in the preceding paragraphs are designed to protect individuals against unfairness or injustice and not to remedy economic ills. We accept however that the closed shop sometimes plays an important part in maintaining restrictions on entry to skilled employments and can as a result have adverse economic effects, which are sometimes serious. However, much more is involved than merely the closed shop. One is concerned here with the whole question of how the craft system operates and how the country's future needs for skilled manpower can be met. We discuss fully the measures we consider necessary in Chapter VI. As we there make clear, once methods of industrial training have been improved trade union rules should be revised so as to ensure that no qualified worker will be arbitrarily denied either the right of admission to the union or the right to use the skills which he has acquired; and that a worker arbitrarily refused membership should have the right of complaint to the independent review body (paragraph 358).

619. Trade union members may need safeguards *vis-à-vis* their unions even in the absence of the closed shop, and these we now consider. As part of the survey of workshop relations conducted for us by the Government Social Survey, a number of questions were put to 494 trade unionists drawn from the register of electors on a random basis. They were asked: " Do you personally know of any case where a member or members of your union were disciplined or punished in some way by the union or members of the union? " Eleven per cent said that they did. They were then asked for details about the case (or the last case) of which they had personal knowledge. When giving such details a total of 4 members considered that a member had been disciplined or punished unfairly. The actual comments were:

" He was working more overtime than allowed, and had to pay some of his overtime to the union."

" He was behind with contributions, and was fined."

" A welder hit another welder, and was fined £5."

" This became a court case and that was taken up by the police, I cannot disclose the offence. The member was removed from his position in the union as a shop steward."

620. Less than 1 per cent of these 494 members professed to know therefore of cases where trade union members had been unfairly treated by the union or by members of their union, and even in these cases there is little evidence that actual unfair treatment occurred. The percentage of trade union members who considered *themselves* to have been unfairly treated by the union would, on the basis of these answers, be lower still.

621. Similar questions were put to another random sample consisting of 412 employees who were non-unionists. None of these professed personal knowledge of unfair disciplinary treatment of an employee at his place of work by a trade union or by fellow trade unionists. Follow-up questions were put to both unionists and non-unionists about appeals within unions against disciplinary decisions. Seven appeals were reported. In five the appellant was said to have had a fair hearing. In one case the person questioned did not know whether there had been a fair hearing. In the remaining one case the person questioned considered that the hearing had not been fair. In three cases the decision appealed from was upheld: in three others it was varied: and in one case the result was unknown.

622. Obviously, too much should not be read into the answers we have quoted, nor into the absence of answers. But the general conclusion can, we think, be drawn with reasonable safety that if the questioning of some 500 trade unionists and 400 non-unionists selected at random yields so little in the way of adverse criticism it is unlikely that abuse of power by trade unions is widespread.

623. There can be little doubt, however, that on occasion it does happen. A number of alleged instances were drawn to our attention by the individuals affected, by Members of Parliament, and by others. In these cases we invited the comments of the trade union concerned, and with one exception the union responded giving us its own version of the affair. This invariably conflicted sharply with the complainant's account; and it was not part of our function to

attempt to hold some kind of inquiry to try and elicit the truth, even if such an inquiry were possible. Our concern was to see whether some issue of principle emerged which was independent of rival versions of the facts and which called for further consideration. Remembering, however, that trade unions, now embracing over 10 million employees, still rely very largely for their day-to-day functioning on the voluntary part-time labour of members at their branches and on the shop floor it is almost inevitable that from time to time instances will occur where members have grounds for complaint of their treatment. The possibility is indeed recognised in the rules of most unions, which give a right of appeal to aggrieved members against disciplinary decisions to designated committees within the union.

624. We received some complaints of a different kind. These were from trade unionists who had become dissatisfied with their union, resigned from it, and sought to join another. This other union, while willing to accept them, nevertheless felt itself debarred from doing so by the " Bridlington principles ". The term refers to a resolution adopted by the TUC in 1939 with the object of ensuring some stability in trade union membership and preventing the " poaching " of members. We discuss the operation of the Bridlington principles fully in our next chapter. Here it is sufficient to indicate that if an applicant is refused admission by a union because of its desire to adhere to the Bridlington principles we envisage that in the event of a complaint the proposed independent review body would accept this as reasonable justification for the refusal.

625. The foundation of a member's rights *vis-à-vis* the union is the contract between himself and his fellow members whereby he agrees to join the union and to observe its rules. The detail of the contract is thus to be found in the rule-book of the union of which, as a rule, each member is given a copy on admission, or can at any time demand a copy on payment of not more than one shilling. The rule-book deals among other things with the objects of the union, the conditions of membership, the appointment and powers of its governing body, the individual rights and obligations of members, the maintenance of discipline, the actions which will constitute offences on the part of members, their rights of appeal against any sanctions imposed upon them, and so on. It is obviously important that these rules should be clear and unambiguous so that the individual member is able to ascertain without undue difficulty what his rights and obligations are. Trade union rule-books generally fall far short of reaching a satisfactory standard in this respect. In many unions they have been altered piece-meal over the years and have become confused, self-contradictory and obscure. We have no doubt that many rule-books need complete revision, and we put forward a number of suggestions for their clarification in a separate section later in this chapter. Our suggestions must be seen in the context of our proposal in Chapter XIV that trade unions should be obliged to register and be granted corporate status.

626. Since the relationship between members of a trade union is based on contract, any member who considers the contract to have been broken to his detriment has a right of action in the courts. This right is at present circumscribed by the provisions of section 4 of the Trade Union Act 1871,

which however a majority of us recommend should be repealed (see Chapter XIV).

627. As in the case of other voluntary associations, if the rules of a trade union are not unlawful, and if the body set up to adjudicate upon alleged offences acts within those rules and also observes the rules of natural justice, courts of law, upon our understanding of the matter, have no jurisdiction to review its findings or to mitigate the penalty imposed. By the contract into which he has entered the member has agreed that he will abide by the rules of the association, which include those for the enforcement of discipline. The control kept by the courts is for the purpose of ensuring that the rules are lawful, that they are adhered to, and that the principles of natural justice are observed.

628. Should there, however, be some independent body which could review the decisions come to by the disciplinary body of a trade union? It can be said that when a trade union, through some committee of its own, sits in judgment upon a member, it is in effect acting as judge and jury in its own cause. Moreover, any appeal against the imposition of a penalty is usually heard by another committee of the union, provision for appeal to a body of independent people outside the union being rare. The decision of this other committee is sometimes but not always subject to review at the union's general conference, which may be held annually or at longer intervals; but this liability to review may mean little, since there is usually a full agenda and delegates will naturally tend to assume that a case already considered before the appropriate committees has been properly and adequately dealt with.

629. Against this, it may be pointed out that a similar situation prevails in most clubs and societies, and in certain professions, so that the case for treating trade unions differently requires special justification. However it must be noted that provision is in fact made in some cases for outside bodies to review the decisions of domestic disciplinary tribunals. Doctors whose names are ordered to be struck off the medical register may appeal to the judicial committee of the Privy Council. Solicitors ordered to be struck off the roll may appeal to the High Court. Barristers ordered to be disbarred may appeal to the judges. In all these cases such provisions are made because the appellant's livelihood is at stake.

630. In our view the connection between membership of a trade union and employees' livelihoods means that trade unions cannot be regarded simply as voluntary clubs from the members' point of view. A man who considers himself unfairly penalised by his union often cannot resort to resignation as a practicable course. If he works in a closed shop he will lose his job. Even if he does not, he may prejudice his prospects of finding suitable jobs in the future. Resignation would also deprive him of benefits earned through membership of the union, sometimes over a considerable period. He would also lose all the other advantages of membership, some of which have a material bearing on the conditions of his working life.

631. We therefore think that any member of a trade union who considers that he has had some penalty unfairly inflicted upon him which amounts to

a substantial injustice should have a right of complaint, in the last resort, to an independent review body. It is necessary to restrict the right to cases of "substantial injustice" so that merely trivial fines and penalties are excluded. The review body would consider the case on its merits. If it found that the expulsion or other penalty was unfair and caused substantial injustice it would so declare. In the case of expulsion the union should then have a reasonable time, say one month, to decide whether it would re-instate the appellant. In the case of some other penalty the review body would recommend such lesser penalty as it thought appropriate. If the union did not within one month after the decision either re-instate the appellant, or substitute the recommended lesser penaly, the appellant should be entitled to ask the review body for compensation (see paragraphs 659 ff.).

TRADE UNION ELECTIONS

Level of Participation

632. The low polls typical of union elections are an unsatisfactory feature of union life. Some unions achieve a better level than others. Thus in the ballot on amalgamation recently conducted in the Amalgamated Engineering Union and the Amalgamated Union of Foundry Workers, 56 per cent of the Foundry Workers' membership seem to have voted but only just over 7 per cent of the Engineers'. The latter figure was about the same as that for participation in the Amalgamated Engineering Union's elections for the General Secretary of the Union in 1957 and 1964—7.9 per cent—and in the first ballot for the recent election of a new President. In this ballot only $8\frac{1}{2}$ per cent of the union's membership voted and none of the candidates secured the votes of even 3 per cent of the electorate. In the second ballot less than $11\frac{1}{2}$ per cent of the electorate voted, less than 6 per cent of it for the successful candidate. Such very low polls are common in national elections in large unions.

633. It would be unreal to expect the degree of participation in union elections to approach that in (say) parliamentary elections; and other factors besides apathy help to produce low polls, such as a constantly changing membership. However a very low level of participation runs the risk of placing power in the hands of unrepresentative minorities and weakening the authority of elected officers.

634. In many unions polls are low because voting in all elections continues to take place at branch meetings, although the focus of union activity has now shifted from the branch to the workplace. To conduct elections at branch meetings in such circumstances is virtually to ensure a low poll. Some alternative method must be found by these unions if more members are to be persuaded to vote.

635. One such method is the postal vote. In several unions ballot papers are sent to every member by post. This means that an impending election is brought to the attention of each member and provides him with an opportunity of voting with the minimum of personal inconvenience. The Electrical Trades Union has recently adopted such a procedure, elections being conducted for the union by the Electoral Reform Society. This

method has resulted in levels of participation significantly higher than those reached by unions when members vote at branch meetings, although a majority still abstain even in a postal ballot. The process is also comparatively expensive; in the case of the election of the union's general secretary the estimated cost is about 1s. per valid vote. Unions considering introducing a postal vote might think that the cost is justifiable only when the election is for senior posts, or where there is some reason to believe that perseverance with postal voting will progressively increase the polls.

636. In some unions many more members would vote if arrangements were made to enable them to do so at the workplace. This is done in the mines, and it results in levels of participation which are far higher than any reached in voting at branch offices. Where union branches are based on the factory this facilitates workplace voting. It is possible however only if the employer grants the necessary facilities, and some might not be willing to do so. Nevertheless arrangements of this sort deserve to be encouraged, and provision for them could appropriately be made in factory agreements in future.

Election Malpractices

637. In the survey referred to earlier which the Government Social Survey conducted for us the 494 trade union members were also asked: " Do you know of any elections in your union which were not carried out fairly? " Four of the 494 said that they did: and in each case referred to a union branch election. In two of these cases it was considered that the elections were unfair simply because too few people were present. Of the other two members, however, one said: " It was a rigged ballot "; and the other: " They counted more votes than there were people to vote ". On the evidence of this survey, there is no general disquiet among trade union members concerning the honesty with which trade union elections are carried out. Election malpractices however occur from time to time. Public attention was drawn to this by the unique case of *Byrne and Chapple v. Foulkes, Haxell and Others* involving the Electrical Trades Union.

638. The method of holding elections is laid down in unions' rules; and while some of the larger trade unions lay down in detail the procedure to be followed, most unions prescribe such procedure in outline only, leaving the detail to be filled in according to practice or custom, or to individual discretion.

639. Some unions make express provision against the contingency that malpractice may occur in the conduct of an election. Thus the rules of the Amalgamated Union of Building Trade Workers provide for a special scrutiny of the votes, and the punishment of any member who falsifies, alters, abstracts, withholds or tampers with forms, or who wilfully mis-states the number of votes. The Amalgamated Engineering Union is one of the unions which has detailed rules designed to ensure the proper conduct of elections: and, as mentioned above, the Electrical Trades Union has in recent years adopted the system of having elections supervised by an outside body—the Electoral Reform Society.

172

640. No rules, however elaborate, would be proof against organised, fraudulent and determined " rigging " of an election such as occurred in the case of the Electrical Trades Union in 1959. But a good deal could be done, we think, by filling gaps in existing rules to reduce the possibility of election irregularities. Dependent as trade unions are on voluntary labour to a large extent, it cannot be expected that their elections will be conducted impeccably in every detail; but a more comprehensive set of rules, and some right of redress in cases of serious irregularity, would provide more adequate assurance of well-conducted elections than exists at present.

641. It is not practicable to prescribe a set of model election rules which would be suitable for every trade union; but there would seem to be no reason why a trade union should not define in reasonable detail in its rules the method of holding elections. Such reasonable detail would cover such matters as the notification of vacancies, the qualification of candidates, the making of nominations, the content of election addresses, the issue and control of ballot papers, the method and supervision of voting, the counting and scrutiny of votes, the declaration and notification of the result. The rules might also specify some officer or officers to be in charge at each stage, and a returning officer to have supervision over the whole election.

642. At present, the Registrar of Friendly Societies has power to insist as a condition of registration under the Trade Union Act of 1871 that the rules of a trade union should provide for certain matters; but these do not include the procedure for the conduct of elections. Whatever be the conditions for registration for the future, we think that a change in the requirements of the law is desirable in this respect and we make suggestions in the following section.

643. The qualifications of candidates and the method of conducting the ballot will normally be among matters governed by the rules of a trade union, whether in detail or in outline only: and since these rules embody the contract of membership, an infraction of them will give an aggrieved member the right to seek redress in the courts, section 4 of the Trade Union Act 1871 having no application to such procedures (see for example *Watson v. Smith* [1941] 2 All ER 725). In the case of *Byrne and Chapple v. Foulkes, Haxell and Others* the action of the complaining members was founded in tort, namely civil conspiracy.

644. But whether the proceedings be in contract or in tort they are likely to be difficult, expensive and, on occasion, protracted. *Byrne and Chapple v. Foulkes, Haxell and Others,* while exceptional in these respects, lasted 42 days, and the total costs were estimated at £80,000. Some less difficult and less expensive method of redress should, we think, be available to a trade union member who has a genuine grievance as to the conduct of a trade union election.

645. For a satisfactory procedure, two elements are required: provision for inquiry into the facts of an allegation of election malpractices, and provision for a trial. Complaints alleging irregular conduct of a trade union election should in our view be dealt with in the first instance by the Registrar, who should be able if necessary to send an inspector equipped with the

necessary powers to make a full inquiry into the facts in any case where a complaint appears to make this necessary. It might be that in the light of the inspector's report the Registrar would be able to obtain a satisfactory settlement of the case on a voluntary basis. However, should this prove impossible, the case should then be brought to trial before the proposed independent review body. That body, the complainant and the defendant union would all have available to them the inspector's report on the case, and the facts as stated in that report would be open to challenge should they be disputed. If the review body found the allegation made out, it would, after giving its reasons, make such order as it thought required by the facts, either declaring some person to be elected other than the one declared to have been elected in the impugned election, or declaring the election void and ordering a fresh election to be held under such conditions as it thought necessary to ensure its proper conduct. If the allegation is not made out, or if it is made out but the irregularity was technical and made no difference to the result of the election, the review body would have power to dismiss the complaint or make no order at all.

646. We suggest that the above procedure should be available to deal with complaints concerning any election to office in a trade union above branch level.

647. At present the Registrar of Friendly Societies has power under the Trade Union Act 1913 and the Trade Union (Amalgamations, etc.) Act 1964 to hear complaints from members of trade unions about infringement of the political fund rules and about irregularities alleged to have been committed in the procedure for amalgamation. We think that it would be desirable to transfer jurisdiction in such cases also to the proposed independent review body.

TRADE UNION RULES

648. We have said that it is very desirable that trade union rule-books should be clear and unambiguous, but that they generally fall far short of a satisfactory standard in these respects. The current requirements as to the rules of a registered trade union are that they should " contain provisions in respect of " certain matters, which are in short:

(a) name and place of business;

(b) objects, purposes for which funds may be applied, conditions of any assured benefits, and any fines and forfeitures;

(c) manner of making and altering rules;

(d) appointment and removal of a general committee of management, a trustee or trustees, treasurer and other officers;

(e) investment of funds and periodical audit;

(f) inspection of the books and names of members by persons having an interest in the funds;

(g) manner of dissolution.

In addition there are the special requirements in relation to the political activities of trade unions which we deal with in Chapter XIV.

174

649. We think that the requirements can and should be revised with a view to ensuring better safeguards for individual members, but without impairing the freedom which trade unions ought to enjoy to frame rules to meet their own circumstances. Our recommendations are set out in the following paragraphs.

Admission

650. The rules should state who is qualified for admission to the trade union, or any separate section of the trade union. They should be framed in such a way as to avoid discriminating arbitrarily against any type of applicant, but unions must be allowed to retain discretion in deciding whom they should admit. The rules should also state who has the power to consider and decide applications for admission; that applicants refused admission should have a right of appeal to the executive committee of the union and should be so informed at the time of refusal of admission; and that the executive committee has the power to admit applicants where an appeal is upheld. (We note that the rules of the Electrical Trades Union for example are in line with this requirement.)

Discipline

651. A separate rule or section of the rule-book should:

(i) set out the offences for which the union is entitled under the rules to expel or take other disciplinary action and the penalties applicable for each of those offences;

(ii) prescribe the procedure or procedures for the hearing of cases in which offences against the rules are alleged, such procedure or procedures to comply with the rules of natural justice;

(iii) prescribe the procedure or procedures for the hearing of appeals against the imposition of penalties, which again should comply with the rules of natural justice.

Disputes between a Union and a Member

652. The rules should also prescribe a procedure for settling disputes between a member and the union or an officer of the union, either generally or in relation only to the payment of subscriptions and benefits.

Elections

653. Rules should prescribe procedures for elections, which should deal with the following matters:

(i)   notification of vacancies and qualifications of candidates;

(ii) making of nominations;

(iii) canvassing and the content of election addresses, where these are permitted;

(iv) in elections in which a ballot is required—

    (a) issue and control of ballot papers;

    (b) method, and supervision, of voting;

    (c) counting and scrutiny of votes;

    (d) declaration and notification of the result; and

(v) designation of officer or officers responsible for the conduct of the election.

Shop Stewards

654. The requirements as to rules in relation to elections should include the rules for the election of shop stewards (or other workplace representatives), if the union has them. In addition the rules should prescribe:

(i) their term of office; and

(ii) the authority charged with, and the manner of, issue and withdrawal of credentials.

(We discuss more fully the question of rules relating to shop stewards in the following chapter.)

655. The Chief Registrar of Friendly Societies suggested to us that registered unions should be required by statute:

(i) to employ professional auditors if they have more than 500 members or funds of more than £5,000; and

(ii) to have their superannuation funds for schemes covering members, if they possess such schemes, valued every five years, and to publish the report to members; also to have any new superannuation scheme certified as solvent by an actuary on its inception.

We endorse these suggestions.

656. The requirements as to rules of registered trade unions will henceforth be rather more extensive, and will call for more supervision on the part of the Registrar, than in the past. The Registrar already advises unions informally on the drafting and re-drafting of rules, and we hope that this beneficial practice will continue. The possibility exists however that disagreement may at times arise between the Registrar and a trade union as to whether its rules comply with the revised requirements of the law. We think that such disagreements should be referred for settlement by the independent review body whose establishment we propose.

657. The rules of many trade unions will need revision in order to comply with new requirements. We suggest that existing trade unions should be allowed a reasonable period in which to accomplish the revision.

THE REVIEW BODY AND THE REGISTRAR

658. We envisage a review body consisting of three members, of whom two would be chosen from a panel of trade unionists appointed by the Secretary of State for Employment and Productivity after consultation with the TUC, and one would be a lawyer who would act as chairman. Members should receive reasonable remuneration for the occasions on which they sit. A small supporting staff would be required. The Secretary of State would have power by statutory instrument to make regulations for the review body's procedure. It would for example be necessary to give the review body powers in connection with requiring the attendance of witnesses and the production of documents and to make it clear whether the final decision on a point of law should rest with the chairman.

659. If the recommendations we make in this chapter are accepted the review body will have jurisdiction over the following:

(i) cases of alleged unfair imposition of penalties resulting in substantial injustice; and cases of alleged arbitrary rejection of an application for admission to a trade union, or a particular section of a trade union;

(ii) cases based on alleged breach of the rules of the union or violation of natural justice (see paragraph 665 below);

(iii) complaints of election malpractices; and complaints under the Trade Union Act 1913 and the Trade Union (Amalgamations, etc.) Act 1964;

(iv) cases in which disagreement arises between the Registrar and a trade union as to whether its rules comply with the requirements of the law.

660. We envisage that all complaints by individuals would be addressed in the first instance to the Registrar, who would have the duty of advising complainants and of promoting the amicable settlement of the matters of which they complain. The Registrar is already able to dispose informally of most of the complaints arising within his existing jurisdiction. It is important that ordinary trade unionists should feel that they can turn to the Registrar for expert and impartial help when they need it.

661. In cases of arbitrary refusal of admission or expulsion the monetary compensation which the review body should have power to award to a successful appellant would in general be measured by the loss occasioned to him by the action of which he complained. But it should be subject to a maximum. It would not be feasible or right, for example, to award in respect of arbitrary non-admission to a union controlling a pre-entry closed shop compensation on the basis of a life-long loss of earnings. The possibility of a different job should be taken into account. A limit of compensation should therefore be fixed. This should, in our view, be in line with the maximum we propose for unfair dismissal. We suggest therefore that in all cases where damages consist wholly or mainly of loss of earnings, actual or prospective, the maximum compensation should be a sum equal to the amount of earnings which the successful appellant could reasonably have expected to earn for two years had the act complained of not occurred, subject to the imposition of an upper limit of £40 a week on the reckoning (and taking into account any sums actually earned or which should reasonably have been earned since the right to bring a complaint arose). Compensation in other cases falling under paragraph 659 (i) will ordinarily amount to far less, for example an amount equal to the sum a member has been unjustly fined, and should in no case be permitted to exceed the equivalent of two years' earnings as aforesaid.

662. Some check would be required to prevent misuse of the procedure by vexatious litigants. It might be provided that no such second or subsequent application by the same persons should be heard without the leave of the review body: and additionally that on the hearing of any such successive application all previous awards of compensation should be taken into account to the extent that the review body thought proper.

663. It is desirable that appellants should exhaust whatever remedies are available to them under the trade union's rules before lodging a complaint with the review body, unless to do this would involve undue delay or damage. It

should therefore be provided that an appeal may be lodged with the independent review body immediately the imposition of the penalty is announced, but that the hearing should be stayed in those cases where the trade union's rules provide for an appeal and for the proceedings by way of such appeal to be completed within three months or less from the time when the penalty was imposed. Proceedings before the review body should also be stayed where the rules of the union provide for the suspension of any penalty pending the completion of its own appeals procedure. In these latter cases however the appellant should be entitled to ask the review body to hear his appeal if long delay is likely, or is being encountered, in the operation of the union's own appeal procedure.

664. Awards made by the review body could be made enforceable by being registered in the appropriate county court and thereafter enforced as if they were judgments of that court.

665. Members of trade unions at present have the right (subject to section 4 of the 1871 Act) to bring an action against a trade union based on alleged breach of the rules or violation of natural justice in the High Court. The independent review body whose establishment we propose in this chapter will have an expert knowledge of internal trade union affairs, and we recommend that it should be given jurisdiction to try any case based on alleged breach of trade union rules or violation of natural justice. Its jurisdiction would be concurrent with that of the High Court, the plaintiff having a right to exercise an option, with one exception: this is that where a trade union member alleges both that a sanction imposed upon him by the union was in violation of union rules or of natural justice and that it was in any event unfair he would be obliged to bring his action before the review body, so that the possibility would be avoided that two sets of proceedings based on essentially the same facts might be brought simultaneously in two different courts. If proceedings have been initiated in the High Court and before the review body as well, the High Court should remit the case to the review body (except where the plaintiff is entitled to, and has asked for, trial by jury).

666. We think that it will be of advantage to trade unions as well as to trade union members that the review body should have the extended jurisdiction we propose because it will enable cases to be disposed of with the minimum of expense and formality. This will be all the more important if section 4 of the Trade Union Act 1871 is to be repealed. There should be a right of appeal to the High Court from the review body by way of case stated on a point of law, provided that the leave of the High Court is first obtained.

667. Contracting out of the right to invoke the jurisdiction of the review body should be prohibited.

668. The independent review body should have power to award costs in its discretion. Legal aid might be granted to individuals who satisfy the regulations of the Legal Aid Scheme.

669. We make further comment and recommendations on the office and functions of the Registrar in the section of Chapter XIV dealing with registration.

Chapter XII
TRADE UNIONS

670. In Chapter III we say that while trade unions have played their part in sustaining the facade of industry-wide bargaining they are not primarily responsible for the decline in its importance and its divergence from the actual conduct of industrial relations; certain features of union structure and government have however produced problems, especially in the way in which they have fostered the autonomy and power of work groups and encouraged a divorce between trade union members and the formal institutions of union authority.

671. Consequently it is necessary to consider what changes in union structure will be required if trade unions are to play their full share in the reconstruction of industrial relations which we envisage. This can best be begun by asking two questions. First, what can be done to reduce multi-unionism? Secondly, what improvements are possible in the internal relationships between shop stewards, work groups and the union? When these questions are answered it will be possible to consider whether there are other ways in which trade unions need to adapt themselves to meet the demands of a more ordered system of industrial relations.

THE REDUCTION OF MULTI-UNIONISM

Two Types of Multi-Unionism

672. It is useful first to distinguish two particular types of multi-unionism. First, there is the common situation in which each one of the main occupational groups in the factory is organised by a different union—e.g. technicians, supervisors, clerks, operatives and various craft groups. Its essential characteristic is that while there are many different unions each has a monopoly of a given group of workers. The second type of multi-unionism arises when there is more than one union competing for membership within a given group of workers within a factory. Both types of multi-unionism are found together, but the second is less common than the first and mainly affects non-craft workers.

Industrial Unionism

673. The most frequently canvassed solution for both types of multi-unionism is industrial unionism, i.e. one union for all employees in the same industry regardless of occupation. In theory industrial unionism would have a number of advantages. Sectional claims on behalf of different occupational groups within a particular factory could be more easily harmonised, and it might be easier for the union concerned to conclude effective company and factory agreements. Demarcation problems between craft groups would be more easy to solve and the temptation for unions to seek to out-do each other in militancy or obduracy would be eliminated. There would also be no need for shop stewards from different unions within the same plant or company to form " unofficial " or " unconstitutional " joint shop stewards' committees.

179

All the union's members in a given factory could be organised into one branch, with appropriate sections for different occupations and groups.

674. On the other hand a number of reservations may be made. In practice sectional claims can still arise within so-called industrial unions. Demarcation problems can exist within one union—as is still sometimes demonstrated by the Boilermakers' Society. The absence of competition between unions is no guarantee of responsibility or against informal, unconstitutional, shop floor organisation divorced from formal union influence—as can be proved from the example of the docks. In other words, while it is arguable that industrial unionism would help management and unions to tackle these problems, it would not necessarily solve them.

675. There are also a number of ways in which industrial unionism might encourage less desirable developments. Many workers, such as craftsmen, clerks or technicians, have an obvious interest in combining on an occupational rather than an industrial basis, so that they are free to take their transferable skills from job to job while remaining within the same union. Occupational unions, for groups of this kind, may in fact facilitate and encourage labour mobility. It is by no means obvious that industrial unionism is appropriate for such expanding and mobile groups as electricians, draughtsmen or skilled engineers.

676. Special problems arise if industrial unionism is taken to the point where it includes white-collar workers. White-collar workers appear to be more readily organised on an occupational basis. Moreover an industrial union which represents workers in an industry which is contracting must inevitably decline along with the industry. By contrast a more widely based union, which has, in effect, diversified its organisational activities, has more chance to survive, and for this reason may be more willing to agree to changes involving reductions in its membership in particular industries. It can also be argued that new technologies are breaking down conventional industrial classifications, and many large companies now straddle traditional industry boundaries.

677. These are mainly theoretical difficulties; the really decisive objection to industrial unionism is a practical one. However defined, industrial unionism would involve a drastic upheaval in the structure of almost every major union in the country and virtually all expanding unions. It would, for example, mean the dismemberment of craft unions and of both the giant general unions (the Transport and General Workers' Union and the General and Municipal Workers' Union) and the cutting off of large sections of the membership of the Amalgamated Union of Engineers and Foundry Workers, the Union of Shop, Distributive and Allied Workers and the Electrical Trades Union. It would entail a reversal of what Mr. John Hughes has called the " natural growth pattern " of British unions[1]. For, as he shows, growth in the last ten years has largely been concentrated among the large and medium-sized " open unions " which " characteristically take a broad definition of their sector of operation and the occupational grades they organise ".

[1]Research Paper No. 5 (Part 1), John Hughes, *Trade Union Structure and Government*, HMSO 1967.

Many of these unions have recently taken an increasingly wide view of their areas of recruitment, and have extended their activities into new industries and processes. This development may well result in still more multi-unionism and it is unlikely to produce a move towards one union for the industry. As Hughes concludes: " There is no sign of any general evolution towards industrial unionism."

678. It is certain therefore that the trade unions will not voluntarily adopt the attainment of industrial unionism as it exists in the Federal Republic of Germany, for example, as their objective; and indeed the Trades Union Congress recently rejected it. Nobody has seriously suggested to us that this reform can be imposed compulsorily by means of legislation, which would mean an end of free trade unions. It is necessary to seek the benefits which are claimed for industrial unionism in other ways.

More Mergers between Unions

679. As we show in Chapter II, although there are 574 trade unions, over four-fifths of all trade unionists belong to the 38 largest unions; and three members out of ten are in membership of the three largest unions, the Transport and General Workers' Union, the Amalgamated Union of Engineers and Foundry Workers and the General and Municipal Workers' Union. The total number of unions is declining, and there is some indication that membership is being concentrated in the larger organisations, but it is obvious that a very real contribution could be made to the problem of multi-unionism if some of the more important and wide-ranging organisations could be induced to combine with each other.

680. In fact there has been a movement towards more amalgamations and transfers of engagement in the last few years. Altogether 53 trade unions have been involved in mergers of one kind or another since 1964. In some cases the mechanics of mergers have been assisted by the Trade Union (Amalgamations, etc.) Act 1964.

681. To take an example in the craft field, the boilermakers, shipwrights and blacksmiths have amalgamated into one single union, the Amalgamated Society of Boilermakers, Shipwrights and Blacksmiths. There have been important mergers among trade unions in the printing industry. These include the formation in 1965 of the Society of Graphical and Allied Trades (as a result of a merger between the National Union of Printing, Bookbinding and Paper Workers and the National Society of Operative Printers and Assistants) and the amalgamation between the Electrotypers and the National Graphical Association. The Foundry Workers' Union has amalgamated with the Amalgamated Engineering Union to form a union with over 1,200,000 members. The Heating and Domestic Engineers have merged with the Sheet Metal Workers and Coppersmiths to establish a National Union of Sheet Metal Workers. In the white-collar field the Association of Scientific Workers has joined with the Association of Supervisory Staffs, Executives and Technicians to form the Association of Scientific, Technical and Managerial Staffs. Other amalgamation movements and " transfers of engagements " have taken place in building, entertainment and the civil service. Taken together these developments represent a readiness to reconsider existing

structural arrangements which is without precedent in recent years, and entirely to be welcomed. Can this movement be accelerated and in what direction are advances most needed?

682. We consider that there is scope for many more mergers between unions. In particular, it seems to us that problems caused by a multiplicity of unions organising in individual factories would be considerably eased in a number of important industries if certain groups of craft unions could be induced to amalgamate. This is particularly true of engineering and of construction. In both there have been important amalgamations in recent years but a number of small but relatively powerful organisations have chosen to stay aloof. It seems to us that it would be practicable as well as useful to work towards the goal of one or at most two craft unions for the great bulk of craftsmen in both industries. In printing, both the National Board for Prices and Incomes[1] and a court of inquiry under the chairmanship of Lord Cameron[2] have urged the need for the amalgamation of all the unions in the industry, both craft and non-craft, into a single union, and we agree that this is highly desirable.

The Elimination of Competition

683. Apart from mergers, the most practical way to reduce multi-unionism is by agreements between unions on recruiting rights and negotiating rights. Where, for example, unions compete for membership among workers of the same grade in a single factory, as is not uncommon among non-craft workers in the engineering industry, it would be possible for the unions mainly concerned, the Amalgamated Union of Engineering and Foundry Workers, the Transport and General Workers' Union and the General and Municipal Workers' Union, to agree that in each factory only one of them would have the right to recruit among these grades in future. Subsequently existing members of the other unions might be persuaded to transfer to the union which has the recruitment rights, and these other unions would be able to give up their rights of representation. The success of the agreement would of course depend on matching losses and gains for each union. The principle is also capable of application on a wider basis. In instances where separate craft unions are not involved it could lead to a single union for manual workers in each factory. It could also be extended to transfers of rights within companies, to produce a single union for each grade of worker, or for all manual workers, throughout a multi-plant company. There are even cases, especially where the two great general unions are concerned, in which transfers of rights between industries might be achieved.

684. Similar arrangements are possible in the white-collar field, but here the opportunity for rationalisation is most readily presented when recognition is being sought. Suppose it were accepted by the three major unions aiming to recruit clerks over a wide range of private manufacturing industry—the Clerical and Administrative Workers' Union, the Transport and General Workers' Union and the General and Municipal Workers' Union—that they would seek to implement the principle of one union for one grade of

---

[1]National Board for Prices and Incomes, Report No. 2, Cmnd. 2750, para. 65.
[2]Cmnd. 3184, paras. 250-1.

work when seeking recognition. It would mean that each union would respect the right of the other to sign an " exclusive jurisdiction " agreement in cases where it was the first to recruit a group of clerks in a particular concern. In instances where two or more unions had members, a form of third party arbitration might be agreed to decide who had the right to demand exclusive jurisdiction rights; the obvious body to perform this function would be the TUC. To avoid the need for arbitration as far as possible the unions concerned would try to allocate future recruitment areas between them in advance.

685.   The major responsibility for reducing multi-unionism falls to the unions themselves, although they will need the co-operation of employers where questions of recognition are involved. Where progress is meeting obstacles the Industrial Relations Commission will be able to play a most important part. The Commission's recommendations can bring persuasion to bear on the trade unions involved and can also greatly influence employers' recognition policies, which as we show in Chapter V are of great importance especially for the development of white-collar unionism. We now turn to the part which the TUC can play.

The TUC and the Reduction of Multi-Unionism

686.   The Bridlington principles for the avoidance of disputes between unions were embodied in a resolution passed by the 1939 TUC. They are primarily designed to avoid competition between unions, and that has been one of their effects. Thus Clause 1 provides that unions which come in frequent contact with each other should consider the possibility of joint working arrangements, the definition of spheres of influence, and conditions for transferring members. Other clauses are designed to prevent unions from poaching members from each other, for example members who are under discipline or in arrears of contributions. It is also provided, in Clause 5, that: " No union shall commence organising activities at any establishment or undertaking in respect of any grade or grades of workers in which another union has the majority of workers employed and negotiates wages and conditions, unless by arrangement with that union." This clause contributes to the elimination of competition by helping to prevent the entry of new unions to areas where there are already recognised organisations with members. In general the limitations on poaching set out in the Bridlington principles are observed and partly as a result of it a number of joint working agreements have been concluded between unions.

687.   Under Rule 12 of the TUC's constitution, the General Council has a duty to use its influence to promote a settlement of disputes between unions. A Disputes Committee of the General Council considers disputes " upon application from an affiliated organisation ". In its evidence to us the TUC stated that over the previous four years unions had reported an average of 25 cases to it annually; an analysis of 100 cases set out in the TUC's evidence indicates that, while nearly half of the cases referred to it are withdrawn or disposed of without a formal meeting under TUC auspices, a very high proportion of the remainder are settled by the TUC's machinery. Rule 13 of the TUC's constitution gives the General Council power to direct members to desist from activities

183

G

detrimental to the trade union movement or contrary to the TUC's declared principles and, failing obedience, to suspend them from membership until the next Congress. The ultimate sanction, which is very rarely used, is expulsion by Congress.

688. When therefore the Bridlington principles have failed to prevent unions from competing with each other and coming into dispute, the matter may be referred to the TUC's disputes machinery by either union involved. The Disputes Committee is free to consider the case on its merits but is bound to be influenced if the conduct of either union appears to have been at variance with the Bridlington principles.

689. Yet although the Bridlington principles have done a great deal to prevent inter-union disputes over conflicting membership rights they have not eliminated all forms of competition, nor were they designed to do so. They are a code of conduct which unions are advised to follow in order to avoid what experience has shown to be the more common causes of inter-union conflicts about membership—not an instrument for achieving trade union reform. The question arises whether the TUC needs to take further measures to help to solve some of the problems which remain. For example, if no union can claim a majority of membership and a recognition agreement, the Bridlington principles will not indicate which of two contesting unions should have priority. The Organisation Committee of the General Council might be able to assist with the difficulty, but Congress has laid down no clear policy to guide it. Nor has it laid down any principle which would prevent a union which can show that it has obtained recruitment and recognition rights in the past from asserting a right to remain even in a situation where its rival may have recruited the great majority of workers.

690. The TUC has for many years given explicit encouragement to joint working arrangements for the elimination of competition. We fully appreciate that in the end the power to make and enforce such agreements rests with individual unions, and that in this respect a special responsibility lies with the three largest unions in the country. Through the activities of their recently-established closer working committee they could make a contribution to the rationalisation of trade union structure second to none. Nevertheless, we think that the TUC should intensify its efforts to encourage the unions concerned to adopt joint working arrangements in particular instances.

691. Secondly, we think that the TUC should consider adopting the principle of " one union for one grade of work within one factory " as a guide for the future development of union structure. If it did so, there are two practical steps the TUC might then take. First, it could bring together suitable groups of unions involved in problems of overlapping and competition in particular industries and companies. The TUC's job would be to act as an honest broker, safeguarding each union's overall interests while seeking to move in the direction of one union for one grade of work in one factory by the creation of closer working agreements. Secondly, the TUC might seek to further the aim of one union for one grade of work within one factory in circumstances where it thought that its intervention might prove acceptable to the parties. Thus a union competing with another for recognition rights could ask the TUC to

pronounce upon its claim, and say whether it ought to be granted an exclusive jurisdiction agreement. Similarly, a union with a majority of membership in a particular grade could ask the TUC to consider whether it ought to be accorded exclusive recruitment rights for the future.

MULTI-UNION CO-OPERATION

692. However rapid the progress made in reducing multi-unionism it will continue for the foreseeable future to exist in many factories and companies. It is therefore necessary to consider whether there are ways of alleviating its effects, especially insofar as they affect work groups and shop stewards and the role which we envisage for the latter in a reconstructed system of industrial relations.

693. In practice multi-unionism evokes inter-union co-operation on the workshop floor. Some idea of the extent of this co-operation can be derived from our workshop surveys. Two-thirds of the joint management-shop steward committees which existed in the firms interviewed were multi-union in character; 39 per cent of stewards said that they had attended workplace meetings with stewards of other unions and 12 per cent said that they had been to meetings attended by stewards of different unions from different places of work. The need for multi-union steward meetings was clearly demonstrated in the answers given to questions concerning the frequency of multi-union grievances and claims. When stewards employed in multi-union situations were asked how often multi-union issues arose, only 21 per cent said " never "; 22 per cent said " very often ", and 19 per cent said " fairly often ".

694. Yet, as our first Research Paper demonstrated, most of these multi-union meetings take place outside the formal framework of union rules, and in some cases it is arguable that in attending them, and abiding by decisions reached, stewards and their members are acting unconstitutionally. The problem of multi-union co-operation outside the framework of union rules is most obvious in the large multi-plant " combine committee ", formed where stewards from many different unions come to feel the need for some form of contact with others of their kind in other plants. As our first Research Paper put it:

> " It is increasingly argued by shop stewards employed in multi-plant firms that the demands of workshop democracy and the need to develop a common response to employer initiatives require the development of regular contacts between work groups in each plant, organised on a multi-union basis. Since unions are not at the moment able to provide such facilities officially a growing number of stewards in multi-plant firms attempt to bridge the gap by forming unofficial ' combine committees '."[1]

695. We think that unions organising in such situations should themselves provide official and constitutionally recognised committees to perform many of the functions now carried out by these unofficial gatherings. Full-time trade union officials concerned should attend their meetings and discuss with leading stewards the formulation of shop floor policy and the way to handle multi-union grievances and claims within the plant or company. Because of

[1]Research Paper No. 1, W. E. J. McCarthy, *The Role of Shop Stewards in British Industrial Relations*, p.52, para. 84.

the constitutional problems involved, the best plan would probably be for the executives of the unions concerned to begin by authorising the establishment of *ad hoc* consultative committees at national level to cover the more important multi-plant companies—especially those where the stewards themselves have already found it necessary to develop their own unofficial contacts through informal " combine committees ". Consultative committees of this kind would have an important part to play in the negotiation and administration of satisfactory company and factory agreements on the lines we recommend in Chapter IV.

WORK GROUPS AND UNION GOVERNMENT

696. Regardless of the number of unions in the plant, we believe that the processes of union government should be modified to accommodate shop stewards and work groups more adequately than they now do. It is often said that the best way to accomplish this is to base the primary unit of union government—the branch—on the place of work. This means abolishing the system of geographically-based branches which bring together workers from many different factories who happen to live in the same area or town. The incomplete evidence of our first Research Paper on this matter can now be supplemented by the findings of our workshop relations survey. It seems that as things now stand the advantages of the factory-based branch can be exaggerated. Although trade union members are slightly more likely to go to union meetings in factory-based branches, there is no difference so far as stewards' attendance is concerned. It is also clear that the factory-based branch does not provide an effective substitute for the informal and unofficial workplace gathering. If full advantage is to be drawn from branches based on the factory, therefore, they must aim to hold their meetings at the place of work. Indeed, where workshop questions are at issue, meetings might on occasion and with safeguards be held in working hours. It was for example a recommendation of the Devlin Committee that in the docks, at least for the period of carrying through modernisation, periodic meetings between full-time union officials and union members might be permitted under proper safeguards during working hours.

697. However, there are two conditions to such a development. First, employers must be willing to grant facilities for formal union meetings, in much the same way as many now grant permission for the calling of informal shop floor gatherings. They must also be willing to allow full-time trade union officials the right to attend these meetings, just as many of them now allow chief shop stewards to attend. It is reasonable that employers should be expected to co-operate, since what we suggest will counter what many employers see as an undue lack of influence of trade unions over their members.

698. The second condition is the revision of union rules on shop stewards. In many rule-books shop stewards, or their counterparts, are mentioned only because the union relies upon them to collect subscriptions. The representative functions of stewards are referred to with surprising infrequency. The rules of the Transport and General Workers' Union and of the Union of Shop, Distributive and Allied Workers, for example, say nothing about such

186

functions. The rules of the Amalgamated Engineering Union leave it to the District Committees to define the powers of shop stewards with the Executive Council's approval " subject to national agreements ". Very few unions make any attempt, in their rules, to provide for the calling of shop floor meetings or seek to prescribe their constitutional powers. The practice of issuing shop stewards' handbooks is no more than a partial remedy for this reticence in the rules. In our previous chapter we make suggestions as to what should be the statutory requirements concerning rules relating to shop stewards (see paragraph 654). If rules are to be really satisfactory they must reach a far higher standard than it would be right or practicable to prescribe by law. We suggest that trade unions should consider covering the following matters at least in their rules:

(1) *The way in which stewards are elected.* Doubtless in many cases formal election will not be necessary, and the results of our workshop survey indicate that the majority of stewards are returned unopposed. Nevertheless, if stewards are to become an integral part of formal structure of union authority provision should be made for the holding of an election where there is more than one candidate for the job.

(2) *The term of office.* No standard period can be recommended in view of the great variety of circumstances which may affect the matter. Wherever possible, however, the period should be long enough to enable the steward to settle down in the job and acquire useful experience.

(3) *The filling of casual vacancies.*

(4) *The bounds of the shop steward's jurisdiction.* The rules should try to give more guidance than is now usual about the action which a steward may take on his own authority or as a result of a meeting of members. This means establishing the relationship between such a meeting and the branch. It should be made clear that neither is entitled to take decisions which are at variance with those arising out of factory, company or industry-wide agreements to which the union is party.

(5) *Relations with other union officials and offices.* In factory-based branches the offices of senior steward and steward should be combined wherever possible with those of branch secretary and branch committee member. The relationship of the branch to its local full-time union officer should also be made clear, together with his right to attend branch meetings and inform those present of union policy and advice.

(6) *The place of the shop steward in the union's organisation.* There should be a clear statement as to the authority within the union to which the shop steward is finally responsible and which can in case of need suspend or dismiss him from office.

(7) *Multi-union committees.* Provision should be made where necessary to ensure that the rules do not hinder the setting up of official multi-union committees of the kind referred to in paragraph 695 above.

699. Such rules will make it reasonable to expect stewards (and their members) to act constitutionally, since they will at last be able to perform their functions within the compass of the rules. They will help to create a

situation in which trade unions could properly be expected to discipline the small minority of shop stewards who at times abuse their position.

OTHER CHANGES

700. The effect of our suggestions so far should be to improve the range and quality of union services to members. But there are other ways in which these services will require improvement and expansion if British unions are to make the most of their future opportunities. We now discuss the most important of these.

More Trade Union Officials

701. Because it has been the tradition of the British trade union movement to rely heavily on the services of voluntary local officers there has always been a relatively low proportion of full-time officers to members compared with other countries. There are about 3,000 full-time trade union officials in Britain, which represents about one union official for every 3,800 trade union members. Equally reliable figures are not available for all other comparable countries, but the evidence suggests that in the United States the ratio of officers to members is of the order of 1 to 1,400 and in the Federal Republic of Germany as low as 1 to 800. Both Italy and France appear to have twice as many officers per member as we do.

702. It is clear that there are wide variations in the ratio of union officials to members in different unions in Britain, even among unions of comparable size organising within a similar range of industries. Some idea of the range among major unions is provided by the table below:

Number of Members per Full-Time Union Officer in Certain Trade Unions — 1966

Union of Shop, Distributive and Allied Workers	1,978
Transport and General Workers' Union	2,762
General and Municipal Workers' Union	3,868
Electrical Trades Union	4,027
National and Local Government Officers' Association ...	4,509
Amalgamated Engineering Union	6,807

703. To judge from our workshop relations surveys these variations in officer/member ratios are also often accompanied by equally marked variations in the number of shop stewards per union official in different unions. This can be seen from the table on the following page. The table also shows that there are very wide variations in the proportion of stewards regularly contacted in different unions, and there appears to be some connection between the proportion contacted and the ratio of officials to stewards. The recent rapid increase in the number of shop stewards of the Amalgamated Engineering Union has not been met by an equivalent increase in full-time union officials. This helps to explain the relatively small proportion of stewards in this union who claimed to have seen a full-time official during the previous twelve months. Our survey indicates that in the six unions covered district officers work on average 60 hours a week. The evidence there-

fore is that there is already a shortage of full-time officers, at any rate in some unions.

FULL-TIME LOCAL OFFICERS: SHOP STEWARD RESPONSIBILITIES AND CONTACTS

Name of Union	Average No. of Stewards for whom each Officer is Responsible	Average No. of Stewards Contacted in last 4 Weeks	Proportion of Shop Stewards Contacted in last 4 Weeks
Transport and General Workers' Union	120	96	80%
Amalgamated Engineering Union	477	132	28%
General and Municipal Workers' Union	169	65	38%
Electrical Trades Union	232	94	41%
Amalgamated Union of Building Trade Workers	33	30	91%
All unions	172	89	52%

Source: Research Paper No. 10 *on Shop Stewards and Workshop Relations.*

704. If the system of formal factory and company bargaining which we envisage is to come about there will be a need for far more frequent and regular contact between shop stewards and their officials. Already the experience of trade union officers responsible for major productivity agreements has been that they take up a great deal of time, and that they sometimes involve frequent meetings with stewards and their members in different parts of a plant or company. In the case of the British Oxygen agreements, for example, months were spent on negotiation and consultation at company and plant level. In addition the union officials involved had to undertake a great deal of propaganda work. After a review of the impact of such agreements on the volume of work of union officials, the conclusion was reached in our Research Paper on the subject that:

> " Productivity bargaining tends to commit unions heavily in terms of the time and effort of its officials. . . . In so far as productivity bargains at the level of plants or undertakings become more common the greater the strain this will put on trade union resources. This is a most important point. There is no doubt that if productivity bargaining is to become more general it will be essential for trade unions to increase the numbers of their officials." [1]

705. All the evidence suggests therefore that the reconstruction of industrial relations which we advocate will require a substantial addition to the number of full-time officers of trade unions.

[1]Research Paper No. 4, *Productivity Bargaining*, HMSO 1967, p.29, para. 132.

189

Trade Union Salaries

706. It is often suggested that it will become progressively more difficult to recruit trade union officials of the necessary calibre unless substantial improvements are made in their remuneration and conditions of employment. There are now greater educational opportunities for talented pupils, some of whom might otherwise have left school at an early age and found outlets for their capacities in service to the trade union movement. Other careers are now open to them when they leave school or university. At the same time unions are feeling the need for qualified specialists as training officers, research officers and information systems experts. Competent applicants will expect competitive salaries.

707. However, the only systematic attempt to investigate the subject so far[1] found little justification for these fears. There were few signs of a shortage of competent candidates for office, especially in unions with well-designed selection systems. The educational standards appeared to be rising rapidly, and the numbers of specialists increasing. On the other hand there were considerable variations in union salaries and career prospects, with no clear notion of the standards by which they should be judged.

708. This study was carried out ten years ago. We ourselves have not been able to conduct a comprehensive survey including all aspects of remuneration, hours of work, job descriptions and methods of recruitment. In any case the reconstruction of industrial relations will alter the situation radically. We think that unions must reconsider their needs both in respect of numbers of officers and their calibre in the light of the changes which follow our report. There is also a need for a general investigation of the subject and we suggest that the TUC is an appropriate body to commission it. It would seek to establish, among other things, how far the tasks allotted to officers at different levels can usefully be compared with work elsewhere, and how far unions offer attractive career prospects to those who wish to serve them in a full-time capacity.

Training

709. To prepare union officers at all levels for the reconstruction of industrial relations will make heavy demands on the available resources, despite a considerable expansion in facilities since the war, in which the TUC has played a notable part. This is another field in which we have conducted no special investigation, and therefore make our comments with some diffidence.

710. We think that trade unions should in the immediate future concentrate on developing courses for junior full-time officers and for shop stewards.

711. Hitherto most full-time officers have received no formal training for their posts. It is our view that there would be value both in a basic course for officers on or shortly after appointment and in a more advanced course for officers with some experience. Some major unions might be able to develop their own courses but smaller unions would have to rely on the TUC.

712. The need for shop steward training is immense. There are about 175,000 shop stewards, of whom more than two-thirds have received no training

---

[1] Clegg, Killick and Adams, *Trade Union Officers*, Blackwell, 1961.

190

of any kind, and turnover runs at about 15 per cent a year. Nevertheless we do not consider that the first need is for indiscriminate expansion. Even when the resources of university extra-mural departments and the minority of technical colleges which assist in shop steward training are added to those of the unions themselves, there is an acute shortage of teachers with the experience and understanding to teach what is required. There is no general agreement on what should be taught. Indeed training in the formal procedures of collective bargaining and trade unionism is likely to be neither successful nor useful where formal rules and procedures are set aside by informal arrangements and by custom and practice. Additional resources are undoubtedly required. They should be used to develop competent teachers and adequate syllabuses with a view to using training of stewards as part of a planned move to more orderly industrial relations based on comprehensive and formal factory or company agreements. This is where shop steward training will be able to make its biggest contribution.

713. Among the various means of providing training, day-release courses appear to offer the best prospect of adequate training on a considerable scale. Day-release courses involve absence from work (on full pay) for a day a week over a period of say 12 or more weeks and the employer's co-operation is therefore needed. It is for this reason that we suggest in Chapter IV (paragraph 182(3)) that this is one of the matters that might be covered in company or factory agreements. It is open to industrial training boards to make grants towards the cost to employers of approved courses for shop stewards, and their grants could be used to increase the number of day-release courses and to improve their standard.

TRADE UNION FINANCES

714. Many of the proposals we suggest in this chapter will require additional expenditure by trade unions. Can they find the money? In 1938 the Ministry of Labour's earnings inquiries showed that adult male manual workers were earning an average of £3 9s. a week. The corresponding figure for April 1967 was £20 11s. 7d., a six-fold increase. Over the period retail prices more than trebled. In 1938 the average annual contribution of members of registered unions was £1 16s. 7d. The latest available figures, which relate to 1966, show that the average annual contribution had risen by then to £4 3s. 3d.—rather over double the previous amount. As a percentage of men's average weekly earnings, weekly trade union contributions had declined from 1.02 per cent in 1938 to 0.39 per cent in 1966.

715. This decline has to some extent been offset by rising membership. The total membership of *registered* unions rose from 4,867,000 in 1938 to 8,584,000 in 1966. This, combined with increased rates of contributions, enabled registered unions to raise their accumulated funds from some £20m. at the end of 1938 to about £122m. at the end of 1966. Between 1938 and 1966 annual expenditure of registered unions rose from £7½m. to nearly £37½m.

716. During this period there was also a decline in the relative importance to trade unions of their friendly society activities, such as the provision of

various provident benefits and other forms of insurance. This trend began earlier in the twentieth century and has no doubt been largely linked with the development of social security provision by the State. The converse of the decline in the importance of provident benefits since 1938 has been the steady increase in the proportion of union funds devoted to what the Chief Registrar of Friendly Societies calls "working expenses". Under these are included the items of trade union expenditure which we wish to see increased, such as salaries and expenses of officials and outlay on training. Today about two-thirds of all union expenditure is devoted to working expenses.

717. Trade union membership expanded rapidly during and immediately after the war. Thereafter increased revenue has had mainly to be found elsewhere. In its evidence to us the TUC records that, partly as a result of its own persuasion, there have been considerable increases in trade union contributions in the last decade. The following table gives some examples:

Union	Weekly Contribution	
	1956	1966
Amalgamated Engineering Union (section 1)	2s. 3d.	3s. 0d.
Electrical Trades Union (skilled)	1s. 7d.	3s. 0d.
'Amalgamated Society of Woodworkers (section 1)	2s. 0d.	3s. 9d.
General and Municipal Workers' Union (male)	8d.	2s. 0d.
Transport and General Workers' Union	8d.	1s. 9d.

Our surveys have shown that most union members are prepared to pay higher contributions provided that there is good reason for doing so. Nearly half of those who were so prepared said that they would agree to contributions being doubled if the result was a more efficient union contributing better services. We believe that a union which explains fully to its members why higher contributions are needed and what improvements will result will be likely to win their consent. Progress need not be held up for lack of money.

The Check-Off

718. While considering the problem of union finances we must refer to the growing practice whereby employers agree to deduct trade union dues from the wages of members in their employment and pay them over to the unions concerned. This arrangement is normally termed a "check-off" and a Research Paper prepared for us[1] estimates that it now affects at least two million trade unionists, i.e. about one trade union member in five. Most of them are employed in the public sector but there are now some 1,200 private companies which have agreed to the arrangement.

719. If there is no check-off, subscriptions are usually collected by shop stewards or collecting stewards. The collection of dues therefore gives union representatives a point of contact with their members which it is sometimes suggested would be lost with the check-off. It has also been suggested that the check-off puts too much power in the hands of the employer. There is

[1]Research Paper No. 8, *Three Studies in Collective Bargaining—Check-off Agreements in Britain*, A. I. Marsh and J. W. Staples, HMSO 1968.

substance in these points, but there are also persuasive arguments the other way. The check-off provides unions with a steady and assured income. It eliminates the need for personal collection of subscriptions, which is often a time-consuming task, unpopular among the voluntary workers who do it, leaving them more time to deal with their members' problems and to communicate information to them. The chance that employers will, as a sanction, withdraw the check-off or threaten to do so, is somewhat remote: and in an emergency collection of subscriptions through shop stewards could be arranged.

720. There has been a significant shift of view on the part of employers in recent years on this subject. A contributory cause has been the introduction of modern accounting methods which have made the deduction of subscriptions from pay relatively simple to arrange. The check-off is a token of acceptance of trade unionism, showing that the employer is willing to assist the union to be organisationally and financially strong. The administrative expense of the check-off is slight, and can be recouped by agreement with the union.

721. On the whole, therefore, we think that the check-off is a useful arrangement, the advantages of which outweigh the disadvantages; that trade unions who do not collect subscriptions in this way might usefully consider doing so; and that employers should sympathetically consider requests from trade unions for the facility.

722. Section 3 of the Truck Act 1831 provides that " the entire amount of the wages earned by or payable to any artificer in respect of any labour done by him shall be paid actually to such artificer in the current coin of the realm and not otherwise . . .". The reason why the check-off does not infringe this provision is that the trade union officer who receives the worker's subscription direct from the employer can be regarded in law as acting as the employee's agent for the collection of the money; the payment is " a payment to the person employed as if the current coin of the realm had been placed in his or her hand " (to quote Lord Herschell, L. C., in *Hewlett v. Allen* [1894] AC 383, the case which provides the authority for the view here stated). This interpretation can be maintained only if the worker has consented to the check-off, as is the normal practice. Consent is therefore desirable not only in itself but also for legal reasons, and it is best for this to be given in writing. In our opinion the law is clear, but it is for consideration by the Government whether it would be desirable to give express statutory authority for the legality of the check-off or whether reliance should continue to be placed on the case law.

THE ROLE OF THE TUC

723. In this chapter we have suggested a programme of action for trade unions, involving a substantial list of proposed reforms. In each instance we have tried to suggest steps which are practicable and realistic, but carrying them through will nevertheless demand considerable effort, imagination and initiative from trade union leaders and executive members, and a willingness to move away from accepted modes of thought and patterns of

behaviour. To generate the initiative and sustain the effort we rely heavily upon the leadership of the TUC.

724. Although it has wider powers over its affiliates than the CBI has over its members, the TUC's authority is more limited than that of many trade union centres abroad, including those of the Federal Republic of Germany and the Scandinavian countries. Nevertheless it has a more comprehensive coverage than any other national trade union centre in the non-communist world, with over five-sixths of British trade unionists affiliated to it. Its unchallenged position as the representative of the unions in dealings with the Government and as their spokesman to the public adds to its influence over its members. In recent years it has taken the lead in several new developments, by far the most important being the working out of its own incomes policy and its own machinery for " vetting " the pay demands of its members. Such an intervention in the autonomy of its members to conduct their dealings with employers to suit themselves is an innovation which would have been barely conceivable even a few years ago; and it has been accomplished without a formal revision of the constitution.

725. We welcome this development, and the expansion in the staff and services of the TUC which has accompanied it. It has often been suggested that the TUC should also seek constitutional authority to intervene in negotiations conducted by affiliated unions. Only the development of incomes policy can determine whether there will be an advantage in reinforcing what is already being done by an extension of formal powers. In any case such powers are largely irrelevant to our proposals for the reform of industrial relations in the factory and the company, for intervention by the TUC is and must continue to be concentrated upon negotiations at industry level. The responsibility for reform therefore rests on the boards of companies and the individual unions which organise their employees.

726. Similarly the responsibility for carrying out the reforms we suggest in this chapter, except for the modification of the Bridlington principles, must rest with individual unions. Decisions to amalgamate, to accept agreements for exclusive recruitment rights, to give recognition to multiunion committees of shop stewards, to reform union rules and branch structure, to appoint more officials and review their salaries and conditions of work, to expand training and to increase subscriptions, can be taken only by the executives and conferences of individual unions. What is required from the TUC is to give a lead, to promote amalgamations and interunion agreements, to guide unions on the reform of rules and structures, to encourage unions to appoint more full-time officers and to continue its campaign for higher subscriptions. This can all be done within its existing powers.

727. While the TUC may not require additional powers beyond those which are needed to develop its incomes policy, the increased scope of its activities suggested in the last paragraph will impose a growing burden on its General Council and staff. The burden on the General Secretary and his senior officers has already become very heavy as a result of the National Economic Development Council and the Economic Development Committees, the Government's incomes policy and associations with the trade union centres

in the European Economic Community and the European Free Trade Area. Practically all the General Council members are chief officials or senior officials of their own unions. We suggest that the TUC will need to develop and adapt its organisation at national and perhaps local level to cope satisfactorily with the many new aspects of its work. It may, if its influence is to extend to local level, need to appoint its own full-time regional officers, who could perhaps act as secretaries of its regional advisory committees.

Chapter XIII

EMPLOYERS' ASSOCIATIONS

728. Our most important observations and proposals concerning employers' associations have already been set out in Chapter IV. This is unavoidable given the close involvement of most important employers' associations in current industry-wide collective bargaining. Proposals for the reform of industry-wide collective bargaining are necessarily proposals for the reform of employers' associations, for, as we have pointed out, trade unions can operate successfully without industry-wide bargaining but industry-wide bargaining requires association among employers.

729. The central responsibility of employers' associations in the reconstruction of industrial relations is to promote and support effective and comprehensive agreements in the company and in the factory. They should, as we have said, assist companies in reviewing industrial relations within their undertakings in the light of the objectives set out in Chapter IV. They should join with trade unions to amend industry-wide agreements so as to facilitate orderly and effective collective bargaining within the company and the factory. Industry-wide agreements should be confined to matters which they are capable of regulating; guide-lines should be provided for satisfactory company and factory agreements; and, where appropriate, exemption from clauses of industry-wide agreements should be granted to agreements which follow these guide-lines.

730. Action on these lines will perhaps demand even greater changes in attitude from employers' associations than from trade unions. The close link between industry-wide bargaining and employers' associations, and the attitudes which it engenders, have both been evident in the development of productivity bargaining. It is significant that many of the companies which pioneered productivity bargaining were not federated. Esso concluded its first productivity agreement at its Fawley refinery, and there is no employers' association which conducts negotiations covering oil refining. It was followed by other productivity agreements at refineries owned by Mobil, Shell and British Petroleum. The productivity agreement concluded by British Oxygen applied to its gases division, which is not covered by membership of an association. ICI has an exceptional arrangement with the Chemical Industries Association whereby it remains free to conduct its own negotiations with the unions, and this arrangement applied to its productivity agreement.

731. In some instances companies have withdrawn from employers' associations in order to conclude productivity deals. Esso was a member of the Welsh Engineers' and Founders' Association in respect of craftsmen at its Milford Haven refinery, and before concluding a productivity agreement applying to this refinery it resigned from the Association. It also resigned from the Employers' Panel of the Oil Companies' Conciliation Committee before concluding the agreement covering its distribution workers, as did Mobil. Alcan withdrew from the South Wales and Monmouthshire Iron and

Steel Manufacturers' Association before negotiating a productivity agreement applying to its Rogerstone plant.

732. It must be admitted that the Employers' Panel of the Oil Companies' Conciliation Committee was an unusual employers' association in several respects; and that the Welsh associations from which Esso and Alcan withdrew were relatively unimportant bodies. A more typical example of the impact of productivity bargaining upon an employers' association can be found in the shipping industry. This industry has in the past attached considerable importance to the negotiation of uniform rates of pay and the employers' association, the Shipping Federation, has expected individual companies to keep closely in line with them. A high proportion of seamen move freely from the employment of one company to another, and it has therefore been thought that disparities in the rates offered by different companies would cause trouble. In the autumn of 1965 Shell (U.K.) Ltd. were discussing the introduction of " general purpose crews " with the National Union of Seamen, having in view a productivity agreement which would result in smaller crews with greater flexibility in their duties in return for higher pay and other advantages. Shell were offering a bonus of £4 a month as part of the bargain but the union were seeking £8. Negotiations broke down at this point because Shell were advised by the Shipping Federation that to go further would prejudice arrangements for the introduction of general purpose crews on other types of ship.

733. In February 1967 the report of the Pearson Court of Inquiry was published. The Court made plain its view that the future of all engaged in the industry depended upon " greater mechanisation of the ships and greater skill and versatility of the crews, coupled with reduction of manning". Referring to Shell's negotiations, the report said that a general decision for the whole industry about general purpose crews would be premature and foolish, but that it would be no less disastrous if Shell were prevented from making an arrangement which was to their own advantage, and to the advantage of their employees, because of a fear that it might at some future date embarrass the Federation in an attempt to reach a uniform settlement on general purpose working for the whole industry. The report went on to say: [1]

> " It will of course be most desirable that any negotiations in individual companies on this and other matters should be conducted with the consent and advice of the Federation. But this will demand a progressive, experimental and sympathetic approach on the part of the Federation. Without that it might be the duty of individual companies to go their own way without regard for the Federation. There is no special virtue in merely keeping in step with one's fellows. In fact in the shipping industry keeping in step has led to frustration and inefficiency. If the Federation sees as its first duty to help shipowners to pursue efficient operation and effective personnel policies, it will continue to play a part of great importance in the industry. In the last resort, however, it would be the duty of each company to seek after these things even if it meant falling out with their fellows."

[1]Cmnd. 3211, para. 145.

734. There are indications that the Federation is developing a more flexible approach. In the course of 1966 a Tanker Committee was formed to enable full consideration to be given to the circumstances of owners operating tankers. These differ in important respects from the circumstances affecting other shipowners. In July 1967 Esso, while remaining a member of the Federation, was able to conclude a productivity agreement with the National Union of Seamen which marked the introduction of a " new marine personnel policy ". It involved, among other things, more flexibility in manning, opportunities for seamen to train for higher skills, and higher pay. Shell had already been permitted to make some experiments which had not involved immediate pay increases and these were followed by the conclusion of a productivity agreement in November 1967.

735. In the past most employers' associations have seen their central task as the protection of their members by insisting as far as possible on common rules for regulating the terms on which labour was to be employed, as did the Shipping Federation. In future they must find their main purpose in the promotion of their members' interests by assisting them to develop orderly and efficient systems of industrial relations within their undertakings and by confining common rules to the areas where they can be applied without hindering this development. Such a revision in attitude is needed both in those associations which, like the Shipping Federation, have been able to maintain a considerable degree of common regulation, but at the expense of the efficient use of labour in individual undertakings, and in those associations where common regulation has been undermined by bargaining within the undertaking, but bargaining which is informal and fragmented.

736. We are the more confident that attitudes can be changed because there are already signs, which we have noted at several points in this report, that the change is beginning to take place. Besides the events in the shipping industry just mentioned we draw especial attention to the recent agreement in the chemicals industry (see paragraph 177 in Chapter IV). What is now needed is a rapid increase in the pace and the scale of the change.

737. A second subject on which employers' attitudes may have to change is the recognition of trade unions, and especially of white-collar trade unions. Collective bargaining, we repeat, is the best method of conducting industrial relations; and this applies to white-collar employment as well as to manual employment. Effective collective bargaining requires strong trade unions. Trade unionism among white-collar workers in private employment is generally weak, and growth is largely dependent upon recognition by employers. The attitude of employers' associations is therefore crucial.

738. We note that a survey conducted by the former British Employers' Confederation in 1963-4 showed that only one out of twenty-three member organisations "was able to state, without reservations, that trade union representation of staff workers is recognised, that this recognition is on a formal basis and that agreements covering the rates of pay etc. of staff workers are made at national or company level", although a few others

granted limited recognition. In giving evidence to us the Director General of the CBI said:[1]

> "At the moment our policy is waiting and seeing. We have not a policy of actively stimulating the membership and recognition of and negotiation with the white-collar unions. On the other hand we have no particular entrenched policy against that development. We are certainly saying to our members that this is a matter largely for them at this stage, because we have no central general policy to press on them. . . . Quite honestly there is such immense diversity of view amongst our members regarding the appointment and treatment of clerical and office workers and about the unions who should represent them, that it is impossible to distil from this diversity anything like a general trend. If there is a general trend it is on the increase, but it is not a general trend of policy."

739. We hope that the CBI and the employers' associations will reconsider their attitudes. We recognise that there are many problems about the recognition of trade unions and particularly of white-collar trade unions. Some of them may be resolved only by the close investigation and analysis of the Industrial Relations Commission. But we think that, given the assistance of the Industrial Relations Commission, employers should be willing to encourage the development of collective bargaining and the trade unions which make it possible.

740. We have no proposals to make concerning the conduct of elections in employers' associations, or the protection of the rights of members, such as we make for trade unions in Chapter XI. There is no evidence of malpractices in the internal affairs of employers' associations, and being organisations who number their members in tens or hundreds, and only in a few instances in thousands, they are subject to fewer pressures in these respects than are trade unions. Moreover we have found no instances of a closed shop among employers' associations, nor any evidence that expulsion could cause a company serious hardship.

741. There is need, however, for changes in the structure of employers' associations, so that they can give adequate support to effective collective bargaining in the company and the plant. We have considered the suggestion that the industry-wide negotiations of the engineering industry should be sub-divided into separate negotiations for different sections of the industry such as motor vehicles, aircraft, electrical engineering, etc. which it is alleged would be more "realistic" units for collective bargaining; and that the Engineering Employers' Federation should be sectionalised on the same basis. While we have some sympathy with the criticism that the collective bargaining machinery of the engineering industry attemps to cover too wide and diverse a field, we do not think that this proposal faces up to the major need, which is to provide effective bargaining in engineering companies. As things stand neither the Federation nor the procedure agreement recognise companies as such, and the factories of multi-plant companies are separately affiliated to the local associations which in turn constitute the Federation.

---

[1]Minutes of Evidence No. 22, *Confederation of British Industry*, p.822, q. 3339.

This arrangement must be changed. Our suggestion is that the Federation should establish a national division to which multi-plant companies could affiliate direct. These companies should have their own internal procedure agreements leading up to joint meetings between the unions and the companies at national level. Local factories of multi-plant companies could be associate members of the local associations, which will continue to serve and represent local engineering companies. Other major employers' associations may also have to revise their constitutions and procedures to give adequate recognition to individual companies and adequate scope for them to develop their own personnel policies.

742. The now-defunct Employers' Panel of the Oil Companies' Conciliation Committee, which has since been replaced by a purely advisory body, operated under "heads of agreement" which prevented individual companies from negotiating any question of principle separately with the unions, and bound every member to observe the standard wages and conditions agreed by the Panel. These provisions prevented companies developing and applying their own personnel policies and made it necessary for companies which proposed to negotiate a productivity agreement first to leave the Panel. It is our opinion that such rules obstruct effective collective bargaining and we suggest that if similar arrangements exist in any other employers' associations they should be amended.

743. If employers' associations are to carry out the functions we suggest, they will need more officials with a high degree of expertise. Some developments in recruiting and training methods are already taking place. A recommendation by the CBI that employers' associations should review the quality and training of their staffs might help.

744. There is a strong case for amalgamations among smaller associations, especially where several independent associations operate in different sections of a single industry as in clothing and distribution. Many small associations lack the resources to provide effective services to their members. Some are virtually run by firms of solicitors or chartered accountants. By pooling their resources the employers concerned could create organisations able to employ staff with experience and training in industrial relations and to offer specialised services to their members. It is also doubtful whether it is in the best interests of employers to have separate organisations for England and Wales and for Scotland, as in the plumbing trade; or to maintain separate associations for municipal bus undertakings and the so-called "company" undertakings.

745. Of the 108 organisations in membership of the CBI, 75 combine the functions of an employers' association with that of a trade association, and 33 operate solely as employers' associations. The number of combined organisations has been growing. Single all-purpose associations have recently been formed in chemicals, in rubber manufacturing and in shipbuilding and ship-repairing. In chemicals and rubber the amalgamations were soon followed by the radical revision of their industry-wide agreements in a progressive direction. Combined organisations have advantages which others should carefully consider. The separation of industrial relations from commercial matters is an unreal dichotomy. It is easier for an employer

to play a full and active part in the affairs of one association than to do so in two separate associations. Combined organisations are thus better able to draw on their members' experience and to profit from their suggestions, and can in turn exercise more influence over members' policies than would otherwise be possible. Economies in operating costs are also feasible.

746. For these reasons the foundation in 1965 of the CBI to centralise in one national organisation the responsibility for dealing with the whole range of matters which affect employers was a considerable step forward. It is a further advantage that the experience of the nationalised industries in matters of industrial relations should be pooled with that of private industry, since so many of the problems in this field are common to both sections of industry. The CBI, in contrast with the previous British Employers' Confederation, admits individual companies into membership as well as employers' associations. Non-federated companies such as Ford and Vauxhall can therefore make a contribution to the work of the CBI.

747. The CBI tells us that " while full membership of the CBI for individual firms is limited to those engaged in productive industry and transport, such membership is open to any employers' association which negotiates with trade unions and there are at present six member organisations covering firms in the services sector ". Banks, insurance companies and some other companies are admitted as " commercial associates ", but this does not at present extend to distribution, and there are no employers' associations from the retail distributive trades at present in membership. This seems to us to be a defect in the constitution of the CBI. The exclusion of companies outside productive industry and transport does not reflect any real distinction in the type of industrial relations issues with which they have to deal. Nor can we see that there is anything in the many other functions of the CBI which would justify the distinction. We are concerned that individual companies as such should be given adequate representation both in individual associations and in the CBI itself. Although in this respect the CBI's constitution is a marked improvement over the constitution of the British Employers' Confederation, we think that the CBI should give consideration to widening its scope to include companies at present excluded from membership. We think this will be to the advantage both of the CBI and of the companies.

748. In certain foreign countries the central employers' organisation has a degree of authority over the actions of its members which is greater than that enjoyed by the CBI. The Swedish Employers' Confederation for example periodically negotiates a " framework agreement " with the central trade union organisation (the LO) in Sweden, and this lays down the lines which subsequent industry agreements are to follow. It also maintains a fund from which payments can be made to members in compensation for losses suffered in industrial disputes. The CBI on the other hand does not enter into collective bargaining nor intervene in the conduct by employers' associations or individual companies of their own affairs. Nor does it maintain a fund to indemnify employers against loss due to industrial disputes.

749. Many of the powers of the Swedish Employers' Confederation go back to the early years of the present century and they are the product of an industrial development widely different from our own. Any attempt by the CBI to imitate the Swedish organisation would be irrelevant to the central need of British industrial relations, which is the promotion of effective and orderly collective bargaining in the company and the factory. Centralised authority cannot accomplish this, since the decisions have to be taken within companies. What the CBI can contribute to this is the use of its influence and persuasion to guide companies in the right direction.

750. The CBI occupies a unique position in relation to employers in this country. Its central position, its resources in staff and money and its access, through its members, to information about the most up-to-date practices in every aspect of management mean that it should be able to exercise a powerful and most beneficial influence in raising standards throughout its membership. Through its agency the experience and knowledge of the most progressive employers can be put at the disposal of employers generally and in this way assist the general raising of standards. It is brought into consultation by the Government on important matters of economic and social policy; these include the prices and incomes policy, on the application of which the CBI makes recommendations to its members. The CBI has therefore a most important part to play in the reconstruction of British industrial relations and will bear a heavy responsibility for its success.

Chapter XIV

CHANGES IN THE LAW

INTRODUCTION

751. The British system of industrial relations is based on voluntarily agreed rules which, as a matter of principle, are not enforced by law. This is an outstanding characteristic which distinguishes it from the systems of many comparable countries. No trade union, no employer in private industry, no employers' association, is under any legal obligation to bargain collectively; and, exceptions apart, the law does not intervene to enforce such a bargain, or any of its terms. The law has done little to restrict or otherwise to regulate the use of industrial sanctions such as the strike and the lock-out. A right to strike has never been formulated in positive terms, but statutes have been enacted to remove obstacles which the common law placed in the way of the use of industrial sanctions. With very few exceptions, the law prevents no one from joining a trade union, and protects no one against attempts made by others to impede the exercise of his freedom of association. The law has never been called upon to help in organising or operating a system of workers' representation at enterprise or at plant level. It has done little to protect individual workers against the exercise by employers of their power of dismissal, or against the exercise by trade unions of their power of expulsion. In short, it has been the traditional policy of the law as far as possible not to intervene in the system of industrial relations.

752. The evidence which we have received shows a wide measure of agreement that this non-intervention should continue to be the normal policy. Most of us arrive at the same conclusion. In the preceding chapters of this report we recommend a number of important legislative measures concerning collective bargaining and agreements, trade unions and employers' associations, and the rights and remedies of individual employers and employees. We do so, however, only where we are convinced that new institutions need to be created in order to strengthen and to improve our system of voluntary collective bargaining or to improve the enforcement of individual rights; or where a clear enunciation of legal principles is required in the public interest; or where some machinery has to be set up for imposing legal sanctions in circumstances in which voluntary action is likely to be insufficient for the solution of urgent social or economic problems.

753. In the present chapter we examine the existing statute law which applies to trade unions and employers' associations, to trade disputes in general, and to the trade dispute disqualification for unemployment benefit, and we make a number of recommendations for the amendment of these statutes.

754. We are, however, also much concerned with the need for simplification of the present law and with measures which should be taken to make the law more easily accessible and understandable. The " law affecting the activities " of trade unions and employers' associations which our terms of reference

require us to consider is scattered over a large number of statutes and of judicial decisions. The statutes were passed in the course of our long legal and economic history in order to deal with practical problems which had arisen at the time of their enactment, and the principal Acts are nearly 100 years old. The law developed piecemeal, as unacceptable judicial decisions were followed by remedial statutes; and one of the main reasons for the somewhat chaotic state of the present statute law is that most of it was enacted in order to remove common law disabilities rather than to enact positive rights. Judicial decisions too have played an important role in the development of the law governing labour relations. Some of these interpret the existing statutes, but others apply to labour relations the principles of the general common law. The application of these general principles is inevitable, but we have interpreted our terms of reference so as to concentrate our attention primarily on those legal principles which particularly affect the activities of trade unions and employers' associations. No attempt has ever been made at a systematic legislative exposition of these principles and the time has now come for doing so.

755. Reform of the law governing labour relations and trade unions and employers' associations has not hitherto been an attractive proposition to Governments with heavy programmes of legislation and limited Parliamentary time. But with the English and Scottish Law Commissions now in being, the task of codification should no longer be delayed, and these Commissions should be requested in due course to undertake it as a matter of urgency. What is needed is to codify in one Act of Parliament the principles relating to collective bargaining, to industrial relations in general (including the new legislation we recommend), and to trade unions and employers' associations. A special Industrial Law Committee should be attached to the Industrial Relations Commission to keep this legislation under constant review and from time to time to recommend its amendment to the Government and to Parliament.

756. If codification were considered premature (which we should regret), we strongly recommend that a comprehensive measure for the consolidation of the statute law should be enacted; and should be taken in hand as early as possible after the passage of such new legislation as may be required to implement such of our recommendations as are accepted. The opportunity should be taken to repeal such statutory provisions, for example in the Trade Union Act 1871 and in the Conspiracy and Protection of Property Act 1875, as have been rendered obsolete by subsequent legislation. Even in the absence of codification the Industrial Law Committee, the establishment of which we recommend in the preceding paragraph, should be set up as part of the Industrial Relations Commission.

757. The legal systems of England, Scotland and Northern Ireland are substantially in agreement where industrial relations are concerned. There are however some differences of detail and procedure, and where these are of significance for the subject under discussion we explain what those differences are. Differences both in the machinery of registration of trade unions and in other respects are also pointed out by Dr. M. A. Hickling in his written evidence, and we suggest that a suitable opportunity should be taken to elimi-

nate these. As Dr. Hickling says: "Unity of the machinery of registration as well as the law applicable in the three parts of the United Kingdom is desirable."

(1) THE DEFINITION OF A TRADE UNION

758. A trade union was first defined in section 23 of the Trade Union Act 1871. The definition was repealed, with the exception of the proviso to s. 23, by section 16 of the Trade Union Act Amendment Act 1876, which substituted another. An amendment to the definition was made by section 2 of the Trade Union Act 1913. The combined effect of these three provisions is to define a trade union as follows:

"Any combination, whether temporary or permanent, the principal objects of which are under its constitution statutory objects, namely, the regulation of the relations between workmen and masters, or between workmen and workmen, or between masters and masters, or the imposing of restrictive conditions on the conduct of any trade or business, and also the provision of benefits to members, whether such combination would or would not, if the Trade Union Act 1871 had not been passed, have been deemed to have been an unlawful combination by reason of some one or more of its purposes being in restraint of trade. Provided that this shall not affect

1. any agreement between partners as to their own business;
2. any agreement between an employer and those employed by him as to such employment;
3. any agreement in consideration of the sale of the goodwill of a business, or of instruction in any profession, trade, or handicraft."

This definition suffers from the defects that it is too cumbrous, too wide, and out of date. Historical reasons account for its being spread over three statutes.

759. In 1871 the Legislature provided, by section 2 of the Trade Union Act of that year, that the purposes of any trade union should not be deemed to be unlawful so as to attract a criminal prosecution merely because those purposes were in restraint of trade. By section 3 of the same Act the Legislature went on to enact that the purposes of a trade union should not render void any agreement or trust, merely because those purposes were in restraint of trade and thus unlawful.

760. When it reached section 23, which defined a trade union for the purpose of the Act, the Legislature seems to have assumed that such combinations would always be unlawful in the ordinary way because one or more of their purposes would be in restraint of trade; and it therefore confined the definition to such combinations. The assumption however was wrong. There were some trade unions with no such unlawful purposes. Accordingly in 1876, by the amending Trade Union Act of that year, the definition of a trade union was made applicable whether or not the combination would, apart from the Act of 1871, have been an unlawful combination by reason of some of its purposes being in restraint of trade.

761. In 1909 the House of Lords decided in the case of *Amalgamated Society*

205

of Railway Servants v. Osborne [1910] AC 87 that since the aforesaid Acts of 1871 and 1876 did not specifically authorise the expenditure for political purposes of the funds of a trade union, it was *ultra vires* a registered trade union to make a levy upon its members for such purposes. Accordingly in 1913 the definition of a trade union was amended again by the Trade Union Act of that year in order to negative the House of Lords' decision. This was done by providing that a trade union might still be a trade union for the purpose of the Trade Union Acts notwithstanding that it had other objects or powers beyond those specifically mentioned in those Acts, so long as these latter objects predominated. Thus a trade union became free to adopt political purposes in its constitution so long as they were not its principal purposes.

762. Apart from the inconvenience of having to consult three Acts of Parliament, allowing for amendments here, and additions there, in order to discover the Legislature's definition of a trade union, the criticisms we have heard of the definition itself are shortly these:

(i) *It is too wide.* It embraces " any combination whether temporary or permanent etc." Thus two shop stewards combining for the purpose of conducting a trade dispute in a particular plant would, provided they have a " constitution " (which it seems need not be written) be a trade union, and immune from all actions for tort so long as their combination continued. The definition is also wide enough to cover employers' associations if their principal objects are any of those specified in the 1913 Act as they well might be, e.g. " the imposing of restrictive conditions on the conduct of any trade or business "; yet no ordinary person would think of such an employers' association as being a " trade union ". The definition could also cover a trade association not concerned at all with labour relations.

(ii) *The definition is out of date.* Thus among the " principal objects " specified as qualifying a combination for the status of a trade union is " the provision of benefits to members "; and section 2 of the Trade Union Act 1913 which first introduced this feature into the definition is unnecessarily ambiguous as to whether such an object is essential to any combination wishing to be a trade union. Thus while the other " principal objects " are separated in section 2 of the 1913 Act by the disjunctive " or ", the " provision of benefits to members " is introduced by the words " and also "; which tends to suggest that the provision of benefits is indispensable if the combination is to be a trade union. The words are not so construed in practice and we think rightly so: because trade unions have always been regarded as having the right to pay benefits to members, and in any event could provide themselves with the powers under section 2 of the 1913 Act itself, even if these specific words were not there. They may have been introduced to remove doubts. Instead they merely create them, and should be removed from the definition.

763. The term " workmen " appearing in the definition is not defined. In practice it is today treated as equivalent to " employee " and in any amendment of the definition it would be preferable to use this term.

764. If, as we think, trade unions should be defined in such a way as to exclude employers' associations, it will be difficult to justify the retention among the principal objects of a trade union of that object now described as " for imposing restrictive conditions on the conduct of any trade or business ". This object would seem to be more appropriate to trade associations, and there seems to be no good reason today why trade associations seeking to benefit themselves by agreeing to restrictive conditions should be regarded as trade unions. They have in some measure been overtaken by the Restrictive Trade Practices Act 1956, which removes in certain proceedings the immunity against suit for tort which would otherwise be available to such associations as trade unions. This part of the definition needs therefore to be reconsidered. *Prima facie* trade unions of employees would not seem to need it.

765. It is also arguable whether it is still necessary to enact that it shall be immaterial whether or not a trade union would if the Act of 1871 had not been passed have been an unlawful combination by reason of some of its purposes being in restraint of trade. But since the doctrine of restraint of trade is still with us, trade unions would probably prefer the retention of those words in the statutory definition as a matter of precaution, and we see no objection.

766. We suggest the following as a possible basis of the new definition— " Trade Union " means any combination of employees the principal activity of which is the regulation of relations between employees and employers, whether such combination is in restraint of trade or not, and which is registered upon the Register of Trade Unions and Employers' Associations.

767. " Employees " could be given a definition in terms similar to that of " workman " in section 8 of the Industrial Courts Act 1919 (see paragraph 821 below): and the term " Register of Trade Unions and Employers' Associations " could be defined by reference to the statute which creates it.

(2) THE DEFINITION OF AN EMPLOYERS' ASSOCIATION

768. We deal with this question in paragraphs 786-787 below.

(3) LEGAL STATUS OF TRADE UNIONS AND EMPLOYERS' ASSOCIATIONS

Trade Unions

769. It is of importance to trade unions and to the public generally that their status at law should be clear. Are they voluntary unincorporated associations or are they, or some of them, legal entities distinct from their members? Upon the answer depends how trade unions may enforce their claims against outsiders; how members and others may enforce claims against trade unions; how far trade unions are liable vicariously for the acts of their officers; and the ownership of monies and properties paid for out of members' subscriptions.

770. At present the situation is far from clear. Dealing first with registered trade unions, the House of Lords in *Taff Vale Railway Co. v Amalgamated Society of Railway Servants* [1901] AC 426 decided that such a union could be sued in its own name in tort with the consequence that the union funds were answerable for the damages awarded, and not the private assets of the members themselves.

771.   The majority of their Lordships held that, while it was true that a trade union was not a corporation or a legal entity distinct from its members, nevertheless the privileges conferred upon registered trade unions by the Trade Union Act 1871 imported a correlative liability upon such a union to be sued in its own name for any torts it committed.

772.   Lord Brampton however said:

"I think a legal entity was created under the Trade Union Act 1871 by the registration of the Society in its present name in the manner prescribed, and that the legal entity so created though not perhaps in the strict sense a corporation, is nevertheless a newly created corporate body created by Statute . . ." (1901 AC at page 442).

773.   In *Bonsor v. Musicians' Union* [1956] AC 104 Lord Morton said that the union was capable of entering into contracts and of being sued as a legal entity distinct from its individual members; and that the contract of membership was between Mr. Bonsor and the union.   Lord Porter took the same view. Lord McDermott and Lord Somervell, however, while agreeing with their colleagues in the ultimate decision of the case, took a different view.   They thought that a registered trade union was not a separate juridical person, and that it could be sued in its own name simply because Parliament (by the Trade Union Act 1871) had, in the result, sanctioned such a course.   Lord Keith appeared to incline to the same view.

774.   Consistently with that view the contract of membership of a trade union is a contract between each member and the other members for the time being, and not a contract between the member and the union regarded as a separate entity.   Nevertheless, in *Bonsor's* case damages were awarded *against the union funds* instead of against the members themselves on the ground, apparently, that since the union ratified Mr. Bonsor's wrongful expulsion the union must pay.   The position of a registered trade union which did not ratify such an unlawful action is still to be decided.

775.   As regards *un*registered unions it is also undecided whether the procedural device which enables a registered union to sue or be sued in its own name applies to them.   In 1965 an action for an injunction was brought by Mr. Lawlor and others against the Union of Post Office Workers, which is described as a registered union in the report of the case (1965 1 All ER 353) but which is in fact an unregistered union.   The irregularity of the action in this respect was not challenged and is doubtful.   The probability is still that for the purpose of legal proceedings an unregistered trade union would be regarded simply as an association of individuals who would have to sue or be sued by means of a representative action.

776.   Order 15, Rule 12 of the Rules of the Supreme Court provides *inter alia* that " where numerous persons have the same interest in any proceedings . . . the proceedings may be begun and continued by or against any one or more of them as representing all or as representing all except one or more of them ".

777.   Such proceedings face formidable difficulties in the case of trade unions. If there were changes in the membership of a trade union between the time the act complained of was committed and the time of the action (as there almost certainly would be) this would defeat the proceedings, since new mem-

bers would not have "the same interest". And if one member successfully pleaded some defence which was peculiar to himself, his fellow defendants could take advantage of it and in this way defeat the action. In the face of such difficulties it is true to say that unregistered trade unions are virtually free from liability to be sued in contract, and virtually unable themselves to sue. In tort, of course, unregistered unions are free from liability to be sued because of the immunity granted by section 4 of the Trade Disputes Act 1906, but even without that section the risk of their being successfully sued is remote.

778.   All registered unions are by statute compelled to hold their property in the names of trustees; and unregistered trade unions must in fact also do so. These trustees might be expected to hold such property for the benefit of the members of the union since the union itself is not a legal entity, and the members' subscriptions have produced the property. Yet section 8 of the Trade Union Act 1871 vests all the property of registered trade unions in their trustees " for the use and benefit of such trade union and members thereof ". This provision was interpreted in the *Taff Vale* case as meaning that the property so held was the property of the union and that the union was the beneficial owner (*per* Lord Lindley, 1901 AC 444).

779.   The position of the unregistered union as regards the ownership of property is still to be decided.

780.   Another source of uncertainty in the present position arises from the language of section 9 of the same Act. This enables the trustees of *registered* unions to sue or be sued in any action " touching or concerning the property right or claim to property of the trade union ". Since the *Taff Vale* and *Bonsor* decisions, this section has been deprived of much of its scope since a registered trade union can now sue or be sued in its own name in such matters. It is thought by some, however, that section 9 in conjunction with section 4(2) of the Trade Disputes Act 1906 would enable the victim of a road accident caused by the negligent driving of a trade union motor car to sue the trustees of the union for damages in tort, though he could not sue the union itself; and that any damages awarded would be payable by the trustees out of the union's property. The reason for this view is that the car would be the property of the union so that the action would be one " touching or concerning the property of the union ". Others doubt this interpretation. If it is right, however, there may be a marked anomaly between the position of registered and unregistered unions in this respect.

781.   The registered trade union has at times been judicially described as a " quasi-corporation "; at others as a " near-corporation "; and at others as the " tertium quid ".

782.   Law apart, we do not think that there is any doubt that most people look upon a trade union as something different from the members who compose it. In 1904 the late Professor Dicey wrote: " When a body of 20, or 2,000 or 200,000 men bind themselves together to act in a particular way for some common purpose, they create a body which by no fiction of law, but by the very nature of things, differs from the individuals of whom it is constituted " (*The Combination Laws, etc.,* 1904 Harvard Law Review, pp. 511 and 513). We think this is true; but even if it were not, we think that the time

has come to clear away the uncertainties and obscurities which surround the position of trade unions at law, and that they should be granted corporate personality. In this we find ourselves at one with the Society of Labour Lawyers.

783. This should impose no hardship or disadvantage. At the present time, registered unions are treated as if they were legal entities for the purpose of suing or being sued and all the largest trade unions, save about three, are registered, and registered unions represent about 85 per cent of trade union membership. Unregistered trade unions would, it is true, lose their virtual immunity from suit but this is something they enjoy not by some conscious decision of the Legislature, but simply by reason of the difficulties surrounding the representative action. Moreover it is something they enjoy in England, but not in Scotland where the law permits all trade unions to sue and be sued in the trade union's name.

784. It was, indeed, suggested to us that English law should be altered so as to enable all unincorporated associations to sue or be sued in the name of the association if they owned property or funds, employed staff and engaged in business transactions. This it is said would solve at one stroke the difficulties of the representative action by or against trade unions. A parallel is drawn in this connection with the position of partnerships, which under Order 81 of the Supreme Court Rules may sue or be sued in the partnership name. A proposal which would affect hundreds of unincorporated associations other than trade unions is one which would require careful prior examination by some other body, for example, the Law Commission. We ourselves could go no further than to recommend its investigation. But in relation to trade unions such a change would achieve little. It would not affect registered trade unions, who represent the great bulk of trade unionists and who can already sue or be sued in their own name. It would, in practice, impose some measure of compulsory registration upon unions at present unregistered since intending claimants would need to consult some register giving the correct name of the union and its address, and possibly the names of its officers. At the same time it would still leave a trade union under the necessity of appointing trustees to hold its property and funds and sign documents of purchase or sale. And above all it would do nothing to clear up the existing doubts about the true legal nature of a trade union and put the matter henceforward on a rational basis corresponding with trade unions' economic and social importance. We think the better solution is the grant of corporate status to all trade unions. This will involve a concomitant liability to register, but the particulars to be registered would be common to all unions.

785. If trade unions were corporations the contract of membership would be a contract between the union and each member. We see no adverse consequences which might flow from this. Indeed it would seem to correspond more to reality than the present doctrine that the contract is between each member and every other member.

Employers' Associations

786. The report of the Chief Registrar of Friendly Societies for 1966 states that 81 employers' associations have registered as trade unions. The Registrar

of Companies informed us in November 1965 that 118 employers' associations were registered under the Companies Acts—all of them as companies limited by guarantee. In law these 118 associations cannot be trade unions. If they were, their registration under the Companies Acts would be invalid—see section 5 of the Trade Union Act 1871. The remaining employers' associations, numbering approximately 1,150 must be unincorporated associations of employers. Some of these may be unregistered trade unions.

787. If trade unions are to receive corporate status, we think the same should apply to their counterparts among employers' associations. These might be defined as being those associations whose principal activity, or one of whose principal activities, is the regulation of relations between employers and employees whether such association is in restraint of trade or not and which is registered upon the Register of Trade Unions and Employers' Associations. Those provisions of the Trade Union Act 1871, the Conspiracy and Protection of Property Act 1875 and the Trade Disputes Acts of 1906 and 1965 which can be invoked by trade unions would apply to employers' associations upon the register. There are at present four employers' associations which have political funds subject to the requirements of the Trade Union Act 1913. These requirements should in future apply to registered employers' associations no less than trade unions.

(4) REGISTRATION OF TRADE UNIONS AND EMPLOYERS' ASSOCIATIONS

Trade Unions

788. The granting of corporate status for trade unions will involve the keeping of a register. This will be necessary so that all who have or wish to have dealings with a union may discover from the register particulars of the union's objects, constitution, rules, chief officers and the address of its headquarters. It will be desirable also to identify those bodies entitled to the various exemptions from the general law granted to trade unions. In addition, a certificate of registration and incorporation will be a ready means by which unions will be able to prove their status.

789. Some 351 trade unions are already registered under the provisions of the Trade Union Act 1871, and these unions together account for over 85 per cent of total trade union membership. The advantages of registration under the Act are not of great importance and no serious detriment is suffered by non-registration. The chief advantage, perhaps, is that a registered trade union is entitled in certain circumstances to exemption from income tax in respect of interest and dividends applicable and applied solely for the purpose of provident benefits. For the rest, the advantages are largely administrative. For example, on a change of trustees the land and other property of the union which is vested in them (other than stock in the public funds) automatically vest in the new trustees without the necessity for a conveyance or transfer. There are summary remedies available to a registered union for the recovery of its property and effects from treasurers and other officers and from any person obtaining possession of union funds, books or other effects by fraud. A registered union may sue and be sued in its own name. On the other hand

there are obligations which a registered union has to undertake. It must send the names of its officers to the Registrar. The rules must contain provision in respect of certain specified matters, though the content of the rules is left to the unions to decide. The union must have a registered office to which all communications may be addressed, and must notify to the Registrar any change in the situation of that office. Every year a general statement of the receipts, funds, effects, and expenditure must be sent to the Registrar showing the assets and liabilities of the union and certain other particulars. Copies of all alterations of rules and changes of officers must likewise be sent.

790. Registration under the Act of 1871 is voluntary; and the chief reason why almost all the large trade unions do in fact register is not that the advantages so far outweigh the obligations that there is virtually no choice, but that the assumption of these obligations is evidence to the public (including prospective members) that the trade union is a stable organisation desirous of conforming to good standards of administration.

791. The reason why trade unions representing rather more than 10 per cent of the total of trade unionists prefer not to register may partly be that under the Trade Union Act 1913 any unregistered trade union may apply to the Registrar of Friendly Societies for a certificate that it is a trade union within the statutory definition; which certificate, when granted, is conclusive evidence of that fact. One of the advantages of registration may then be secured without any obligation being incurred. For the rest, the unregistered trade union may consider that the benefits of registration are not worth the duties which registration entails. Yet it cannot be said that these duties are onerous or vexatious. They do not go beyond what any well-run trade union would do in any event: and while nobody likes having to do something which previously was optional, a law which obliged the unregistered trade union in future to become registered would not, in our opinion, impose a hardship, work any injustice, or deprive unregistered unions of some valuable liberty.

792. We think therefore that all trade unions should as from some convenient future date receive corporate status and be registered. As regards those trade unions which are already registered this need call for no immediate action on their part. The register now kept by the Registrar of Friendly Societies could be named the Register of Trade Unions and Employers' Associations and existing registered unions would simply remain upon it. Existing unregistered unions could be given a period of time, for example a year, in which to become registered. As from some convenient future date all unions on the register would be given corporate status. The definition of a trade union would be exclusively related to registered unions. New unions would be required to register within a stated period after formation.

793. The conditions of registration would be the same as they are at present under existing legislation, modified by such alterations as Parliament hereafter thinks fit to make as a result of this report or for any other reason. For example, future conditions might include filing a copy of the union's constitution (unless this is already embodied in the rules) and proof of a fee-paying membership. Again, we make recommendations in Chapter XI as to how the requirements of the law in relation to the rules of trade unions might be revised. All the existing provisions of the law would continue to apply to

trade unions, including the protective provisions of the Trade Union Act 1871, the Conspiracy and Protection of Property Act 1875, the Trade Disputes Acts 1906 and 1965 and the Trade Union Act 1913.

794. The present definition of a trade union includes temporary combinations the principal objects of which, under their constitution, are the statutory objects of regulating relations between workmen and masters or between workmen and workmen, etc. Thus, assuming that a temporary combination of six or seven employees in a particular shop in a factory were formed, and had a constitution (which it is assumed need not be written) with the object of regulating relations between them and their employer, then no matter how short-lived, this combination would be, while it lasted, a " trade union " entitled, among other things, to immunity from liability for any tort committed in pursuit of its objects. If the definition of a trade union were altered, so as to refer exclusively to trade unions on the new register, this situation would cease. If however the ephemeral combination wished to become a trade union, with the advantages which this would bring, it could take steps to bring itself within the new definition of a trade union and register.

795. There are, however, certain exemptions from the ordinary law which have been enacted by Parliament in favour of " persons " acting in combination in contemplation or furtherance of a trade dispute. Thus:

(i) section 3 of the Conspiracy and Protection of Property Act 1875 provides that an agreement or combination of two or more persons to do or procure to be done an act in contemplation or furtherance of a trade dispute is not to be indictable as a conspiracy if such act, committed by one person, would not be punishable as a crime; and

(ii) section 1 of the Trade Disputes Act 1906 provides that an act done in pursuance of an agreement or combination by two or more persons is not to be actionable if done in contemplation or furtherance of a trade dispute unless the act if done without any such agreement would be actionable.

796. These two sections give protection respectively against prosecution for criminal conspiracy and against actions for civil conspiracy to persons combining together to further their legitimate ends in a trade dispute. These provisions should be continued as a protection for employees not yet organised in trade unions.

797. The like recommendation is made with regard to section 2 of the Trade Disputes Act 1906, which makes peaceful picketing as therein defined lawful not only by trade unions but by " any person acting on his own behalf ".

798. Another statutory provision needing consideration in this context is section 3 of the Trade Disputes Act 1906, the first part of which provides that no action may be brought against any person who induces another to break his contract of employment if this is done in contemplation or furtherance of a trade dispute. This provision should continue to apply for the benefit of trade unions on the suggested new register. Is it still necessary, however, for persons who will not be trade unions?

799. The problem can be envisaged as arising, for example, in a case where

213

an effort is being made to organise employees who are not members of a trade union. If the effort is on behalf of a trade union already on the new register, the benefit of section 3 will apply. This could be made clear by a suitable addition to the section as it now stands. If however an attempt is being made to organise workers into some proposed new trade union, the time may come when the organisers find themselves faced with a trade dispute. Should they then be able, without risk of suit, to endeavour to induce employees to break their individual contracts of employment by coming out on strike without giving whatever notice that contract requires of an intention to cease work?

800. A majority of the Commission (Lord Donovan, Lord Robens, Lord Tangley, Dame Mary Green, Sir George Pollock, Mr. Andrew Shonfield and Mr. John Thomson) think that such immunity is no longer necessary or desirable in such circumstances. In order to avoid a breach of their contracts most employees will need to do no more than give a week's notice of their intention to cease work; and it would not seem unreasonable to ask that they should do so. If the persons who are organising the employees feel for some reason that the protection of section 3 is vital to them, they can secure it by framing a constitution for themselves with the requisite objects and rules and register themselves as a trade union.

801. Moreover persons who are in process of organising a nascent trade union are not the only persons or combinations to be borne in mind in this connection. Unofficial bodies such as those in the construction industry and in the docks at present qualify for the protection given by section 3, and are therefore collectively and severally immune from suit if, in contemplation or furtherance of a trade dispute, they induce workers to break their contracts of employment. The same members consider that the time has come when this immunity should cease; and the suggestion receives added force in their view if section 3 is extended so as to protect those who in contemplation or furtherance of a trade dispute induce breaches of commercial contracts.

802. The Trade Disputes Act 1965 was passed to counteract the effect of the decision of the House of Lords in *Rookes v. Barnard* and provides, in effect, that the protection of the Act of 1906 against actions in tort is not to be lost simply because a person threatens the breach of a contract of employment, or threatens that he will procure another person to break such a contract. Whether the proposals in this section are adopted or not the Act should remain in force. It will remain necessary for the protection of trade union officials and probably for individual employees too.

803. In outline therefore what is proposed is as follows:

(1) All trade unions to be given corporate status and to register.

(2) The definition of a trade union to be amended so as to comprise combinations of employees only, and to include, as part of the definition, being registered as aforesaid.

(3) The conditions of registration to be the same for the time being as those now governing registration under the Act of 1871. In this connection however we make proposals relating to trade union rules in Chapter XI.

(4) The existing register kept by the Registrar of Friendly Societies to be

continued so that trade unions already on it will not need to take any immediate action to continue being registered. Existing unregistered unions, and new unions, to register within a stated time.

(5) All existing laws relating to trade unions to continue to apply to them.

(6) Section 3 of the Conspiracy and Protection of Property Act 1875 and sections 1, 2 and 3 of the Trade Disputes Act 1906 (which in terms apply to persons or combinations of persons) to be made expressly applicable for the benefit of trade unions as well. This may not be strictly necessary, as an incorporated trade union will be a " person " anyway, but it may be desirable to allay any doubts.

(7) The same sections to continue to apply to persons and combinations who are not trade unions with the exception of the first part of section 3 of the Trade Disputes Act 1906. As to this, however, see paragraph 804 below.

(8) The Trade Disputes Act 1965 to remain in force.

(9) No penalty is contemplated for failure to register. It is thought that it would be enough to provide that registration was essential in order that a body should be a trade union.

804. A minority of the Commission (Lord Collison, Professor Clegg, Professor Kahn-Freund, Mr. Eric Wigham and Mr. George Woodcock) cannot support the recommendation that the immunity of the first limb of section 3 of the Trade Disputes Act 1906 should be restricted to registered trade unions and to those acting on their behalf. If unofficial strikers were deprived of the immunity from actions for inducing breaches of contract, they would thereby also automatically be deprived of the protection of section 1, i.e. they would be exposed to actions for civil conspiracy, if they agreed and acted upon an agreement to induce or procure a breach of contract. Such actions would then lie in the case of many, perhaps of most, unofficial strikes. They might lie even if the proper notice were given in the event, for example, of a breach of contract by a supplier or customer of the employer having been procured. As long as our system of collective bargaining is in its present state, these members cannot see any justification for exposing unofficial strikers to a measure of this kind, and they think that it is incompatible with the proposals made in this report for the reform of the collective bargaining system. They are therefore opposed to the recommendation that the sanction for a refusal to register should be the risk of being faced with claims for damages in the event of strikes. The need for compulsory registration could be met by a provision that the members of the Executive Committee of a body which should, but does not, register as a union should be liable to a penalty for each day of default.

805. *Sections 2 and 3 of the 1871 Act.* Notwithstanding that the purposes of a trade union may be in restraint of trade, section 2 of the Trade Union Act 1871 negatives any liability to criminal prosecution on that account of any member of the union: and section 3 of the same Act preserves the validity of agreements and trusts. The benefit of these provisions might be lost by any combination of persons which is a " trade union " within the present definition, but which would cease to be such under the suggested new law if it did not register and satisfy the proposed new definition. We think however that the protection of these two sections should continue in favour of all such combinations as are or would be entitled to them under the present law.

H

806. Employers' associations whose principal activity, or one of whose principal activities, is the regulation of relations between employers and employees should also, in addition to receiving corporate status, be registered. It would be convenient to give these associations a distinctive name, and we suggest that they might be called " Registered Employers' Associations ". One register, to be called " The Register of Trade Unions and Employers' Associations " would probably suffice.

807. Some such associations are already registered under the Companies Acts as companies limited by guarantee. Under the proposed new arrangements we think that they should be registered only on the new Register of Trade Unions and Employers' Associations. The principal advantages which these associations acquired by registration under the Companies Acts were corporate status and limited liability: and these will be available under the new arrangements.

808. It should be expressly provided that the liability of both trade unions and employers' associations registered under the proposed arrangements should be limited to their assets and not extend to the assets of their members.

(5) ENFORCEABILITY OF BINDING CONTRACTS ENTERED INTO BY TRADE UNIONS: SECTION 4, TRADE UNION ACT 1871

809. The purposes of most trade unions in 1871 were, as they still are today, unlawful as being in " restraint of trade ". The common law regards it as unlawful that unreasonable obstructions should be placed in the way of trade, and this includes trade in labour as well as in other things. Accordingly an agreement by a workman, evidenced by his joining a trade union and consenting to obey its rules, whereby he accepts restrictions on his freedom to work for whatever wages and under whatever conditions he pleases, and agrees further not to work when his union orders him to strike, has hitherto been regarded as being in unreasonable restraint of trade and therefore unlawful at common law.

810. One of the purposes of the Act of 1871 was to relieve trade unions from some of the consequences of this doctrine, which could not only expose their members to the risk of prosecution for criminal conspiracy, but also render agreements designed to effect their purposes void and of no effect. Sections 2 and 3 of the Act therefore provided as follows:

> *Section* 2. " The purposes of any trade union shall not, by reason merely that they are in restraint of trade, be deemed to be unlawful, so as to render any member of such trade union liable to criminal prosecution for conspiracy or otherwise."
> *Section* 3. " The purposes of any trade union shall not, by reason merely that they are in restraint of trade, be unlawful so as to render void or voidable any agreement or trust."

If no more had been said, then under section 3 disputes among members as to their rights and obligations under the rules of the union, which rules constitute an agreement between them, might have been made the subject of legal action in the courts. This possibility the Legislature wanted to avoid, and in consequence enacted section 4 of the Act which reads as follows:

Section 4. "Nothing in this Act shall enable any court to entertain any legal proceeding instituted with the object of directly enforcing or recovering damages for the breach of any of the following agreements, namely,

1. Any agreement between members of a trade union as such, concerning the conditions on which any members for the time being of such trade union shall or shall not sell their goods, transact business, employ or be employed:

2. Any agreement for the payment by any person of any subscription or penalty to a trade union:

3. Any agreement for the application of the funds of a trade union—

(a)   To provide benefits to members; or,

(b)   To furnish contributions to any employer or workman not a member of such trade union, in consideration of such employer or workman acting in conformity with the rules or resolutions of such trade union; or,

(c)   To discharge any fine upon any person by sentence of a court of justice; or,

4. Any agreement made between one trade union and another; or,

5. Any bond to secure the performance of any of the above-mentioned agreements.

But nothing in this section shall be deemed to constitute any of the above-mentioned agreements unlawful."

811. This enumeration of specific agreements which were to come within the terms of section 4 makes it clear that the section was not intended to deny to trade unions or their members access to the courts in matters relating to all trade union agreements or relating to all disputes which might arise from trade union rules. In the first place a trade union whose purposes were not in restraint of trade would not need the Act of 1871 to "enable" it to sue; and the restrictive provisions of section 4 apply only to proceedings the object of which was "directly" to enforce an agreement or "directly" to recover damages for its breach. Proceedings having these objects "indirectly" are not within the literal words of the section. Exactly what constitutes "indirect enforcement" is a problem which has caused the courts some difficulty. But on the general scope of section 4 it is pertinent to quote Lord Wrenbury's words in *Amalgamated Society of Carpenters and Joiners v. Braithwaite* [1922] 2 AC at page 470:

"It is plain that under the Act of 1871 a trade union is not outside the jurisdiction of the Court altogether. It is within the jurisdiction as regards contractual obligations other than those specified in section 4."

812. Proceedings which have the objects next specified are among those held by the courts to be outside the prohibitions contained in section 4:

1. To restrain a trade union from dealing with its funds in violation of its rules (*Wolfe v. Matthews* (1882) 21 ChD 194; *Yorkshire Miners' Association v. Howden* [1905] AC 256).

217

2. To prevent a trade union from raising members' subscriptions, or imposing a levy on members, in contravention of the union's rules (*Edwards v. Halliwell* [1950] 2 All ER 1064).

3. To prevent expulsion from the union in violation of its rules (*Amalgamated Society of Carpenters and Joiners v. Braithwaite* [1922] 2 AC 440).

4. To recover damages for wrongful expulsion (*Bonsor v. Musicians' Union* [1956] AC 104).

5. To recover payment of a salary or superannuation benefit owing by a union to one of its officials under a contract of employment.

6. To compel payment to a union's trustees of funds held by a seceding branch.

7. A judgment merely declaring the plaintiff's rights under the rules of trade unions, without an accompanying injunction to enforce an agreement of the type caught by section 4 (*Boulting v. ACTAT* [1963] 2 QB 606 at pp. 629-30).

813. These instances make it plain that a considerable part of trade union affairs is left 'subject to the jurisdiction of the courts by section 4. The question now arises whether the restrictive provisions of the section continue to serve a useful purpose or whether any alteration should be made.

814. The following alternatives are open:

(1) Leave the section entirely as it is, that is to operate according to its present terms, any difficulties of interpretation which remain to be resolved as hitherto by judicial decision as occasion arises.

(2) Repeal the section *in toto*, leaving a trade union and its members as free to resort to the courts upon any question arising between them as would be members of any other similarly constituted body.

This could lead to the somewhat bizarre consequence that a union might seek an injunction against one or more of its members to compel them to come out on strike in fulfilment of their obligation under the union's rules to do so; or alternatively for damages for breach of their contract in this respect. An injunction being a discretionary remedy would probably be refused by the court even if one can envisage a trade union ever seeking it; and damages in such circumstances might also be very difficult for a trade union to prove. Not much harm is likely to be done therefore if the possibility of such proceedings were left to take care of itself.

(3) Re-write section 4 so as to allow complete freedom of access to the courts in matters where it is now restricted, but excluding such matters (e.g. those last mentioned) where it is stil thought desirable to exclude the court's jurisdiction.

We have received representations favouring each of these alternatives.

815. A majority of the Commission favour the complete repeal of the section. In their view its scope has been very greatly cut down by judicial decisions, and there would seem to be no compelling reason today why legal contracts entered into by trade unions should be placed on a different footing from other contracts as regards enforceability. A minority of the Commission (Lord Collison, Lord Tangley and Mr. George Woodcock) favour the retention

of the section. In their view it is still sound policy to minimise the intervention of the law in matters which concern the relations of trade unions with their members and with others. Section 4 does not oust the jurisdiction of the courts altogether, but restricts it as regards certain specified matters only, and these restrictions should remain. Lord Collison and Mr. Woodcock would, however, like to see the section clarified if possible. In this connection we all think that if the section is retained the words " directly enforcing " should be replaced by the words " specifically enforcing ".

(6) DEFINITION OF " TRADE DISPUTE "

816. The definition of a trade dispute is of considerable importance since the existence of such a dispute is indispensable if the provisions of section 3 of the 1875 Act and of sections 1, 2 and 3 of the 1906 Act are to be invoked as a shield against criminal and civil proceedings. The definition in section 5 (3) is this:

> " In this Act and in the Conspiracy and Protection of Property Act 1875 the expression ' trade dispute ' means

> *any dispute between employers and workmen,*
> *or between workmen and workmen,*
> *which is connected with*
> *the employment or non-employment*
> *or the terms of the employment,*
> *or with the conditions of labour,*
> *of any person,*
> *and the expression ' workmen '*
> *means all persons employed*
> *in trade or industry,*
> *whether or not in the employment*
> *of the employer with whom a trade dispute arises."*

817. We do not think that this definition needs any substantial alteration. Fears have however been expressed in some quarters that recent judicial decisions have thrown doubt upon whether a recognition dispute is a trade dispute within this definition. One of these decisions is said to be that of the House of Lords in *Stratford v. Lindley* [1965] AC 269.

818. In that case, however, the union concerned (the Watermen's etc., Union) had remained quiescent for about a year after the employer, Bowker and King Ltd., had declined to negotiate with them over the wages and conditions of the three men, out of 48 in its employ, who belonged to the union. When, however, at the end of this period Bowker and King Ltd. recognised the T&GWU for negotiating purposes (it represented the other 45 employees) the Watermen's Union struck, not at Bowker and King Ltd., but at its subsidiary company, Stratford Ltd., in which the Watermen's Union had no members. It did this without inquiring whether, since the T&GWU had now been recognised by Bowker and King Ltd., the Watermen's Union might also now be recognised by that company. In these circumstances it was held by the House of Lords in interlocutory proceedings that the existence of *any* dispute

had not yet been proved. It was not known what the reaction of Bowker and King Ltd. would have been if there had been a fresh request by the Watermen's Union for recognition. But some members of the House of Lords indicated that, if there had been such a fresh request and a fresh refusal, a trade dispute would then have existed. Thus Lord Pearce:

> " When a union makes a genuine claim on the employers for bargaining status with a view to regulating or improving the conditions or pay of their workmen and the employers reject the claim a trade dispute is in contemplation even though no active dispute has yet arisen (see, for instance, *Beetham v. Trinidad Cement Co. Ltd.* [1960] AC 132)."

819. The case cited is a decision of the Judicial Committee of the Privy Council to the effect that a dispute over recognition was a trade dispute within the words of the present definition. While the decision would not bind a court in the United Kingdom it has great persuasive authority. The latest decision to the effect that a recognition dispute is a " trade dispute " appears to be that in *Square Grip Reinforcement Company Ltd. v. Macdonald and Others* [1968] SLT 65. We see no need therefore for express provision to be made declaring a dispute over recognition to be a " trade dispute ". If this view is, for any reason, mistaken however, such a provision can easily be made.

820. The following members of the Commission, namely Lord Robens, Sir George Pollock and Mr. John Thomson, are of the opinion that demarcation disputes between trade unions in which the employer is neutral (that is, is indifferent as to which of the contending parties' members do the particular job) should be excluded from the statutory definition of trade dispute, and that this should be achieved by deleting the words " or between workmen and workmen ". They point out that the dispute they have in mind is not of the employer's making, that he can do nothing to resolve it and that in these circumstances it is unjust that he should be debarred from exercising legal remedies which might otherwise be open to him. The remaining members of the Royal Commission consider that it would be difficult to distinguish and define a demarcation dispute in which an employer was completely neutral and that as productivity bargaining spreads employers are likely to become more involved in defining the duties of particular workers. Demarcation disputes moreover are not nearly so costly in terms of working days lost as they used to be, and the problem is not so pressing as to justify altering the definition of a trade dispute in the way proposed. To do so would, in any event, not solve the dispute: it would merely leave the employer free to sue for damages in certain cases where he cannot sue now. Whether he would take advantage of such freedom is doubtful.

821. Section 5(3) defines the expression " workmen " which is contained in the definition as meaning " all persons employed in trade or industry ". The TUC in its evidence questioned whether this phrase would cover those " in the public sector ". It would, we suggest, clearly cover those in the nationalised industries, but, at first sight, hardly those employed by local authorities, by the National Health Service, by educational or other charitable institutions, or by other non-profit-making bodies. It is true that in an *obiter dictum* in *National Association of Local Government Officers v. Bolton Corporation* [1943]

AC 166 at pp. 184-185 Lord Wright placed a wide interpretation on the words "trade or industry". Nevertheless the matter remains open to doubt, and the Irish courts have adopted a narrow construction in a number of cases. We are of the opinion that the scope of the 1875, 1906 and 1965 Acts should be co-extensive with that of the Industrial Courts Act 1919, which deals with the settlement of trade disputes, but that, as in the Redundancy Payments Act 1965, words should be added to make it clear that the termination of the contract of employment does not remove the protection given by the Acts. The definition would then read as follows:

"The expression 'employee' means any person who has entered into or works under (or, in the case of a contract which has been terminated, worked under) a contract with an employer, whether the contract be by way of manual labour, clerical work, or otherwise, be expressed or implied, oral or in writing, and whether it be a contract of service or of apprenticeship or a contract personally to execute any work or labour."

822. Under the present law, a dispute over the matters specified in section 5(3) between an employers' association representing employers and a trade union representing workmen is regarded as a dispute "between employers and workmen" so as to qualify as a "trade dispute". If such employers' associations and trade unions become incorporated bodies it would perhaps be desirable to add words to the definition which would make it clear that the change in their status made no difference in this respect.

(7) CONSPIRACY AND PROTECTION OF PROPERTY ACT 1875

823. The policy of abstention from intervention in trade disputes was exemplified in the criminal law well before it influenced the law of tort. The above Act of 1875 was one instance. Another was the abolition, subject to some important exemptions, of criminal prosecution of workers for breach of their contracts of employment. This was the effect of the above Act of 1875 and of the Employers and Workmen Act passed in the same year. Since then the criminal law has played a minor role in the regulation of trade disputes, although of course its provisions have to be observed.

824. Section 2 of the Trade Union Act 1871 declared that the purposes of a trade union should not, merely because they were in restraint of trade, render any member of the trade union liable to criminal prosecution; and the Criminal Law Amendment Act 1871 by restricting the definition of "threats" and "intimidation" made a mere threat to strike no longer a statutory offence. Nevertheless a threat by certain London gas stokers to go on strike unless a fellow workman, discharged for union activity, was re-instated resulted in their conviction in 1872 on a charge of criminal conspiracy and in a sentence of 12 months' imprisonment (see *Reg. v. Bunn* (1872) 12 Cox 316). The common law had not been abrogated by the Acts of 1871, said Brett J. (who tried the case), so as to permit an act done with improper intent and amounting to an unjustifiable annoyance and interference with the employer's business. The consequence of this decision was that a strike or a threat to go on strike might lead to a criminal prosecution for conspiracy to coerce.

825. This decision led to the appointment of the Royal Commission on

Labour Laws of 1874, and after its report the Conspiracy and Protection of Property Act 1875 was passed. Its long title is:

"An Act for Amending the Law Relating to Conspiracy, and To The Protection of Property and for Other Purposes ".

826.   Section 3 provides that an agreement or combination by two or more persons to do or procure to be done any act in contemplation or furtherance of a trade dispute shall not be indictable as a conspiracy if such act, committed by one person, would not be punishable as a crime.

827.   To strike, or to threaten to do so, was no longer therefore a criminal offence and the decision in *Reg. v. Bunn* ceased to be law. This change in the law of criminal conspiracy was a turning point in the law governing labour relations.

828.   Until 1875 manual workers were, in certain circumstances, liable to criminal prosecution for breach of their contracts of employment. The relevant statute then in force was the Master and Servant Act 1867, which was repealed by the above Act of 1875. Its place was taken by the Employers and Workmen Act 1875, which put employers and workmen on a footing of equality by providing civil instead of criminal remedies for breach by either party of a contract of employment.

829.   There were however a number of exceptions to this rule. Two of them are contained in the Conspiracy and Protection of Property Act itself, the relevant provisions being sections 4 and 5. These we now consider (Mr. Shonfield's differing views being expressed in his note at the end of our report).

Section 4

830.   Section 4 makes it a criminal offence for any person to break a contract of service in the following circumstances:

1.   He is employed by a gas undertaking, or a water undertaking, which supplies gas or water to the inhabitants of a city, borough, town or place.
2.   He wilfully and maliciously breaks a contract of service with the gas or water undertakers.
3.   He knows or has reasonable cause to believe that the probable consequence of his so doing, whether alone or in combination with others, will be to deprive the inhabitants concerned wholly, or to a great extent, of their gas or water.

831.   The punishment prescribed is a fine of £20 or imprisonment not exceeding 3 months. The section goes on to impose a duty upon gas and water supply undertakers to post, and keep posted, a printed copy of the section in some conspicuous place in the works.

832.   It is no offence under this section for an employee to terminate his contract of service with a gas or water undertaking by proper notice; but for such an employee to go on strike in breach of his contract without giving such notice would contravene the section, provided that the other conditions which it stipulates were present.

833.   In 1919 the provisions of the section were extended so as to cover persons employed by authorised electricity undertakers.

834.   The Chairman of the Gas Council, who gave evidence before us, could recollect only one case where proceedings under the section were taken.

This was in 1950, when the men involved were prosecuted both under section 4 and under the Emergency Powers Regulations. A conviction having been obtained under those regulations the proceedings under the section were withdrawn. In his opinion the section served a useful purpose still, as being a reminder to those engaged in the industry of its importance to the safety of the public: and while the great majority of the Boards' employees have a very high sense of their responsibility to the public, this particular legislation may well have a deterrent effect on a small pocket of discontented people. On the whole he would not be willing to see it go.

835. The Chairman of the Electricity Council took a similar view. We had no evidence from any water supply undertaker.

836. Some witnesses on the other hand took the view that the section should now be repealed on the grounds that in principle it was wrong to visit criminal sanctions upon breaches of contract. Among trade unions the National and Local Government Officers' Association considered that the section discriminated unfairly against employees in public utility under-takings; and that there was today no valid reason for it, since many other industries and occupations were also of great public importance.

837. The London Transport Board in its evidence asked the Commission to consider the desirability of extending section 4 to cover public transport undertakings. The Board did not envisage that, if this were done, it would necessarily prosecute large numbers of its drivers or conductors who went on strike without notice, but thought that the possibility would have a restraining influence on such impulsive conduct.

838. We do not recommend that the section should be either repealed or extended. The section does not make it an offence to participate in a strike. It penalises certain breaches of contract. If, by giving the contractual or statutory notice (usually a week), the employees concerned terminate their contracts, they commit no offence. The effect of the section is therefore to give to the employer and through him to the public previous warning of a stoppage which, in view of the nature of these industries, may expose the public to special danger. The difference between these public utility industries and other service industries (such as public transport) is that they affect every household, and that a stoppage of supplies without warning (and also, for example in the case of gas, their resumption) may have serious conse-quences as regards the health and safety of the population. The fact that the employer is under a statutory obligation to exhibit the wording of the section at the place of work brings this home to the employees. This alone would justify its continued existence even if section 5 of the Act (which deals with danger to life and health and which we discuss below) is also continued. We were also told, however, by the Chairmen of two of these three industries that the section does have a useful restraining influence by imposing, in effect, a short period of delay equal to the length of the period of notice required to terminate the contract of employment.

839. It might be suggested that section 4 should be extended to other industries of vital and immediate concern to the public, such as transport. The specific risks to the public inherent in stoppages in water, gas or

electricity supply are not however present in stoppages in these other industries; and if future technical development should lead to the creation of similar risks connected with other services or supplies, the section could be extended to them as, in 1919, it was extended to electricity. Moreover, it was one thing to introduce section 4 into an Act of 1875 when Parliament was taking what must have seemed at the time bold steps towards the legalisation of trade union and strike action, and no doubt thought it prudent to provide safeguards for the public in matters of special importance. It would be another thing altogether to introduce the like criminal sanctions today for breaches of contract in a new field. The evidence falls far short of convincing us that this is necessary, or even desirable. The chief value of section 4 today is, we think, that it imposes a short period of delay before work ceases. The public is thus assured of getting adequate warning before supplies are stopped and an opportunity for final negotiations is presented.

Section 5

840. This section imposes criminal liability over a wider field than section 4. It applies to " any person " who
    (1) wilfully and maliciously breaks a contract of service or of hiring,
    (2) knowing or having reasonable cause to believe
    (3) that the probable consequences of his so doing, either alone or in combination with others, will be
    (4) (a) to endanger human life, or
        (b) to cause serious bodily injury, or
        (c) to expose valuable property to destruction or serious injury.
The penalty on conviction is a fine of £20 or imprisonment not exceeding 3 months.

841. In contradistinction to section 4, section 5 applies to both parties to a contract of service, and not merely to the employee. An employer who broke an obligation on his part under a contract of service and thereby provoked a stoppage of work having the probable consequences specified in the section might be criminally liable thereunder. The section, unlike section 4, also applies to " contracts of hiring ", and there appears to be no good ground for restricting this term to contracts of hiring of services; *prima facie* it covers contracts for the hire of goods, e.g. machinery and equipment.

842. So construed the section covers a very wide field; and persons who would not be covered by section 4 might well be within section 5. *Citrine's Trade Union Law* instances drivers, signalmen, pilots, surgeons, hospital staffs, sewage workers, haulage contractors, etc., the breach of whose contracts might endanger life or expose valuable property to destruction or serious injury. So far as we are aware, however, there has not yet been a prosecution for an offence under this section.

843. We have considered whether it is necessary to preserve both sections 4 and 5; or whether on the other hand it would be better simply to have one statutory provision based on the principle that it was a public wrong to break contracts wilfully and maliciously where the probable and foreseeable consequences were those mentioned in both the existing sections, and that commission of this wrong should be visited by criminal sanctions. If

however the Legislature proceeded upon this basis, the question would at once arise why such criminal sanctions should be dependent on a breach of contract by the offender? Why should the giving of (say) seven days' notice to terminate his contract make all the difference, notwithstanding that the consequences of his action might remain the same? There might well be cases where seven days' notice would not avert them or at any rate all of them. On the other hand to extend the criminal law to cases where a person lawfully terminated his contract of service would be open to serious objection.

844. Short of such extension, to have one section instead of two would no doubt make for tidiness and could be achieved by suitable additions to section 5, but we see no other advantage.

845. It might be recalled that by section 6(4) of the Trade Disputes and Trade Union Act 1927 the provisions of section 4 of the 1875 Act were extended to cover certain breaches of contracts of service with local or public authorities. This extension was repealed by the Trade Disputes and Trade Union Act 1946.

846. The repeal of either of these sections involves the risk that it might be construed as an express licence to do that which the criminal law now forbids. On the whole, we think that these two sections should be left undisturbed.

847. We have not dealt in this report with the special position of seamen in relation to strikes. Separate legislation is here in question dealing with the circumstances of employment at sea, and it is for those with knowledge of the special problems involved to suggest how they may best be solved. The general principle should be that to the extent compatible with their calling seamen should have the same rights as other employees.

(8) LIABILITY FOR CIVIL CONSPIRACY AND OTHER TORTS: THE TRADE DISPUTES ACTS 1906 AND 1965

848. Criminal prosecutions have long ceased to play a major role as a reaction of the law to the use of industrial sanctions, but actions for tort continue to be of great importance. The difference between criminal and civil liability is well understood and fundamental, but in practice it may not be as far-reaching as appears at first sight. A person who is liable in tort may be ordered to pay damages, but he may also be subjected to an injunction. If he violates this he may be committed to prison for contempt of court and this may be a penalty as serious as, or more serious than, that following upon a criminal prosecution. It is thus very largely for the law of tort to draw the line between the protection of the right to strike which, as Lord Wright said in a celebrated judgment, is " an essential element in the principle of collective bargaining ", and the protection of the rights of others which may be adversely affected by its exercise. No " right to strike " has ever been formally proclaimed by our law. What Lord Wright referred to is a freedom to act without interference by the law. Much the most significant aspect of that freedom is the immunity from liability for tort based on the principles of the common law.

849. The borderline between that which is permissible and that which is prohibited in industrial relations is therefore for the most part drawn by

those statutes which define the immunity from liability of persons acting " in contemplation or furtherance of a trade dispute ". These statutes are the Trade Disputes Acts of 1906 and of 1965.

850. The Trade Disputes Act 1906 was passed after the publication of the Report of the Royal Commission on Trade Disputes and Trade Combinations under the Chairmanship of Lord Dunedin. The Royal Commission had been appointed to consider the effect and if necessary the reform of the law as it had emerged from a number of important decisions on common law liability in tort given around the turn of the century. Of these the decisions of the House of Lords in *Taff Vale Ry. Co.* v. *Amalgamated Society of Railway Servants* [1901] AC 426 and in *Quinn v. Leathem* [1901] AC 495 had the most far-reaching effect. The first established that trade unions could be sued in their registered name and that they were liable to satisfy out of their funds liabilities in tort incurred by those acting on their behalf. The second affirmed that the protection which the Conspiracy and Protection of Property Act 1875 gave to those acting " in contemplation or furtherance of a trade dispute " against prosecutions for criminal conspiracy did not extend to actions for civil conspiracy. It was this case which also decided that those using industrial sanctions as a result of an agreement, that is by way of collective action, could be liable in tort in circumstances in which an individual acting alone would not be liable.

851. The Trade Disputes Act 1906 was intended to deal with these two decisions. It provided by section 1 that an act done in pursuance of an agreement by two or more persons and in contemplation or furtherance of a trade dispute should not be actionable unless the act done without any such agreement or combination would be actionable. It also enacted that an act done by a person in contemplation or furtherance of a trade dispute should not be actionable on the ground only that it induced another person to break a contract of employment. It went on to enact by section 4 that no action in tort should be brought against any trade union. The rights of pickets were enlarged by section 2 so as to enable them peacefully to persuade any person to work or not to work.

852. The protection afforded by the statute in respect of acts done in contemplation or furtherance of a trade dispute is in terms which preclude the use of unlawful means. In 1964 in the case of *Rookes v. Barnard* [1964] AC 1129 the House of Lords held that a threat by persons that contracts of employment would be broken unless the employer conceded their demand was a threat to do something unlawful and constituted the tort of intimidation. Consequently the persons concerned, when sued for damages for civil conspiracy, could not rely on the protection afforded by the 1906 Act. This decision was nullified by the Trade Disputes Act 1965. We think that this last statute was necessary for the protection of trade union officials in the reasonable performance of their functions and do not recommend its repeal.

853. The common law now seems to have been brought largely into line with section 1 of the 1906 Act. Cases such as the *Mogul Steamship Company v. McGregor Gow and Co.* [1892] AC 25, *Sorrell v. Smith* [1925] AC 700 and *Crofter Hand Woven Harris Tweed Co. v. Veitch* [1942] AC 435 have established the proposition that the tort of civil conspiracy is not committed where,

226

although some person is injured, those who combined and caused the injury were acting with the predominant object of advancing their own legitimate interests and used no unlawful means. Section 1 nevertheless contains special advantages for those whom it covers. First, proof that there is a trade dispute, and that the act complained of was done in contemplation or furtherance of it, dispenses with the need for establishing anything about the predominant motive of the actors. Secondly, the definition of a trade dispute, covering as it does sympathetic action, means that the protection of the section can be invoked even if the predominant motive was to promote someone else's legitimate interests. Subject to the point next to be mentioned we recommend no alteration in section 1.

854. In consequence of the decision in *Rookes v. Barnard* [1964] AC 1129, however, it has been suggested that liability for civil conspiracy might arise where a number of persons agreed together, in contemplating or furtherance of a trade dispute, to break their contracts of employment in combination, since they would be parties to an agreement to do an " unlawful " act. If done by one person alone, the act, i.e. breach of his own contract, would be actionable, and accordingly the protection of section 1 would not be available. Nor would the combination be protected by the Trade Disputes Act 1965. This possibility is one which we think should be removed by legislation.

(9) PICKETING

855. Where a strike occurs it is obviously in the interests of the strikers to dissuade, if they can, other workmen from replacing them and customers of the employer from dealing with him while the strike continues. This involves that such other workmen and such customers must know that a strike is taking place and the men's side of the case. From the strikers' point of view the most effective means for this purpose is the placing of pickets outside the place of work.

856. It has, we think, never been illegal under the law simply to communicate information to a person in order to persuade him not to enter into or to renew contractual relations with another. In the atmosphere engendered by a strike, however, men who are enduring the privations which may accompany it would hardly be human if they viewed with composure the spectacle of other workmen endeavouring to take over their jobs or the apparent uninterrupted flow of custom to their employer. The law therefore has had to deal with the problems that picketing may sometimes go beyond mere attempts at peaceful persuasion and erupt into a variety of forms of intimidation in violation of the rights of others.

857. Thus in 1824 the Combination Laws Repeal Act, while removing criminal liability for the act of combining to increase wages or decrease hours of work, specifically provided by section 5 that it should be an offence punishable by imprisonment to resort to violence, threats or intimidation in order *inter alia* to force a person to desist from work or to prevent him from accepting work, or to force any master to make any alteration in the mode of carrying on his business. Threats and intimidation were not however defined.

858. In 1825 the Combination Laws Repeal Act (Amendment) Act repealed

the above Act of 1824: but provided by section 3 that it should thenceforward be an offence punishable by imprisonment to resort to violence, threats, intimidation, molestation or obstruction in order to force any workman to leave his work or to prevent him from accepting work, or to force any manufacturer or trader into any alteration in his mode of carrying on his business.

859. Again, threats and intimidation remained undefined, as did " molestation " and " obstruction ", which were now added to the kind of conduct which was proscribed. These last two words could obviously be construed in such a way as to make picketing which was free from violence, or threats, or intimidation, still a criminal offence. Thus although men might lawfully combine to improve their wages and conditions, a strike for this purpose might well be rendered ineffective by the section.

860. The Molestation of Workmen Act 1859 ameliorated the position to the extent of enacting that merely to endeavour peaceably to persuade others, without threats or intimidation, to cease work in order to obtain the rates of wages or hours of labour being sought was not to be deemed to be " molestation " or " obstruction " and was not therefore to be a ground for a prosecution for conspiracy.

861. Following the report of the Royal Commission on Trade Unions appointed in 1867, the Criminal Law Amendment Act 1871 was passed. This repealed the Acts of 1825 and 1859 above mentioned. In relation to picketing it provided by section 1 a definition of threats, intimidation, molestation and obstruction. The section made it an offence to use violence, or such threats or intimidation as would justify a justice of the peace in binding the offender over to keep the peace, in order, among other things, to coerce a workman into quitting any employment or a master into altering the mode of carrying on his business.

862. A person was to be deemed to molest or obstruct another if he persistently followed such other person from place to place, or hid his tools or clothes, or watched or beset his house or place of work or business, or, with others, followed such other person in a disorderly manner through any street or road. The Act expressly provided however that no person was to be liable to any punishment for doing any act tending to restrain the free course of trade, unless it was one of the acts specified in section 1 and was done for the purpose of the coercion therein mentioned. It was apparently thought unnecessary in those circumstances specifically to declare that peaceful picketing was lawful.

863. The Criminal Law Amendment Act 1871 was in its turn repealed by the Conspiracy and Protection of Property Act 1875. By section 7 of that Act it was declared to be a criminal offence for any person, wrongfully and without legal authority and with a view to compelling another to do or not do any act which that other had a legal right to do:

1. To use violence to or intimidate such other person or his wife or children, or to injure his property.
2. Persistently to follow such other person about from place to place.
3. To hide any tools, clothes or other property owned or used by such other person or deprive him of them, or hinder him in the use thereof.

4. To watch or beset such other person's house or place of work or business or the approach thereto.

5. To follow such other person with two or more other persons in a disorderly manner in or through any street or road.

864. A further provision enacted that attending at a person's house or place of work or business merely to obtain or communicate information was not to be deemed a " watching or besetting ". This provision was however replaced by a wider one in the Trade Disputes Act of 1906. Otherwise section 7 of the 1875 Act remains law today.

865. Section 2 (1) of the Trade Disputes Act 1906 provides as follows:
" It shall be lawful for one or more persons, acting on their own behalf or on behalf of a trade union or of an individual employer or firm in contemplation or furtherance of a trade dispute, to attend at or near a house or place where a person resides or works or carries on business or happens to be, if they so attend merely for the purpose of peacefully obtaining or communicating information, or of peacefully persuading any person to work or abstain from working."

866. The important addition made by this section is the liberty which it gives to attend at a person's house or place of work etc. in order peaceably to persuade him to work or not to work. Section 7 of the 1875 Act had referred merely to the purpose of obtaining or communicating information.

867. So far as the right to picket rests on statute it now rests upon section 2 of the Act of 1906. The provisions of section 7 of the 1875 Act which still remain are a statement of offences which pickets, as well as others, must avoid committing.

868. From the workers' point of view the defect in the law up to 1906 was that it gave protection to pickets only when they were obtaining or communicating information. If they went beyond this and endeavoured to persuade other persons either not to accept work or to discontinue work, they might commit the offence of " watching or besetting " within section 7 of the 1875 Act.

869. Since this omission has been rectified by section 2 of the 1906 Act, there is little point in reciting the judicial decisions on the earlier legislation. They will be found conveniently collected in Professor Grunfeld's recent book on trade union law.[1] Those cases, and also the cases which have been decided upon section 2 of the 1906 Act, show that it has not been easy for the courts to distinguish clearly the boundary between action by pickets which stays on the right side of the line and that which constitutes an invasion across the line of the rights of others.

870. Two recent cases on section 2 of the Act of 1906 might be mentioned. In *Piddington v. Bates* [1960] 3 All ER 660 a police constable told Piddington, a would-be picket, that the two existing pickets at the particular entrance to the employer's premises were enough. Piddington however insisted on attempting to join them as a third picket and was arrested. There was no obstruction of the highway, no violence and no disorder. Piddington

---

[1]Cyril Grunfeld, *Modern Trade Union Law*, Sweet & Maxwell, 1966.

was, however, convicted of obstructing a police constable in the execution of his duty contrary to the Prevention of Crimes Amendment Act 1885, section 2: and, on appeal to the Divisional Court of the Queen's Bench Division, the conviction was upheld. The magistrates accepted that on the evidence (not set out in the report of the case) the police constable was reasonably justified in expecting a breach of the peace unless he thinned out the picket line. The Lord Chief Justice said:

> " The law is reasonably plain. First the mere statement of a constable that he did anticipate that there might be a breach of the peace is clearly not enough. There must exist proved facts from which a constable could reasonably have anticipated such a breach. Second, it is not enough that his contemplation is that there is a remote possibility, but there must be a real possibility of a breach of the peace. Accordingly in every case it becomes a question whether, on the particular facts, there were reasonable grounds on which a constable charged with this duty reasonably anticipated that a breach of the peace might occur."

871. In *Tynan v. Balmer* [1965] 3 All ER 99 and [1966] 2 All ER 133 forty pickets outside the main entrance to a factory moved about in a continuous circle thus obstructing vehicles and pedestrians. There was no violence. Tynan, who was in charge of the pickets, was asked by a constable to stop the circling, but refused. He was arrested and later convicted by a magistrate for wilfully obstructing the police constable in the execution of his duty. The conviction was upheld in the Crown Court at Liverpool and in the Court of Appeal. It was held:

(1) that the powers of the police to interfere with picketing were not confined to cases where a breach of the peace was feared;

(2) that the circling was not justified by section 2 of the 1906 Act; and

(3) that the circling was an unjustified obstruction of the highway.

872. It should be noted that section 2 of the 1906 Act, in relation to customers and suppliers whose business the strikers may wish to cut off from the employer, permits picketing only for the purpose of peaceably obtaining or communicating information. It does not of itself sanction attempts to persuade customers and suppliers to cease to do business with the employer. Such attempts will be subject to the general law outside the 1906 Act.

873. We received a number of suggestions for the alteration of the law relating to picketing, ranging from its complete abolition to considerably more freedom for pickets.

874. The TUC asked that section 2 be amplified so as to permit communication by pickets with a person " whether that person is in a vehicle or on foot ". There is however at present nothing in the section to preclude this. The Society of Labour Lawyers went further and suggested that a limited right should be given to pickets to stop vehicles so as to communicate with the drivers, due regard being had to other users of the highway. It seems to us, however, that it would be impossible to define such a right in terms which would avoid considerable obstruction to the highway and serious risk

of personal injury to the pickets themselves. Others urged that "mass picketing" should be protected by the law. It is not clear however why mass picketing is required simply to communicate information, and the advocates of this proposal did not suggest that they desired it for any other purpose than to demonstrate solidarity, which can be done equally well by other means. The National Federation of Building Trades Employers on the other hand complained that the provisions of section 2 enabled a handful of pickets during the recent disputes at the Horseferry Road and Barbican building sites to hold up work for many months there in defiance of the decision of their trade unions, and would wish to see some appropriate curtailment of the right to picket in such circumstances. As to this we might say that information given to us suggests that the fault lay not with the provisions of section 2 but with the action of the pickets in going, upon occasion, beyond what section 2 permits, and being allowed to do so with impunity for many months.

875. In considering these and other similar suggestions, it should be recalled that the prime objects of picketing are to make known the existence and the facts of the dispute and peaceably to persuade persons to abstain from working. Obstruction or intimidation of those wishing to work is unlawful and no change in the law in this respect has been advocated by anybody. In the circumstances, and subject to the exception next to be mentioned, it seems to the majority of us that the law as contained in section 2 and as further explained by the Lord Chief Justice in *Piddington v. Bates* (*supra*) is reasonably satisfactory. The exception is that section 2 does not expressly permit the peaceful persuasion of any customer or potential customer of the employer in dispute not to deal with him while the dispute continues. Such persuasion is however frequently attempted, and most persons, we think, regard it as legitimate. In our opinion section 2 should be amplified so as to make such peaceful persuasion lawful.

876. The following members of the Commission, namely Lord Donovan, Lord Robens, Dame Mary Green and Sir George Pollock, consider however that picketing should not be allowed at a person's home where this is not also his place of work. They consider that in such cases it is quite unnecessary: information can be peaceably communicated or sought by post. The liberty to picket a person's home involves the risk of threats to his family which are quite unjustifiable, and may cause much distress. No doubt such threats are a breach of the law, but the victims are unlikely in most cases to bring proceedings. Section 2 should therefore be amended so as to preclude the picketing of a person's home.

877. A majority of members consider that the Commission has had no evidence of abuse of the right to picket sufficient to justify such a restriction.

(10) INDUCEMENT OF BREACH OF CONTRACT IN CONTEMPLATION OR FURTHERANCE OF A TRADE DISPUTE: SECTION 3, TRADE DISPUTES ACT 1906

878. Trade union officials who induce their members to come out on strike without giving the requisite notice to end their contracts of employment

commit a tort for which, in the ordinary way, they could be sued personally for damages. The trade union itself could not be sued, being protected by the provisions of section 4 of the Trade Disputes Act 1906. But if the trade union paid the damages awarded in such a case against its officials, the cost might be heavy.

879. Prior to the passing of section 4 of the 1906 Act a number of trade unions were themselves successfully sued for damages for inducing breaches of contracts of employment. Examples are the *Taff Vale Railway* case [1901] AC 426; *Read v. Friendly Society of Operative Stonemasons* [1902] 2 KB 732; and *South Wales Miners' Federation v. Glamorgan Coal Company* [1905] AC 239.

880. The law was altered by what is now section 3 of the Trade Disputes Act 1906. This provides *inter alia* that

"an act done by a person in contemplation or furtherance of a trade dispute shall not be actionable on the ground only that it induces some other person to break a contract of employment . . ."

This provision is commonly referred to as the "first limb" of section 3: and it provides a defence to trade union officials and other persons in the circumstances above envisaged.

881. When the Trade Disputes Bill was introduced by the Government of 1906, clause 3 did not contain this first limb. It provided simply that an act done by a person in contemplation or furtherance of a trade dispute should not be actionable on the ground only that it was an interference with the trade, business or employment of some other person or with the right of some other person to dispose of his capital or labour as he willed.

882. This provision is now the concluding part of section 3 and we have some observations to make upon it later. It is usually called the "second limb" of the section.

883. The first limb owes its origin to an amendment moved on the Committee stage of the bill by Sir Charles Dilke, the then Liberal member for the Forest of Dean, which the Government accepted, and which was carried on a division.

884. It will be seen that it refers only to a contract of employment. Trade union officials and others who induce a breach of any other kind of contract, whether in contemplation or furtherance of a trade dispute or not, still commit an actionable tort. We have received a number of representations to the effect that this situation should be altered and that section 3 should be amended so as to extend to all contracts and not merely to contracts of employment. These representations come from the TUC, a number of trade unions, some legal authors having a close knowledge of trade union law, and the Bar Council. The Law Society opposes the suggestion. So also does the CBI, which fears that it would lead to a considerable extension of the disruption of commercial affairs caused by strikes.

885. When giving evidence before us the CBI was asked to explain its objection in more detail. It then said that if the protection given by section 3 were extended to persons who in contemplation or furtherance of a trade

dispute induced the breach of a commercial contract, an employer in dispute with his workpeople might find his sources of supply of materials, or his outlet for sales, cut off by breach of such contracts so induced, and be without redress.

886. This is true. Indeed the very object of trade union officials or others who induced such breaches of commercial contracts would be to bring about such additional economic pressure on the employer in dispute. It is argued by those in favour of extending section 3 that there is no essential difference between embarrassing an employer by persuading his employees to break their contracts of employment in contemplation or furtherance of a trade dispute, and embarrassing him in the like circumstances by persuading his suppliers or his customers to break their contracts of sale or purchase.

887. It is not possible at this distance of time to say why the protection afforded by section 3 was confined to breaches of contracts of employment. The first limb of the section owes its origin, as we have said, to a private member's amendment. The contracts of which trade union officers were most likely to induce a breach were contracts of employment; and the cases decided in the courts against trade unions seem to have been cases of that kind. It may therefore have seemed to Sir Charles Dilke at the time that this was the situation which called for some immediate action and that there was no present need to go further. Limited as it was, his amendment aroused strong opposition.

888. At the present time, however, it is a familiar aspect of trade disputes that trade unions not only call out their members on strike but also endeavour to exert additional economic pressure on the employer in dispute by sealing off his sources of supply of materials or his outlet for sales, or both: and unless unlawful means are used to secure these ends, such action is permissible.

889. Lawful means are, in fact, available to achieve both the foregoing purposes; and if in this field trade union officials and others collide with the law, it is not because they have kept supplies away from an employer or stopped his sales, but because they have used for these purposes methods which the law regards as wrongful. If the law upon the subject were clear, any trade union official or other person who adopted wrongful means would have only himself to blame. The law, however, upon this subject is far from clear.

890. Beginning with the comparatively straightforward case of *Lumley v. Gye* (1853) 2 E & B 216, where an opera singer was directly induced to break her contract to sing at Covent Garden by a rival impresario, the law has found itself confronted, very largely in trade union cases, by a variety of other steps which have led to breaches of contract and upon the legality of which the courts have had to pronounce. They include the tendering of advice, a statement of possible consequences if the relevant contract is maintained, and the persuasion of a third party into taking some action having the effect of causing the relevant contract to be broken. In the result the law has become complicated and irrational. The one element in it which might

233

be said to be constant is that the method by which the breach of contract is brought about is the all-important factor.

891.   In the context of a trade dispute the position would appear to be as follows:

(1) Mere advice is not inducement; so that a trade union official who advises a customer of the employer in dispute that he should consider his business relations with that employer in the light of the dispute commits no tort even if in consequence of such advice the customer breaks his contract.

(2) Such advice will not constitute an inducement to break a contract even if it calls attention to the possible dangers for the customer of continuing to deal with the employer in dispute.

(3) If, however, a trade union official threatens a customer of the employer in dispute that, unless he ceases to deal with him, the customer's own employees will be called out on strike, and in consequence the customer breaks his contract with the employer in dispute, the trade union official commits the tort of inducing the breach of such contract.

(4) If the trade union official ignores the customer altogether and goes directly to the customer's employees and persuades them to come out on strike without giving due notice under their contracts of employment to cease work, and this is done successfully in order to persuade the customer to cease to deal with the employer in dispute, the latter may sue the trade union official for inducing the customer's breach of contract.   This is a case of " indirect inducement " or " procuring " and is actionable because unlawful means were counselled and employed, to wit the breach of their contracts of employment by the customer's employees.

(5) If in the last instance, however, the trade union official had persuaded the customer's employees first to give the due notice under their contracts of employment, and to strike only when such notice had expired, the employer in dispute could not sue the official if the customer gave in and broke his contract.   The reason is that no unlawful means have been counselled or used.   The strikers were entitled to cease work on giving due notice, and the exercise of a legal right gives no cause of action to a person injured by the exercise.

892.   Thus any trade union official today who wishes to cause a breach of a commercial contract between the employer in dispute and one or more of his customers can do so without risk of committing a tort, simply by using methods (1), (2) or (5).   It may well be asked in these circumstances why there is any need to extend the provision of section 3 in the manner proposed.   The answer in our opinion is that the law upon the subject ought not to be left in such a state that all persons, whether they be employees, employers or trade union officials should be so uncertain of their position. For example, one Judge has said that " advice which is intended to have persuasive effect is not distinguishable from inducement " (1940 Ch. at p.366), while another has said that advice may properly extend to warnings which draw attention to the facts and the dangers for the party advised (1952 Ch. at

p.686). These statements pose an almost insoluble problem for the trade union official seeking to "advise" a customer of the employer in dispute without being persuasive at the same time. Employers themselves apparently misunderstand the law. We are told that some of them, as soon as a strike is threatened, serve the officials of the union or unions concerned with a list of their commercial contracts and intimate that, if because of the strike they have to break them, the officials will be liable in damages for inducing their breach. This is a fallacy. The tort is not committed in such circumstances. Such breaches of contract would be the incidental, even if inevitable, consequences of the strike, and not the result of any "inducement" such as would found a right of action. Finally more doubt has been recently introduced into the law by certain dicta in the case of *Stratford v. Lindley* [1965] AC 269.

893. Seeing that it is possible in the existing state of the law for trade unions or other persons to take action leading to a breach of commercial contracts without incurring any liability for damages, and that such liability is incurred only if a complicated state of the law is either unappreciated or misunderstood, the straightforward course appears to us to be that the law should be clarified and simplified: so that liability in achieving an end which the law regards as legitimate is not avoided or incurred according to whether a legal maze is successfully threaded or not. In the light of these considerations we recommend that the protection of section 3 be extended so as to cover all contracts. This can be done by deleting from the first limb the words "of employment". A consequential amendment would presumably be required in section 1 (b) of the Trades Disputes Act 1965.

894. A majority of the Commission, namely Lord Donovan, Lord Robens, Lord Tangley, Dame Mary Green, Sir George Pollock, Mr. Andrew Shonfield and Mr. John Thomson, consider that the protection of any extension of section 3 should, like that of the section itself—see paragraph 800 above—be restricted to those bodies which will be trade unions under the suggested new arrangements for incorporation and registration. They do not think it should apply to temporary combinations. Lord Collison, Professor Clegg, Professor Kahn-Freund, Mr. Wigham and Mr. Woodcock are opposed to any such restriction.

895. The second limb of section 3 was enacted following a recommendation by the majority of the Royal Commission on Trade Disputes of 1903. They said that an Act should be passed to declare *inter alia* that an individual should not be liable "for doing any act not in itself an actionable tort, only on the ground that it is an interference with another person's trade, business or employment".

896. The House of Lords had decided in 1898 in the case of *Allen v. Flood* [1898] AC 1 that no action lay against a person for interfering with another's trade, business or employment unless he did so by means unlawful in themselves. Lord Herschell said (1898 AC at p. 138):

"I do not doubt that everyone has a right to pursue his trade or employment without 'molestation' or 'obstruction' if those terms are used to imply some act in itself wrongful. This is only a branch of a much wider proposition, namely that everyone has a right to do any lawful act he pleases without molestation or obstruction. If it be intended to assert that an act not otherwise wrongful always becomes so if it interferes with another's trade or employment and needs to be excused or justified, I say that such a proposition in my opinion has no solid foundation in reason to rest on."

Nevertheless after this decision judicial doubts upon the point continued to be expressed. See for example *Quinn v. Leathem* [1901] AC 495 *per* Lord Brampton, and *Giblan v. National Amalgamated Labourers' Union* [1903] 2 KB 600 *per* Romer L.J. Hence the foregoing recommendation of the Royal Commission of 1903.

897. Since that time other decisions of the House of Lords have proceeded upon the basis that mere interference with another's business is not actionable if no unlawful means are used (see *Sorrell v. Smith* [1925] AC 700 and the *Crofters'* case [1942] AC 425).

898. Strictly speaking therefore there would seem to be no need today for the second limb of section 3. Mere interference by itself is not actionable anyway. Accordingly protection is not needed for such interference in contemplation or furtherance of a trade dispute. If illegal means are used to bring about the interference then the section gives no protection and never has. The illegal means, e.g. libel, slander, violence etc., would be actionable in themselves.

899. However, in *Rookes v. Barnard* [1964] AC at pp. 1215-6 Lord Devlin said:

> "I do not think it is necessary for the House to decide whether or not malicious interference by a single person with trade, business or employment is or is not a tort known to the law. But I must at least say what I mean by such a tort. I mean, putting it shortly, *Quinn v. Leathem* without the conspiracy. If one man, albeit by lawful means, interferes with another's right to earn his living or dispose of his labour as he wills, and does so maliciously, that is with intent to injure without justification, he is, if there is a tort, liable in just the same way as he would undoubtedly be liable if he were acting in combination with others. The combination aggravates but it is not essential. As I say I do not think your Lordships need decide this point."

900. It would seem to us nevertheless that the House of Lords had already decided this question in *Allen v. Flood* back in 1898 when they laid down that a lawful act which interfered with another person's employment was not actionable when done by an individual, whatever his motive. It is true there is nothing very positive in Lord Devlin's statement, but since the House of Lords has recently decided that it will no longer treat itself as bound by its own previous decisions, and could therefore, in theory, reverse *Allen v. Flood* some day, we think that the second limb of section 3 should be retained as part of our statute law.

901. A doubt has been raised whether the Trade Disputes Act 1906 (and other extant statutes dealing with trade unions) bind the Crown, since the Crown is not expressly named therein and there would appear to be no necessary implication that the Crown is bound. If this is so, then the protective provisions of section 3 of the 1906 Act, for example, would not

236

be available as a defence against the Crown suing as plaintiff for damages in a case where the defendant had induced a breach of contract. It is not for us, we think, to pronounce any opinion upon the validity of the doubt thus raised, but if it is well-founded we think it should be removed: and that it should be made clear in the new consolidated statute we have recommended that the Crown is bound.

(11) FREEDOM OF TRADE UNIONS FROM ACTIONS FOR TORT: SECTION 4, TRADE DISPUTES ACT 1906

902.   Before the decision in the *Taff Vale* case [1901] AC 426 it was generally supposed that trade unions, like other unincorporated bodies, could be sued at law, if at all, only by means of the representative action. Earlier in this chapter we referred to the formidable difficulties in the way of such an action against a trade union having frequent changes in its membership. The virtual immunity against being sued to which such difficulties led may have fostered a mistaken impression before 1901 that trade unions were not liable to be sued at all.

903.   The House of Lords decided in that year that registered trade unions could be sued in their own name for damages for tort. In the case of such unions, therefore, the difficulties of the representative action did not arise, and the funds of the union became answerable for any damages awarded.

904.   Parliament decided in 1906 that the immunity from actions in tort which trade unions had, prior to the *Taff Vale* decision, enjoyed in practice should be restored and made into a legal right: the view being that trade union funds ought not to be put to the risk of being depleted or absorbed by hostile litigation. Section 4 of the Trade Disputes Act 1906 therefore enacted:

" (1) An action against a trade union, whether of workmen or masters, or against any members or officials thereof on behalf of themselves and all other members of the trade union in respect of any tortious act alleged to have been committed by or on behalf of the trade union, shall not be entertained by any court.

(2) Nothing in this section shall affect the liability of the trustees of a trade union to be sued in the events provided for by the Trade Union Act 1871, section 9, except in respect of any tortious act committed by or on behalf of the union in contemplation or in furtherance of a trade dispute."

905.   The following points may be noted:

(a) The section does not sanction the commission of torts by a trade union. It simply removes a remedy.

(b) The form of the section is such that it applies to torts committed by unregistered and registered trade unions alike.

(c) The section applies to any tort committed by or on behalf of the trade union, whether in contemplation or furtherance of a trade dispute or not.

(d) On the other hand trustees of a trade union remain liable to be sued for any tort " touching or concerning the property, right, or claim to property " of the union (the words quoted are from section 9 of the

237

Trade Union Act 1871) unless the tort were committed in contemplation or furtherance of a trade dispute.

906. As a result of a number of representations made to us we have considered the question whether trade unions still need, for the proper discharge of their functions, the complete immunity from actions for tort conferred upon them in 1906. We think that such immunity should still continue in respect of torts alleged to have been committed by or on behalf of a trade union in contemplation or furtherance of a trade dispute, since without this protection trade union funds might be put in jeopardy when industrial action was taken against an employer in the circumstances of such a dispute; though the risk would be materially lessened if the protection of the first limb of section 3 of the Trade Disputes Act 1906 were extended to all contracts, as we have recommended.

907. Whether trade unions still need protection against actions for tort committed by them or on their behalf in circumstances unconnected with any trade dispute is questioned by a number of witnesses who submitted evidence to us. It has been pointed out that no other body of persons enjoys such immunity; and that since the Crown Proceedings Act 1947 even the Crown does not possess it. Further, that it is entirely anomalous that employers' associations which are also trade unions within the present statutory definition enjoy it. It is said that the onus is on trade unions to show that outside the sphere of a trade dispute it is necessary for their proper functioning that they should be free to commit torts without being answerable for the consequences.

908. We have tried to envisage the position of trade unions if their immunity were confined to torts committed in contemplation or furtherance of a trade dispute, and are not convinced that they would be seriously prejudiced. Whatever may happen in a trade dispute, it is not the case that trade unions frequently commit torts when no trade dispute is involved, or that they need to do so. Their officials remain liable at all times to be sued for any torts they commit: and when these are committed while acting in the course of their employment as trade union officials the union sometimes pays any damages which may be awarded out of its own funds. To that extent the immunity conferred by section 4(1) is waived. Again, when no trade dispute is involved, and the tort touches or concerns the union's property (a phrase of wide potential import), the trustees of the union may be sued and the funds of the union made answerable for any damage awarded. Trade unions are themselves able to sue others for damages for tort, and on occasions have done so.

909. In all the circumstances we think it would be right and proper to confine the immunity of trade unions so that it applies as regards torts committed in contemplation or furtherance of a trade dispute but not as regards any other tort; and we so recommend.

910. There is a further matter which arises upon the literal language of section 4. It grants immunity from action in respect of any tortious act alleged " to have been committed by or on behalf of a trade union ".

911. It is thought by some judges that this wording does not cover torts *about to be committed*: so that an injunction can be sought and granted

against a trade union to prevent a tort which is simply threatened or apprehended. See for example *Boulting v. ACTAT* [1963] 2 KB at p.644. Other
judges appear to take the opposite view; and indeed it would be an anomalous
situation if protection were confined to the case where damage was done
but withheld from the case where, so far, it had not. We think the section
should be amended so as to make it clear that actions against trade unions
are precluded also where the tort was simply threatened or apprehended,
again in contemplation or furtherance of a trade dispute.

(12) TRADE UNION ACT 1913: POLITICAL ACTION

912. The promotion of their members' interests by way of legislative reform
has long been one of the objectives of trade unions. In the 19th century
their aim was to secure election to Parliament of members sympathetic to the
needs and aspirations of labour. For this purpose, trade unions drew upon
their general funds. In 1874 two trade union candidates were elected to
Parliament and were supported financially by their unions. The Royal
Commission on Labour of 1894 noted that one of the objects for which trade
unions used their funds was to secure Parliamentary representation. The
Independent Labour Party was founded by Keir Hardie in 1893, and in 1900
the Labour Representation Committee was formed with the support of the
TUC. This was re-named the Labour Party in 1906. Trade union funds
continued to be used to support Labour Party candidates and to maintain
them if they secured election to the House of Commons. This was regarded
as legitimate at the time even though a minority of members might object
to such use of the funds. This view was confirmed by the decision of a
divisional court of the King's Bench in 1907 (*Steele v. South Wales Miners'
Federation* [1907] 1 KB 361).

913. In 1910, however, in *Amalgamated Society of Railway Servants v.
Osborne* [1910] AC 87, the House of Lords decided that the statutory
definition of a trade union then to be found in the Trade Union Acts of 1871
and 1876 was exhaustive of the objects which trade unions could lawfully
pursue, and that as political objects found no place in that definition their
pursuit by trade unions was illegal.

914. This decision was nullified by the Trade Union Act 1913, which revised
the statutory definition of a trade union in a manner which now empowers a
trade union to pursue any lawful object including political objects. As regards
certain political objects, however, specified in the Act, conditions are laid
down which trade unions must fulfil if monies are to be expended upon them.
These provisions are designed to secure that members who object to their
contributions being used in part to finance such objects shall have their
objections respected.

915. The political objects in question are specified in section 3(3) of the
Trade Union Act 1913 and may be summarised as being representation in
Parliament and local government, the holding of meetings and the distribution
of literature to achieve these aims.

916. In order to be able to finance these objects, a trade union is required
by section 3 of the 1913 Act among other things to secure that a resolution
approving the furtherance of these objects is passed on a ballot by a majority

239

of members voting; and, if such resolution is so passed, to incorporate in its rule-book rules which have been scrutinised and approved by the Registrar of Friendly Societies.

917. One of these rules must provide for payments in respect of the political objects specified in the Act to be made out of a separate political fund; and another rule must provide for the exemption from any obligation to contribute to that fund of any member who gives notice in accordance with the Act that he objects to contributing.

918. Section 5 of the Act confers upon any member so objecting the right to claim exemption by giving notice to that effect in the form set out in the schedule to the Act or in a form to the like effect. The notice set out in the schedule to the Act reads: " I hereby give notice that I object to contribute to the political fund of the .... union and am in consequence exempt in manner provided by the Trade Union Act 1913 from contributing to that fund."

919. This procedure has become known as " contracting-out " and it lasted from 1913 to 1927. In that year, following the general strike of 1926, the Trade Disputes and Trade Union Act 1927 substituted a procedure of " contracting-in ". In other words no member of a trade union was to contribute to the political fund unless he had specifically agreed in writing to do so. In 1946, by the Trade Disputes and Trade Union Act of that year, the procedure of " contracting-out " was restored, so far as Great Britain is concerned, and has remained the law since.

920. The average annual contribution to unions' political funds in 1966 was 2s. 11d. per member contributing.

921. We received a few representations that " contracting-in " should by law again be substituted for " contracting-out ". The argument was that for many people today membership of a trade union is a virtual necessity in following their occupations; and that it is wrong that they should have to contribute towards the funds of a political party with whose aims and policies they may disagree. It is recognised, the argument continues, that there is statutory provision for " contracting-out " but this it is claimed is not sufficient. Pressures can be and are successfully exerted, it is alleged, to prevent the exercise of this right.

922. We had no evidence of instances where such pressures have been used either successfully or unsuccessfully, though we have sought it. In May of 1967 the Rt. Hon. Robert Carr, Member of Parliament for Mitcham, when making a speech to a conference of trade unionists in Birmingham, said: " I am prepared to express a strong personal view that contracting out as at present practised is indefensible. It creates pressures and inequities which should, in justice, be removed."

923. We asked Mr. Carr whether he had specific instances in mind, and if so, whether he would be prepared to give details to the Royal Commission, if necessary in confidence. In a courteous reply, he made it clear that he was not basing his remarks on detailed examples but was speaking in general terms. He thought, however, that he might be able to supply details of specific cases if given the time—an expectation apparently not fulfilled.

Mr. Carr did say that any such evidence would in the nature of things be difficult to come by because the persons who had been subjected to such pressures might be unwilling to give evidence about it. This we understand, but in the continued absence of such evidence we are unable to say that the case for substituting " contracting-in " for " contracting-out " has been established. Considerations which tell the other way are that a very considerable number of trade unionists do in fact contract out. The Chief Registrar of Friendly Societies has reported that 113 trade unions with a total membership of 7,997,000 had political funds in 1966, but the total number of members contributing was over $1\frac{1}{2}$ million less, namely 6,423,000. The Act of 1913 requires that it shall be a rule of any trade union setting up a political fund that no member who is exempt from the liability to contribute should be discriminated against in any way (except in relation to the control or management of the political fund itself). The Act further provides that, if any member considers himself aggrieved by any breach of the rule, he may complain to the Registrar of Friendly Societies. We understand that there are very few such complaints. Between the years 1951 and 1964 the state of political power in Parliament was such that the law could have been changed so as to revert to the system of " contracting-in ", but this was not done.

924. When " contracting-in " was substituted in 1927 for " contracting-out " the result was to diminish very considerably the amount of money received by the trade unions' political funds; whereas when " contracting-out " was restored in 1946 the contributions rose again. We have no doubt that this is due very largely to the innate reluctance of people to take positive steps involving the filling up and despatch of a form when only a very small sum is involved: and that the problem of " contracting-in " or " contracting-out " is not so much a question of industrial relations as a political question, namely whether the Labour Party shall get the benefit of this reluctance or not. Parliament in 1913 enacted provisions (which were restored in 1946) in favour of members of trade unions who object to paying a political levy, enabling them to " contract out " if they wished, and we have no evidence to show that these are ineffective, and that the protection conferred by the Act of 1913 is illusory. In the circumstances, we do not recommend any change.

925. The Trade Disputes and Trade Union Act of 1927 was followed in Northern Ireland. Most of the provisions of the Northern Ireland Act of 1927 have now been repealed—see the Trade Disputes and Trade Union (Northern Ireland) Act 1958—but " contracting-in " has been retained. The fact that " contracting-in " remains the law in Northern Ireland whereas " contracting-out " is the law in Great Britain is something of an anomaly and may be accounted for by the fact that there has been no such change in political power in Northern Ireland as occurred in Great Britain in 1945. We have already said that we regard the matter more as a question of politics than of industrial relations.

926. It is right to record that we received from Mr. Robert Carr and others complaints that trade unionists who wished to " contract out " encountered difficulties at times in getting the necessary forms from their unions, and suggestions were made for overcoming these hindrances. These complaints are founded upon a misconception. No stereotyped form is necessary. The

Act of 1913 prescribes a form, but enacts that any other form "to the like effect" will do. Any trade unionist so minded can therefore write out his own, saying that he objects to contributing to the political fund of his trade union and claiming exemption accordingly.

927. We received from the Society of Conservative Lawyers a detailed memorandum suggesting other changes in the Trade Union Act 1913. We deal with these suggestions fully in Appendix 7, our conclusion being that no change in the law is required except as regards the auditing of trade union accounts, on which we make a recommendation in paragraph 655.

(13) THE RIGHT TO STRIKE

928. We use the expression "strike" to mean "the cessation of work by a body of persons employed acting in combination, or a concerted refusal or a refusal under a common understanding of any number of persons employed to continue to work for an employer in consequence of a dispute, done as a means of compelling their employer or any person or body of persons employed, or to aid other employees in compelling their employer or any person or body of persons employed, to accept or not to accept terms or conditions of or affecting employment ".

929. This quotation is from the Contracts of Employment Act 1963, Schedule I paragraph 11 (i), and is, we think, the only current statutory definition of a strike.

930. In some occupations strike action would be a criminal offence, for example in the armed forces, and, at certain times, in the merchant navy. In other occupations, where strikes are not subject to similar prohibitions, there is nevertheless no law expressly conferring a right to strike.

931. Every employee has, however, the right to withdraw his labour upon giving to his employer the notice called for in that event by his contract of employment. He may then lawfully leave when the notice expires. The same is true of several employees acting in combination.

932. If an employee ceases to work without giving such notice his action, in the absence of legal justification, is unlawful in the sense that it is a breach of contract. It is not, however, a criminal offence except in the circumstances specified in sections 4 and 5 of the Conspiracy and Protection of Property Act 1875, dealing (as regards section 4) with gas, water and (since 1919) electricity undertakings, and (as regards section 5) with possible damage to human life and valuable property.

933. If a number of persons acting in combination likewise withhold their labour in breach of contract, and go on strike, while each of them remains individually liable to a civil action for breach of contract, their action is no longer regarded as a criminal or (subject to what is said in paragraph 854) a civil conspiracy.

934. The change is the result of a succession of statutes passed in the last hundred years, and designed to relieve persons who combine to improve their wages and conditions, and to withhold their labour as a means to that end, from the sanctions which would otherwise attach to their actions under the criminal and the civil law. The history of the matter will be found set out in *Citrine's Trade Union Law*.

935. The right to strike thus derives from the language of statutes passed to protect combinations of persons who act to improve their wages and conditions, and from the implication to be drawn from such legislation that the combined withholding of labour is a lawful means to that end. It is urged by some that a right to strike should be granted by statute in express terms. In this context it should be remembered that every individual employee has the legal right to cease to work for his employer on giving whatever notice is required by his contract of employment. The right to strike is, basically, a right to withdraw labour in combination without being subject to the legal consequences of acting in combination which would, in the past, have followed. This situation is now well recognised and we do not think it can be improved by granting the right in express terms. No doubt, however, if the law relating to trade disputes is codified, as we recommend, the matter will receive further consideration.

(14) EFFECT OF STRIKES ON THE CONTRACT OF EMPLOYMENT

936. Strikes may be preceded by no notice or some notice given by or on behalf of the employees concerned.

937. If no notice is given, then ignoring special cases such as an engagement from day to day where no notice is required, a breach of the contract of employment will normally result. The same is true even if notice of the intention to strike is given, whether the notice be shorter, or longer, or the same length as the notice required by the contract for its termination.

938. If however the notice is in terms a notice to terminate the contract and is of the required length, and the employee works the notice out before ceasing work, no breach of contract occurs. On the contrary the contract has been fulfilled according to its terms.

939. It is sometimes said that this situation does not reflect the true intentions of the parties. Where notice of a stoppage of work is given, not being a notice to terminate the contract, it is true that the employees concerned are in breach of the contract. Under that contract they are bound to go on rendering service until some event has occurred upon which it was agreed that the contract should end, as for example the giving of due notice to terminate it. Yet by ceasing to work without giving such a notice, the employees are not, it is argued, really intending to repudiate the contract altogether—they simply want it modified. Nor does the employer in such a case regard the cessation of work as a repudiation of the contract, entitling him to rescind it. He really wants the contract to continue and he hopes to be able to come to terms over the modification which his employees are seeking. Only if this hope is finally dashed will questions of repudiation and consequent rescission arise.

940. Similarly when due notice to end the contract is given prior to the strike, the notice being to the effect that the employee will cease work on its expiry, neither side, it is said, really wishes to put an end to the contract. One party simply wants different terms; the other hopes to come to some agreement about them.

941. It has accordingly been proposed by some that this situation should be

reflected in the law and that, if the intention of the parties is simply to suspend the contract for the period of the strike, then the law of contract should produce that effect; for one of the purposes of the law, after all, is to give effect to the intentions of the contracting parties.

942. To this end it has been suggested that strikes should merely suspend the contract of employment without breaking it, or terminating it. In practice this would mean creating a new right of unilateral suspension, since either side to the contract of employment could exercise the right without the consent of the other, the employee by striking, the employer by locking out.

943. The concept is not as simple as it sounds: and before any such new law could be formulated problems of some difficulty would have to be faced and solved. They include the following:

(a) To what strikes would it apply? To unofficial and unconstitutional as well as to official strikes? How would strikes be defined for this purpose?

(b) Would it also apply to other industrial action such as a ban on overtime in breach of contract or to a " go-slow "?

(c) Would it apply to " lightning strikes " or only to strikes where at least *some* notice was given, though less than the notice required for termination of the contract? If so, what length of notice should be required?

(d) Would the new law apply to the gas, water, and electricity industries, which at present are subject to the special provisions of section 4 of the Conspiracy and Protection of Property Act 1875? What also would be the position under section 5 of the same Act?

(e) Would the employer still be allowed instantly to dismiss an employee for grave misconduct during the course of the strike? (Note: this is the case under French law where strikes are treated as suspending the contract of employment.) If so, what kind of acts would constitute " grave misconduct "?

(f) Would " contracting out " of the new law be permissible, e.g. in collective bargains, or in individual contracts of employment?

(g) Would strikers be free to take up other employment while the contract was suspended? If so, would any obligations of secrecy in the suspended contract be suspended too?

(h) If all efforts to end the strike failed, upon what event would the suspension of the contract cease and be replaced by termination?

944. This list is not exhaustive, but is perhaps sufficient to show that considerable technical difficulties would be encountered if the doctrine of unilateral suspension of contracts of employment by strike action were to be made part of our law.

945. Nor are we convinced that such a fundamental change in the law of contract is really called for. It is advocated on the basis of the argument that it would represent the true intention of the parties. This proposition needs further examination.

946. The position at common law, as we understand it, is that a contract cannot be terminated unilaterally. If an employee refuses to carry on working

under his contract of employment, this gives the employer the option either to ignore the breach of contract and to insist upon performance of it, or alternatively to accept such a fundamental breach as a repudiation of the contract and to treat himself as no longer bound by it. In this latter event he can sue for damages at once. If however he refuses to regard the contract as at an end, the employee is thus given an opportunity to reconsider his attitude.

947. When an employee goes on strike in breach of his contract it may well be that he does not intend finally to end it. But this is true of many other breaches of contract, whether the contract be one of employment or otherwise, and there is no problem arising out of this particular situation which calls for a doctrine of unilateral suspension. Where strikes are concerned the parties will, as a rule, try to settle their differences. While there is hope that this may come about, management will not want to treat the contract as at an end and to sue for damages for its breach.

948. When notice is given pursuant to the contract to terminate it, again it may be true that the parties hope that the employer-employee relationship will soon be resumed and not ruptured for good. But nevertheless it seems to us reasonable to say that in such a case the employee *does* wish to put an end to the existing contract, even though he remains ready to conclude another on terms more favourable to him; and the employer has no choice but to accept the situation that the old contract is at an end, however much he may wish to retain his employee's services. He can do this only by entering into another contract on new terms. So far there seems to us to be no need and no justification for ignoring the plain language of the notice to terminate the contract given by the employee. Indeed if this were to be construed merely as a notice that he was about to break his contract, serious difficulties might arise under sections 4 and 5 of the Conspiracy and Protection of Property Act 1875, which make certain breaches of contract criminal offences. It has always been assumed, we think, that no criminal liability can attach under those sections if the employee gives due notice to terminate his contract and discontinues work only when the notice has expired. It would seem to us to be an impossible situation that such an employee should be liable to criminal penalties on a construction of his notice which contradicts its plain terms.

949. Some legal commentators appear to suggest that notice of an intention to cease work which is of the same length as the required notice for termination of the contract ought to be treated as such a notice of such termination even though it does not use express words to this effect. This must be a question of construction in each particular case and we can make no useful pronouncement upon it. It has also been suggested that the effect of certain dicta in the cases of *Rookes v. Barnard* and *Stratford v. Lindley* is that every notice of intended strike action is a notice of intended breach of contract and cannot be regarded as a notice of termination of the contract. We have referred to those dicta, which do not seem to us to support the construction thus put upon them; and we have reason to believe that their authors disavow the interpretation in question.

950. However that may be, the chief problem which seems to arise from the dissonance between the terms of a valid notice of termination to end the employment, and the desire of both sides to continue it if new terms can be

245

arranged, is the problem of rights or benefits which depend upon continuity of service. This has already been the subject of legislation with regard to statutory rights to minimum periods of notice, and to redundancy payments—see section 37 of the Redundancy Payments Act 1965, which provides that strikes should not break continuity of service for those purposes.

951. In the case of other benefits which depend upon length of continuous service and which are provided for by the contract of employment itself, it is always possible for the parties, if they wish to do so, to agree that strikes shall not be treated as breaking such continuity, and to do so either by means of a provision in the contract itself or as one of the terms of a settlement of the strike.

952. In our opinion a fundamental change in the law such as the creation by statute of a unilateral right to suspend a contract of employment should not be introduced except after prior examination of the whole problem and its possible repercussions by an expert Committee. The same Committee might also examine the question whether it would be practicable to enact that every notice given by an employee to cease work which was not less in length than a notice required to determine the contract should, in the absence of any contrary intention clearly expressed, be regarded as a notice of termination of the contract rather than as a notice of intended breach.

(15) THE TRADE DISPUTE DISQUALIFICATION FOR UNEMPLOYMENT BENEFIT

953. Shortly after our appointment we were asked by the Minister of Social Security (then Miss Margaret Herbison) whether we would examine the conditions under which unemployment benefit was at present withheld from persons who became unemployed by reason of a stoppage of work resulting from a trade dispute at their place of employment. This we agreed to do, on the view that the relevant legislation was part of " the law affecting the activities " of trade unions, and so within our terms of reference. This was, perhaps, rather a wide view: and our examination of the problem leads us to the conclusion that the matter raises issues of social policy rather than of industrial relations.

954. The law which affects the matter and the nature of the problems to which it gives rise may first be briefly summarised.

955. Insurance against unemployment was introduced by the National Insurance Act of 1911. In return for contributions, the persons insured became entitled to money payments during periods of unemployment. The scope of the Act was at first confined to certain trades, broadly engineering and shipbuilding.

956. At the outset the problem presented itself as to what was to happen when persons became unemployed, not through the ordinary fluctuations of trade or business, but because of industrial dispute. The purpose of the insurance scheme was to protect those who lost their employment because of such fluctuations, and not because of strikes or lock-outs.

957. Accordingly it was provided, in the Act of 1911, that:

" A workman who loses employment by reason of a stoppage of

work which was due to a trade dispute at the factory workshop or other premises at which he was employed shall be disqualified for receiving unemployment benefit so long as the strike or lock-out continues."

958. An important exception was made to this general disqualification. It could happen that different branches of work, which would normally be carried on at separate premises, might, in some cases, be carried on in separate departments on the same premises. It would obviously be unfair, in such a case, that a man in Department " B " who had no interest in a strike taking place in Department " A ", but who was thrown out of work in consequence of that strike, should be disqualified from receiving unemployment benefit. Accordingly the Act of 1911 provided that where different branches of work, which were commonly carried on as separate businesses in separate premises, were in fact carried on in separate departments on the same premises, then each of those departments was to be regarded as a separate factory or separate premises. Sir John Simon explained: " It is not fair on the workman that you should put him under a special penalty merely because he happens to have as fellow workmen a lot of people who normally would not be his fellow workmen at all ".

959. In 1920, by the Unemployment Insurance Act of that year, the coverage of insurance against unemployment was extended to all employments under a contract of service, with certain exceptions, one of which was agriculture. The disqualification relating to trade disputes remained substantially unchanged.

960. The wording of this disqualification had, over the years, been criticised on the ground of undue harshness, since it disqualified persons who often had no real interest in the dispute which occasioned the stoppage of work. For example, in 1919-1920 there was a strike of skilled moulders. The moulder's labourers were not concerned in the dispute, but were thrown out of work because of it. They were disqualified from receiving unemployment benefit because they worked in the same establishment as the moulders. The strike lasted four months.

961. Accordingly in the Unemployment Insurance (No. 2) Act 1924 the scope of the disqualification was narrowed. The Act provided that an insured contributor should not lose his right to unemployment benefit if he proved that he was not participating in the trade dispute which caused the stoppage of work, nor financing it, nor directly interested in it: and, further, that he did not belong to a grade or class of workers, some members of whom *were* participating in the dispute, or financing it, or directly interested in it. This latter provision has become known as " the grade or class provision " and henceforth we so refer to it.

962. In 1927, by the Unemployment Insurance Act 1927, the grade or class provision was narrowed, so that it applied only in respect of workers of the same grade or class employed at the premises where the stoppage occurred.

963. In 1936, by the Unemployment Insurance (Agriculture) Act of that year, insurance against unemployment was extended to agricultural workers,

and "farms" were added to the description of places of employment where stoppages of work might occur. Subject to minor drafting amendments the conditions under which disqualification for unemployment benefit occurs have remained unchanged since 1927. They now appear in the consolidating measure of 1965—the National Insurance Act 1965—as section 22.

964. In summary therefore a person who is thrown out of work by reason of a trade dispute will not lose his title to unemployment benefit unless the dispute occurs " at his place of employment ". If it occurs elsewhere, it will not matter for this purpose that he loses his employment in consequence. He will still be entitled to benefit. Moreover if at his place of employment separate branches of work are carried on in separate departments, which are commonly carried on in separate premises or at separate places, each of those separate departments is to be regarded, for the purpose of unemployment benefit, as a separate place of employment. This means that a man employed in one department of the same works who is thrown out of work by reason of a strike in another department can, where the extended definition applies, still qualify for unemployment benefit.

965. Since an employee may not be disqualified in any event from receiving unemployment benefit unless the stoppage is due to a trade dispute at his place of employment, and since " place of employment " is exclusive in certain cases of separate departments on the same premises, the provisions just summarised constitute perhaps the main limitation on the right to withhold unemployment benefit in cases of industrial disputes.

966. There are, however, others. Even though the stoppage of work may be due to a trade dispute at the place of employment, a person thrown out of work in consequence may still qualify for unemployment benefit if he proves:

(a) that he is not participating in, or financing or directly interested in the trade dispute; and

(b) that the " grade or class provision " described above is inapplicable.

967. While the burden of proof of these matters is put upon each applicant for benefit, we understand that in practice the adjudicating authorities assemble all the evidence themselves and decide, in the light of it, which workers are and which are not disqualified.

968. Notwithstanding that the position with regard to disqualification has been ameliorated over the years as above described, it still evokes criticism. The TUC for example thinks that the conditions under which disqualification may be incurred are too severe. The CBI on the other hand wishes to see them broadened. The problem is how to ensure that the insurance fund, which is financed by contributions from employees, employers and the State, is confined to relieving hardship resulting from unemployment due to causes other than industrial disputes, while at the same time not denying relief to those losing employment because of such a dispute if their connection or interest in the dispute is non-existent, indirect or remote. In this context it is useful to recall the observations upon the matter made by Lord Blanesburgh's Committee of 1925-1927 set up to consider the working of the unemployment insurance scheme. Speaking of the clause which restricted

248

payment of benefit when unemployment resulted from a trade dispute, the Committee said:

> " This clause can never assume a form which will be entirely satisfactory. Frame it as you will, many will be entitled to benefit who, if the whole truth could be known, ought to be excluded as much as actual participants in the dispute, and some will be excluded from benefit who, if the whole truth could be known, ought to have it."

969. The criticisms we have received deal with specific aspects of the problem and we consider them in turn in the following paragraphs.

The Definition of " Place of Employment "

970. The CBI considers that disqualification for receiving unemployment benefit should be broadened so that it will be imposed in some cases even though the stoppage of work which causes the unemployment is due to a trade dispute occurring elsewhere than at the claimants' own place of employment, provided it occurs within one company. The Confederation says that " a feature of industrial development in recent years has been the tendency to break down the production process between a number of establishments with a high degree of inter-dependence ". The implication is that the " place of employment " ought not to be determined simply by geography. The tendency mentioned involves that an employee at one factory of a company may easily be directly interested in the outcome of a trade dispute at another factory belonging to the same company, and accordingly ought not to be paid benefit if the dispute involves him in unemployment. This alleged community of interest may be true in some cases but it would certainly not be true in all, and the determination of the point in disputed cases might not be easy. Other difficult questions of fact might arise such as whether the dispute at factory " A " really caused the lay-off of employees at factory " B ". This might take some time to resolve, and yet it is important that unemployment benefit, where due, should be paid as soon as possible. Other objections to the proposal seem to us to be that the tendency to which the CBI refer is not so recent an innovation. In 1946 it was no doubt discernible, but Parliament made no alteration in the disqualification provision when enacting the National Insurance Act 1946. Again, such an amendment might lead to an industrial group unintentionally extending the scope of the disqualification materially by grouping additional establishments within one company.

971. The TUC wishes the definition of place of employment still further narrowed. At the moment, separate departments are regarded as separate places of employment only if the work there done is commonly carried on as separate businesses in separate premises or at separate places. It is argued that today branches of production which formerly were commonly carried on in separate workplaces are now often carried on in one workplace as part of an integrated process. In addition a larger trade union membership is concentrated in fewer unions, so that those at risk of losing unemployment benefit as the result of a single stoppage has grown. Accordingly the TUC propose that where an integrated process is carried out under one roof the separate departments in which these operations are carried out should

each be treated as a separate place of employment. The result would be that nobody could be disqualified for unemployment benefit by reason of a trade dispute occurring in a department other than his own.

972. The serious objection to this is that it would open the door to selectivity in the matter of strikes. A union which organised the workers in a factory of the kind instanced would need, on the occasion of a trade dispute, to call out only the workers in one department. Production being integrated, the probability is that work would have to stop in the other departments too. But the employees there would qualify for unemployment benefit, and the union need pay strike benefit to its members in one department only. Yet all the employees might have a direct interest in the outcome of the dispute. Lord Collison, Mr. Woodcock and Mr. Shonfield take the view that the risk of such selectivity, which they think to be slight, ought to be accepted in order to avoid the greater injustice of penalising men who are not concerned in a trade dispute simply because it is the common practice of an industry to locate people doing their work in a particular way. The remainder of us think that the present definition of place of employment should stand.

The Grade or Class Provision

973. The purpose of the Unemployment Insurance (No. 2) Act 1924, which first introduced this provision, was benevolent from the worker's point of view. Up to that time a person thrown out of work by reason of a trade dispute at his place of employment could not claim unemployment benefit. Now he was enabled to do so provided he proved certain things, namely, that he was not participating in, or financing, or directly interested in the dispute: and that he did not belong to a grade or class of worker, some of whom were doing one or other of these things. In 1927, as above narrated, the grade or class provision was narrowed so that it operated only if there were members of the same grade or class as the unemployed person at the premises where the stoppage occurred, some of whom were participating in, financing, or directly interested in the dispute.

974. The principle underlying the grade or class provision is thus stated in the evidence of the Ministry of Social Security: [1]

> " *Principle of the grade or class provision*
> The grade or class provision considers the position of workers in relation to a particular trade dispute, not according to whether they are personally involved in the dispute in the sense that they are individually participating in, financing or directly interested in the dispute, but according to whether they belong to a group of workers containing workers who are personally involved. It assumes that a group of workers doing much the same kind of work in the same place and under the same conditions and circumstances have a corporate identity and a special relationship one with another—a ' community of interest '—quite apart from their position in relation to any particular trade dispute. The argument runs that just as members of a particular grade or class are treated alike in so many other aspects of their working life in the factory so they

---

[1]Minutes of Evidence 54, *Ministry of Social Security*, Seventh Memorandum, pp.2334-5.

should also be treated alike for purposes of the trade dispute disqualification. Thus if any member of the grade or class is personally involved in the dispute as participating, financing, or directly interested in it, all the other members of the grade or class are deemed to be involved by virtue of their corporate identity as members of the same grade or class, and cannot therefore escape disqualification. In some cases, a high proportion of the grade or class will be personally involved. In others this proportion will be small. The principle of treating the whole grade or class alike however applies irrespective of the proportion of members personally involved."

The Ministry goes on to say:

"The grade or class provision does not assume that workers disqualified under it are in fact 'interested' in the *dispute* in the same way and to the same extent as workers personally involved as participating, financing or directly interested in the dispute may be regarded as having an 'interest' in the dispute. It operates on the principle that members of a grade or class have a mutual 'interest' as *members of that grade or class* which justifies treating them alike for unemployment benefit purposes in trade disputes."

And later the Ministry comments:

"The present law was based on the assumption that this special relationship, or community of interest, between a group of workers identified as a grade or class is a reality of sufficient importance to justify treating them all alike in the matter of entitlement to unemployment benefit where work is lost as a result of a trade dispute. Whether this assumption is valid in modern industrial conditions may be open to doubt and certainly there is evidence that its validity is not generally recognised or accepted by those who are adversely affected by it."

975. In our view the reasoning thus said to underlie the grade or class provision is fallacious. In order to ascertain whether a class of persons has a common interest simply because it is a class one needs to know what common attribute it is which marks such persons off as a class. This the law makes no attempt to do. It simply assumes, apparently, that if a group of workers in the same place of employment can by some means be identified as a " class " or " grade " then automatically they possess a common interest as such: and no investigation is required to disqualify them from receiving unemployment benefit beyond discovering whether there is at least one of the class participating in the trade dispute, or financing it, or directly interested in it. This seems to us not so much the recognition of an interest as the invention of it. The capricious results which the provision can and does produce are themselves some indication of the invalidity of the assumption which underlies it. If for example the process workers at a particular works go on strike on an issue which concerns them alone and one member out of a total of 100 maintenance workers strikes in sympathy, the remaining 99 if laid off will all be disqualified from receiving unemployment benefit, though they have no interest in the strike and indeed are hostile to it.

976. Moreover the grade or class provision will operate if only one member

of the grade or class is "financing" the trade dispute. A member of a trade union which is paying the strikers their strike benefit is normally regarded as "financing" the dispute. Thus if "A" were a storeman in a works comprising different departments and a dispute occurred in the foundry shop which led to a stoppage of work, during which the union concerned paid strike benefit, "A" would be disqualified for receiving unemployment benefit if he happened to belong to the same union. So also would all the other storemen, although they might belong to a different union or unions.

977. The term "grade or class" is not defined in the Act. A literal interpretation could treat all manual workers or all unskilled workers as a class and thus involve wholesale disqualifications. In practice, however, a narrower interpretation is normally adopted by the independent adjudicating authorities and "grades" and "classes" are determined by reference to some aspect of the work performed. "Grades" and "classes" are not considered as interchangeable terms, but neither are they treated as mutually exclusive. Difficult borderline cases are bound to arise. For example, in 1965 a claimant's "grade" was said to be either a fettler or a grinder and his "class" that of a semi-skilled production worker. He was first disqualified from unemployment benefit on the ground that he was a grinder, some of whom were financing the dispute through their unions. He appealed to the local tribunal, who allowed his claim on the ground that he was a fettler, none of whom were financing the dispute. The local insurance officer then appealed on the ground that in any event the "grade" was irrelevant. The man's "class" was that of a semi-skilled worker: and accordingly he fell to be disqualified along with a few thousand other semi-skilled workers because members of that "class" were financing the dispute. (Many of these had however already received benefit on the basis of their "grade".) The appeal was after much argument dismissed by the Chief Insurance Commissioner.

978. The grade or class provision has an administrative advantage, that once the grade or class is identified, and once it is established that any member of it is participating in, financing, or directly interested in the dispute, detailed inquiries into the position of other members can be avoided. They are disqualified forthwith. Administrative convenience however is not much of a commendation for a provision which is also capable of considerable injustice.

979. The abolition of the provision would not have the consequence of allowing unemployment benefit to large numbers of undeserving cases. Any employee who became unemployed by reason of a stoppage of work due to a trade dispute at his place of employment would still have to prove that he was not participating in the dispute, not financing it, and not directly interested in it. On the other hand such an employee would not be debarred from benefit merely because one member of his "grade or class" was doing one or other of these things.

980. For the reasons which we think sufficiently appear above, we are of the view that the grade or class provision should now be abolished. Some suggestions were made to us that it should not be wholly abolished, but only that part of it which disqualifies the whole class if some members are financing the dispute. The Ministry of Social Security considers that this

would produce worse anomalies still. Thus a whole grade or class would continue to be disqualified by the presence of one striker among them, but not by the presence of a large number of members who by money contributions of one kind or another helped to keep the dispute going. The Ministry considers that the grade or class provision should stand or fall as a whole, and we agree.

981. This would leave as the sole tests for disqualification:

(i) Whether the stoppage of work which caused the unemployment is due to a trade dispute at the claimant's place of employment, as that place is defined in the Act.

(ii) If so, whether the claimant is participating in, or financing, or directly interested in the dispute.

As to " Participating "

982. There is general agreement that a person participating in a trade dispute at his place of employment and becoming unemployed in consequence ought not to be supported by the insurance fund during such unemployment. Such support would be foreign to the purposes for which the fund was created and is maintained.

As to " Financing "

983. It may be wondered how a person who is out of work and wishes to claim unemployment benefit is able at the same time to " finance " a trade dispute. The answer lies in the interpretation which has been placed on the relevant statutory provision. It is construed as disqualifying from unemployment benefit any person who is unemployed as the result of a trade dispute at his place of employment if he is a member of a trade union which is paying strike pay to other members being participants in the dispute.

984. It is regarded as immaterial whether such a claimant is continuing, while unemployed, to pay his usual contributions as a member to such trade union; and a decision to this effect has, in fact, been given by the Insurance Commissioner. It is also regarded as irrelevant that the funds from which the trade union is paying strike pay are funds to which the claimant has contributed in the past, and may, if he keeps up his subscription while unemployed, still be contributing. The theory upon which the disqualification is based is that the act of the union in paying strike benefit, and thus financing the trade dispute, is the act of each and every one of its members. As members of an unincorporated association of individuals bound by a common contract providing *inter alia* for financial support for fellow-members on strike, all must be regarded as involved in the act individually as well as collectively. Expressed in another way, the union acts as agent for its members.

985. There is clearly logic in such an interpretation. But the logic squares very uneasily at times with reality. It must be obvious beforehand in most cases that a strike in one department at a place of employment is likely to throw out of work employees in another department who may have no interest in the dispute whatever. If one of the employees in this other

253

department is a member of the union supporting the strike, it is again a little unreal to treat him automatically as a party to the union's action if he knows full well in advance that the result will be to bring considerable financial hardship upon himself, and also perhaps upon his family. Of course, such a man may be willing to accept such hardship in the interests of union solidarity; on the other hand he may regard the strike as quite unjustified and unworthy of support. At the present time he is penalised whatever view he takes.

986. In considering how far individual members of trade unions should be regarded as party to union decisions, it may be of interest to recall the decision in *Bonsor v. Musicians' Union* [1956] AC 104. Mr. Bonsor had been expelled from the union. He claimed that he had been expelled wrongfully. One answer to his claim made on behalf of the union was that being a member at the time he was, as such, a party to the decision to expel himself, and therefore could not recover damages even if the expulsion were wrongful. This argument succeeded in the Court of Appeal but was summarily rejected in the House of Lords. It was there held to be too farfetched to regard Mr. Bonsor as being responsible together with all the other members of the union for a decision to expel himself—a decision which would bring considerable hardship upon him. The case, though dealing with facts different from those now being considered, does show that the doctrine that all members are identified with union decisions has its limits.

987. It could presumably happen that the trade dispute occurs in a key department of a factory, and the ensuing strike throws out of work a very much larger number of men in a dependent department. If these men are all members of the same trade union as the comparatively few members on strike, and strike pay is being paid, it is perhaps easier to regard the many as involved in the decision to finance the few. There is, however, as it seems to us, no sufficient reason for distinguishing such a case from the case where only a few men are rendered unemployed in the dependent department. Moreover such a situation as above described may occur where all the strikers and all those thrown out of work in consequence may be members of the same union, and yet no disqualification of any of the latter class will occur. This is the position in all cases where the trade dispute occurs at a place of employment other than the claimant's: and a different department in the same works may be such another place.

988. It is open to a claimant for unemployment benefit to evade the disqualification now being considered simply by resigning from his trade union at any time during the trade dispute. He is entitled to benefit if he can show that he " is not " financing the dispute. This use of the present tense involves that the question must be decided, if need be, each time the claimant applies for benefit, which he will usually do each week. On the basis that membership of the union paying strike pay is a " financing " of the trade dispute, the claimant can cease to finance by ceasing to be a member. This of course may involve him in difficulties with the union if he is entitled to benefits dependent on continuous membership; but no union, we think, would have

254

any great legal difficulty in devising a rule to meet such a case, providing that the member rejoined after the trade dispute was over.

989. A situation can arise in which claimants may be refused benefit if a strike by their fellow union members is official and therefore financed by their union, but may be granted benefit if the strike is unofficial and there is therefore no financing by the union. In such circumstances an advantage is given to unofficial action which might not always be marginal and which should if possible be removed.

990. The theory that a member must be regarded as automatically involved in union decisions will be much more difficult, if not impossible, to sustain if and when trade unions are given corporate status.

991. For all these reasons all of us except Mr. John Thomson think that a claimant for unemployment benefit should no longer be regarded as financing a trade dispute simply because he is a member of a trade union which is paying strike pay to those on strike. Mr. Thomson thinks that the " financing " disqualification should continue to be operated as at present, because whether or not corporate status is granted to trade unions it is and will continue to be important that all members should bear a measure of individual responsibility for union actions and that they should in particular accept full involvement in strike decisions at their place of work. He also thinks that the incentive for trade unionists to participate actively in the affairs of their unions would be lessened by the proposed change.

As to " Directly Interested "

992. There is no suggestion from any quarter that a person directly interested in the result of a trade dispute at his place of employment which has led to his being unemployed should receive unemployment benefit. The TUC however complains of the way in which the term " directly interested in the dispute " is at times interpreted and applied by the adjudicating authorities. Cases have been cited to us in which the decisions on the point seem to conflict or are at any rate very difficult to reconcile; and it is suggested that there are periodical trends during which a clear distinction is drawn between direct and indirect interests, while at other times the distinction becomes blurred. The TUC recommends that a claimant should not be disqualified unless his terms or conditions of employment are the subject of, or are immediately in issue in, the trade dispute and that any " minor " interest should be disregarded. This would mean that a claim recognised as potentially of general application in a place of employment might be advanced and made the subject of a dispute by one section alone. Even though workers in all the other sections were laid off in consequence, their terms or conditions of employment might be said not to be the subject of, or immediately in issue in, the dispute. The TUC also asks that the distinction between direct and indirect interests should be re-established, and that any merely minor interest should be disregarded. By " re-established " is presumably meant that the adjudicating authorities should follow the words of the statute, which are " directly interested " and which contain no reference to indirect interest. Or it may mean that Parliament should define direct interest in such a way as clearly to exclude indirect interests. Or, again, that the

adjudicating authority should do this. Upon none of these matters do we feel we should make pronouncements. The statute is there: the problem of distinguishing between direct and indirect interests is notoriously difficult, and the line between major and minor interests could also not be drawn with precision. These are all matters of interpretation and therefore matters for the courts alone, unless Parliament wishes to attempt the task of clarification itself which so far it seems studiously to have avoided. We ourselves are not able to suggest a definition of " directly interested " which will put all doubts to rest. It may be, however, that the Government's advisers may be able to devise a formula which will, at least, improve the present position on the lines proposed by the TUC.

Other Matters

993. In 1924 when the Unemployment Insurance (No. 2) Act was in progress through the House of Commons, an amendment proposed by a back-bencher, Mr. George Spencer, was accepted by the Government on the Report stage, after having been rejected on the Committee stage. This was to the effect that there should be no disqualification for unemployment benefit where the claimant proved that the stoppage of work was due to the contravention by the employer of some provision of a collective bargain. This clause, after being rejected in the House of Lords but restored in the Commons, eventually became the second part of section 4 (1) of the Act.

994. The Blanesburgh Committee of 1925-1927 recommended that this provision should be dropped, and it ceased to be law in 1927. The main reason for the Committee's recommendation was that those responsible for operating unemployment insurance should not enter into the merits of industrial disputes, nor into disputed questions of interpretation of collective bargains. We think this reason still holds good; and we would add that if insurance officers, or the Industrial Court, had to decide whether a collective bargain had been breached, and if so by whom, much delay would result, and delay in the matter of paying unemployment benefit should be avoided as far as possible. We are not able therefore to recommend that a similar provision should be re-introduced into the law as proposed by the TUC.

995. The TUC finally asks that supplementary benefit should be available to all persons disqualified from seeking unemployment benefit. At present this is available only to the wives and children of such persons, or of the unemployed person himself in cases of real emergency. The claim is supported on the grounds that supplementary benefits are available to those who leave their employment without just cause, or who are dismissed for industrial misconduct. Whatever the reason may be for this, we do not think it follows that all those on strike should be entitled to draw supplementary benefits for themselves and we cannot endorse this suggestion.

996. It is sometimes suggested that the sources of income open to strikers and those laid off as a result of strikes in the form of refunds of income tax, supplementary benefits for their dependants and so on is such that it makes little difference to them if they are unable to draw unemployment benefit. We believe this suggestion to be ill-founded. The facts of the situation are explained in Appendix 8.

Chapter XV

WORKERS' PARTICIPATION IN MANAGEMENT

997. In this report we have dealt mainly with collective bargaining, with individual rights and with the law on trade unions and industrial disputes. We have not so far touched upon another important area of industrial relations, namely the participation by workers and their representatives, over and above issues dealt with in collective bargaining, in decisions concerning the running of the undertaking and the linking of this participation with the work of such bodies as the National Economic Development Council and the Economic Development Committees in which trade unions already play their part. This is a subject to which we all attach great importance, but even at this stage we deal with it only briefly, for two reasons: first, we are agreed that any changes which might be made in order to facilitate and encourage such participation should be subsidiary to our main proposals for the reform of collective bargaining; and, secondly, we have been unable to agree upon changes which might be expected to have the desired effect.

998. The TUC have made proposals to us for securing increased participation by workers in management. They propose its introduction at three levels. First, at plant level they would like a workpeople's representative, e.g. a shop steward, to sit on "whatever is the normal body which regularly meets at plant level to take decisions on the running of that plant". Secondly, they suggest that there should be trade union representation at intermediate levels, for example at regional level or "at a level which represents the functional authority for the particular product within the enterprise". Thirdly, at top level there should be legislation to allow companies, if they wish, to make provision for trade union representation on boards of directors. The TUC seek no compulsory powers, and wish progress on a voluntary basis. If progress is to be substantial, they believe that the CBI must take a strong lead in encouraging its members to follow the spirit of their proposals.

999. As regards the suggestion for workers' representatives to be included in managerial bodies in the factory and at other levels of management apart from the board, we believe that our proposals for the reform of collective bargaining on the basis of comprehensive agreements at factory and company level will do more than could any other change to allow workers and their representatives to exercise a positive influence in the running of the undertakings in which they work. In addition representation on management bodies of this kind might even be harmful. Although managers, if they are wise, will keep in close touch with shop stewards, they must also be free to discuss policy without being preoccupied with the risk that what they say may be misunderstood and lead to confusion on the shop floor, just as stewards must be free to meet on their own. Consequently if workers' representatives were

included in management bodies there would be a serious danger that meetings would become perfunctory with the real decisions taken beforehand by managers alone.

1000. As regards workers' representation on boards we have little experience in this country to guide us. Trade union officials have been appointed to the boards of nationalised industries under the relevant statutes, which provide for the appointment of members with experience, among other things, of the organisation of workers. But many of them have been selected from unions wholly or mainly concerned with industries other than the nationalised industry in question; if appointed full-time they have relinquished their trade union posts; and in any case they have not, as members of the board, been asked to act or sought to act as workers' representatives. The appointment of employees to group boards in the iron and steel industry is a recent innovation.

1001. There are, however, provisions for workers' participation in management in some other countries, notably in the Federal Republic of Germany. On our visit there we were able to discuss the German arrangements with many people of experience, both employers and trade unionists. The structure of their companies differs from ours. Control is shared between a " supervisory board " which decides major questions of policy, and an " executive board " of the directors who actively manage the enterprise. In most industries in Germany two-thirds of the members of the supervisory boards represent shareholders and one-third represent workers. In the coal and steel industries the two groups have equal representation and in addition the workers' representatives have the right to nominate the " labour director " (personnel manager) to the executive board. We found no consensus about the value of these arrangements. In particular the structure of the coal and steel boards was particularly unwelcome to most employers and strongly defended by most trade unionists. Our brief stay does not enable us to pass any reliable judgment on workers' participation as there practised. All we can do is to note that the German coal and steel industries do not appear to function conspicuously more or less efficiently than those of other countries.

1002. A majority of us feel unable to recommend the appointment of " workers' directors " to the boards of companies: and have reached this conclusion for a number of reasons. One is that such an office might expose its holder at times to an almost intolerable strain when decisions unfavourable to workers (for example on redundancy) had to be taken because they were in the interests of the company as a whole. A concurring vote by the workers' director might be unavoidable if he is to do his duty as a director; and yet could easily be misunderstood or misrepresented. The result might be to open a gap between the workers and the workers' director which it would be extremely difficult thereafter to bridge. In effect he would cease to represent them. Another reason is the difficulty of finding an equitable definition of the extent to which a workers' director should bear personal responsibility jointly with the other members of the board for their decisions or for any misfeasances on their part. A third reason is that the appointment of workers' directors in the near future would divert attention from the urgent task of reconstructing company and factory collective bargaining. Finally the majority of us cannot see that the appointment of a small number of workers' directors would be likely to give workers a real share in or control over the work of the boards they joined.

1003. Five of our members, however, take the view that the present position in which the shareholders in a concern have the exclusive right to elect directors is inappropriate. Persons whose daily work and livelihood are bound up with a company are more personally involved in its well-being than those to whom it is merely something in which they have a financial share capable of being bought and sold; and meantime yielding dividends. The interests of shareholders themselves can conflict with the interests of the company as much as can the interests of the workers. In an extreme example, a majority of shareholders might favour selling a company to a competitor who wants to close it down. The interests of workers in the companies for which they work cannot find adequate expression in a collective bargaining relationship, however fully developed.

1004. Lord Collison, Professor Kahn-Freund and Mr. Woodcock believe that, while the appointment of workers' directors will not lead to immediate and dramatic results, it is desirable to encourage and facilitate experiments. The difficulties over such questions as the accountability of workers' directors are not insuperable. They suggest therefore that legislation should be passed to enable workers' directors to be relieved of those legal and financial responsibilities which it would be wrong to ask them to share with other directors. Apart from this they believe that progress should at this stage be on a voluntary basis.

1005. Mr. Shonfield and Mr. Wigham regard these proposals as insufficient because they think little progress is likely if reliance is placed on voluntary arrangements. Even though no immediate and startling results would ensue, they consider change is necessary. There should be directors appointed to act as guardians of the workers' interest at the stage when company policy is being formulated; they should participate in this process on the same footing as directors appointed by the shareholders, and should in all other respects exercise the rights and responsibilities of non-executive directors of companies to which they are appointed. The power of appointment should rest with the trade unions active in the company concerned, who would consult the TUC. It is envisaged that those chosen would be more likely to be men with industrial or financial experience or knowledge, or trade union officials, than workers from the bench. (Any trade union official appointed would of course be barred from any collective bargaining involving the company while he was a director of it.) The number of workers' directors should vary with the size of the board but should not be less than two. They would be concerned no less than other directors with the prosperity of the company as a whole. They would report annually to their constituency in the same way as other directors report to shareholders' meetings, and opportunities would be provided for the workers in the establishment to discuss with and urge upon the workers' directors particular policies on matters of interest to them. However, the actual decisions of workers' directors would be their personal responsibility; they would not be bound as delegates to obey a set of instructions. Nor would they be subject to summary dismissal by the workers in the company. Their appointment would be for a fixed term. Their legal responsibility would have to be defined, but should approximate as nearly as possible to that of other directors. The details of any changes required in company law should be the subject of further inquiry, but it should now be decided in principle to legislate on these lines. It is suggested that a start should be made with companies above a certain size—say employing 5,000 workpeople or more —that is of the same size as those subject to the proposal for the registration of collective agreements (see paragraph 191).

1006. We have also received evidence concerning profit-sharing and co-partnership schemes. We do not doubt that in the right circumstances such schemes can be useful, and there are a number of well-known concerns which operate them successfully. There are also dangers, which should not be overlooked. In particular, schemes of this kind have suffered in trade union eyes from a suspicion that they have in some cases been designed to attract the loyalty of workers to their employers at the expense of the unions. It is evident that such schemes cannot be an acceptable substitute for the reform of industrial relations through comprehensive factory and company agreements. If they are to play a part in the wage structure of an under-taking we believe that this should be decided by negotiation through the relevant collective bargaining procedure along with the other elements in wage structure.

Chapter XVI

SUMMARY OF MAIN CONCLUSIONS AND RECOMMENDATIONS

THE SYSTEM OF INDUSTRIAL RELATIONS (CHAPTER III)

1007. Britain has two systems of industrial relations. One is the formal system embodied in the official institutions. The other is the informal system created by the actual behaviour of trade unions and employers' associations, of managers, shop stewards and workers (paragraph 46).

1008. The keystone of the formal system is the industry-wide collective agreement, in which are supposed to be settled pay, hours of work and other conditions of employment appropriate to regulation by agreement (paragraphs 50-52).

1009. The informal system is often at odds with the formal system. Actual earnings have moved far apart from the rates laid down in industry-wide agreements; the three major elements in the " gap " are piecework or incentive earnings, company or factory additions to basic rates, and over-time earnings. These are all governed by decisions within the factory (or other establishment such as a construction site or an office, the word " factory " not being used in the report in a restricted literal sense). At the same time, disputes procedures laid down in industry-wide agreements have been subjected to strain by the transfer of authority to the factory and workshop (paragraphs 53-64).

1010. The bargaining which takes place within factories is largely outside the control of employers' associations and trade unions. It usually takes place piece-meal and results in competitive sectional wage adjustments and chaotic pay structures. Unwritten understandings and " custom and practice " predominate (paragraphs 65-69).

1011. These developments help to explain why resort to unofficial and unconstitutional strikes and other forms of workshop pressure has been increasing (paragraphs 70-73).

1012. This decentralisation of collective bargaining has taken place under the pressure of full employment, which in Britain has had special consequences because of the way our industrial organisations have reacted to it (paragraph 74).

1013. The authority of employers' associations has declined. At one time they were innovators, but from 1914 until very recently nearly every important innovation in industrial relations which was not the work of the unions came from the Government or from individual companies (paragraphs 75-82).

1014. Despite this decline, however, most individual companies do not have comprehensive and well-ordered agreements for regulating terms and conditions over and above industry-wide minima. There has been a growth in the importance of personnel specialists, but many companies have no effective personnel policy to control methods of negotiation and pay structures, and perhaps no conception of one (paragraphs 83-95).

1015. Shop stewards are to be found in most factories where unions are strong. The basis of the shop steward's power is the work group. Full employment would in any case have increased the influence of work groups, but the way managements have chosen to act has also augmented it (paragraphs 96-110).

1016. Trade unions have, like employers' associations and managers, helped to sustain the façade of industry-wide bargaining, but cannot bear primary responsibility for the decline in its effectiveness. However, certain features of trade union structure and government have helped to inflate the power of work groups and shop stewards. One is the existence of multi-unionism in most British industries and factories (paragraphs 111-122).

1017. The Government's influence has generally been used to support the arrangements which have developed in private industry, and statutory wage fixation and systems of wage settlement in the public services for the most part yield results not very dissimilar from those achieved by collective bargaining elsewhere (paragraph 142).

1018. Many of those who conduct industrial relations in Britain are content with things as they are, because the arrangements are comfortable and flexible and provide a very high degree of self-government. Existing arrangements can be condemned only because these important benefits are outweighed by the disadvantages: the tendency of extreme decentralisation and self-government to degenerate into indecision and anarchy; the propensity to breed inefficiency; and the reluctance to change. All these characteristics become more damaging as they develop, as the rate of technical progress increases and as the need for economic growth becomes more urgent (paragraphs 123-130).

THE REFORM OF COLLECTIVE BARGAINING (CHAPTER IV)

1019. The central defect in British industrial relations is the disorder in factory and workshop relations and pay structures promoted by the conflict between the formal and the informal systems. To remedy this, effective and orderly collective bargaining is required over such issues as the control of incentive schemes, the regulation of hours actually worked, the use of job evaluation, work practices and the linking of changes in pay to changes in performance, facilities for shop stewards and disciplinary rules and appeals. In most industries such matters cannot be dealt with effectively by means of industry-wide agreements (paragraph 162).

1020. Factory-wide agreements can however provide the remedy. Factory agreements (with company agreements as an alternative in multi-plant companies) can regulate actual pay, constitute a factory negotiating committee and grievance procedures which suit the circumstances, deal with such subjects as redundancy and discipline and cover the rights and obligations of shop stewards. A factory agreement can assist competent managers, many current industry-wide agreements have become a hindrance to them (paragraphs 163-167).

1021. Industry-wide agreements should be limited to those matters which they can effectively regulate; but there would be advantage in agreements between employers' associations and trade unions which set out guide-lines for acceptable company or factory agreements and exempt the latter from the obligation to uphold all the terms of the existing industry-wide agreements. But if the basis of British industrial relations is to become the factory agreement, the change must be accomplished by boards of directors of companies. Employers' associations can continue to have a most important role in a system of factory and company agreements. In particular they could provide advice to members, many of whom are at present poorly equipped for the purpose, on the negotiation of their own agreements (paragraphs 168-180).

1022. The Commission recommends that boards of companies should review industrial relations within their undertakings, with six objectives in mind: to develop comprehensive and authoritative collective bargaining machinery; to develop joint procedures for the rapid and equitable settlement of grievances in a manner consistent with relevant collective agreements; to conclude agreements regulating the position of shop stewards; to conclude agreements covering the handling of redundancy; to adopt effective rules and procedures governing disciplinary matters; and to ensure regular joint discussion of measures to promote safety at work (paragraph 182). In pursuit of these objectives companies should welcome the exercise by employees of their right to join trade unions, develop positive management policies on specified matters and collect systematic information, which should be made available to workers' representatives insofar as they may reasonably require it (paragraph 184).

1023. Trade unions and employers' associations should assist (paragraphs 185-187).

1024. An Industrial Relations Act should be passed. Companies of a certain minimum size should be obliged to register their collective agreements with the Department of Employment and Productivity or if they have none to state why. This requirement would have a dual purpose: to emphasise that the primary responsibility for the conduct of industrial relations within a concern, and for the framework of collective agreements within which those relations are conducted, lies with the board of directors; and to draw attention to the aspects of industrial relations which the public interest requires should be covered wherever possible by clear and firm company and factory agreements (paragraphs 191-196). Initially only companies with say 5,000 employees would be covered, but the number should be progressively reduced—paragraph 199. The Act should apply also to the nationalised industries and public services, other than the civil service (paragraph 197).

1025. The Act should provide for the establishment of an Industrial Relations Commission, with a full-time chairman and other full-time and part-time members and its own staff. The Commission would, on a reference from the Department of Employment and Productivity, investigate and report on cases and problems arising out of the registration of agreements (paragraph 198). The Department of Employment and Productivity's industrial relations service should handle problems up to the point at which a reference is thought advisable (paragraph 199). The Industrial Relations Commission should also consider problems referred to it concerning companies not large enough to be covered by the obligation to register agreements (paragraph 200) as well as carrying out inquiries into the general state of industrial relations in a factory or industry (paragraph 201). Principles to guide the work of the Industrial Relations Commission are suggested (paragraph 203). There would be no penalties for non-compliance with the Commission's recommendations, though this question would have to be reviewed in the light of experience (paragraphs 204-205).

1026. These proposals will assist an incomes policy to work effectively by exposing the whole process of pay settlement to the influence of policy. The functions of the Industrial Relations Commission and the Prices and Incomes Board are different but the work of each will assist the other (paragraphs 208-209).

THE EXTENSION OF COLLECTIVE BARGAINING (CHAPTER V)

1027. New measures are needed to encourage the extension of collective bargaining (paragraphs 213-241).

1028. Any stipulation in a contract of employment that an employee is not to belong to a trade union should in law be void and of no effect (paragraph 245). So also should any stipulation in a rule of a Friendly Society that members may not belong to trade unions (paragraph 252).

1029. The Industrial Relations Commission should deal with problems of trade union recognition (paragraph 256).

1030. The Wages Councils Act 1959 should be amended with the object of encouraging the development of voluntary arrangements: the requirements as to the abolition of Wages Councils should be eased (paragraph 262) and the Wages Inspectorate might be enabled to enforce statutory minimum rates for a limited period following abolition (paragraph 264); it should be possible for undertakings with satisfactory collective bargaining arrangements of their own to be excluded from the scope of Wages Councils (paragraph 263); and Wages Councils should be empowered to establish voluntary disputes procedures (as also should Agricultural Wages Boards) (paragraph 266).

1031. Section 8 of the Terms and Conditions of Employment Act 1959, under which an employer may be required to observe the relevant terms and conditions for his industry, should be amended: it should be made available for use in Wages Council industries (paragraph 265); and in the consideration of claims not only the particular term or condition to which the claim relates but the terms and conditions laid down by collective agreement as a whole should have to be taken into account (paragraph 275).

1032. Compulsory unilateral arbitration by the Industrial Court should be made available in industries, sections of industry or undertakings in which the Secretary of State for Employment and Productivity has certified, on the advice of the Industrial Relations Commission following an inquiry, that it can contribute to the growth or maintenance of sound collective bargaining machinery (paragraph 274).

1033. Incomes policy raises problems in relation to Wages Councils and to arbitration. The only adequate long-run solution to the former is the extension of voluntary collective bargaining to Wages Council industries. In the short run it is for the Government, having reviewed such possibilities as a national minimum wage or the fixing of statutory minimum earnings for broad groups of industries, to formulate and state in clear terms what its policy is in relation to the lowest paid and how it is to be pursued. So far as arbitration is concerned, there should be legislation placing on all arbitrators an obligation to take incomes policy into account. Arbitrators should also be encouraged to give reasons for their awards or, in cases where they do not feel that they can, to state so plainly (paragraphs 277-287).

THE EFFICIENT USE OF MANPOWER (CHAPTER VI)

1034. There is great scope for the better use of manpower and this represents not only a challenge but a major opportunity (paragraph 295).

1035. Most important restrictive labour practices can be understood only in relation to particular circumstances in particular undertakings or plants. Many are simply the result of changed circumstances and technological advance; and work groups seek their retention as a means of protection. But it is in any case misleading to suggest that the primary responsibility for the wasteful use of manpower rests upon work groups or trade unions. Even where restrictive labour practices exist their removal is only one element in securing the efficient use of resources, which is the task of management (paragraphs 297-304).

1036. The formal system of industrial relations is especially ill-fitted to accomplish improvements in the use of manpower, since it offers no means for negotiating about the relaxation of restrictive practices enforced by work groups (paragraphs 305-311).

1037. The possibility of dealing with restrictive labour practices by means of a tribunal is rejected (paragraphs 312-317).

1038. Experience of productivity bargaining shows what can be accomplished by the conclusion of company and factory agreements. The proposals made for the reform of the collective bargaining system are therefore fundamental to the improved use of manpower. They will put in management's hands an instrument—the factory agreement—which, properly used, can contribute to much higher productivity; and the work of the Industrial Relations Commission can give an impetus to change and progress which has been lacking hitherto (paragraph 329).

1039. Training is an area in which restrictive traditions have especially deep roots in British industry and where the pressure of technological advance makes the need for a radical change in outlook particularly urgent. The present craft system can be very prejudicial to efficiency and to the needs and aspirations of workers outside the craft, and the gathering speed of technological change will make it still more obsolete (paragraphs 330, 337).

1040. Certain specific obstacles in the way of access to skilled work must be removed. "Dilution" agreements, under which if craftsmen are not available other workers may do skilled work, should be revised so that "dilutees" can become skilled workers for all purposes. As regards the training of women, a revolution in attitudes and in practical performance is needed from all concerned—education authorities, the Youth Employment Service, industrial training boards, the Department of Employment and Productivity, employers and trade unions (paragraphs 348, 356).

1041. The future of training is largely in the hands of industrial training boards. There is urgent need to secure the rapid and general adoption of systems of training which accord with the social and economic needs of a modern industrial society, with the following basic features: the laying down of objective standards by which to judge qualifications; a person who has attained those standards to be universally accepted as qualified and eligible to do the work in question; apart from introductory training and further education for young people, the content and duration of training courses to be determined by what is required to enable trainees to reach the set standards; no artificially restrictive barriers to be placed against access to training, for example on grounds of age, sex or colour (paragraph 357).

1042. Once objective standards have been laid down, trade unions should revise their rules as necessary to ensure that no qualified worker is arbitrarily denied admission or the right to use his skills; any worker alleging that he is denied admission although qualified should have a right of appeal to an independent review body (paragraph 358).

1043. Aided by the other departments concerned, the Department of Employment and Productivity will have to take the major responsibility for rousing the country to the gravity of the issues surrounding principles and practice in training and for carrying through the required reforms in time (paragraph 359).

STRIKES AND OTHER INDUSTRIAL ACTION (CHAPTER VII)

1044. Official strikes tend to be much more serious individually than unofficial strikes in terms of working days lost, but they are relatively infrequent and their number shows no consistent tendency to grow (paragraphs 368-370).

1045. Some 95 per cent of stoppages are unofficial, and unofficial strikes are becoming more common. About half concern wages and over 40 per cent concern "working arrangements, rules and discipline" and "redundancy, dismissal, suspension, etc.", matters usually dealt with at workplace rather than at industry level (paragraphs 379-380).

1046. Investigation of unofficial strikes in the motor industry shows that the causes are complex and that employers and unions both bear a considerable responsibility. Above all, they have failed to develop adequate institutions in changing circumstances. Wages structures, the engineering industry's disputes procedure and trade union communications are all defective (paragraphs 396-397).

1047. The motor industry's difficulties arise in the main not so much from special factors peculiar to the industry as from factors present in many other

266

industries, although to a less marked degree. Unofficial strikes and other types of unofficial action in industry are above all a symptom of a failure to devise institutions in keeping with changing needs (paragraph 398).

1048. Because of their unpredictability unofficial strikes have a damaging effect on managerial initiative, and the economic consequences are obvious and serious (paragraphs 413-415).

1049. Various means of reducing the number of official and unofficial strikes are examined. The possibility of introducing a new procedure for dealing with stoppages " creating grave national loss or widespread hindrance to public health and safety " is examined but rejected; so also is the possibility of making strike ballots compulsory (paragraphs 425, 430).

1050. The tendency to appoint inquiries into industrial relations problems which are able to examine long-term problems as well as immediate causes of dispute is welcomed, but in future the resources available to the bodies concerned will need to be increased. The Department of Employment and Productivity should have its own industrial relations research section. While the Industrial Relations Commission would normally be given responsibility for carrying out inquiries into long-term problems of industrial relations, it is desirable that the Secretary of State should still be able to appoint *ad hoc* inquiries. The Conciliation Act 1896 and the Industrial Relations Act 1919 should be amended to enable statutory inquiries to be appointed, irrespective of whether a dispute or difference exists or is threatened, by the Secretary of State acting alone or in conjunction with other Ministers. The Secretary of State should also, in appropriate cases, place on an industrial relations officer or officers the duty of obtaining the full facts about unofficial and unconstitutional stoppages in any industry, region or undertaking where they are causing particular difficulties, the Conciliation and Industrial Courts Acts being widened as necessary for this purpose; at the same time it would be appropriate to consider whether the powers which may be conferred on Courts of Inquiry, for example to require witnesses to give information and to attend and give evidence on oath, need to be brought up to date (paragraphs 436-451).

1051. A number of the Commission's recommendations will have an important effect on certain specific causes of strikes, including disputed claims to recognition and dismissals alleged to be unfair (paragraph 453).

1052. By far the most important part in remedying the problem of unofficial strikes and other forms of unofficial action will however be played by reforming the institutions of whose defects they are a symptom. The proposals for the reform of the collective bargaining system in Chapter IV are therefore fundamental to the solving of the problem (paragraph 454).

THE ENFORCEMENT OF COLLECTIVE AGREEMENTS
(CHAPTER VIII)

1053. Collective agreements are not legally binding contracts, and this is the intention of the parties themselves. If existing agreements were to be made into legal contracts this would have to be done by a statute attaching the force of law to the terms of a bargain contrary to the wishes of the parties. This would be a new departure in the law of contract and a breach with a long tradition of our industrial relations. The case for it might be argued if it could be shown to promise a decisive turn for the better in our industrial relations and in particular a substantial reduction in the number of unofficial strikes. But to make the present inadequate procedure agreements legally enforceable would be irrelevant and would divert attention from, and hinder, action to remedy the real causes (paragraphs 458-475).

1054. The implications of making collective agreements into binding legal contracts are examined. A measure which had the effect of putting on unions a legal obligation to use their best endeavours to secure the observance of procedure agreements would be more likely to lead to internal union disruption than to fewer unofficial strikes (paragraphs 480-482). In present circumstances, no proposal to impose legal sanctions on individuals who strike in breach of procedure agreements is practicable if it relies on enforcement by the employer (paragraphs 483-485). Experience shows that criminal proceedings would not be successful (paragraphs 486-487). An " automatic " sanction such as loss of statutory rights to notice and to redundancy pay would also not succeed: it would not in fact be automatic but would depend on employer enforcement, and would be ineffective for other reasons as well as being unfair (paragraphs 489-499).

1055. The effect of the reform of collective bargaining will be to reduce greatly the problem of unconstitutional strikes, which may not however disappear. It will then be possible to identify any circumstances in which it would be neither unjust nor futile to apply legal sanctions, because satisfactory disputes procedures are available and because legal penalties are appropriate where irresponsibility or ill-will is the root cause of their breach. If legal sanctions have to be applied—and whether this will happen cannot be predicted at present—it will have to be done *ad hoc*, and the machinery will have to be employed as an emergency device for use from case to case and in exceptional situations, after consultation with both sides and with the Industrial Relations Commission. The Industrial Relations Commission should be instructed to keep the matter under review in the light of progress with the reform of industrial relations in general and of disputes procedures in particular, with a view to advising the Secretary of State whether legislation for the enforcement of procedure agreements has become imperative and, if such legislation is enacted, to making such proposals for its application in exceptional cases as it thinks fit (paragraphs 500-518). (A note expressing the differing view of two members in relation to procedure agreements is added—paragraph 519.)

SAFEGUARDS FOR EMPLOYEES AGAINST UNFAIR DISMISSAL (CHAPTER IX)

1056. It is desirable that satisfactory voluntary procedures governing dismissals should be developed and extended (paragraph 532).

1057. A majority of the Commission recommend early legislation to establish statutory machinery to safeguard employees against unfair dismissal. This will encourage employers to improve their arrangements for handling dismissals, and may well spur employers and trade unions to establish satisfactory voluntary joint procedures which can be exempted from the coverage of legislation (paragraphs 539-544).

1058.   The legislation should state that dismissal is justified only if there is a valid reason for it connected with the capacity or conduct of the worker or based on the operational requirements of the undertaking, establishment or service; and that in the absence of such valid reason it is unfair. Certain specific reasons which are not valid should be specified, namely trade union membership or activity, race, colour, sex, marital status, religious or political opinion, national extraction or social origin (paragraph 545).

1059.   An employee who considers himself unfairly dismissed would have a right to complain within five working days of dismissal to the labour tribunal (for which see the next chapter), seeking either compensation or, if both parties agree, reinstatement.   No scale of compensation would be fixed, but there would be a ceiling of an amount equal to the employee's wages or salary for two years, wages or salary in excess of £40 a week being ignored (paragraphs 546-554).

1060.   The Secretary of State for Employment and Productivity should have power, on the recommendation of the Industrial Relations Commission, to exempt from the statutory machinery industries or undertakings which apply an agreed voluntary procedure, provided that it reaches satisfactory standards (paragraphs 559-560).

LABOUR TRIBUNALS (CHAPTER X)

1061.   In addition to the improvement of collective bargaining, it is desirable to improve the present machinery for the judicial determination of disputes arising out of individual contracts of employment and of statutory claims between employers and employees, and to avoid a multiplicity of jurisdictions (paragraph 573).

1062.   The existing industrial tribunals should be re-named " labour tribunals " and have their jurisdiction extended to cover disputes arising between employers and employees from contracts of employment or from statutory claims they may have against each other as employers and employees (paragraphs 572-573).   However, actions for damages arising from accidents at work should continue to go to the ordinary courts (paragraph 574).

1063.   The labour tribunals should (with a minor exception—see paragraph 580) have exclusive jurisdiction where statutory rights are concerned, but their jurisdiction should be concurrent with that of the ordinary courts where other matters arising from the employment relationship are concerned (paragraph 579).   They should have a primary duty to promote the amicable settlement of disputes by means of conciliation (paragraph 584).   Recommendations are made on other more detailed matters of procedure.

1064.   The Bar Senate, the Law Society and the universities should provide facilities for the training of lawyers in labour law (paragraph 583).

SAFEGUARDS FOR INDIVIDUALS IN RELATION TO TRADE UNIONS (CHAPTER XI)

1065.   The possibility of prohibiting the closed shop is rejected.   It is better to recognise that under proper safeguards a closed shop can serve a useful

269

purpose and to devise means of overcoming the disadvantages which accompany it (paragraph 602).

1066. An unsuccessful applicant for admission to a trade union, or the skilled section of a trade union, should be able to lodge a complaint that his application has been arbitrarily turned down. The complaint should lie in the first instance to the executive committee of the trade union. Thereafter a rejected applicant who still considers that his application has been arbitrarily rejected and that he is being caused substantial injustice should have a further right of complaint to a new and independent review body. If this body upholds his complaint it may issue a declaration that he should become and remain a member, and if rights of membership are withheld from him thereafter he will have the same legal right to obtain redress as any other member (paragraphs 610-613).

1067. A majority recommend that a worker declining to join a union who is dismissed following the introduction of the closed shop, or as a result of shop-floor pressure, should have a right of complaint to the labour tribunal against unfair dismissal (paragraph 614: also paragraphs 563-564).

1068. Once a person has been a member of a union for a specified period, say two years, his admission should not be questioned on any ground other than fraud at the time of application (paragraph 617).

1069. The results of research justify the general conclusion that it is unlikely that abuse of power by trade unions in relation to individuals is widespread. It does happen. Because of the connection between union membership and members' livelihoods trade unions cannot be regarded simply as voluntary clubs from the members' point of view. It is therefore recommended that there should be a right of complaint to the independent review body if a trade union member claims that he has been unjustifiably expelled and has suffered damage in consequence or has had any penalty inflicted upon him by the union which amounts to a substantial injustice (paragraphs 630-631).

1070. Members should be given a statutory right to complain to the Registrar of Trade Unions and Employers' Associations of alleged election malpractices and he should be able to send an inspector to investigate. The independent review body should hear complaints not disposed of by the Registrar. The jurisdiction of the Registrar of Friendly Societies to hear complaints about the infringement of political fund rules of trade unions and about irregularities connected with trade union mergers should be transferred to the independent review body (paragraph 645).

1071. The requirements relating to the rules of trade unions should be revised with a view to ensuring better safeguards for individual members but without impairing the freedom which trade unions ought to enjoy to frame rules to meet their own circumstances. The revised requirements suggested relate to admission, discipline, disputes between a union and a member, elections and shop stewards. Trade unions should also be required to employ professional auditors if they have more than 500 members or funds of more than £5,000 and to fulfil certain requirements as to superannuation funds for schemes covering members. Any disagreement between the Registrar and a union as to whether its rules comply with the revised requirements should be settled by the independent review body (paragraphs 649-656).

1072. The independent review body attached to the office of the Registrar should consist of three members; the chairman would be a lawyer and the other two would be chosen from a panel of trade unionists appointed by the Secretary of State after consultation with the TUC. In addition to the matters already mentioned, it should have jurisdiction concurrently with the High Court to try any case based on alleged breach of trade union rules or violation of natural justice (paragraphs 658-659). All complaints would be made in the first instance to the Registrar, who would have the duty of advising complainants and of promoting the amicable settlement of their complaints (paragraph 660). The independent review body would be able to award compensation (subject in some cases to a maximum—paragraph 661).

1073. Recommendations are also made on certain more detailed aspects of the operation of the independent review body.

TRADE UNIONS (CHAPTER XII)

1074. Means of reducing multi-unionism are examined. Industrial unionism —one union for all employees in the same industry regardless of occupation— would in theory have a number of advantages, though there would be theoretical difficulties too; but in any case there are decisive practical objections. It is necessary therefore to seek the benefits claimed for industrial unionism in other ways (paragraphs 673-678).

1075. There is scope for many more mergers between trade unions. It would in particular be useful to work towards the goal of one or at most two unions for the great bulk of craftsmen in engineering and in construction, and of one union for the printing industry (paragraph 682).

1076. Apart from union mergers, the most practical way to reduce competition between unions for members in the same group of workers in a factory is for the unions concerned to conclude agreements on rights of representation. The major task here falls to the unions themselves, although they will need the co-operation of employers where questions of recognition are involved. The Industrial Relations Commission will also be able to play a most important part (paragraphs 683-685).

1077. It is suggested that the TUC should intensify its efforts to encourage the unions concerned to adopt closer working arrangements. The TUC should also consider adopting the principle of " one union for one grade of work within one factory " as a guide for the future development of structure and taking practical steps to further observance of the principle (paragraphs 690-691).

1078. Trade unions should provide constitutionally recognised committees to perform many of the functions now carried out by unofficial shop stewards' " combine " committees (paragraph 695).

1079. The processes of union government should be altered to accommodate shop stewards and work groups more adequately. It is desirable for union branch organisation to be based on factories and for branch meetings to be

271

held at the place of work. This will require the co-operation of employers. Union rules relating to shop stewards should also be revised in relation to such matters as elections, term of office, the filling of casual vacancies, the bounds of the shop steward's jurisdiction, his relations with other union officials and his place in the union's organisation (paragraphs 696-698).

1080. The reconstruction of industrial relations (and especially the growth of factory bargaining) will mean that more full-time union officials are required; unions must reconsider their needs as regards both numbers and calibre in the light of changes following the report and it is suggested that the TUC should commission a general investigation of the subject (paragraphs 705-708).

1081. So far as training is concerned, trade unions are urged to concentrate on developing courses for junior full-time officers, both on or shortly after appointment and after some experience, and for shop stewards. For the latter day-release courses with the employer's co-operation offer the best prospects; grants by industrial training boards could be used to increase the number and raise the standard of these courses (paragraphs 710-713).

1082. Trade unions which do not already collect subscriptions by means of the check-off might usefully consider doing so and employers should consider requests for the check-off sympathetically (paragraph 721).

1083. The TUC should give a lead in all the matters covered by the chapter, which it can do within its existing powers. It will need to develop and adapt its organisation to cope satisfactorily with the many new aspects of its work (paragraphs 726-727).

EMPLOYERS' ASSOCIATIONS (CHAPTER XIII)

1084. In future employers' associations must find their main purpose in the promotion of their members' interests by assisting them to develop orderly and efficient systems of industrial relations within their undertakings (paragraph 735). Any rules which obstruct effective collective bargaining should be amended. Attitudes are already changing but a rapid increase in the pace and scale of the change is needed (paragraph 736).

1085. Employers' attitudes may have to change as regards recognition of trade unions, especially white-collar unions. The CBI's present policy as regards white-collar unions is " waiting and seeing ". The hope is expressed that the CBI and employers' associations will reconsider their attitudes with a view to encouraging the development of collective bargaining and the trade unions which make it possible, aided by the work of the Industrial Relations Commission (paragraph 739).

1086. It is suggested that the Engineering Employers' Federation should establish a national division to which multi-plant companies can affiliate direct. Other major employers' associations may have to revise their constitutions and procedures to give adequate recognition to individual companies (paragraph 741). There is a strong case for amalgamations among smaller associations (paragraph 744). Organisations which combine the functions of an employers' association with those of a trade association have advantages which others should carefully consider (paragraph 745).

1087. The CBI should consider widening its scope to include companies at present excluded from membership (paragraph 747).

CHANGES IN THE LAW (CHAPTER XIV)

1088. It is suggested that in due course the English and Scottish Law Commissions should be requested to undertake the task of codifying the law governing labour relations and trade unions and employers' associations (including such new legislation as is enacted to implement recommendations of the Royal Commission) as a matter of urgency. If codification is considered premature, a comprehensive consolidating measure should be enacted as soon as possible after implementing legislation. A special Industrial Law Committee should be attached to the Industrial Relations Commission to keep the law under review (paragraphs 755-756).

1089. The term " trade union " should in law be reserved for employees' organisations, and it is suggested that a trade union might be defined on the lines: " any combination of employees the principal activity of which is the regulation of relations between employees and employers, whether such combination is in restraint of trade or not, and which is registered upon the Register of Trade Unions and Employers' Associations " (paragraph 766).

1090. In future trade unions should be granted corporate personality and should register. The existing register kept by the Registrar of Friendly Societies can serve as a new Register of Trade Unions and Employers' Associations. New unions would be required to register within a stated period after formation. The conditions of registration would be the same as at present, modified as Parliament may think as a result of the report (recommendations as regards rules, for example, being made in Chapter XI) (paragraph 803).

1091. Section 3 of the Conspiracy and Protection of Property Act 1875 and sections 1-3 of the Trade Disputes Act 1906, which give certain immunities to persons from criminal prosecutions and civil actions in respect of acts committed in contemplation or furtherance of a trade dispute, should be made expressly applicable for the benefit of trade unions; and the Trade Disputes Act 1965 should remain in force (paragraph 803).

1092. The provisions referred to in the previous paragraph have hitherto applied for the benefit of any person (or combination). It is recommended that they should continue to do so, with one exception; a majority of the Commission recommend that section 3 of the Trade Disputes Act 1906 (which prevents an action being brought for an act done in contemplation or furtherance of a trade dispute on the ground only that it induces some other person to break a contract of employment) together with the relevant provision of the Trade Disputes Act 1965 should no longer apply to persons and combinations other than trade unions and employers' associations on the new register (paragraphs 787, 800, 802).

1093. The protection which sections 2 and 3 of the Trade Union Act 1871 give trade unions against consequences which might flow from their purposes being regarded as unlawful because they are in restraint of trade should continue to apply to all combinations which are or would be entitled to it under the present law (paragraph 805).

1094. Employers' associations whose principal activity, or one of whose principal activities, is the regulation of relations between employers and employees should also be granted corporate personality and should register; such associations would not be registered under the Companies Acts. Legal provisions analogous to those relating to trade unions would apply to registered employers' associations (paragraphs 806-808).

1095. A majority of the Commission recommend the repeal of section 4 of the Trade Union Act 1871, which precludes the direct legal enforcement of various kinds of trade union agreement (paragraph 815).

1096. Section 5 (3) of the Trade Disputes Act 1906, which defines the term " trade dispute " for the purpose of that and other Acts, does not need any substantial alteration (paragraph 817). However the term " workmen " (which is used in it) should be clarified (paragraph 821). It should also be made clear that the incorporation of trade unions and employers' associations is to make no difference so far as the definition is concerned (paragraph 822).

1097. The Commission recommends, with one dissentient, that sections 4 and 5 of the Conspiracy and Protection of Property Act 1875, which make breach of contract a criminal offence in certain circumstances, should be left undisturbed (paragraph 846).

1098. There is a possibility that a liability for civil conspiracy may arise where persons have agreed together, in contemplation or furtherance of a trade dispute, to break their contracts of employment, and that the protection of section 1 of the Trade Disputes Act 1906 and of the Trade Disputes Act 1965 would not be available; it should be removed by legislation (paragraph 854).

1099. Section 2 of the Trade Disputes Act 1906 (relating to picketing) should be amplified to make lawful the peaceful persuasion of customers not to deal with an employer in dispute (paragraph 875).

1100. The protection which section 3 of the Trade Disputes Act 1906 gives in relation to inducement of breach of a contract of employment (see paragraph 1092 above) should be extended so as to cover inducement of breach of any contract; but in the opinion of a majority this extended protection, like the existing protection given by this section, should be restricted to trade unions and employers' associations on the new register (paragraphs 787, 893-894).

1101. If doubt as to whether the Trade Disputes Act 1906 and other relevant statutes bind the Crown is well-founded it should be removed (paragraph 901).

1102. The immunity from actions in tort conferred on trade unions by section 4 of the Trade Disputes Act 1906 should be confined to torts committed in contemplation or furtherance of a trade dispute (paragraph 909). It should also be made clear that actions are precluded not only if they are

274

brought for damages in respect of past torts but also if they are for injunctions in respect of torts threatened or apprehended in the future (paragraph 911).

1103. No change is recommended in the law relating to " contracting-out " of liability to contribute to trade unions' political funds (or to " contracting-in " where Northern Ireland is concerned), since the Commission regards the matter more as a question of politics than of industrial relations (paragraphs 924-925). Nor are any changes recommended in the requirements of the Trade Union Act 1913 relating to the political funds of trade unions, except as regards the auditing of accounts (paragraph 927 and Appendix 7).

1104. Changes are recommended in section 22 of the National Insurance Act 1965, which concerns the disqualification of persons for receipt of unemployment benefit when there is a trade dispute at their place of employment. A claimant for benefit should no longer have to prove that he is not a member of a " grade or class " of workers any of whom are participating in or financing or directly interested in the dispute (paragraph 980). The Commission also recommends, with one dissentient, that a claimant should not be regarded as " financing " a trade dispute simply because he is a member of a trade union paying strike pay to those on strike (paragraph 991).

WORKERS' PARTICIPATION IN MANAGEMENT (CHAPTER XV)

1105. The importance of the question of workers' participation in management for industrial relations is acknowledged, though any changes to encourage such participation should be subsidiary to reforms in collective bargaining. However, a majority of the Commission feel unable to recommend the appointment of " workers' directors " to the boards of companies. If a profit-sharing and co-partnership scheme is to play a part in the wage structure of an undertaking, this should be settled by negotiation (paragraphs 1002, 1006).

. . . . . .

THE MAIN TASKS FOR THE DEPARTMENT OF EMPLOYMENT AND PRODUCTIVITY

1106. If our recommendations are accepted, their implementation will impose a formidable programme of legislation and practical action on the Department of Employment and Productivity, in addition to the heavy burden it already has. It is therefore appropriate in conclusion to draw together in a single list the main tasks for the Department.

1107. As regards legislation, we propose in this report that there should be an Industrial Relations Act providing for the registration of collective agreements with the Department and for the establishment of an Industrial Relations Commission; revision of the Wages Councils Act 1959 and the re-introduction of unilateral arbitration on a selective basis; statutory protection for employees against unfair dismissal, and for trade union members (or applicants for membership) in relation to the trade unions; revision of the law relating to trade unions and employers' associations, including provision for registration and incorporation; revision of the law relating to trade disputes; the transformation of the industrial tribunals into labour tribunals; and legislation on a number of other related matters.

1108. Practical implementation of the report involves putting into effect a scheme for the registration of collective agreements and for their scrutiny. The Industrial Relations Commission has to be established. The Department's industrial relations officers will have to undertake further advisory work both in connection with the recommended review by companies of their industrial relations policies and as an integral part of implementing the Industrial Relations Act. Some Wages Councils will have to be wound up, and the functions of the remainder expanded. There will be added work on industrial training, especially so far as opportunities for women are concerned. An industrial relations research section will have to be established.

1109. We emphasise that we are not suggesting a sharp break with the policies which the Government have hitherto pursued. The policy of providing support for the collective bargaining system has long been established and remains as sound today as it was at the end of the last century. We suggest rather how that policy can be made fully effective in modern circumstances.

1110. Likewise we propose only one completely new permanent institution —the Industrial Relations Commission—and otherwise aim in our proposals to modernise existing institutions and give them new functions to meet new needs. Thus the Industrial Court, which unlike the Industrial Relations Commission is concerned with quick solutions for existing differences, will in future provide unilateral arbitration as well as adjudicating in an enlarged range of cases under section 8 of the Terms and Conditions of Employment Act 1959. The existing industrial tribunals will be transformed into labour tribunals whose jurisdiction will be extended to include disputes between individual employer and employee arising out of the contract of employment and also complaints by employees of unfair dismissal. The trade union work of the Chief Registrar of Friendly Societies will be divided off from the other functions he performs, a separate Registrar of Trade Unions and Employers' Associations being appointed; the latter will be assisted by an independent review body whose jurisdiction will cover cases previously dealt with by the Chief Registrar as well as cases arising out of the exercise of further rights of appeal granted to individuals. The pattern of public institutions concerned with industrial relations which will result from all these changes is set out in tabular form in Appendix 9.

1111. It will be the duty of the Department of Employment and Productivity, as the Government Department responsible for industrial relations, to maintain close links with the other public institutions in this field. This applies particularly where the Industrial Relations Commission is concerned: the work of the Commission and the work of the Department will be complementary, and to function efficiently each will greatly depend on the other. Responsibility for the speedy and successful reconstruction of British industrial relations will lie largely in their hands.

1112. We have been extremely fortunate in having as our Secretary Mr. John Cassels and owe to him a very considerable debt of gratitude. The amount of evidence and other material which the Commission has had to study has been immense, and it has lightened our task considerably to have had it abstracted, classified and indexed in the efficient and expeditious manner in which this essential work has been done. Mr. Cassels has however gone further than simply seeing that the administrative arrangements have worked smoothly and well. He has placed at our disposal his specialised knowledge of industrial relations and has contributed to our research programme by writing and publishing a paper on productivity bargaining and restrictive labour practices. He has also helped materially in the drafting of this report. He has been ably assisted from the start by our Assistant Secretary Mr. John Brownsort, to whom our thanks are likewise due. Together they have supervised a small staff whose work, though not so prominent, has nevertheless been indispensable, and who never failed us when urgent tasks had to be performed with all possible speed. We are also greatly indebted to Dr. William McCarthy, our Research Director, for the skill and energy with which he organised and directed our programme of research and for the valuable contribution which the papers he himself prepared made to our work. Altogether we could not have been better served by those appointed to assist us, and to all of them we express our gratitude.

ALL OF WHICH WE HUMBLY SUBMIT FOR YOUR MAJESTY'S GRACIOUS CONSIDERATION

DONOVAN* *(Chairman)*

ROBENS*

TANGLEY*

COLLISON

GEORGE WOODCOCK

MARY GREEN

GEORGE POLLOCK*

ERIC L. WIGHAM

H. A. CLEGG

OTTO KAHN FREUND

ANDREW SHONFIELD*

JOHN THOMSON*

J. S. CASSELS *(Secretary)*

J. S. BROWNSORT *(Assistant Secretary)*

24th May, 1968

---

*Signed subject to the views expressed in the note which appears hereafter under the name of the signatory.

ADDENDUM BY LORD DONOVAN

1. I desire to add a few observations on the subject of the legal enforcement of collective agreements.

2. I am in full agreement with my colleagues that there is no case for legislation which would transform such agreements into legal contracts, contrary to the will of the parties, so far as such agreements lay down terms and conditions of work. These are very seldom dishonoured, and the legal difficulties involved in the proposal are such that its advocates made no real attempt to meet them in any evidence given to us.

3. As regards " procedure " agreements I recognise the force of the argument deployed in Chapter VIII to the effect that the root cause of unofficial and unconstitutional strikes is the absence in many parts of industry of satisfactory procedures for the peaceful settlement of disputes; and that once this defect has been made good, a substantial improvement in the situation may be expected. I agree that this ought to follow.

4. The agreement and institution of such procedures seems unlikely, however, to be a rapid process, and indeed may take some considerable time. In the meantime if present trends continue, the number of unofficial and unconstitutional strikes, which we describe as a serious and urgent problem, will continue to grow.

5. In these circumstances I have been reluctant to trust entirely to the expected effect of better procedure agreements; and have sought some interim remedy which would be both workable and just. I have found it very elusive.

6. Fines, whether called " damages " or not, are open to the objections set out in paragraph 486, and if, as is usually proposed, they are to be deducted from pay by instalments, some machinery must be set up to trace employees who leave before paying in full, and to oblige the new employer to deduct the balance. If the employee became self-employed instead, proceedings for the balance would have to be taken against him directly. Imprisonment, or distraint upon an employee's goods and chattels, as the ultimate sanction are consequences from which the proponents of fining invariably shrank.

7. I was initially much attracted by the idea that participation in an unofficial or unconstitutional strike should break the continuity of service of an employee, and so affect, among other things, his entitlement to any future redundancy payment. In the end however I have reached the conclusion that this is not a practicable remedy. The objections to it are elaborated in Chapter VIII and I would add only this: that any punishment of this kind must be accompanied by a right of appeal. There may be issues of fact in dispute: there may have been provocation on the part of the employer: there may be mitigating circumstances of other kinds which ought fairly to be taken into account. If this be accepted, the consequence is that there must be a trial of each case. The appellants could be numbered in scores, and sometimes in hundreds. The employer or his representatives would have to attend and give evidence. And all in all the effect on production might be worse than was the strike itself. In these circumstances the employer is unlikely to co-operate in the scheme, as he must do if it is to work.

8. De-registration has been suggested of a trade union whose members, or some of whose members, persistently break a procedure agreement. The consequences of de-registration would need to be carefully considered. We propose that trade unions should be given corporate status and in consequence have to register. On this basis de-registration would not, *per se,* amount to dissolution of the union. It would continue as a corporate body and, though not now a " trade union " by legal definition, would still be performing the functions of one. And it would be doing this free from the obligations imposed by registration in the interests of its members and of the public. If it were made a consequence of de-registration that the union concerned lost the protection of sections 1-4 of the Trade Disputes Act 1906 the position would seem to be as follows. As regards section 1, reliance could be placed on the Common Law instead, which is now largely in harmony. As regards section 2, there is much that is lawful, apart from the terms of the section, in the way of peacefully obtaining or communicating information by way of picketing, and of peacefully persuading persons not to work. As regards section 3, the tort of inducing breaches of contracts of employment would not be committed if proper notice to terminate them were given. Section 4 of the Act would be more important, since even if the section is restricted as we propose, the withdrawal of its protection would leave a union exposed to the risk of damages for torts committed on its behalf in contemplation or furtherance of a trade dispute. The *Taff Vale* judgment of 1901 which Parliament over-ruled in this respect in 1906 would be revived. The effect of this on industrial relations generally is hardly likely to be beneficial. Moreover, in the face of such a prospect a de-registered union might well decide to shed its corporate status: and become instead an unincorporated association. A suit for tort against such an association would then be faced with all the hazards of the representative action which we refer to in paragraph 777.

9. Apart altogether from these considerations, de-registration as a sanction for unions some of whose members break procedure agreements would seem to be less than just until the system of industrial relations is reformed so as to give unions the requisite measure of control of the situation.

10. We comment in Chapter VIII on the unwillingness of employers to pursue the legal remedy which the law already provides in the shape of an action for damages for breach of the contract of employment. Such unwillingness does not end there. After the lengthy unofficial dock strike last autumn, which involved breaches of contract which must have exposed valuable property to destruction or serious injury, the Liverpool Chamber of Commerce and Industry wrote to us with suggestions for changes in the law. Their attention was drawn to the existing law contained in section 5 of the Conspiracy and Protection of Property Act 1875, and they were asked whether proceedings thereunder had been considered, and if so why they had not been taken. The Chamber replied that one trade association represented on its Council had considered such action but, after discussion with other associations, had decided that it would merely have served " to exacerbate the relations between the two parties " and " act as an irritant ".

11. This reluctance by employers to pursue remedies already provided both by the civil and by the criminal law is, of course, perfectly understandable.

But the reason, namely that such a course might simply make industrial relations worse, is one which the Commission likewise has had to keep constantly in mind when considering other remedies which it has been urged to recommend.

12. Occasions may however arise when the employer does not need to take the initiative in legal proceedings. He could, for example, defend a claim for a redundancy payment by means of a counterclaim for damages for any breach of contract by the claimant within the preceding six years. The same could be true in relation to any claim for compensation for unfair dismissal if Parliament hereafter allows such claims to be made. These possibilities of themselves are probably not significant, though they should not be overlooked.

13. The recommendation of a majority of us that the first limb of section 3 of the Trade Disputes Act 1906 should not in future extend to unofficial and temporary groups might, however, well have a material effect, although the recommendation is made on grounds of general principle. For the rest I must subscribe to the conclusion that the need for further measures should be considered when procedure agreements have been improved as proposed, and the results of this necessary reform are available.

SUPPLEMENTARY NOTE BY LORD TANGLEY

1. I regret that I cannot without some qualification join my colleagues in presenting our Report. I have however over the last twelve months co-operated fully in its preparation and except as recorded in the Report itself do not dissent from its recommendations. My qualifications are twofold, one minor and one major. The minor is that paragraph 18 of Chapter I does not in my opinion do justice to the change that has come over the ownership and consequently the organisation of companies. There is a great deal of confusion between the functions of Shareholders, Board and Management, a confusion which our Report does not wholly avoid. The major qualification relates to the powers of the proposed Industrial Relations Commission (IRC). I deal separately with each of these qualifications.

2. As to the first qualification I make the following comments: —

The organisation of industrial companies has changed greatly since 1871 and even since 1893 or 1906. The phrase ' Masters and Men ' dates from an early stage of industrial development and fairly described the situation at a time when businesses were directly owned and managed by individuals or families even in instances where the newly invented device of a limited liability company was utilised.

Even today there are many businesses where this situation persists. Most of them are of small or medium size but some of the largest and most successful industrial undertakings are still of this type. These large undertakings have been outstandingly successful in their industrial relations. Even amongst those which have many shareholders amongst the public there are some where the individual or family influence both in ownership and management is strong.

However none of these companies can be said to be typical of the organisation of most large industrial concerns today. The typical large company is owned by a large number of individual shareholders each with a relatively small stake who cannot be expected to concern themselves directly with the management of the company. Instead of direct participation these shareholders rely upon their directors who are appointed by them to ensure the good management of the company. The directors are in a fiduciary relationship with their shareholders. Indeed in many respects they can be properly regarded as Trustees for the general body of shareholders. As Trustees for the shareholders, directors as such direct the business of the company but do not directly manage its business. They are responsible for the raising of funds, for the investment of those funds, and for ensuring that the company is managed in accordance with the policy laid down by the board. As part of their duty directors must appoint proper managers or executives, must ensure that those managers or executives remain efficient and be prepared if necessary to replace them. It is also the duty of the board to ensure that the managers bring before the board at the right time matters that should receive the attention of the board. The board is also responsible for seeing that proper accounts and information are laid before the shareholders at the proper time. Strictly speaking the chairman of the company has the special duty only of taking the chair at general meetings of the company and at board meetings. In practice however in a large concern the chairman has the duty of keeping in close touch with the managers and executives and on behalf of the board ensuring that they are carrying out their duties in a proper manner.

It frequently happens that managers or executives are appointed directors of the company. Indeed the board may consist entirely of managers or executives, though usually there is a mixture of managers or executives and outside directors who bring to the business of the company experience they have gained in other walks of life. However, the manager or executive who becomes a director must remember that as a director he is performing quite different functions from those he performed as a manager or executive. Indeed much confusion and bad organisation can result unless everyone concerned keeps these two functions separate. The manager or executive is responsible to the board, the board are responsible to the shareholders.

There is another change also that should be noticed. Largely as a result of taxation and particularly death duties the proportion of shares held by private individuals is diminishing and the proportion of shares held by the so-called institutional shareholders is increasing. These institutional share-holders are mainly Insurance Companies, Investment Trusts, Pension Funds and Unit Trusts. In a large public company the institutional shareholdings are usually also large. The investments are made by the managers of the institutions subject to the direction of their own boards. But the funds invested are the aggregate of the savings of innumerable small investors. For the most part an Insurance Company will be investing the premiums paid by numerous life policy holders who rely upon their life policies for the security of themselves and their families. Similarly the Investment Trusts and the Unit Trusts have entrusted to them for investment the funds of a large body of savers, most of them small, who hope through this method of investment to secure themselves against the evils of inflation which the normal life policy does not do. The Pension Funds are investing the contributions of employees and employers so as to build up a fund out of which retire-ment pensions will ultimately be paid. Most of the shareholders of a public company whether institutional or otherwise are looking to the long term growth of the company in which they have invested. If this long term growth does not take place a vicious circle sets in which makes it impracticable for growth to be financed, with the consequence that growth is diminished, stagnation or recession sets in and the prospects of employment for those who work for the company are diminished. It is the duty of the directors to ensure that the company is so managed as to secure the objects of the shareholders' investment. It is the duty of the managers so to manage the company as to secure this end. The end cannot be secured unless the managers succeed in satisfying customers' requirements in securing and maintaining a contented and productive labour force and in making adequate profits.

In a real sense, therefore, the major interests of all parties coincide and it is noticeable that the most successful leaders amongst managers set them-selves to emphasise the unity of the interests of all parties. In doing so they often have to face the charge of being paternalists particularly from those

283

who have not had the responsibility of leadership and management thrust upon them.

Within this ultimate unity of interest however there can be and usually are conflicts of immediate interest between the different groups concerned. For example, an increase of wages may diminish the amount immediately available for dividend, or a productivity agreement may result in an immediate increase in costs which will not be offset by economies for some time to come. The managers therefore may often have to perform a balancing act in the interests of the long-term prosperity of the concern. What is being balanced is the interests of customers, the interests of the employees and the interests of innumerable people whose life savings are directly or indirectly invested in the company. This fact makes it all the more necessary to keep distinct the functions of the managers and the directors and also necessitates a full and free understanding between the directors and the managers as to what is in the best long-term interests of the company.

3. I turn now to my major qualification which relates to the powers of the proposed IRC.

(i) I am in agreement with the analysis of the situation as set out in the Report and with the general tenor of the recommendations. The essence of the situation is that national or industry-wide agreements (including disputes procedures) have become increasingly less effective and meaningful; that the most important and relevant arrangements are made at workplace level; that these arrangements derive from unorganised and even unadmitted negotiations; and that in consequence there is an air of makebelieve about the whole state of industrial relations.

The object of the recommendations is to substitute reality for make-believe by (a) seeing that national or industry-wide agreements deal with matters that can be effectively dealt with at that level and are capable of being given effect to at the workplace; (b) regularising and institutionalising workplace negotiation; and (c) ensuring that national or industry-wide agreements and workplace agreements are compatible with one another and together form a rational and comprehensible code of conduct.

The main function of the IRC is to secure these ends. If they are not secured the United Kingdom will no doubt continue to fall behind other countries in industrial efficiency, an efficiency upon which the growth of the prosperity of all classes of the community depends.

(ii) The decisive question therefore must be: "What powers does the IRC need to enable it to perform its functions?" The Report appears to assume that the IRC will rely wholly on persuasion and publicity. I agree that persuasion should be the principal mode of procedure and that where it succeeds it is the most effective and productive. Publicity can also be helpful and sometimes produces results. But there are plenty of instances in which there have been ample persuasion and publicity that have produced no results at all, as for example the scandalous history of the printing industry. I fear therefore that if we leave the IRC as powerless as is proposed in the Report it will become yet another voice crying in the wilderness.

284

(iii) The most specific of my reasons for believing that the proposals for an IRC as set out in the Report will lead to its being an ineffective body is that there do not exist today institutions representing either employees or employers that are capable of producing the results we have in view and which we expect the IRC to achieve. There are exceptions in certain trades and certain companies. The conception of national or industry-wide agreements and institutionalised workplace agreements so linked together as to make a rational and comprehensible code carries with it the corollary that on the employees' side there is a trade union organisation and on the employers' side an employers' association capable of negotiating and seeing to the carrying out of the hierarchy of agreements. In general this organisation is lacking. There are yawning gaps on the trade union side between national, branch and workplace levels. The same may be said of employers' associations. Far-reaching changes of structure, organisation and procedure are needed on both sides. Having read many rules and constitutions of trade unions and employers' associations and having heard the evidence of so many people on both sides I am regretfully driven to the conclusion that the necessary reforms will not come about by mere persuasion unbacked by active authority. If we want the IRC to be effective its persuasive function must be supported by real power. In the following paragraphs I set out what I believe this power will have to be.

(iv) a. All national or industry-wide agreements must be registered with the IRC.

b. If any company fails within the prescribed time to register a plant or company agreement as required by the Report it must report its failure and the reasons for it. The union or unions concerned must report their reasons. The IRC must then have power to draft and submit to the Minister a disputes procedure code which the Minister may by order make binding on the parties. A minority of the Commission seem to support this view.

c. On the application of any employer or trade union the IRC may certify to the Minister which union or unions should be recognised as negotiators for a company or workplace agreement and the Minister may by order require that negotiations proceed accordingly.

(v) a. The IRC should take over the functions of the Registrar with regard to trade unions and employers' associations.

b. Separate Registers of Trade Unions and Employers' Associations should be kept, but employers' associations which do not conduct labour negotiations should not be registered.

c. For a trade union the IRC shall require that existing rules shall within a prescribed period be amended or new draft rules submitted covering matters dealt with in the Report and in addition rules as to admission, expulsion, suspension or other disciplinary action including a right of appeal to an independent body. I consider that there is no need to set up a separate review body for this purpose. The labour tribunals are to consider questions of unfair dismissal by employers. Unfair dismissal may have serious consequences. Unfair

285

loss of a union card may amount to a life sentence of unemployment and I can see no justification for reserving such a question to a tribunal consisting of two trade unionists and an independent chairman. In default the Minister at the request of the IRC may promulgate rules to be adopted.

d. A new union may be registered provided that the IRC is satisfied (i) that it represents a substantial proportion of employees in any industry, company or plant, (ii) that those employees are not adequately represented by an existing registered trade union and (iii) that the membership of the new union would be large enough to make it a viable concern.

e. For both a trade union or an employers' association the IRC may require alterations of rules as far as in the IRC's opinion such alterations may be necessary or desirable to facilitate the negotiating or carrying out of agreements of the kind referred to in the Report. If the requirement is not complied with the Minister may by order enjoin compliance.

(vi) The IRC may deregister a trade union (i) for failure to comply with any of the foregoing provisions as to rules and (ii) for breaches of registered agreements on the part of the union, its officers or members of such frequency or gravity as in the opinion of the IRC justifies deregistration. There should be an appeal to the Industrial Court.

Some explanation of this recommendation is needed. The Report puts upon certain employers a proposed statutory obligation to register comprehensive agreements. I agree that the sort of agreements we have today are not really capable of being made legally enforceable. I agree also that the sort of agreements proposed by the Report should not be made legally enforceable. The difficulties are too great. On the other hand it is, in my opinion, too much to require employers to register agreements if they are to be treated as they are today. Today any breach by an employer leads to industrial action; the employees choose for themselves the conditions under which they will or will not treat the agreement as binding. It is this one-sidedness that gives rise to the demand for the legal enforceability of collective agreements. I cannot see my way to acceding to this demand.

But the new kind of agreement proposed by the Report (even if it is part industry-wide and part plant- or company-wide) will have involved all levels of employees' representatives, national district branch and workplace. Such an agreement so arrived at should be observed. No doubt there will from time to time be slips up or local loss of temper which should not be visited by legal consequences. But where a union permits its members to act flagrantly or frequently to break such an agreement it is flouting the whole conception of collective bargaining and cannot expect to retain immunities designed to support and encourage collective bargaining.

(vii) The IRC may deregister an employers' association for the same reasons and subject to the same right of appeal.

(viii) The "immunities" from civil proceedings in section 3 of the Trade

Disputes Act 1906 should continue to apply in case of a trade dispute (with the extensions and limitations proposed in the Report) to
  (a) registered trade unions
  (b) registered employers' associations
  (c) individuals acting in an authorised capacity on behalf of a registered trade union or employers' association.

As I understand the Report a majority of the Commission concur in this recommendation.

SUPPLEMENTARY NOTE BY LORD ROBENS, SIR GEORGE POLLOCK and MR. JOHN THOMSON

We agree with the view expressed by Lord Tangley in his supplementary note that the Industrial Relations Commission should have power to de-register a trade union or employers' association for failure to comply with its own rules or for breaches of registered agreements on the part of the union (or association), its officers and members of such frequency or gravity as in the opinion of the Industrial Relations Commission justifies de-registration, with a right of appeal against this decision to the Industrial Court.

NOTE OF RESERVATION BY MR. ANDREW
SHONFIELD

1. The main Report addresses itself to the immediate situation in British industrial relations and proposes a number of remedies which I heartily support. But it barely concerns itself with the long-term problem of accommodating bodies with the kind of concentrated power which is possessed by trade unions to the changing future needs of an advanced industrial society. There are a number of questions that ought to be asked at this stage about the degree of regulation which should properly be applied to organisations wielding great authority in communities where the average citizen becomes progressively more vulnerable to what they do. With the growing dependence of people on the reliable performance of services required for tolerable living in crowded urban communities, the employment of collective power of groups of producers to disrupt the lives of people who have no means of helping themselves raises new problems. One has to contemplate a situation in which the typical city dweller has been forced into relying on collective services for things that he is no longer able to provide for himself privately. This has happened, or is happening, with light and heat, and is likely to happen with transport and other services. It will become less possible in the circumstances which are unfolding to distinguish, in the sharp traditional style of the English Common Law, between public authority and power and the ' private ' power of organisations with collective functions, which control the supply of essential goods and services not obtainable from any alternative source.

2. Although the argument applies with special force to the direct relations between the producer and the private citizen, it is also relevant to the supply and service relationships in the earlier stages of the production process. It is no longer possible to accept the traditional notion of the individual workplace as a separate and largely autonomous estate, where employers and employees are able to conduct their quarrels with little or no regard to the effects of what they do on other workplaces. In recent years we have seen how a large complex of interrelated industrial operations located in different concerns may suddenly be placed at the mercy of the impulse of some small work group somewhere along the line. The degree of industrial interdependence is certain to increase. Meanwhile the proportion of capital costs in the total outgoings of modern firms, especially of those in the advanced industries, is constantly on the increase. An enforced shut-down caused by a strike in a small plant in a quite different part of the country may hit the earnings of such a highly capitalised firm very hard. Its willingness to accept the risks of heavy investment in the production of specialised products dependent on the chain of other operations will be influenced by the view that it takes of the reliability of the engagements made by its suppliers of essential goods and services. If the flow is constantly subject to unpredictable interruption, business initiative in important fields of activity is likely to be discouraged. There is also the effect on wage-earnings; the demand for total autonomy by a work group which has banded together

to stop or slow down production in one place results in the loss of wages and the disruption of the working lives of many times their number elsewhere. These workers and their employers both have a right to expect the effective intervention of trade unions in plants where labour is organised, to ensure that frivolous or minor disputes are not allowed to cause excessive damage.

3. They have no right to demand that the strike weapon shall never be used. The existence of a threat of this kind, whether it is the complete withdrawal of labour or a change in work practices, such as a go-slow to the detriment of the employer, will continue to be a necessary element in the bargaining power of wage and salary earners for as far ahead as one can see. But all those who have to rely on the output of a particular body of workers for their livelihood are entitled to a clear assurance about the status and purposes of the organisations in whose name the order to use the strike or other weapons of industrial dispute is issued, and about the responsibilities of those in charge of them.

4. Hitherto no distinction has been made in British law between the activities of an organised trade union with a permanent base and a temporary association of employees in an autonomous work group. A majority of the Royal Commission has proposed that in future the immunities (under section 3 of the 1906 Act) from legal penalties for certain offences, which would be actionable if done in the ordinary way by an individual person but are not actionable so long as they are done as part of a trade dispute, shall in future apply only to registered trade unions. This is an essential first step in the process of reform. But the distinction between labour organisations which explicitly accept certain responsibilities towards society as a whole, as well as towards their own members, and those which refuse or are unable to do so, needs to be pressed further. This should be done by demanding of trade unions the fulfilment of certain minimum standards of behaviour as a condition for being registered. Again, the Report makes a beginning, notably in its recommendation that the rules of unions governing admission and expulsion shall be subject to judicial control (via the Review Body attached to the Registrar of Trade Unions and Employers' Associations). But there are other obligations, notably those which express the duty of trade unions to conduct their industrial relations in such a way as not to hold back improvements in the standard of living of the community as a whole, which need to be spelt out.

Towards a Regulated System

5. It seems inconceivable in the long run that in a society which is increasingly closely knit, where the provision of services to meet the elementary needs of a civilised daily life depends more and more on the punctual performance of interrelated work tasks of a collective character, trade unions will be treated as if they had the right to be exempt from all but the most rudimentary legal obligations. This is the traditional view, which has bitten deep into the British system of industrial relations. It is what the TUC in their evidence to the Royal Commission referred to as the principle of ' abstention, of formal indifference ' on the part of the state (paragraph 174).

The principle has been breached over a widening area, largely as a result of the advance of the welfare state and the effort to guarantee for work-people by law more rights and benefits — redundancy payments, better industrial training, fairer contracts of employment—than collective bargaining had been able to secure for them. It will be breached further if the recommendations of the Royal Commission, especially on the regulation of dismissals from employment, are accepted.

6. But all the while the myth that the act of regulation is a falling from grace and that each case is to be treated as a regrettable exception, which must not in any circumstance be generalised, continues to influence power-fully the judgment of many of those concerned with industrial relations. Since my own view differs profoundly from this received opinion, it is necessary to say something briefly on the general topic of the place of law in an industrial system.

7. I start from the proposition that the deliberate abstention of the law from the activities of mighty subjects tends to diminish the liberty of the ordinary citizen and to place his welfare at risk. If organisations are powerful enough to act the bully then very special grounds are necessary to justify the decision not to subject their behaviour to legal rules. The legal rules need not be much brought into play in practice; if such organisations enforce their own systems of rules and these work in the public interest there will be little actual labour for the law to do. But the content of the rules and the way that they operate in particular cases must not be allowed to escape from close public surveillance. I therefore regard the principle which is stated in para-graph 471 of the Report to be characteristic of the British system, that collec-tive bargaining should remain " outside the law ", to be wrong. The special grounds for treating trade unions in this way which seem to have influenced the 19th and early 20th century legislators, who laid down the framework of rules which govern British industrial relations today, were essentially that trade unionism was an unpleasant conspiracy—of a kind which would be reprehensible if practised by anyone else but which had to be tolerated in this particular instance as the only available means of conducting relations between employers and the representatives of workpeople. However, it was felt to be wrong for the law to do anything to support such a conspiracy, e.g. by making any of the agreements among the conspirators enforceable as ordinary legal contracts. The only course was to leave the trade unions to their own devices.

8. Historically the doctrine of the " licensed conspiracy " served a useful social purpose. The trade unions were weak and vulnerable at the time, and the respectable prejudice against them, which was shared by judges, would almost certainly have meant that legal decisions on matters affecting their affairs would have tended to inhibit their growth. The removal of these matters from the purview of the courts therefore helped the British trade unions to establish themselves as the large and influential bodies which they are today. But now that they have evolved to this dominant role, it would be highly anomalous if the legal prejudices of an earlier generation were to continue to be used to encourage them to avoid undertaking ordinary con-

tractual obligations in their relations with employers or to permit their actions to escape the public regulation which has come to be accepted as the common lot of corporate bodies wielding economic power.

9. It is true that the trade union is in the last resort a fighting organisation; its business is to be equipped to be able to make a nuisance of itself in pursuit of the interests of its members. The reform suggested here is not intended to reduce its capacity to fight. But the trade union is also a regulative body: it makes rules about the way in which certain economic activities are to be conducted and about who is to be allowed to conduct them. Where these rules appear to run counter to the welfare of the community, e.g. in sustaining restrictive work practices which make things more expensive than they need be, they should be subjected to public scrutiny. And the trade union concerned should be placed under an obligation to justify these rules, if it wishes to maintain them, by reference to a set of criteria established by legislation which take account of the public interest as well as the interest of the particular group of workers directly involved. A specific proposal on the control of restrictive practices is made later in this note.

The Criminal Law

10. The existing legal framework of industrial relations is not only meagre, it is also rather too free in its application of the criminal law. The category of industrial crimes ought now to be narrowed down to the minimum that is absolutely necessary for the protection of people's lives and safety. This means that section 4 of the Conspiracy and Protection of Property Act of 1875, and its extension by the Act of 1919 (see Chapter XIV, paragraphs 830 ff.), should be repealed. This law singles out the employees of three industries, gas, water and electricity, for criminal penalties if they engage in a lightning strike, on the ground that sudden stoppages here may pose a special threat to health and safety. This is true; but their case is not unique. It is not clear why it is a worse offence for a group of maintenance workers to shut down the supply of gas in a district which is provided with electricity and other alternative fuels than it would be, for example, for nurses in a hospital to stage a sudden walk-out. The criterion, it is clear, should not be whether workers are employed in a particular industry but what are the likely consequences of a sudden stoppage in their particular job.

11. This is the criterion which is applied—to employers as well as to employees—by section 5 of the 1875 Act. Indeed what section 5 does in essence is to say that actions known to be likely to endanger life, limb or valuable property, which we would recognise as criminal if done by an individual, are also a crime if done by a combination of people who break their contracts by staging a strike without proper notice. I find the arguments advanced in the Report for retaining the special additional penalties under section 4 unconvincing. It does not seem to me that the narrowing of the criminal law would be construed as " an express licence " to behave irresponsibly by workers in gas, water and electricity (Chapter XIV, paragraph 846). On the contrary, by narrowing the law to its true purpose and making it more rational it would be given more credibility and persuasive

power. Moreover, the criminal penalty should apply to people who act dangerously, regardless whether they are formally breaking their contracts or not. I fail to see the difficulty, referred to in Chapter XIV, paragraph 843, of punishing someone for criminally irresponsible behaviour even if this behaviour took place when he " lawfully terminated his contract ". Indeed it would seem to be a valuable contribution to our laws to make it clear that in our kind of society, in which people are increasingly dependent on the punctual performance of services by one another, the duty to avoid doing people or property serious damage, when the risk is clearly apparent, is what counts—regardless of the precise nature of the contractual obligation undertaken in one's job. Section 5 should, therefore, be elaborated to establish this principle.

12. I anticipate that a law of this kind will be of more relevance to industrial relations in the future than section 5 has proved to be in the past. Safety and health will depend more than ever on the functioning of the communications system, and organised workers who contemplate lightning strikes will have to think carefully about the effect of what they do on the ability of ordinary people to look after themselves without danger to life and limb when a particular service is suddenly denied them. This is not an argument for the total prohibition of the use of the strike weapon by certain workers simply because the service which they supply is one which people cannot do without, even during a short period. It is, however, reasonable to demand first, that the enterprise supplying the service concerned should be placed under an obligation to do everything possible to ensure that its denial through strike action causes the minimum of physical harm to consumers, and secondly that this obligation should also be reflected in the terms of the collective agreement between the enterprise and its workpeople. The trade union involved would be bound not only to refrain from lightning strikes of a dangerous character, but also to avoid impeding the employer in his efforts to minimise the risk to life and health resulting from a stoppage which occurred after due notice had been given. Thus, for example, in a strike of nurses in a hospital the trade union, or any other group of persons, would commit a crime if it impeded the efforts of the management to mobilise a skeleton staff of substitutes to carry out an emergency operation. That is an extreme case which is employed to make the principle clear. It is a principle which is likely to have a wide application in a society which one can foresee some years ahead, when there will be many more older people, some of them living in the upper stories of high blocks of flats where they will be completely dependent for the necessaries of their daily life on a minimum of lift and telephone service. One of the tasks of the Industrial Relations Commission, when it examines collective agreements subject to registration, should be to ensure that both parties to any agreement have made arrangements to safeguard vulnerable consumers where these are likely to be subjected to serious risk of harm in case of a strike.

Disputes over Trade Union Recognition and Jurisdiction

13. One of the purposes of a more regulated system of industrial relations would be to supply a check, in cases of doubt, on the representative character

of trade unions. These organisations derive their right to interfere with the way in which people conduct themselves at their workplace not, as is sometimes suggested, from the brute fact that the leaders are determined men who happen to be in occupation of the terrain and are in a position to make life awkward for employers who refuse to fall in with their wishes. It is not just a matter of effective power in conditions of "abstention of the law". In case of a dispute between two rival organisations claiming to bargain exclusively on behalf of the workers in a plant, it would surely be felt to be a wrong outcome if a majority of the organised labour there had to accept that bargaining on its behalf was to be conducted by a union representing the minority, simply because the latter had been able, through its greater power or greater readiness to disrupt the business of the employer, to persuade him to accept this arrangement. Collusion between an employer and an aggressive labour organisation would, in these circumstances, have robbed the organised workers in the plant of the right to exercise majority rule over the conduct of their own affairs. No doubt this occasionally happens. But in the end the legitimacy of trade unions depends on the elective principle: they are accepted as bargaining agents because of the belief that they command the voluntary assent of a majority of those on whose behalf they bargain.

14. Thus in the case of a jurisdictional dispute between rival unions there should be an arrangement, if attempts at conciliation fail, for the automatic reference of the dispute to a judicial body—a special section of the Industrial Relations Commission should be set up for this purpose—which, having established the wishes of the workers concerned in the dispute, would decide which union or unions were the appropriate bargaining agent for specified groups of employees and would issue an order to this effect. In contrast to the proposal in paragraph 256 of the Report, which confines the IRC's power to the making of a "recommendation", failure to comply with the order would lay the union or the employer open to a monetary penalty. It would be the prerogative of the IRC to determine the "bargaining unit" in which any ballot of the members of rival trade unions should be held, i.e. to identify the group of persons in the workplace who are involved in the particular issue in dispute between the unions, and also to frame the questions to be asked in the ballot. There will clearly be differences of opinion about the definition of the appropriate "bargaining unit" in any particular case, and the decision about which classes of worker in a plant are to be included or excluded from a ballot may sometimes determine the outcome. This cannot be avoided.

15. The IRC's power to intervene in this way would probably not be used very frequently, after an initial period in which those concerned became used to the fact of its existence. The knowledge that it existed would add persuasive force to the IRC's prior efforts to achieve a settlement by conciliation. But in the last resort the IRC would have to take the responsibility for deciding how the rival claimants to jurisdictional authority should divide the field of negotiation with an employer.

16. The same power would be exercised by the IRC against an employer who refused to accord recognition to a union which it judged to have estab-

lished a representative position in a plant. The IRC would, in such a case, order the employer to bargain with the union in good faith, meaning that he must genuinely seek a settlement and not use frivolous excuses for breaking off the negotiation or declaring it deadlocked. Indeed, it is a prior condition for the exercise of authority by the IRC in jurisdictional disputes that it should be able to order an employer to enter into negotiation with a union which is seeking an agreement with him.

A More Powerful Industrial Relations Commission

17. In order to fulfil the role outlined here, the IRC will have to be equipped in a different way and with more powers than those envisaged for the body proposed in the Report of the Royal Commission. The Report (paragraphs 198-206) sees the IRC essentially as an advisory body, responding to requests for counsel from the Secretary of State for Employment or making recommendations to trade unions and employers about ways of improving the conduct of industrial relations. The main defects of this scheme are, in my view, first that the pace of reform will be determined by the extent to which the Secretary of State finds it expedient, in the light of current political and other circumstances, to refer particular problems and cases to the IRC for an opinion; and secondly, that altogether too much depends on the personal performance of the man appointed to head the IRC. It would be unwise to be over-impressed by the performance of the Prices and Incomes Board with comparable powers in the second half of the 1960s, when both of these conditions have been extremely favourable. There are other precedents for advisory bodies appointed since the war to press forward some process of desired social or economic change which are much less encouraging.

18. For these reasons I propose that the body to be established should have a more autonomous function than that which is set out in the Report. Firstly, its powers of investigation should be exercised without waiting for the Secretary of State's orders, whenever there is evidence of serious friction in industrial relations or of inefficiencies in the employment of manpower. Secondly, the IRC should have a section exercising independent judicial authority in certain matters concerned with the conduct of collective bargaining, including the following: — jurisdictional disputes between unions and disputes with employers about recognition; the range of subject matter to be covered in collective agreements that are liable to compulsory registration; restrictive practices. The IRC's judicial task would be designed to supplement collective bargaining, not to replace it. It would ensure that genuine bargaining would take place in circumstances where the resistance of an employer or the presence of rival unions threatened to stultify it, and it would ensure that employers and trade unions extended their bargaining to certain matters which one side or the other might otherwise be inclined to regard as being within its own exclusive prerogative. The effect of the reform would therefore be to increase the amount and enlarge the scope of collective bargaining.

19. The chief instrument used by the IRC Tribunal would be the order to "bargain in good faith". Paragraph 317 of the Report raises objections to this device. But other proposals of the Royal Commission involve an arrange-

ment which is in practice indistinguishable from it. Thus the important reform which would impose compulsory arbitration on employers who reduce the process of collective bargaining "to a mockery" (paragraph 273) would require that a judgment be passed on the bargaining behaviour of the persons involved. The question to be answered before compulsory arbitration could be legitimately imposed would be: Was the employer bargaining in good faith or not? The Report refers briefly to the means to be employed for the examination of this question—" an inquiry " by the IRC " in which both sides have had an opportunity to put their point of view " (paragraph 274). Here in embryo is the judicial organ of the IRC, which should in my view be given a more generalised function extending to cases where either side in a dispute, not the employer only, is preventing the orderly and efficient conduct of industrial relations by refusing to bargain seriously on a particular matter or with a particular organisation. The Royal Commission's proposal on compulsory arbitration, in fact, goes further than anything I am proposing here for the IRC Tribunal, since it would create the legal power to impose on the parties the actual content of a collective agreement brought up for compulsory arbitration. Although I endorse this arrangement in the particular circumstances envisaged, I wish to make it quite clear that the judicial power to be given to the IRC by the reform outlined here would be much more limited, being confined to a judgment (a) on matters that require to be bargained about, and (b) on the manner in which the bargainers have conducted themselves—not on the substance of the bargain itself.

20. The jurisdiction of the IRC Tribunal would be confined to the parties to collective bargaining—trade unions, employers and employers' associations —and would not apply to disputes with individual persons. (The judicial bodies concerned with the rights and obligations of individuals are the Review Body attached to the Registrar of Trade Unions and Employers' Associations and the proposed Labour Tribunals.) The IRC Tribunal, which will be the usual mixed body consisting of a trade unionist, an employer and a legal chairman, will, in order to enforce its judgments in jurisdictional and recognition disputes, have to consider complaints that an order to " bargain in good faith " has been disobeyed either by an employer or a trade union. American experience suggests that it is not too difficult to establish some commonsense ground rules which would make it possible to decide whether one of the parties, while pretending to engage in negotiation, was intent on not making a bargain—e.g. by withholding certain kinds of information.

21. The order to bargain would be made when a collective agreement subject to official registration (as proposed in the Report) was found, on examination by the IRC, to have failed to cover some important subject—like the arrangements for the notification of anticipated redundancies or the office and shop-floor facilities to be provided for shop stewards. If one of the parties then claimed that it had been impossible to include these matters because the other refused to bargain about them, the IRC would first use conciliation to try to effect a settlement, and if this failed proceed to impose a monetary penalty on one or possibly both of the parties if it judged them to be responsible. The size of the maximum penalty should be moderate in terms of the resources available to the parties, say something of the order of £500. It is to be

295

expected that this would be enough to make union members or company shareholders feel that their representatives were unnecessarily wasting their money and to put pressure on them not to defy the Tribunal. The main sanction would not be the size of the monetary loss—though this could mount up if there were persistent defiance—but the consequences of the publicity attaching to the penalty.

22. The decisions of the IRC about the subjects to be included in collective agreements would result in a body of case law which would evolve further with changing industrial conditions. It is probable that the range of issues deemed to be proper subjects for collective bargaining, rather than the sole prerogative of either management or of trade unions, will in any case tend to grow in future. From time to time the IRC would issue a directive for the guidance of employers and trade unions whose agreements are subject to official registration and scrutiny, on the matters to be included in industrial bargaining.

Control of Restrictive Practices

23. One such matter where the need for a new set of rules is apparent now is collective bargaining on restrictive practices that have been shown to cause a significant loss of production. The first requirement is a definition which will allow such practices to be reliably identified; this will involve some approximate measurement of the unnecessary loss of production for which they are responsible. The standard of comparison should not be the theoretical maximum output per man-hour obtainable from a piece of machinery or equipment, but the actual amount of output known to have been secured by efficient methods already in operation elsewhere and which can be shown not to result in unusual strain or discomfort to the workers involved.

24. The last proviso plainly leaves scope for a good deal of argument. One of the departments of the IRC would specialise in the problem of work practices, using where necessary the advice of industrial consultants to make international and inter-firm comparisons. The Prices and Incomes Board has begun to examine some of these matters in a preliminary way; the IRC's Office of Restrictive Practices would carry the matter further and do so in a more systematic fashion. International comparisons would be especially important, since it might well be found in some cases that methods of work practised by competitors abroad could not, in fact, be employed here, because they were in conflict with some accepted standard of behaviour. In that case other questions of general economic policy would arise; the IRC in making its recommendations would have to consider whether the industry should receive tariff protection at the expense of the British consumer, who would have to pay higher prices for its products, or whether it would be in the public interest to allow foreign competition to force the home industry out of business and transfer the manpower employed in it to some other branch of production where Britain was not at an international competitive disadvantage.

25. Where investigation indicated that restrictive work practices were in use, the case would go to the IRC Tribunal, which after hearing the evidence would decide whether to issue an order to the trade union and the employer

to negotiate about the elimination of the restrictive practice. The Tribunal would not lay down the terms of any new arrangement; its power would be limited to an order to the parties to bargain in good faith about a particular set of work practices. After a reasonable interval, the Tribunal would expect a report on progress, and if this was unsatisfactory, the two sides would be called upon to state the reasons why they had failed to advance. If the Tribunal found there was no adequate justification for their inactivity, it would, in the last resort, have the power to impose a monetary penalty on a recalcitrant trade union or employer.

26. It is argued in the main Report that trade union negotiators would be able " to parry almost indefinitely " any accusation that they were deliberately avoiding serious negotiation. If this were really so, it is hard to see why it would not apply with equal force to employers, who are going to be given the opportunity of going before the IRC and arguing against the introduction of compulsory arbitration as proposed by the Royal Commission in circumstances where collective bargaining is being reduced " to a mockery ". The judgment in such a case must clearly depend in the end on whether the Tribunal is able to say that the demands of either party are so unrealistic as to imply an unwillingness to engage in serious bargaining on the subject. There will undoubtedly be occasions when it will be impossible to make a judgment of this sort—either because the two parties have in fact negotiated in good faith and honestly failed to reach agreement or because it is impossible to demonstrate that the bargaining position of either side, although very tough, amounts to a deliberate attempt to sabotage the negotiation. But there will be other cases where the Tribunal will be able to say, on the basis of what is being demanded, that one or the other party has no serious intention of making a bargain on the subject in question. It should not be forgotten that the IRC Tribunal will start with a benchmark—in the form of the data on wages, etc., provided by the investigation of more efficient work practices actually in force elsewhere, on which the original case will have been brought—and it will therefore be able to apply some measure of what would constitute a wholly unreasonable demand. It is in any case not to be supposed that a trade union would relish the experience of being put in the position of publicly justifying work practices known to be causing inconvenience or higher costs or both, and doing so on the ground that the terms for their elimination had to be vastly better than those conceded to people doing comparable work with the same equipment elsewhere.

27. Since the IRC procedure would apply only to established organisations wielding significant market power—trade unions, employers' associations and firms—it would be on all fours with the principle governing the existing regulation of monopolistic and restrictive business practices. A group of individuals who banded together in a plant to run their own restrictive practice could not be reached by this means. Moreover, if individuals refused to abide by a collective agreement made between the employer and their trade union in response to the IRC's urging, there would be nothing that the IRC would be able to do about it. The deterrent to the leaders of any such unofficial movement which carried resistance to the point of strike action would be the removal of their present legal immunities under section 3 of the 1906

Act, as recommended by the majority of the Royal Commission. The sole purpose of the present proposal is to compel the trade union and the employer to acknowledge their responsibility for *trying* to achieve certain improvements. If they were able to demonstrate that their authority was insufficient to ensure that a negotiated agreement on the elimination of a restrictive practice would be carried out, this would absolve them from any penalty. It would then be the duty of the IRC to explore other possibilities of negotiation between the employer and the workers responsible for the maintenance of restrictive practices in defiance of the wishes of their trade union.

28. The effect of the proposed reform would therefore be limited. Its intention is to use the law in the same spirit as it has been used, for example, to persuade people to change their practices of burning fuel which are also often hallowed by long-standing custom, in a smoke-controlled zone. The law helps first of all by setting a clear timetable for change, which will usually be faster than the pace that is likely to be achieved by relying exclusively on the spontaneous response to reasoned argument. Secondly, the existence of legal authority makes it much easier to identify and investigate any persistent obstacles to change. Thirdly, because a social rule is set out in the form of a law from which there are no exceptions, the main body of those who wish to abide by the rule in any case will not be deterred from doing so, or be tempted to indulge the occasional impulse to disobey, by the sense that someone else who is not motivated in the same way is ignoring the rule and getting away with it.

29. It may be said that this measure would not touch those who are chiefly responsible for restrictive labour practices in British industry—the unofficial groups of trade unionists who organise themselves at plant level and decide what they are going to do on the spot, with little or no regard for the policies laid down at trade union headquarters. There are two points which are worth making about this aspect of the problem. First, although it is true that many restrictive practices have been established as a result of unofficial action, this does not mean that unions do not take the initiative sometimes in negotiating the terms on which they are to be eliminated. Several productivity agreements bear witness to the fact that they do. It is to be expected that unions will take such initiatives more frequently in the future if, as a result of the reforms proposed in the main Report, they re-establish their authority over what happens at the workplace and take back the effective power over industrial relations from the informal work groups which at present dominate a wide area of British industry. Secondly, while it is true that trade unions do not, for the most part, officially support restrictive practices—though there are important exceptions to this rule (see paragraph 300)—there is plenty of evidence that the action of workshop leaders who force the wasteful use of manpower on employers by insisting on inefficient methods of work is condoned by trade unions. At any rate the shop floor leaders are not made to feel that what they are doing is in conflict with the aims of their trade unions. On the contrary, the maintenance of restrictive practices is too often seen as a worthy and profound way of expressing trade union solidarity at the grass roots. At the present time it requires an unusually strong and determined union leadership to take the risks of friction which accompany an

agreement for the large-scale elimination of restrictive practices, like the Electrical Trade Union's agreement of 1967 in the electrical contracting industry. Without some additional pressure on trade unions, too few of them will take these risks. The pressure, under the proposed reform, will take the form of demanding of the trade union leadership that it defines its position in relation to restrictive practices. It is, of course, assumed that it will be doing this in the context of the measures proposed in the main Report for the reform of the whole process of collective bargaining. Without these measures the attempt to apply some additional pressure for the removal of restrictive practices through the IRC Tribunal would almost certainly be frustrated.

30. It should be made clear that the present proposal is not regarded as being in any sense a substitute for the negotiation of productivity agreements, which are one of the most promising developments in British industrial relations during the past few years. On the contrary, the IRC's action would serve as a forcible reminder to those industries which were laggard in productivity bargaining that they were judged to be failing the community by their inefficient and wasteful use of manpower. In other cases the IRC directive would be the means of spreading the improved work practices negotiated by one firm in a productivity agreement throughout an industry. No doubt the process of imitation among firms competing with one another would in any case tend to result in the spread of more efficient practices—in time. The order to the laggards to bargain in good faith about matters which have been settled in negotiation by more progressive firms is a device for accelerating the pace of change. The ultimate sanction of the law would simply be an extra bit of persuasive power. The judgments of the IRC, being public, would be that much more persuasive; and the penalties, although they would be limited in such a way as not to put any organisation's capacity to function in jeopardy, would be substantial enough to exercise financial pressure on the recalcitrant.

31. Underlying this proposal, as well as the earlier proposal for the intervention of the IRC in jurisdictional disputes which cause a loss of production, is the notion that bodies which wield significant economic power should be subject to new forms of accountability to the community about the way in which they use, or influence the use of scarce resources. Productive manpower in Britain is such a resource: it ought to be husbanded at least as carefully as agricultural land or any other valuable natural asset. If it is used wastefully in one form of employment then this limits the possibility of doing other desirable things elsewhere. The " opportunity cost " involved should be registered, because it affects the standard of living of the whole community.

32. It needs to be emphasised, however, that this whole argument rests on the assumption that there is full employment and a clear public commitment to its maintenance. It would be unjust to demand the collaboration of trade unions in a policy which made industry more efficient at the cost of higher unemployment. No principle of social accountability could be held to apply in that case. The proposed reform is conditional on effective Government action to secure work at good wages for people who are made redundant by improved methods of production.

The IRC and Parliament

33. The IRC should report to Parliament annually on the state of industrial relations. This Report would include a review of judicial decisions by its own tribunal and by all other courts concerned with industrial relations. The IRC would recommend to Parliament any alterations in the law that it judged were necessary in order to meet changing circumstances. Technological and social change is likely to throw up many fresh problems during the coming decades, and it is to be hoped that British industrial relations will not be left to be governed in the future, as they have been too often in the past, by the vagaries of judge-made law. With the help of a specialist parliamentary committee on labour questions, it should be possible for Parliament to legislate expeditiously on problems as they arise. One of the lessons to be drawn from the experience of the past 50 years is that a special effort needs to be made to ensure that the laws about the rights and obligations of trade unions and employers, as well as the collective agreements between them, are made much more precise and kept up to date.

Collective Agreements in the Form of Contracts

34. One of the reasons why collective agreements have lacked precision is that they have not been treated as enforceable contracts. As the Report makes clear, the typical agreement at present in operation is of a kind that could not be made legally enforceable. However, the same disability would not attach to a new kind of collective agreement which, it is hoped, will emerge as the reforms proposed in the Report take effect.

35. The arguments that are commonly advanced for the contention that the contractual form is an inappropriate one for collective agreements are not persuasive. They are regarded as having binding force in other countries, and no special difficulties arise from that fact. Of course it should be open to the two parties to a collective agreement to avoid making promises to one another about fulfilment if they specifically state, at the time that the agreement is signed, that neither side regards it as being a contractual obligation. But otherwise it should have the character of a normal undertaking, in which each party has a claim for redress if it suffers loss because the other fails to keep its side of the bargain.

36. The proposal in essence is that the bias of English law, as it has been hitherto, should be changed. Instead of making it complicated and difficult for unions to enter into contractual obligations which are enforceable at law, so that it has become an eccentric thing for a union to do, unions and employers should be encouraged to treat it as the normal thing to do.

37. The traditional bias has had some unfortunate effects on the attitudes of trade union officials towards agreements which they make with employers. By many of them such an agreement is not thought of as being an undertaking about future behaviour, not even as something which they feel bound in honour to try to carry out. If circumstances change in such a way as to offer the union the opportunity of compelling the employer to go beyond the conditions or terms agreed, then it is thought proper to take advantage of the situation regardless of any agreement to the contrary. No doubt atti-

300

tudes to collective agreements vary between different trade union leaders, but it has been made clear in the course of the investigation of the Royal Commission that the predominant view in Britain, as opposed to the view taken in other advanced industrial countries, is that a collective agreement does not set up any obligation on the part of the trade union to do anything which in the event turns out to be less convenient than the framers of the agreement anticipated. At the very least the proposed reform would induce trade unions which were offered more advantageous terms, on condition that they were prepared to treat their side of the bargain as a genuine promise, to consider their own attitudes more closely and critically. At the moment the inducement to promise anything seriously is weak; it should be strengthened.

38. If this happens there will be two consequences. First as regards the observance of disputes procedure, the objective set out in paragraph 457 of obtaining the widespread acceptance of binding arbitration by trade unions will be achieved that much faster. Secondly, on the substance of collective agreements, the attitude of management towards innovations dependent on the support of trade unions will grow more confident. At present innovations which would reduce costs in industry or greatly increase output per head are delayed, because employers feel that they cannot rely on trade unions to ensure that the necessary agreements on new methods of work, without which it would be too costly to install new machinery, will in fact be carried out. To this extent the atmosphere of uncertainty generated by the absence of precise and dependable commitments is a factor holding back the pace of British economic growth. It may be that employers are mistaken in their beliefs, but it is enough that many of them are convinced that they would go ahead faster with the process of re-equipment involving the negotiation of changes in work practices, if they knew that agreements reached with unions had the force of a contractual obligation. By this they do not mean that they want the automatic right to obtain damages from a union if some of its members refuse to carry out any part of a collective agreement which the union has made on their behalf. The contract would simply commit the union officials who have accepted it to use their best endeavours to ensure that the terms of the bargain were carried out by their members. The activities covered by the phrase " best endeavours " can be given clear and concrete form, even though there would almost certainly be some matters of interpretation on which opinions might well differ. But after a time a body of useful case law would be built up. Unions and employers would be expected to contribute to this because they would go out of their way in their agreements to define, in as precise terms as possible, the nature of the undertakings that they would make towards one another.

39. It is worth making the point that evidence of the use of its " best endeavours " by a union in an unofficial strike situation would not be pushed to the point of requiring it to prove that it had threatened rebellious members of the union with expulsion. This might well be too drastic a penalty in an industry or trade with a closed shop. The union would be asked, above all, to demonstrate that it had not connived at the use of its authority by any of its officials, including its shop stewards, to defeat the purposes of the agreement which it had made.

40. It is the long-run consequences of the habit of entering into binding agreements which are the main objective of the proposed reform. The probability is that those unions which are able to promise reliably to perform their part of a collective agreement will obtain better bargains from employers for their members than weaker or less determined unions. The assumption underlying this proposal is that there are dynamic employers in British industry who would be inclined to innovate more rapidly, if the orderly introduction of new methods had the active support of strong trade unions carrying out contractual obligations which they had freely undertaken. After a time binding agreements would be seen to confer benefits on members of trade unions which had accepted them. Their chief benefit would be that a wider range of management decisions would be subject to negotiation with the workpeople affected by them. Management would be induced to enlarge the scope of the collective bargain, if the reward for doing so were to allow it to plan for more rapid change in a climate of security.

41. It would probably not be appropriate to subject these contractual agreements to the processes of the ordinary courts. For one thing, decisions on disputed matters would need to be arrived at expeditiously; for another, the persons making the judgments would require to have a close knowledge of industrial relations. The usual mixed group of judges—a trade unionist and an employer sitting side by side with a lawyer—would seem to be the proper arrangement. Perhaps the Industrial Court, whose functions it is in any case proposed to enlarge by making it responsible for unilateral arbitration, might be adapted to fulfil this function.

APPENDIX 1

(see paragraph 8)

SURVEY OF PROBLEMS TO BE CONSIDERED
UNDER EACH HEAD OF THE INQUIRY

INTRODUCTION

The Royal Commission has prepared for its own guidance the annexed survey of the field covered by its terms of reference. This survey may also assist those wishing to prepare evidence for the Commission. The survey is cast in the form of questions which formulate the problems, and those preparing evidence are asked to regard it in this light rather than as a series of questions to which a series of answers is sought. It is not of course possible to indicate every aspect of each problem which the Commission will be considering, and the survey is not therefore exhaustive. The Commission will also consider evidence on any other subjects within its terms of reference although not referred to explicitly in the survey.

The Commission hopes that those preparing written evidence will feel free to do so in whatever form is most convenient to them, addressing themselves only to those problems on which they are able to assist. *They are invited both to supply factual information and to express any views they may wish about the present situation together with any suggestions as to how it might be improved.*

It would be appreciated if replies would, where appropriate, bring out differences in the situation as between men and women.

The Commission's terms of reference are:—

" To consider relations between managements and employees and the role of trade unions and employers' associations in promoting the interests of their members and in accelerating the social and economic advance of the nation, with particular reference to the law affecting the activities of these bodies; and to report ".

The survey has been divided into five parts corresponding to the broad heads under which the Commission's task as defined by these terms of reference can be classified, as follows:

Part (1): the role of trade unions and employers' associations in accelerating the social and economic advance of the nation;

Part (2): relations between managements and employees;

Part (3): the role of trade unions in promoting the interests of their members;

Part (4): the role of employers' associations in promoting the interests of their members;

Part (5): the law affecting the activities of trade unions and employers' associations.

Part (1): The Role of Trade Unions and Employers' Associations in Accelerating the Social and Economic Advance of the Nation

Definitions

" *The Social advance of the nation* " is taken to indicate such matters as:—

(a) improvements in the standard and extent of education;

(b) greater liberty and opportunity for the individual to lead a fuller life;

(c) more adequate leisure and the proper use of it;

(d) diminution of class distinction;

(e) willingness on the part of the citizen to take his share in civic duties;

(f) reform of oppressive laws;

(g) the awakening of the public conscience in relation to wrongs suffered by any section of it.

303

" *The economic advance of the nation* " is taken to indicate such matters as:—

    (*a*) increase in the national wealth, in real terms;

    (*b*) increase in the citizens' standard of living;

    (*c*) adoption of new and more efficient methods of production and distribution.

Problems

1. What social purposes do trade unions and employers' associations serve, and what economic purposes?

2. How does their role in accelerating (a) the social and (b) the economic advance of the nation differ in present circumstances from their role earlier in the century and before that?

3. In particular, how does full employment affect their role?

4. In what ways, if any, do trade unions and employers' associations hinder (a) the social, and (b) the economic advance of the nation?

5. In what ways, if any, could their contribution to such advance be improved?

6. What contribution in particular do their political activities make?

7. Do trade unions through collective bargaining raise wages and salaries relatively to other incomes?

8. If so, what are the economic and social consequences of the shift in the distribution of incomes?

9. If collective bargaining raises relative wages and salaries does this impede or accelerate the rate of economic growth?

10. In particular do rising wages and salaries cut down the funds available for investment and so hinder economic development, or do they encourage employers into a more rapid investment in new equipment in an effort to offset rising wage costs?

11. Is the cause, or one of the causes, of inflation that under conditions of full employment or near full employment collective bargaining raises money wages faster than productivity?

12. If so, why do trade unions try to raise wages faster than increases in productivity?

13. To what extent do trade unions encourage or maintain practices which restrict the use of labour?

14. Do these practices hinder economic development?

15. To what extent are these practices justified by social considerations?

16. Apart from *general* inflation, do unions hinder exports in *particular* industries by raising labour costs, either by means of wage advances above the general level or by restrictive practices or both, so as to give a competitive advantage to overseas producers?

17. Do trade unions add to the individual liberties of workers by restraining the autocratic power of employers?

18. Do trade unions diminish the individual liberties of workers by imposing restrictions upon them?

19. Do employers' associations unnecessarily limit the freedom of firms to follow the personnel policies which they think most desirable?

20. Do trade unions improve the functioning of society by providing a means for the representation of workers' views and a discussion of their affairs with government and other public authorities and agencies?

21. Do employers' associations perform a similar service to society by representing their members to government and public authorities and agencies?

22. Are trade unions today in a position to extract undue consideration from public authorities to the detriment of other groups?

23. Are employers' associations in a similar position?

24. Do trade unions, through collective bargaining and joint consultation, provide an effective form of democracy within the enterprise?

25. Do trade unions, through collective bargaining and joint consultation, unduly limit the scope of employers to manage their own enterprises?

26. Does collective bargaining yield more desirable economic and social results if it is carried on on an industry-wide basis with employers' associations, or if it is conducted firm by firm (or plant by plant) without the intervention of employers' associations?

Part (2): Relations between Managements and Employees

Definitions

" *Relations* " means those relations which arise out of the common association of managers and employees in the work of an undertaking. They include the arrangements for the settling of wages and conditions of work and for the settlement of disputes.

" *Managements* " mean those by whom the business is managed. The term has to be used in preference to " employer " for in so many businesses today the employer is a limited company. It is not perhaps an altogether satisfactory word, since many managers are themselves employees. But it suffices to indicate those who, when claims for improvement in pay and conditions are made by employees, would normally be regarded as " the other side".

" *Undertaking* " means any business in which persons are employed, including, for example, manufacturing and service industries, commercial businesses, Government Departments and local authorities, but not the Armed Forces.

" *Employees* " includes both wage and salary earners and also apprentices.

Problems

ENGAGEMENT OF EMPLOYEES: FINDING A JOB

27. How do employees, including apprentices, obtain their employment? Through a Ministry of Labour Employment Exchange, a Youth Employment Office, a private employment agency, a trade union, an advertisement, a relative or friend already employed by the undertaking, enquiry at the undertaking or in any other way?

28. Are there any employments where a father, for example, is regarded as having a pre-emptive right in favour of a son?

29. Are there any employments (including apprenticeships) for which the number or proportion of new recruits who may be engaged is subject to limitations under an agreement or understanding between a management or employers' association and a trade union or trade unions?

30. Or as a result of pressure exercised unilaterally by a trade union or trade unions?

31. What, if any, are the age limits for entering apprenticeships?

32. Are there any employments which are reserved to men, to skilled workers or to workers who have served an apprenticeship?

33. Are there any jobs which an applicant can obtain only if he is already a member of a trade union or of a particular trade union or section of a trade union before applying?

34. If entry to jobs is limited in any of the ways mentioned in questions 28-33, is this as a result of (i) unrecorded trade practices or (ii) formal written agreements? In either case what is their scope—national or local?

35. If not already a member of a trade union on starting work, is the employee (a) invited to join a trade union or one of a number of trade unions, or (b) made to do so, as a result of an informal or formal understanding or agreement between the management and a trade union or unions?

36. Is he in some cases compelled to do so by the union itself acting on its own?

37. Are any exceptions made on the grounds of conscientious objection?

38. Are there any agreements or understandings whereby preference is given to union members in filling vacancies (or in selection for promotion or security against dismissal)?

39. Where managements and trade unions come to an understanding or agreement that all employees in a particular undertaking shall be members of a trade union, are any exceptions allowed e.g. for those who were non-unionists at the time the understanding or agreement was reached?

40. If managements do co-operate in making membership of a trade union a condition of employment, what is the effect of such co-operation on relations between employees and managements?

41. What would be the effect of requiring all employees to join trade unions?

TRADE UNION RECOGNITION

42. What is comprised in the term " recognition of a trade union "?

43. How do trade unions set about obtaining such recognition from managements?

44. What criteria are used by managements in deciding whether to give or withhold recognition?

45. What advantages accrue to (a) trade unions and (b) managements from recognition?

46. Are there any disadvantages?

47. Are there undertakings which discourage or prohibit some or all of their employees from joining a trade union?

48. If so, how do they do this?

49. Do undertakings discriminate in any way against " leading " members, e.g. members chosen by their fellow members to speak on their behalf?

50. What effect does refusal of recognition have on relations between the management and the employees concerned?

SETTLEMENT OF TERMS AND CONDITIONS OF EMPLOYMENT

51. What are the various types of payment which may be made to employees by managements as a reward for labour? [Presumably they will include basic pay, time and overtime rates, piece-rates, bonuses, the pay for particular jobs, etc.?]

52. What matters are in practice included in the term " conditions of employment—"? [Presumably they will include hours of work: environment: refreshment breaks: amenities: holidays, etc., etc.?]

53. Which of these matters are settled by individual agreement between the employee himself and the management?

54. Which are settled by agreement between the management and one or more trade unions?

55. To what extent are such agreements formal or informal?

56. To what extent are the formal agreements expressed in writing, for example in written agreements with union representatives or in works rules?

57. Which matters are settled by agreement between an employers' association and one or more trade unions?

58. When they are settled between an employers' association and one or more trade unions what circumstances decide whether they are settled

    (a) at district level:

    (b) at national level?

59. Is the scope of machinery for negotiating terms and conditions of employment generally adequate, or are there cases where, for example, it is geographically too wide or too narrow? Or where the sector of industry or range of occupations covered could be extended or reduced with advantage?

60. Are conditions of work ever governed by a combination of the methods indicated in questions 53, 54 and 57?

61. If so, what terms and conditions are settled by each such method?

62. What proportion of earnings is based on terms settled at national level, what proportion on terms settled at district level and what proportion on terms settled at plant level, and how are district and plant agreements affected by national agreements?

63. To what extent are arrangements for settling terms and conditions of employment affected by the state of the labour market?

64. What criteria are normally employed in deciding what the terms and conditions of employment should be? To what extent is the principle of fair comparison with other industries used?

65. What difference, if any, exists in such terms and conditions where the relevant trade union organisation is

(*a*) strong,

(*b*) weak,

(*c*) non-existent?

66. What effect does it have on terms and conditions of employment if the employee is (a) not a member of a trade union at all, (b) not a member of the trade union conducting the negotiations?

67. What is the effect both as regards collective bargaining and in other ways if employees in an industry or undertaking are organised by more than one trade union?

68. What is the effect if there is only one union organising the employees in a particular industry or undertaking?

69. What effect does it have on terms and conditions of employment if the employer is

(*a*) not a member of any employers' association,

(*b*) not a member of the association conducting the negotiations?

70. In industries subject to statutory regulations as regards minimum wages, to what extent are these minimum wages supplemented by collective or individual bargaining?

71. What is the general attitude of employers' associations and trade unions to the various methods of determining the terms and conditions of employment?

72. How can the interests of the national economy be brought into consideration by managements and employees, or their respective representatives, in settling terms and conditions of employment by negotiation?

NEGOTIATING PROCEDURES AND SETTLEMENT OF DISAGREEMENTS

73. What, in outline, is the typical procedure for the negotiation of terms and conditions of employment?

74. What, in outline, is the typical procedure for resolving deadlocks which may arise in the course of negotiations?

75. If there are no procedures which can be described as typical, what, in outline, are the most common procedures?

76. If these procedures, being followed, lead nevertheless to deadlock, by what means short of a strike or lockout is the deadlock resolved?

77. How much time normally elapses between the making of a claim for improved terms and conditions of employment and its final settlement?

78. What statutory powers does the Minister of Labour have designed to ensure good industrial relations?

79. What are the Ministry of Labour's arrangements for conciliation, arbitration and fact-finding?

80. Are they affected by the establishment of the National Prices and Incomes Board?

81. How do they relate to other independent conciliation and arbitration arrangements?

82. As methods of preventing or settling disputes, what are the respective merits of conciliation, arbitration and fact-finding?

83. Is arbitration by standing arbitration bodies (such as the Industrial Court, the National Reference Tribunal in the coalmining industry, and the Civil Service Arbitration Tribunal) preferable to the appointment of *ad hoc* arbitrators or arbitration boards, or is the latter preferable, and why?

84. What professional group provides the best arbitrators? Civil Servants? Lawyers? Academics? Businessmen?

85. Can statistics be given of the incidence of strikes and lockouts over a past convenient period, e.g. number of working days lost, number of workers involved, etc.?

86. How do the nationalised industries compare in this respect with other industries, and what accounts for any differences?

87. Is there any one cause of strikes or lockouts which can be said to be more common than the rest? If so, what is it?

COMMUNICATIONS AND CONSULTATION

88. By what means do managements communicate with their employees and with what results?

89. To what extent do managements consult their employees about matters which are not the subject of joint negotiations?

90. When such consultation takes place how are the employees' representatives chosen? Do they have to be shop stewards or union members?

91. Are such consultations held simply to elicit the employees' views or to reach a joint decision?

92. Are there agreements in any undertakings providing for such consultations and prescribing the procedure?

93. Are such agreements the rule or the exception?

94. Where there are no such agreements do managements decide for themselves when and over what matters consultations should take place?

95. Are works rules the subject of agreement between employees and managements or are they drawn up by managements alone?

96. What disciplinary rules are imposed by managements?

97. What effect in practice does the Truck Act 1896 have?

98. To whom do managements delegate their authority in dealing with employees? To what extent do managements include specialists in dealing with personnel matters? What are the effects?

99. To what extent are decisions of junior management liable to be reversed by senior management, and what are the implications for relations between employers and employees?

APPEALS AND GRIEVANCE PROCEDURES

100. What provision is there for appeals against disciplinary action, and what part, if any, do trade union representatives play in assisting appellants?

101. What machinery, if any, is there for the settlement of grievances arising on the shop floor? What part do trade union representatives play in this?

102. What is the attitude of trade unions and employers and employers' associations to the introduction either by voluntary agreement or statutorily of a system of grievance arbitration, with or without impartial chairmen of grievance arbitration boards? Would such a system reduce the number of unofficial strikes?

103. Could such a system be used for the speedy settlement of differences arising out of the interpretation or application of existing collective agreements or practices?

SECURITY AND STATUS OF EMPLOYEES

104. What security do employees have against dismissal? Can they appeal and if so what is the procedure?

105. Does the typical individual contract of employment adequately define the relationship between the employee and the employer? Should the employee be regarded as having some property in his job? If so, what effect does this have?

106. What provision is there for sick pay, pensions, redundancy pay, etc., and what effect do these have on relations between managements and employees?

107. What effect do profit-sharing and co-partnership schemes have on relations between managements and employees?

108. What distinctions of status are drawn between employees in different grades or occupations? What is their justification? What effect would their removal have?

109. What distinctions are made between employees of different sex, race, colour and creed? What effect would their removal have?

GENERAL

110. Do National Insurance benefits and other benefits, grants and payments provided by the State have any effect on relations between managements and employees, and if so what effects?

111. How is entitlement to such benefits, etc., affected by industrial disputes, and what is the effect on relations between managements and employees?

112. Is legislative intervention increasing in matters previously regarded as the preserve of collective bargaining or management decision? What is the effect on relations between managements and employees?

113. What is the role of the National Joint Advisory Council?

114. What kind of relations between managements and employees most conduce to the efficiency of the undertaking?

115. What facilities are there for management and trade union training in industrial relations? To what extent are they used?

116. What contribution do shop stewards in particular make towards good industrial relations?

Part (3): The Role of Trade Unions in Promoting the Interests of their Members

Definitions

" *Interests* " here is taken to mean the interests of the members of a trade union as such members. Such interests will include:—

(a) Wages and conditions of work;

(b) Effective consultation with managements at national, district, and shop level;

(c) 100% trade union membership;

(d) Participation in the conduct of the union's affairs, at all levels;

(e) Fidelity to union rules and decisions;

(f) Help in personal problems;

(g) Help in dealing with grievances;

(h) Help in legal matters;

(i) Maintenance of full employment;

(j) Maintenance of the real value of wages.

Problems

CONSTITUTION OF TRADE UNIONS

117. How are trade unions constituted?

118. Are there different forms of constitution? If so, what, in brief, are the different forms?

119. Is there a common form precedent for the rules of a trade union, or do they vary so much from union to union that no set of rules can be taken as typical?

120. What objects are commonly expressed in the rules as being the objects of the union?

121. What other matters are commonly provided for in the rules?

ORGANISATION OF TRADE UNIONS

I. Officers

122. What officers does a trade union have
  (a) at its Headquarters
  (b) at its branches
  (c) at shop level?

123. How are these various officers appointed?

124. Are some of them, and if so which, elected by the votes of members?

125. If so how is the ballot conducted?

126. How is it scrutinised?

127. How often are such elections held?

128. How in particular are shop stewards elected?

129. What qualifications and training do trade union officers usually have?

130. What training do they receive after appointment?

131. Which of these are paid and which unpaid?

132. In the case of paid officers what are the scales of their remuneration?

II. Members

133. How does a trade union recruit members?

134. Are all applicants accepted?

135. If not, by what criteria are applicants accepted or rejected?

136. In what ways if at all do unions seek to secure that all employees in a particular undertaking
  (a) are members of a trade union:
  (b) are members of one particular trade union?

137. What advantages accrue to the members of a trade union if all the employees in a particular undertaking
  (a) are members of a trade union:
  (b) are members of one particular trade union?

138. What sanctions are employed by a trade union or its members against a fellow employee in any particular undertaking who
  (a) refuses to join any trade union:
  (b) refuses to join a particular trade union?

139. On what grounds are any such sanctions considered to be justified?

140. In what ways do unions compete for members?

OPERATIONS

I. Generally

141. How is the business of a trade union managed?

142. How is its policy decided?

143. When policy has been decided who is responsible for carrying it out?

144. What, normally, are the functions of a General Secretary?

145. Are general meetings or delegate conferences held? If so, who is entitled to attend?

146. How often are general meetings or delegate conferences held?

147. What is the kind of business transacted at such meetings or conferences?

148. What proportion of members, on an average, attend?

149. How often do members (1) of a district or regional organisation (2) of a local branch meet together to transact business?

150. What is the kind of business transacted at such meetings?

151. What proportion of branch members, on an average, attend branch meetings?

152. What functions do shop stewards perform?

153. When there is a committee of shop stewards in an undertaking, how is the committee organised?

154. On what occasions does such a committee meet and what kind of business is transacted at such a meeting?

155. To what extent do managements assist shop stewards to function, e.g. by provision of facilities, allowing time off, and making up pay?

156. Do difficulties arise at times in reconciling the actions of a shop stewards' committee with the policies of the unions to which they belong? Can instances be given?

157. How are any such difficulties resolved?

II. Claims on behalf of Members

158. In what ways do trade unions seek to improve wages and conditions of work?

159. Who, in a trade union, would normally take the initiative in putting forward a claim for increased wages or better conditions or both?

160. How is such a claim

    (a) initiated,

    (b) pursued,

    (c) eventually resolved?

161. Does any research work have to be carried out in support of such claims? If so, of what kind? Who does it?

162. Who decides whether to accept or reject an offer made by an employer or employers' association? Are there cases in which a ballot is taken?

163. How does a trade union whose members represent only a small proportion of those engaged in a particular trade or manufacture or undertaking seek to promote the interests of its members?

164. Would legislation enabling one trade union only to bargain on behalf of all workers in a particular concern or in a particular industry be acceptable?

FINANCE

165. What sources of income do trade unions possess other than

    (a) members' subscriptions:

    (b) income from invested funds?

166. What are the rates of members' subscriptions?

167. Looked at as a proportion of earnings, how do the present rates of members' subscriptions compare with subscriptions before the 1939-1945 War?

168. Do trade unions have enough income to fulfil adequately their role in promoting their members' interests?

169. If not, what more could be done in this way if such income were increased?

311

170. What reasons are there against increasing members' subscriptions so as to provide an adequate income?

171. What funds are at the disposal of

    (a) Districts or Regions:

    (b) Branches:

    (c) Shop Stewards?

COMMUNICATIONS

172. In what ways do trade unions seek to establish effective consultation with managements

    (a) at national level:

    (b) at district level:

    (c) at shop level?

173. In what ways do trade unions keep their members informed of matters affecting members' interests, and keep themselves informed of members' feelings?

174. Are these ways effective?

175. How do shop stewards keep in touch (a) with members and (b) with the union?

176. What steps do trade unions take to encourage members to take part in the conduct of the unions' affairs?

177. How effective are such steps?

DISCIPLINE

178. What steps are open to trade unions to ensure that union rules and decisions are obeyed by members?

179. In cases of disobedience, what considerations are material in deciding whether such steps shall be taken or not?

180. On what grounds, speaking generally, may a member be expelled?

181. Is there, as a rule, a right of appeal against any such a decision to expel?

182. If so, to whom does it lie?

183. Is it possible for a member, once expelled, to be reinstated?

184. If so, under what conditions could this happen?

STRIKES

185. Before a trade union member goes on strike, do trade union rules commonly prescribe any preliminary conditions such as the holding of a ballot, or a specially convened meeting of, say, an Executive Council?

186. To what extent are these conditions observed?

187. When observed, do they on occasions prevent or delay a strike?

188. If a strike is called is prior notice always given to the management? In what cases, if any, is no such notice given?

189. How is strike pay

    (a) determined in amount, and

    (b) paid out?

190. In what way, in practice, do unions and managements keep in touch with each other during a strike in order to facilitate a settlement?

191. In what ways do trade unions seek to prevent victimisation of their members, e.g. a member who had been prominent in securing the strike?

192. What instructions are normally given to pickets, and how is picketing usually carried out?

193. What are unofficial strikes?

194. How common are they?

195. Why do they happen?

196. To what extent are they successful?

197. Who call unofficial strikes?

198. What steps do unions take to prevent or resolve them?

199. What disciplinary action do unions take against leaders of unofficial strikes?

200. How do unions seek to prevent victimisation of a member who has refused to join in an unofficial strike?

OTHER FORMS OF INDUSTRIAL ACTION

201. When, in support of members of other unions, certain objects or operations are declared " black ", how does the union keep control of such declarations?

202. What are the features of a " go slow " movement?

203. And of an overtime ban?

204. And of a " working to rule "?

205. Do managements ever seek to alter their rules so as to make them conform to actual working, and thus frustrate in whole or in part the " work to rule " weapon?

206. What attitude would a trade union usually adopt towards any such alterations?

207. What other forms of industrial action do unions take?

OTHER TRADE UNION ACTIVITIES

208. In what ways do trade unions help their members or dependants in personal afflictions, e.g.

unemployment,

sickness,

personal injuries at work,

death?

209. What help do trade unions give their members in dealing with grievances?

210. What help with legal matters do trade unions provide for their members?

211. Do trade unions seek to arouse and sustain an interest on the part of their members in (a) national and (b) municipal affairs? If so, how is this done?

212. In what way does trade unionism contribute at the present time

    (a)   to the maintenance of full employment,

    (b)   to the maintenance of the real value of wages?

Or are these objectives considered to be the sole concern of the Government?

TRADES UNION CONGRESS

213. What is the function of the Trades Union Congress?

214. What is its constitution?

215. To what extent has it been altered to meet changing conditions?

216. Has the TUC sufficient power to carry out its objects? If not, in what respects are these powers deficient?

217. Do some trade unions refuse to affiliate to the TUC? If so, on what grounds?

218. Does the TUC at times refuse requests from trade unions for affiliation? If so, on what grounds?

TRADE UNION FEDERATIONS AND INTER-UNION RELATIONS

219. What federations of trade unions exist today? How do they promote the interests of the members of the federated unions?

220. To what extent do they have powers, acting on behalf of their members, (a) to make agreements and (b) to call strikes? Is there a case for increasing their powers?

221. What procedure is followed when one trade union wishes to negotiate with another on some matter of common interest to the members of both?

222. How do demarcation disputes arise between trade unions?

223. How are disputes between unions settled or avoided?

DIFFERENT TYPES OF UNION

224. Is there any difference between the following types of trade union in the degree of efficiency with which they promote their members' interests—

    (a) craft unions

    (b) general unions

    (c) industrial unions

    (d) " white collar " unions?

225. If so, what are these differences, and what is the explanation?

226. What effect on relations between managements and employees do the different types of union have? Is one preferable to another?

227. Does the general structure or pattern of the trade unions affect their ability to promote their members' interests?

228. Could this structure or pattern be improved? If so, how?

STATISTICS

229. Can statistics be given of the number of trade unionists in the working population and in particular industries?

230. To what extent are members of the following kind (a) organised into trade unions and (b) productive of problems special to themselves:

    (1) " white collar " workers:

    (2) women workers?

231. Can figures be given of the number of working days lost through strikes of all kinds over a past convenient period, together with a comparison of the figures with other industrial countries?

REGISTRATION

232. What in practice are the functions of the Chief Registrar of Friendly Societies in respect of trade unions?

233. What are the advantages and disadvantages to a union of registration?

234. Are there any respects in which the Registrar's powers could be altered or enlarged with advantage?

Part (4): The Role of Employers' Associations in Promoting the Interests of their Members

Problems

CONSTITUTION

235. What is an employers' association?

236. How did such associations come into being?

237. What is their purpose?

238. How are they constituted?

239. What objects are commonly expressed in the rules as being the objects of employers' associations?

240. What other matters are commonly provided for in the rules?

314

241. Do employers' associations have special provision for the representation of major firms on their governing bodies? If so, what kind of provision?

ORGANISATION
I. Officers

242. What officers does an employers' association normally have?

243. How are the various officers appointed?

244. Are some of them, and if so which, elected by the votes of members?

245. If so, how is the ballot conducted?

246. How is it scrutinised?

247. How often are such elections held?

248. What qualifications and training do officers of an employers' association usually have?

249. What training do they receive after appointment?

250. Which of them are paid and which unpaid?

251. In the case of paid officers what are the scales of their remuneration?

II. Members

252. How does an employers' association recruit members?

253. Are all applicants accepted?

254. If not, by what criteria are applicants accepted or rejected?

255. Is membership of employers' associations entirely voluntary?

256. Are there cases in which although, on the face of things, membership is voluntary, yet it is virtually compulsory?

257. If so, how does this come about?

258. What advantages and disadvantages accrue from membership?

259. And from non-membership?

260. Is any, and if so what, discrimination practised in the case of any employers' association against any person or company who

    (*a*) refuses to join; or

    (*b*) resigns and refuses to rejoin?

261. On what grounds is any such discrimination considered to be justified?

OPERATIONS
I. Generally

262. How is the business of an employers' association managed?

263. How is its policy decided?

264. When policy has been decided who is responsible for carrying it out?

265. Who is, generally, the association's Chief Executive officer, and what are his functions?

266. How often do members meet in a general meeting of the Association?

267. What is the kind of business transacted at such general meeting?

268. What proportion of members, on an average, attend?

269. Do some such associations have local branches, or other local organisations?

270. If so, what is their purpose?

271. Do any such local branches or organisations hold meetings?

272. If so, how often, and what kind of business is transacted?

273. What proportion of members usually attend?

L*

274. Do some employers' associations cover a wide range of undertakings?

275. If so, how are the interests of small undertakings reconciled with those of large undertakings if there is a risk of conflict?

276. Do employers' associations at any time take steps to prevent any particular person or persons from being employed by their members?

277. If so, in what circumstances?

II. Conduct of Negotiations

278. What is the machinery, inside a typical employers' association, for dealing with claims for improved wages and conditions put forward by employees of its members or by trade unions on their behalf?

279. Does any research have to be carried out at times in connection with such claims? If so, of what kind? By whom is it done?

280. Do employers' associations regard wages and conditions which they agree with unions as minima which any employer is free to exceed or as fixed provisions which all its members should observe?

281. If they regard such agreements as settling minima, do they try to exercise control over the remuneration paid by members?

282. If they regard their agreements as establishing fixed wages and conditions, what steps do they take to ensure that members observe them?

283. What steps, if any, do employers' associations take in relation to concerns which are not members and which may be observing terms and conditions of employment which are at variance with those negotiated by the employers' association?

FINANCE

284. What sources of income do employers' associations possess other than

    (a) members' subscriptions

    (b) income from invested funds?

285. What are the rates of members' subscriptions?

286. On what basis are they fixed?

287. What proportionate increase has there been since the 1939-1945 War?

288. In general, do employers' associations have enough income to fulfil adequately their role in promoting their members' interests?

289. If not, what more could be done in this way if such income were increased?

290. Is there any reason against increasing members' subscriptions so as to secure an adequate income?

291. What funds are at the disposal of branches or other local organisations?

COMMUNICATIONS AND DISCIPLINE

292. In what ways do employers' associations keep their members informed of matters affecting members' interests, and keep themselves informed of members' feelings?

293. Do employers' associations possess disciplinary powers over their members, and if so what are they?

294. How far are these powers used to ensure the observance of agreements with unions?

295. In what other circumstances are they exercised?

296. To whom does any appeal lie?

INDUSTRIAL DISPUTES

297. Do lock-outs still occur?

298. If so, how often? In what circumstances?

299. At what stage in disputes between unions and member firms does an employers' association generally intervene?

300. Do employers' associations provide strike indemnity funds?

301. How do employers' associations seek to prevent or resolve unofficial disputes?

OTHER ACTIVITIES

302. What services not covered by the foregoing questions do employers' associations provide for members?

303. Are there ways in which those services could be improved or extended with advantage to the interests of members?

FEDERATIONS AND RELATIONS BETWEEN ASSOCIATIONS

304. What federations of employers' associations now exist?

305. Do such federations promote the interests of the associations federated, and of the members of these associations? If so, how?

306. What are the functions and powers of such federations?

307. What liaison is there between various employers' associations?

308. To what extent do employers' associations represent wider commercial interests of their members as distinct from their interests purely as employers?

309. What are the relations between employers' associations and associations formed by firms for other trade purposes in the same industry?

310. What will be the constitution, functions and powers of the Confederation of British Industry?

311. How will it be financed and staffed?

312. How will it promote the interests of its members?

STATISTICS

313. How many employers' associations are there?

314. Are statistics available showing

    (1)   the distribution among industries of employers' associations:

    (2)   how membership is distributed among them:

    (3)   the extent to which such associations are representative of particular trades or industries:

    (4)   whether they are on the increase or not?

REGISTRATION

315. Are some employers' associations, and if so how many, registered as trade unions?

316. Are some, and if so how many, registered as corporations under the Companies Acts?

317. What are the advantages and disadvantages of either kind of registration?

318. Are there any respects in which the powers of the Chief Registrar of Friendly Societies or of the Registrar of Companies in relation to employers' associations could be altered or enlarged with advantage?

Part (5): The Law Affecting the Activities of Trade Unions and Employers' Associations

Definition

The leading activities of trade unions are taken to be

    (1)   the formation of workers into organised bodies with the object of maintaining and improving pay and conditions of work;

317

(2)   the pursuit of this object by bargaining with employers, by political action, and in the last resort by industrial action.

There are other activities of some trade unions, e.g. the provision of social benefits. They are also consulted on various matters by the Government of the day.

The leading activity of employers' associations is taken to be formation of employers into organised bodies with the object of securing, maintaining, and improving the profitable conduct of their members' undertakings. They may have other activities constituting means to this end.

In the context of the Royal Commission's terms of reference the term " *activities* " is taken to refer primarily to the activities described above as leading activities.

Problems

319.   What is the present law relating to the right of workers to combine together into trade unions, and how has it developed?

320.   What is the present law regarding trade unions themselves as regards the part they play in organising and managing such combinations of workers, e.g. are they corporate or incorporate bodies, can they sue in contract and tort, are they subject to restrictions or disabilities, or possessed of privileges, etc.? How has such law developed?

321.   In what respects is a trade union, or its officers, answerable in law

   (a)   in contract;

   (b)   in tort?

322.   What is the present law regarding agreements come to between trade unions on the one hand and employers or employers' associations on the other? Are they binding in law

   (a)   on the parties to the bargain;

   (b)   on the individual worker or employer?

323.   What is the present law regarding the right to strike, and how has it developed?

324.   What is the present law regarding the right to picket, and how has it developed?

325.   What is the present law regarding the right of employers to combine together into employers' associations and how has it developed?

326.   The like question in relation to employers' associations as at 320 above.

327.   The like question in relation to employers' associations and their officers as at 321 above.

328.   What is the present law regarding the right of employers' associations to declare a lock-out, and how has it developed?

329.   As regards any of the foregoing matters should the law be amended, and if so how?

330.   To what extent is British practice in relation to the matters covered in this survey in line with international standards as reflected in International Labour Conventions and Recommendations, the Universal Declaration of Human Rights, etc.?

ROYAL COMMISSION ON TRADE UNIONS AND EMPLOYERS' ASSOCIATIONS,
LACON HOUSE,
THEOBALD'S ROAD,
LONDON, W.C.1.
July 1965

APPENDIX 2
(see paragraph 10)

LIST OF THOSE WHO SUBMITTED WRITTEN EVIDENCE

1. The list of those who submitted written evidence to the Royal Commission is divided into the following categories:

    (1) Government Departments and other official bodies;

    (2) trade unions, trade union federations and other organisations representing employees;

    (3) employers' associations and other employers' organisations;

    (4) the nationalised industries;

    (5) companies and other employers;

    (6) other organisations, including political, professional and voluntary bodies and educational institutions;

    (7) others who have made written submissions.

2. The papers referred to in the list include both formal memoranda, submitted in response either to the Commission's general invitation or to specific invitations addressed to particular individuals or organisations, and other written communications, including for example letters from members of the general public and notes commenting on submissions made by others.

3. Most of the written evidence of witnesses who gave oral evidence in public has already been published by HM Stationery Office on behalf of the Royal Commission (Minutes of Evidence Nos. 1-69) and the number of the relevant Minutes is here listed together with the Royal Commission's own reference number. The written evidence of the Ministry of Labour and of the Chief Registrar of Friendly Societies was published by HM Stationery Office in separate volumes.

4. The remaining written evidence of witnesses who gave oral evidence in public, together with certain other submissions, is to be published shortly by HM Stationery Office in a separate volume of Selected Written Evidence, and this is recorded by the letters " SWE " in the list against the names of the witnesses concerned.

5. A complete set of all the written evidence received by the Royal Commission, including evidence not being published by HM Stationery Office, is being deposited at the Public Record Office and will—with the exception of submissions made in confidence—shortly be available for reference there. In addition copies of many of the more important written submissions are being lodged with libraries as follows:

British Museum

Department of Employment and Productivity

Queen's University, Belfast

Marshall Library of Economics, Cambridge

University College of South Wales and Monmouthshire, Cardiff

Glasgow University

Brotherton Library, Leeds University

British Library of Political and Economic Science, London School of Economics and Political Science

Manchester University

Nuffield College, Oxford

Warwick University.

(1) GOVERNMENT DEPARTMENTS AND OTHER OFFICIAL BODIES

	Commission's Ref. No.	Minutes of Evidence Ref. No.
Chief Registrar of Friendly Societies	WE/91 & (Supp. 1)	8 (WE/91 published separately)
Department of Economic Affairs	WE/199	18
Department of Education and Science	WE/380	—
Director of Public Prosecutions (in confidence)	WE/287	—
General Post Office	WE/348	—
Isle of Man Government	WE/347	—
Ministry of Agriculture, Fisheries and Food and the Department of Agriculture and Fisheries for Scotland	WE/273	—
Ministry of Defence (Navy Department)	WE/178	—
Ministry of Health	WE/257 & (Supp. 1)	—
Ministry of Health and Social Services, Northern Ireland	WE/212	—
Ministry of Labour	WE/75 & (Supps. 1, 2, 3, 4 & 5)	2 & 3 (WE/75 published separately, also SWE)
Ministry of Social Security (formerly Pensions and National Insurance)	WE/70 & (Supps. 1, 2, 3, 4 & 5)	54
National Board for Prices and Incomes	WE/307	51
Registrar of Companies	WE/153	—
Scottish Education Department	WE/301	—
Treasury	WE/113 & (Supp. 1)	10

(2) TRADE UNIONS, TRADE UNION FEDERATIONS AND OTHER ORGANISATIONS REPRESENTING EMPLOYEES

	Written Evidence Ref. No.	Minutes of Evidence Ref. No.
Trades Union Congress	WE/322 & (Supps. 1, 2, 3, 4 & 5)	61 & 65, SWE
Scottish Trades Union Congress	WE/342	—
General Federation of Trade Unions	WE/40	58
Aeronautical Engineers' Association	WE/159 & (Supp. 1)	—
Amalgamated Central Association of Colliery Overmen, Deputies and Shotfirers	WE/96	—
Amalgamated Engineering Union (Supp. 2 submitted in confidence)	WE/111 & (Supps. 1 & 2)	24
Amalgamated Slaters, Tilers and Roofing Operatives	WE/60 & (Supps. 1, 2, 3, & 4)	—
Amalgamated Society of Woodworkers	WE/272	—

Amalgamated Union of Building Trade Workers	WE/340	64
Associated Metalworkers' Society	WE/53	—
Associated Society of Locomotive Engineers and Firemen	WE/64	—
Association of Cinematograph, Television and Allied Technicians	WE/391	—
Association of Local Government Financial Officers	WE/140	—
Association of Managerial Electrical Executive	WE/86	—
Association of Managerial Electrical Executive (comments on evidence of Mr. W. Davies)	WE/83	—
Association of Official Architects	WE/368	—
Association of Scientific Workers	WE/62 & (Supp. 1)	—
Association of Supervisory Staffs, Executives and Technicians (Association of Scientific, Technical and Managerial Staffs)	WE/219 & (Supps. 1, 2, 3, 4 & 5)	53
Association of University Teachers	WE/114	—
British Association of Chemists	WE/148	—
British Association of Colliery Management	WE/110	—
British Iron and Steel Management Association	WE/150 & (Supp. 1)	—
British Medical Association	WE/211	—
Central Council of Bank Staff Associations	WE/388	—
Chief Fire Officers' Association	WE/32	—
Civil Service Clerical Association	WE/133	—
Civil Service National Whitley Council (Staff Side)	WE/20	—
Clerical and Administrative Workers' Union	WE/296	—
Coopers' Federation of Great Britain and Ireland (Northern)	WE/154	—
Draughtsmen's and Allied Technicians' Association	WE/119 & (Supp. 1)	36
Draughtsmen's and Allied Technicians' Association (comments on evidence of " Aims of Industry ")	WE/370 (Supp. 1)	—
Draughtsmen's and Allied Technicians' Association (members employed at Vauxhall Motors Ltd.)	WE/384	—
Educational Institute of Scotland	WE/161	—
Electrical Power Engineers' Association	WE/127	—
Electrical Power Engineers' Association (comments on evidence of Mr. W. Davies)	WE/83	—
Electrical Trades Union	WE/329 & (Supps. 1, 2, & 3)	57
Electricity Supply Union	WE/344	—
Engineer Surveyors' Association	WE/183 & (Supp. 1)	—
Engineers' Guild Ltd.	WE/186	—

	Written Evidence Ref. No.	*Minutes of* Evidence Ref. No
Federation of Insurance Staff Associations	WE/232	—
Federation of Telecommunications Sales Associations	WE/115	—
Friendly Association of Craft Trade Societies	WE/160	—
General & Municipal Workers' Union (National Union of General and Municipal Workers) (Supp. 1, comments on evidence submitted by Mr. T. McGlade, Mr. A. V. Pallett and 21 others)	WE/277 & (Supp. 1)	42
General & Municipal Workers' Union (comment on evidence of Kores Manufacturing Co. Ltd.)	WE/237	—
General & Municipal Workers' Union (comment on evidence of Mr. O. Sanderson & 3 others)	WE/369	—
Greater London Council Staff Association	WE/210	—
Guild of Insurance Officials	WE/132	—
Health Visitors' Association	WE/142	—
Institute of Hospital Administrators	WE/229	—
Institute of Journalists	WE/169	—
Joint Four (Associations of Head Masters, Head Mistresses, Assistant Masters and Assistant Mistresses)	WE/188	—
Junior Hospital Doctors' Association Ltd.	WE/367	—
Kodak Joint Trade Union Recognition Committee	—	—
Lloyds Bank Staff Association	WE/131 & (Supp. 1)	—
London Industrial Shop Stewards' Defence Committee	WE/291	—
Martins Bank Staff Association	WE/57	—
Metropolitan Water Board Staff Association	WE/35	—
Midland Bank Staff Association	WE/179 & (Supps. 1 & 2)	—
"Midland Shop Stewards" Study Group	WE/371	—
National and Local Government Officers' Association (comments on evidence of Mr. W. Davies)	WE/170 & (Supps. 1 & 2) WE/83	26, SWE —
National and Local Government Officers' Association (Long Eaton Branch) (in confidence)	WE/6	—
National Association of State Enrolled Nurses	WE/180	—
National Federation of Building Trades Operatives	WE/126	19
National Federation of Professional Workers	WE/182	27, SWE
National Provincial Bank Ladies' Guild	WE/69	—

	Written Evidence Ref. No.	Minutes of Evidence Ref. No.
National Provincial Bank Staff Association	WE/87	—
National Union of Agricultural Workers	WE/385	—
National Union of Bank Employees	WE/118	—
National Union of Commercial Travellers	WE/218	—
National Union of Flint Glassworkers (submitted jointly with Stourbridge Crystal Glass Manufacturers' Association)	WE/235	—
National Union of Gold, Silver and Allied Trades	WE/278	—
National Union of Insurance Workers	WE/141	—
National Union of Journalists	WE/194	—
National Union of Portworkers	WE/207	—
National Union of Railwaymen	WE/176 & (Supps. 1 & 2)	17
National Union of Seamen	WE/334	—
National Union of Sheet Metal Workers and Coppersmiths (comment on evidence of Mr. J. Crawford)	WE/136	—
National Union of Sheet Metal Workers and Coppersmiths (comment on evidence concerning Mr. R. G. Smith forwarded by Mr. Jim Prior, M.P.)	WE/387	—
National Union of Teachers (in confidence)	WE/195	—
National Union of Vehicle Builders	WE/155	—
Post Office Departmental Whitley Council (Staff Side)	WE/375	—
Post Office Engineering Union	WE/288	—
Printing & Kindred Trades Federation	WE/65	—
Refuge Field Staff Association	WE/81	—
Royal College of Nursing and the National Council of Nurses of the United Kingdom	WE/61	—
Scottish Joint Council for Teachers' Salaries (Teachers' Panel)	WE/255	—
Scottish Schoolmasters' Association	WE/189	—
Scottish Secondary Teachers' Association	WE/250	—
Scottish Lace and Textile Workers' Union	WE/29	—
Shop Stewards' Committees:—		
Austin Motors Joint Committee (in confidence)	WE/299 & (Supp. 1)	—
Ford, Dagenham (in confidence)	WE/308	—
Garringtons of Bromsgrove Joint Committee	WE/293	—
Showmen's Guild of Great Britain	WE/208	—
Society of Clerks of Rural District Councils	WE/162	—
Society of Goldsmiths, Jewellers and Kindred Trades	WE/82	—
Society of Graphical and Allied Trades (comments on evidence of Mr. E. M. Amphlett)	WE/373	—
Society of Telecommunication Engineers	WE/145	—
Student Nurses' Association	WE/89	—

	Written Evidence Ref. No.	Minutes of Evidence Ref. No.
Transport and General Workers' Union (Supp. 3 submitted in confidence)	WE/198 & (Supps. 1, 2 & 3)	30
Transport Salaried Staffs' Association	WE/192	—
Union of Railway Signalmen	WE/31	—
Union of Shop, Distributive and Allied Workers	WE/193 & (Supp. 1)	29
Union of Skilled Engineers	WE/327	—
United Patternmakers' Association	WE/90	—
Variety Artistes' Federation	WE/290	—
Watermen, Lightermen, Tugmen and Bargemen's Union	WE/269	—

(3) EMPLOYERS' ASSOCIATIONS AND OTHER EMPLOYERS' ORGANISATIONS

	Written Evidence Ref. No.	Minutes of Evidence Ref. No.
Confederation of British Industry	WE/112 & (Supps. 1, 2, 3, 4, 5 & 6); (WE/144)	6 & 9, 22, 69, SWE
National Association of British Manufacturers (now merged in CBI)	WE/1	—
Belfast and Ulster Licensed Vintners' Association	WE/19	—
British Federation of Master Printers	WE/185 & (Supp. 1)	—
British Furniture Manufacturers' Federated Associations	WE/167	—
British Hotels and Restaurants Association	WE/92	—
British Insurance Association & Lloyd's	WE/355	—
British Iron and Steel Federation	WE/268	—
British Shipping Federation Ltd. (in confidence)	WE/356	—
British Spinners' and Doublers' Association	WE/39	
Central Council of Irish Linen Industry Ltd.	WE/49	—
Chair Frame Manufacturers' Association	WE/77	—
Cocoa, Chocolate and Confectionery Alliance	WE/135	—
Committee of London Clearing Bankers	WE/130	—
Conference of Omnibus Companies	WE/184	—
Co-operative Union Ltd. (submitted jointly with the Co-operative Wholesale Society Ltd., the Scottish Co-operative Wholesale Society Ltd. and the Co-operative Productive Federation)	WE/156	—
Covent Garden Tenants' Association Ltd.	WE/63	—
Engineering Employers' Federation	WE/197 & (Supps. 1, 2 & 3)	20, SWE
Engineering Employers' Federation (comment on evidence of Henry Wiggin & Co. Ltd.)	WE/390	—

	Written Evidence Ref. No.	Minutes of Evidence Ref. No.
Federation of Associations of Specialists and Sub-Contractors	WE/172	—
Federation of London Wholesale Newspaper Distributors	WE/34	—
Federation of Master Builders	WE/98	—
Federation of Master Organ Builders	WE/66	—
Federation of Municipal Passenger Transport Employers	WE/139	—
Federation of Painting Contractors Ltd.	WE/231	—
Food Manufacturers' Industrial Group	WE/204	—
Hinckley and District Hosiery Manufacturers' Association	WE/78	—
Heating and Ventilating Contractors' Association	WE/196	
Hull Fishing Industry Association	WE/123	—
Incorporated Guild of Hairdressers, Wigmakers and Perfumers	WE/117	
Joinery and Woodwork Employers' Federation	WE/25	—
Local Authorities: Associations of Local Authorities in England and Wales, the Greater London Council and the Local Authorities' Conditions of Service Advisory Board	WE/221 (Supps. 1 & 2)	60
Local Authority Associations in Scotland	WE/202	—
Longbridge Group of Delivery Agents	WE/354	—
Mastic Asphalt Employers' Federation	WE/16	—
Motor Agents Association Ltd.	WE/67	—
Motor Industry Employers	WE/200 & (Supp. 1)	23
National Association of Master Bakers, Confectioners and Caterers	WE/279	—
National Association of Retail Furnishers	WE/137	—
National Brassfoundry Association	WE/58	—
National Chamber of Trade	WE/104	—
National Cooperage Federation	WE/116	—
National Federated Electrical Association National Electrical Contractors' Trading Association (the N.E.C.T.A. Ltd.) Electrical Contractors' Association (Incorporated)	WE/177 & (Supp. 1)	—
National Federation of Builders' and Plumbers' Merchants	WE/241	—
National Federation of Building Trades Employers	WE/128 & (Supps. 1, 2 & 3)	16, SWE
National Federation of Demolition Contractors	WE/22	—
National Federation of Master Steeplejacks and Lightning Conductor Engineers	WE/21 & (Supp. 1)	—
National Federation of Master Painters and Decorators in Scotland	WE/37	—
National Federation of Meat Traders' Associations (Incorporated)	WE/201	—

	Written Evidence Ref. No.	Minutes of Evidence Ref. No.
National Federation of Master Window Cleaners	WE/79	—
National Federation of Plumbers and Domestic Heating Engineers	WE/121	—
National Federation of Retail Newsagents, Booksellers and Stationers	WE/109	—
National Federation of Wholesale Grocers and Provision Merchants	WE/120	—
National Grocers' Federation	WE/108	—
National Joint Industrial Council for the Seed Crushing, Compound and Provender Manufacturing Industries (Employers' Side)	WE/122	—
National Sawmilling Association	WE/43	—
National Union of Retail Confectioners	WE/105	—
National Union of Retail Tobacconists	WE/174	—
Newspaper Proprietors' Association	WE/216	—
North Lincolnshire Roofing Tile Makers' Association	WE/76	—
Organisation of Employers' Federations & Employers in Developing Countries	WE/326	—
Pianoforte Manufacturers' Association Limited	WE/147	—
Retail Distributors' Association Incorporated	WE/107 & (Supp. 1)	—
Scottish Grocers' Federation	WE/168	—
Scottish House Furnishers' Federation	WE/59	—
Scottish Licensed Trade Association	WE/230	—
Scottish Retail Drapers' Association	WE/106	—
Shipbuilding Employers' Federation	WE/311 & (Supp. 1)	48
Soap, Candle and Edible Fats Trades Employers' Federation	WE/239	—
Society of Independent Manufacturers	WE/129 & (Supp. 1)	32
Stourbridge Crystal Glass Manufacturers' Association (submitted jointly with the National Union of Flint Glassworkers)	WE/235	

(4) THE NATIONALISED INDUSTRIES

	Written Evidence Ref. No.	Minutes of Evidence Ref. No.
British European Airways	WE/27 & (Supp. 2)	—
British Overseas Airways Corporation	WE/27 & (Supp. 1)	—
British Railways Board (Supps. submitted in confidence)	WE/146 & (Supps. 1, 2 & 3)	14
British Transport Docks Board	WE/313	—
British Waterways Board	WE/30	—
Electricity Council	WE/73 & (Supp. 1)	21
Electricity Council (comments on evidence of Mr. W. Davies)	WE/83	—
Gas Council	WE/94 & (Supp. 1)	11
London Transport Board (Supp. 2 submitted in confidence)	WE/56 & (Supps. 1 & 2)	5

	Written Evidence Ref. No.	Minutes of Evidence Ref. No.
National Coal Board	WE/99, WE/151	4
Transport Holding Company	WE/52	—
United Kingdom Atomic Energy Authority	WE/46	—

(5) COMPANIES AND OTHER EMPLOYERS

	Written Evidence Ref. No.	Minutes of Evidence Ref. No.
Alcan Industries	WE/319	—
Austin Motor Co. Ltd. Longbridge (in confidence)	WE/312	—
C. H. Bailey Ltd.	WE/397	—
British Electric Traction Co. Ltd. (in confidence)	WE/242	—
British Motor Corporation	WE/254	—
British Oxygen Company	WE/267 & (Supp. 1)	—
Co-operative Wholesale Society Ltd. Scottish Co-operative Wholesale Society Ltd. Co-operative Productive Federation (submitted jointly with Co-operative Union Ltd.)	WE/156	—
Dunlop Rubber Co. Ltd.	WE/281 & (Supp. 1)	—
English Clays Lovering Pochin & Co. Ltd. (in confidence)	WE/266	—
Esso Petroleum Co. Ltd.	WE/143 & (Supps. 1 & 2)	39
Ford Motor Co. Ltd. (in confidence)	WE/298	—
Glacier Metal Co. Ltd.	WE/314	—
Hebron & Medlock Ltd. (comments on evidence of " Aims of Industry ")	WE/370 (Supp. 1)	—
Howard & Holder Direct Mail Ltd. (in confidence)	WE/395	—
I.C.I. (in confidence)	WE/261	—
International Publishing Corpn. Ltd.	WE/318	59
Kodak Limited (Supp. 2 comments on evidence of Association of Cinematograph, Television and Allied Technicians)	WE/382 & (Supps. 1 & 2)	67
Kores Manufacturing Co. Ltd.	WE/237	—
John Lewis Partnership	WE/97	—
Lewis's Investment Trust Ltd.	WE/134	—
Lloyds Bank Ltd.	WE/88	—
Joseph Lucas Ltd.	WE/265	—
Marriott Magnetics Ltd.	WE/378	—
Massey Ferguson (United Kingdom) Ltd.	WE/103	25

	Written *Evidence Ref. No.*	*Minutes of* *Evidence Ref. No.*
Mobil Oil Company Ltd.	WE/270 & (Supp. 1)	49
Montague Burton Ltd.	WE/262	—
Morris Motors Ltd., Tractor & Transmissions Branch (in confidence)	WE/306	—
National Provincial Bank Ltd.	WE/44	—
Philips Industries	WE/102	28
Rolls-Royce Ltd., Derby	WE/374 & (Supp. 1)	—
Roll-Royce Ltd., Derby (comments on evidence of " Aims of Industry ")	WE/370 (Supp. 1)	—
Rootes Group (Rootes (Scotland) Ltd., Linwood) (in confidence)	WE/280	—
Messrs Rossi & Rossi (Chartered Accountants)	WE/33	—
Rover Co. Ltd.	WE/396	—
Schreiber Wood Industries Ltd.	WE/68	—
Scottish & Newcastle Breweries Ltd.	WE/328	—
Scott Bader Commonwealth Ltd.	WE/285	—
Shell Petrochemicals Ltd.	WE/264	—
Steel Company of Wales	WE/251 & (Supp. 1)	—
Tilling Association Ltd.	WE/225	—
Unilever Ltd.	WE/246	46
United Glass Ltd.	WE/284	—
Vauxhall Motors Ltd. (Supp. 1 submitted in confidence)	WE/205 & (Supp. 1)	—
Vickers Ltd. (in confidence)	WE/309 & (Supps. 1 & 2)	—
Westminster Press Provincial Newspapers Ltd.	WE/349 & (Supp. 1)	—
Henry Wiggin & Co. Ltd.	WE/390	—

In addition one company which submitted evidence in confidence requested that its identity should not be disclosed.

(6) OTHER ORGANISATIONS, INCLUDING POLITICAL, PROFESSIONAL AND VOLUNTARY BODIES AND EDUCATIONAL INSTITUTIONS

	Written *Evidence Ref. No.*	*Minutes of* *Evidence Ref. No.*
" Aims of Industry "	WE/370	—
Association of Liberal Trade Unionists	WE/224	—
Bar Council	WE/295	43
Bar Association for Commerce, Finance and Industry	WE/271	—
British Housewives' League	WE/45	—
Campaign against Racial Discrimination	WE/351	—
Christian Socialist Movement	WE/214	—
Communist Party of Great Britain	WE/100	—

	Written Evidence Ref. No.	*Minutes of* Evidence Ref. No.
Conservative Trade Unionists' National Advisory Committee	WE/220	—
Consumer Council	WE/258	—
Council of Liverpool Chamber of Commerce	WE/398	—
Fabian Society	WE/297	55
Foremen and Staff Mutual Benefit Society	WE/294	—
Haldane Society	WE/310 & (Supp. 1)	56
Harrow Public Transport Users' Association	WE/50	—
Independent Labour Party	WE/372	—
Industrial Co-partnership Association	WE/346	—
Industrial Law Society	WE/323	—
Inns of Court Conservative and Unionist Society—see Society of Conservative Lawyers		
Institute of Personnel Management	WE/253	40
Certain members of the Editorial Staff of Newspapers in the International Publishing Corporation Group	WE/10	1
Joint Council for the Building & Civil Engineering Industry (Northern Ireland)	WE/158	—
Justice (British Section of the International Commission of Jurists)	WE/17	13
Labour and Industrial Correspondents' Group	WE/316	—
Law Society	WE/304	52, SWE
Liberal Party Organisation	WE/223	—
Management Strategists Ltd.	WE/240	—
National Citizens' Advice Bureaux Council	WE/377	—
National Council for Civil Liberties	WE/350	—
National Joint Council for the Building Industry	WE/125	—
Ruskin College, Oxford	WE/215	—
Slough College Residential Centre	WE/152	—
Socialist Medical Association	WE/236	—
Society for Individual Freedom	WE/341	—
Society of Conservative Lawyers (formerly Inns of Court Conservative and Unionist Society)	WE/226 & (Supp. 1)	35
Society for Democratic Integration in Industry	WE/228	—
Society of Labour Lawyers	WE/317 & (Supp. 1)	63
Workers' Educational Association	WE/360	—
Young Fabian Group	WE/244	—

(7) OTHERS WHO HAVE MADE WRITTEN SUBMISSIONS

	Written Evidence Ref. No.	Minutes of Evidence Ref. No.
Mr. E. M. Amphlett, C.B.E., M.C.	WE/373 & (Supp. 1)	—
Mr. E. G. Andrews	WE/181	—
Mr. J. H. Armitt	—	—
Mr. J. H. Arrowsmith-Brown	WE/400	—
Mr. B. Ashton	WE/48	—
Mr. Tom Beardsley (submitted by B. M. Birnberg & Co., Solicitors, on his behalf)	—	—
Mr. J. E. Beattie	WE/393	—
Mr. R. N. Beer (statement forwarded by Mr. Tam Dalyell, M.P.)	WE/164	—
Mr. D. F. Bellairs (Slough College)	WE/263	—
Mr. R. W. Berwick-Gooding	—	—
Judge A. P. Blair (in confidence)	WE/321	—
Mr. T. Booth	—	—
Mr. Donald Box, M.P.	WE/190 & (Supp. 1)	—
Mr. T. P. Bowman (Chairman, P.A. Management Consultants Ltd.)	WE/343	—
Mr. Bernard Braine, M.P. (forwarding the statement of Mr. O. Sanderson & 3 others)	WE/369	—
Mr. P. Breuer	WE/157	—
Mr. J. Brightman	WE/243	—
Lord Brown (in confidence)	WE/206	—
Mr. N. Bruce, B.A., F.R.Hist.S. (University of Sheffield)	WE/234 & (Supp. 1)	—
Mr. A. E. Bryant	WE/3, WE/7	—
Mr. W. Buckley	—	—
Mr. E. C. Burr and Mr. A. J. E. Welch	WE/149	—
Miss K. N. Busfield	WE/325	—
Mr. E. Byford	WE/353	—
Mr. G. A. H. Cadbury	WE/336	—
Professor G. H. Camerlynck	WE/320 & (Supp. 1)	66
Professor A. D. Campbell	WE/238 & (Supp. 2)	—
Rt. Hon. Robert Carr, M.P.	WE/381	—
Mr. E. Carroll	WE/124	—
Mr. Donald Chapman, M.P.	WE/11	—
Mr. G. de N. Clark	WE/365	—
Mr. T. Clark	—	—
Mr. J. Clarke	WE/245	—
Mr. A. G. H. Collins	—	—
Mr. R. G. Collins and Miss A. O. J. Crichton	WE/93	—
Mr. P. M. Colvin-Smith, M.I.Mar.E., A.M.I.E.E., A.I.Mech.E. (Colvin-Smith Pipework Ltd.) (in confidence)	WE/2	—
Mr. C. Conway	—	—
Mr. W. J. Coombs	WE/26	—
Mr. D. Covey	WE/399	—
Mr. J. A. Crawford	WE/4	—
Mr. D. H. Dale	WE/332	—
Mr. D. Daley	WE/362	—
Mr. Tam Dalyell, M.P. (forwarding the statement of Mr. R. N. Beer)	WE/164	—

	Written Evidence Ref. No.	Minutes of Evidence Ref. No.
Mr. J. C. G. Davies	—	—
Mr. W. Davies	WE/15	—
Mr. T. L. DelaPorte	WE/8	—
Mr. D. A. C. Dewdney (in confidence)	WE/300	—
Mr. D. Dickens	WE/42	—
Mr. R. Dixon	WE/379	—
Mr. L. Dodd	WE/54	—
Mr. A. R. Drane	—	—
Sir Harold Emmerson, G.C.B., K.C.V.O.	WE/203	Appendix 6
Mr. J. E. Evans	—	—
Mr. S. M. Fernando	WE/256	—
Mr. Allan Flanders	WE/333	62, SWE
Mr. E. Fletcher, M.A., F.C.A., F.B.I.M.	WE/358	
Mr. John Garnett (Director of the Industrial Society)	WE/101	7
Mr. F. G. Gates	WE/352	—
Mr. R. H. Gill	—	—
Mr. A. Gillett	WE/222	—
Mr. H. Goodhind	—	—
Mr. J. Gorman	—	—
Mr. Cyril Grunfeld, M.A., LL.B.	WE/95 & (Supp. 1)	12
Mr. N. G. Gunton	WE/330	—
Mr. C. K. Hakim	—	—
Commander M. B. Hale	WE/274	—
Lord Hankey	WE/283 & (Supp. 1)	—
Mr. J. Hendy, LL.B.	WE/357	—
Dr. M. A. Hickling	WE/359	SWE
Mr. J. Hodgson	WE/9	—
Sir George Honeyman, C.B.E., Q.C.	WE/282	50
Mr. T. R. Hosking	—	—
Mr. J. Hotchkis (in confidence)	WE/91 & (Supp. 1)	—
Mr. H. J. Jackson	—	—
Mr. B. Johnson	—	—
Mr. B. P. Johnson, M.A., F.S.A. (Ben Johnson & Co. Ltd.) (in confidence)	WE/175	—
Mr. K. B. Johnson	WE/12 & (Supp. 1)	—
Mr. R. C. Kirk	—	—
Sir John Langford-Holt, M.P.	—	—
Mr. W. J. Lawson	WE/227	—
Mr. D. Layton (Incomes Data Services)	WE/302	—
Mr. J. A. Lincoln	WE/74 & (Supp. 1)	—
Mr. F. C. Lindon	—	—
Mr. A. P. Locke	WE/13	—
Mr. W. Lowry	—	—
Professor Tom Lupton	WE/191 & WE/249	SWE
Mr. A. McElwee	—	—
Mr. T. McGlade, Mr. A. V. Pallett and 21 others	WE/233	—
Dr. Angus Maddison	P/225	SWE
Mr. A. I. Marsh	WE/247	—

	Written Evidence Ref. No.	*Minutes of* Evidence Ref. No.
Mr. J. W. Martin	WE/376	—
Mr. J. Matthews, O.B.E.	WE/361	—
Mr. S. Mercer	WE/47	—
Mr. F. W. H. Miles	WE/366	—
Mr. A. H. Milnes	WE/18	—
Mr. D. Mitchell, M.P.	WE/331	—
Mr. Roger Moate	WE/187	—
Mr. N. K. Mousley	WE/363	—
Mr. E. F. Mundin and 29 others	WE/14	—
Mr. T. B. Naik	WE/85	—
Mr. E. Nelson	—	—
Mr. G. Nurse	WE/71	—
Mr. R. O'Brien & Mr. A. J. Nicol	WE/303	47
Mr. J. O'Leary & Mr. H. McComisky	—	—
Mr. A. W. T. Pearson	WE/84	—
Mr. N. Pearson	WE/213	—
Professor E. H. Phelps Brown, M.B.E.	WE/276 & (Supp. 1)	38
Mrs. W. M. Philip	WE/165	—
Councillor Alan Pickup	WE/392	—
Mr. Glyn Picton, M.Com.	WE/386	—
Mr. C. E. Pitman (Pitman Press)	WE/23	—
Mr. A. Portman	WE/51	—
Mr. J. Prior, M.P. (forwarding the statement of Mr. R. G. Smith)	WE/387	—
Rt. Hon. Enoch Powell, M.B.E., M.P. (forwarding the statement of Mr. J. W. Stevenson)	—	—
Mr. G. A. Quinn (statement forwarded by Mr. Sydney Silverman, M.P.)	WE/36	—
Sir Halford Reddish, F.C.A. (Rugby Portland Cement Co. Ltd.)	WE/383	68
Mr. S. E. Richards (in confidence)	WE/138	—
R. W. Rideout, LL.B., Ph.D.	WE/24 & (Supp. 1)	15
Professor B. C. Roberts	WE/248	33
Mr. T. Roberts	—	—
Brigadier W. P. T. Roberts, C.B.E.	WE/337	—
Professor D. J. Robertson	WE/238 & (Supps. 1 & 2)	44, SWE
Mr. Douglas Rookes	WE/289	—
Mr. L. F. Rose	WE/338	—
Mr. J. J. Rough	—	—
Mr. O. Sanderson & 3 others (statement forwarded by Mr. Bernard Braine, M.P.)	WE/369	—
Mr. N. Selwyn (University of Aston)	WE/305	—
Mr. W. R. Sheffield	—	—
Mr. Sydney Silverman, M.P. (forwarding the statement of Mr. G. A. Quinn)	WE/36	—
Mr. J. Silvester	—	—
Mr. J. Simpson	WE/5	—
Sir Leonard Sinclair	WE/345	—
Mr. A. J. Sjogren (in confidence)	WE/111 (Supp. 3)	—

	Written Evidence Ref. No.	Minutes of Evidence Ref. No.
Mr. R. G. Smith (statement forwarded by Mr. J. Prior, M.P.)	WE/387	—
Mr. W. H. Smith	WE/163	—
Mr. J. Sofer	WE/324	—
Mr. J. W. Stevenson (statement forwarded by the Rt. Hon. Enoch Powell, M.B.E., M.P.)	—	—
Mr. R. J. Stone	WE/72	—
Mr. C. B. J. Story	WE/166	—
Mr. T. Swinfen	WE/171	—
Mr. A. G. Tanner	—	—
Mr. M. J. Taylor	WE/389	—
Mr. J. S. Thomson	WE/339	—
Mr. E. L. J. Thorne, A.M.I.Prod.E., A.M.I.W.M.	WE/292	—
Rear Admiral W. G. S. Tighe, C.B. (Retired)	WE/55	—
Mr. J. Toothill	—	—
Professor H. A. Turner	WE/364 & WE/260 & (Supp. 1)	SWE
Mr. Justice Tyndall (in confidence)	WE/335	—
Mr. W. C. Vine	—	—
Mr. Gavin Waddell	WE/80	—
Mr. W. Walker	—	—
Mr. A. Warren	WE/315	—
Mr. J. Watson	WE/28	—
Professor K. W. Wedderburn	WE/217	31
Professor Harry H. Wellington	WE/286	41
Lt. Col. J. B. White	WE/38	—
Mr. W. Whitelaw, M.P. (forwarding the statement of Mr. J. Wilde)	WE/173	—
Mr. J. Wilde (statement forwarded by Mr. W. Whitelaw, M.P.)	WE/173	—
Sir Roy Wilson, Q.C.	WE/252	45
Miss Joan Woodward	WE/259	—
Mr. W. L. Wright	WE/394	—
Mr. T. Wylie and 8 shop stewards at the College of Advanced Technology, Aston	WE/209	—

APPENDIX 3

(see paragraph 11)

LIST OF WITNESSES WHO GAVE ORAL EVIDENCE

The list of witnesses who gave oral evidence to the Royal Commission is divided into two parts. The first part lists all those who gave oral evidence in public. The record of this evidence has been published by HM Stationery Office on behalf of the Royal Commission (Minutes of Evidence Nos. 1-69). The second part lists witnesses who gave evidence in private: this evidence was given in confidence and is not being published.

Part 1: Witnesses who gave Oral Evidence in Public

	Minutes of Evidence Ref. No.
Amalgamated Engineering Union	24
Amalgamated Union of Building Trade Workers	64
Association of Supervisory Staffs, Executives and Technicians	53
Associations of Local Authorities in England and Wales, the Greater London Council and the Local Authorities' Conditions of Service Advisory Board	60
Bar Council	43
British Railways Board	14
Professor G. H. Camerlynck	66
Chief Registrar of Friendly Societies	8
Confederation of British Industry	6 & 9, 22, 69
Department of Economic Affairs	18
Draughtsmen's and Allied Technicians' Association	36
Electrical Trades Union	57
Electricity Council	21
Engineering Employers' Federation	20
Esso Petroleum Co. Ltd.	39
Fabian Society	55
Mr. Allan Flanders	62
Mr. John Garnett, Director of the Industrial Society	7
Gas Council	11
General and Municipal Workers' Union	42
General Federation of Trade Unions	58
Mr. Cyril Grunfeld, M.A., LL.B.	12
Haldane Society	56
Sir George Honeyman, C.B.E., Q.C.	50
Inns of Court Conservative and Unionist Society	35
Institute of Personnel Management	40
Certain Members of the Editorial Staff of Newspapers in the International Publishing Corporation Group	1
International Publishing Corporation Ltd.	59
" Justice " (British Section of the International Commission of Jurists)	13
Kodak Ltd.	67
Law Society	52
London Transport Board	5
Massey-Ferguson (U.K.) Ltd.	25
Ministry of Labour	2 & 3
Ministry of Social Security	54

Mobil Oil Co. Ltd.	49
Motor Industry Employers	23
National and Local Government Officers' Association	26
National Board for Prices and Incomes	51
National Coal Board	4
National Federation of Building Trades Employers	16
National Federation of Building Trades Operatives	19
National Federation of Professional Workers	27
National Union of Railwaymen	17
Mr. Richard O'Brien and Mr. A. J. Nicol	47
Professor E. H. Phelps Brown, M.B.E.	38
Philips Industries	28
Sir Halford Reddish, F.C.A. (Chairman and Managing Director, The Rugby Portland Cement Co. Ltd.)	68
R. W. Rideout, LL.B., Ph.D.	15
Professor B. C. Roberts	33
Professor D. J. Robertson	44
Shipbuilding Employers' Federation	48
Society of Independent Manufacturers	32
Society of Labour Lawyers	63
Swedish Employers' Confederation	34
Trades Union Congress	61 & 65
Transport and General Workers' Union	30
HM Treasury	10
Unilever Ltd.	46
Union of Shop, Distributive and Allied Workers	29
Professor K. W. Wedderburn	31
Professor Harry H. Wellington	41
Sir Roy Wilson, Q.C.	45
Mr. N. S. Woods, M.A., Dip.Ed., Dip.Soc.Sci. (Otago)	37

Part 2: Witnesses who gave Oral Evidence in Private

1. The Royal Commission took oral evidence in private on a number of occasions either in response to requests from witnesses who had reason to ask for their evidence to be treated as confidential or because it appeared likely that private hearings would be more fruitful.

2. Private hearings were held in connection with the Royal Commission's investigations of the causes of unofficial strikes in the motor vehicle manufacturing industry in addition to the evidence given in public bearing on this matter. Those heard were:—

Sir Jack Scamp, Chairman of the Motor Industry Joint Labour Council

The Motor Industry Sub-Committee of the Confederation of Shipbuilding and Engineering Unions

Professor Tom Lupton

Mr. A. I. Marsh

Professor H. A. Turner, Dr. Garfield Clack and Mr. G. Roberts

Miss Joan Woodward

Members of management, local full-time trade union officials and shop stewards concerned with the following plants: Austin Motor Co. Ltd., Longbridge; Ford Motor Co. Ltd., Dagenham; Morris Motors Ltd., Tractors and Transmissions Branch, Birmingham; Rootes (Scotland) Ltd., Linwood; Vauxhall Motors Ltd., Luton.

3. The following also gave oral evidence in private:—

Sir Henry Bland, C.B.E., Permanent Secretary of the Australian Department of Labour and National Service

Mr. W. Coutts Donald, Miss Nancy Taylor, Mr. G. Wood (Urwick, Orr and Partners Ltd.), Mr. E. Fletcher (Associated Industrial Consultants Ltd.) and Mr. Brian P. Smith (P.A. Management Consultants Ltd.)

Mr. D. A. C. Dewdney

Ministry of Labour

Vickers Ltd.

One witness who requested that his identity should not be disclosed.

APPENDIX 4

(see paragraph 12)

RESEARCH PAPERS PUBLISHED BY THE ROYAL COMMISSION

1. The Role of Shop Stewards in British Industrial Relations, by W. E. J. McCarthy.

2. (Part 1) Disputes Procedures in British Industry, by A. I. Marsh.
   (Part 2) Disputes Procedures in Britain, by A. I. Marsh and W. E. J. McCarthy.

3. Industrial Sociology and Industrial Relations, by Alan Fox.

4. 1. Productivity Bargaining; 2. Restrictive Labour Practices. Written by the Commission's secretariat.

5. Trade Union Structure and Government, by John Hughes. Part 1: Structure and Development. Part 2*: Membership Participation and Trade Union Government.

6. Trade Union Growth and Recognition, by George Sayers Bain.

7. Employers' Associations: The Results of Two Studies: 1. The Functions and Organisation of Employers' Associations in Selected Industries, by V. G. Munns. 2. A Survey of Employers' Association Officials, by W. E. J. McCarthy.

8. Three Studies in Collective Bargaining: 1. Grievance Arbitration in the United States, by Jack Stieber. 2. Compulsory Arbitration in Britain, by W. E. J. McCarthy. 3. Check-off Agreements in Britain, by A. I. Marsh and J. W. Staples.

9. Overtime Working in Britain, by E. G. Whybrew.

10. Shop Stewards and Workshop Relations, by W. E. J. McCarthy and S. R. Parker.

11. Two Studies in Industrial Relations*: 1. The Position of Women in Industry, by Nancy Seear. 2. Changing Wage Payment Systems, by Robert B. McKersie.

* With the exception of those marked thus, the Research Papers listed above have already been published by HM Stationery Office on behalf of the Royal Commission. The others will be published shortly.

APPENDIX 5

(see paragraph 152)

THE EFFECTIVENESS OF INDUSTRY-WIDE WAGE REGULATION

1. In Chapter III of our report we discuss the declining effectiveness of industry-wide agreements and the extent to which they no longer determine actual pay levels. This Appendix aims to present further evidence for the statements in Chapter III by means of an analysis of the position of workers in different industries and occupations. It must be stressed that the figures it contains are only approximations and often rely on an element of guess-work, although as a result of reports of the Prices and Incomes Board much more is known about the relationship between national rates and pay than was the case even two or three years ago.

2. In trying to assess the position in different industries it helps to distinguish five different situations. They are:—

A. Where actual pay (excluding overtime) of most workers is thought to be well in excess of such nationally determined rates as exist.

B. Where there are substantial groups of workers whose pay (excluding overtime) is thought to be well in excess of such rates, but these are not thought to be the majority.

C. Where industry-wide rates exist and are generally followed, but average overtime pay is high enough to add something like 50 per cent to average earnings and much more in some cases.

D. Where existing industry-wide rates are generally followed and most workers do not receive overtime payments which approach the levels of Category C.

E. Where there is not sufficient information available to justify any estimate of the relationship between nationally determined rates and actual levels of pay.

3. The following table attempts to allocate industries according to their most appropriate category:—

	No. of employees (UK June 1967)
A. Engineering, electrical goods, vehicles, shipbuilding Distribution Food, drink, tobacco Metal manufacture Paper, printing and publishing Other metal goods Chemicals Bricks, pottery, etc. Timber, furniture, etc. Other manufacturing (including rubber, plastics) Port and inland water transport	10¾m.
B. Construction (rates fixed by industry agreement exceeded especially on large construction sites in most trades*) Textiles (rates fixed by industry agreement exceeded in hosiery and some sections of wool and cotton manufacturing) Mining and quarrying Railways Gas Motor garages, etc.	4m.

*Electrical contracting being a notable exception.

	No. of employees (UK June 1967)
C. Road haulage, road passenger transport, shipping	½m.
D. Educational services Local government service National government service (including Post Office) Clothing Agriculture Electricity supply	4½m.
E. Financial, professional and scientific services (excluding educational services) Catering Miscellaneous	4 m.
	23¾m.

4. It should be noted that in the industries included in the first three categories there are usually differences between the pay position of men and women and the situation affecting manual workers and white-collar workers. Most women covered by industry-wide agreements or statutory regulations in these industries are employed on manual work and receive payments which are much closer to those laid down at industry level than their male counterparts. However, this does not greatly affect the total numbers since in most cases women are very much in the minority in these categories: altogether they constitute less than an eighth of the total labour force employed in Categories A, B and C. (Over three-quarters of women employed are to be found in Categories D and E.)

5. Most white-collar workers employed in Categories A, B and C are not covered by industry-wide agreements or statutory regulations of any kind. Moreover, those who are, for example in engineering and paper and printing, usually receive actual rates of pay well in excess of basic rates. Differences between groups in these industries do not therefore affect the main conclusions of Chapter III.

6. In summary it may be said that, on the basis of the evidence available, about half the workers covered by industry-wide agreements or statutory wage regulations are employed in industries where the rates specified are generally exceeded and most of the rest work in jobs not covered by any form of wage fixing at industry level. Even where rates fixed at industry level are fairly closely followed, more often than not they are supplemented by high levels of overtime earnings. On any reasonable estimate the effective regulation of pay levels by industry-wide agreement is now very much the exception rather than the rule in Britain and is largely confined to the public sector.

APPENDIX 6

(see paragraph 486)

WRITTEN EVIDENCE OF
SIR HAROLD EMMERSON, G.C.B., K.C.V.O.[1]

MASS PROSECUTION IN WAR TIME

1. Doubts about the practicability of prosecuting large numbers of men for going on strike illegally were put to the test at the Betteshanger Colliery, in Kent, in December 1941. There had been trouble at this colliery about allowances for work in a difficult seam where working conditions changed almost weekly. After all else had failed the company and the men agreed to go to arbitration and to abide by the award. An experienced arbitrator decided that the allowances offered by the management were reasonable and erred, if at all, in being excessive. The men rejected the award and work stopped. About 4,000 men were idle.

2. Under the National Arbitration Order the strike was illegal and to make matters worse it was backed by local Union Officials. In the Ministry of Labour we felt that the great value of the Order lay in its moral effect. Any quick resort to prosecution could only weaken its authority, we might possibly lose Union support, and the work of the Chief Industrial Commissioner and his staff would be made more difficult. But in coal mining the Mines Department decided on action under the Order and we were only their agents when it came to legal action. The Secretary for Mines, who was himself a former miners' leader decided on prosecution, and he had Cabinet backing. Reluctantly we set the machinery of the law in motion.

3. The prosecution of 4,000 men seemed a tall order, but as the dispute had started with 1,000 underground workers we decided to concentrate on them. Extra supplies of forms for the serving of summonses were rushed down to the Chief Constable of Kent. Then several Justices of the Peace had to be found willing to sign 1,000 forms in duplicate and extra police were drafted to serve them. After these preliminaries a special hearing was arranged. Charges against 1,000 persons could only be handled satisfactorily if the men pleaded guilty. If each man pleaded " not guilty " the proceedings might last for months. The Union was asked if they would instruct their members to plead guilty, and accept a decision on a few test cases. The Union obligingly did so.

4. The magistrates met in Canterbury. The news had spread to other coalfields and colliery bands decided to accompany the culprits. Local colliery workers made it an outing for their families and chartered coaches to take wives and children. The Mines Department authorised the Regional Petroleum Officer to allow petrol for the journeys.

5. Everything on the day was orderly and even festive. Bands played and women and children cheered the procession on its way to the Court. The proceedings in Court went smoothly; everyone pleaded guilty. The three Union officials were sent to prison. The Branch Secretary was sentenced to two months with hard labour; the local President and a member of the local executive each received one month with hard labour. Thirty-five men were fined £3 or one month's imprisonment, and nearly one thousand were fined £1, or fourteen days.

6. Protests came against the severity of the sentences, particularly against the imprisonment of three union officials. Many of the miners in the area were in the Home Guard, and Kent was in the front line. " Was this the way to treat good citizens?" There was talk of sympathetic strikes. But the real trouble was that the only men who could call off the strike were now in gaol. The Secretary for Mines went down to Kent to see them accompanied by Mr. Ebby Edwards, then the National President of the Miners' Union. Negotiations were re-opened and five days after the hearing an agreement was signed, in prison, between the colliery management and

---

[1] Sir Harold Emmerson is a former Permanent Secretary of the Ministry of Labour and in 1942-44 was the Ministry's Chief Industrial Commissioner.

the Kent Miners' Union. Apart from some face-saving words, it gave the men what they wanted. Then the Secretary for Mines took a deputation to the Home Secretary asking for the immediate release of the three local officials. The men would not start work until their leaders were free. After eleven days in prison they were released. The mine reopened and in the first week the normal output of coal was nearly trebled.

7. In the Ministry of Labour there was gloom and apprehension. Certainly we had shown that it was possible to prosecute on a large scale if everyone co-operated. But even if the remissions were necessary for work to start, they were bound to weaken the authority of the Order. Also what would be the effect on the men who had been fined? We were soon to know; for the Clerk to the Justices reported that of the men who had been fined only nine had paid. Before he went to the trouble of preparing nearly a thousand commitment warrants the Clerk asked whether it was proposed to recommend remission. The County gaol could only accommodate a few at a time and it would take several years to work through the list. He understood that the men had been at work for some weeks, they had made good the lost output and he believed the country needed coal. There might be an outcry if men were sent to prison for not paying the fines, when the original sentences of imprisonment on the leaders had been remitted. He asked for guidance.

8. The company also wanted to avoid further trouble. They asked if they could pay the fines on behalf of the men; the cost to them would be so much less profits tax! They were told on no account to do this. The Court was advised not to enforce the unpaid fines.

9. Of course someone asked: "What about the nine men who paid their fines? Should they have their money back?" But it was not until 1950—eight years later— that the National Union of Mineworkers asked formally that the paid fines should be returned. The Union was told, in appropriate official language, to forget it.

6th January 1966.

APPENDIX 7

(see paragraph 927)

TRADE UNIONS AND THE POLITICAL LEVY

1.   The Society of Conservative Lawyers submitted to us in 1967 a supplement to their main evidence: the supplement dealing with the law affecting the political funds of trade unions and making certain proposals for its amendment.   Even though these proposals may owe something to party political considerations, we feel that we should deal with them, since the law in question is part of the law affecting the activities of trade unions.   Because the matter is rather detailed we have embodied the Society's proposals and our comments in this Appendix.

2.   We have described elsewhere how trade unions originally regarded themselves as free (if the majority of their members wished it) to spend their money on party political objects in the same way as many other voluntary societies, and in particular as a means towards the attainment of trade union objectives.   This freedom was eventually negatived by the decision of the House of Lords in *Amalgamated Society of Railway Servants* v. *Osborne* [1910] AC 87, but restored subject to certain conditions by the Trade Union Act 1913.   The Society of Conservative Lawyers wishes that Act to be amended.   We set out below their proposals and our comments.   (References to sections are references to sections of the said Act of 1913.)

3.   *Proposal.*   It should be made clear in section 3(3) that a donation or subscription to a political party must come out of the political fund.
   Comment.   The opening words of section 3(1) taken in conjunction with the terms of section 3(3) already, in our opinion, produce this result.

4.   *Proposal.*   It should also be made clear that affiliation fees paid to a constituency Labour Party by a trade union must come out of the political fund.
   Comment.   The Registrar of Friendly Societies says that this is the first time he has heard it responsibly suggested that such fees could properly be paid from a trade union's general fund: but that if the law does allow this it should be amended.   Again, in our opinion, section 3(1) and 3(3), read together, already require payment of such fees out of the political fund.

5.   *Proposal.*   Since many topics must " lie squarely on both the political and ' industrial and social ' fields ", section 3(3) which defines the political objects which must be paid for out of the political fund should be altered so as to require much more to be paid for out of the same fund.   At the moment a trade union may apply its general funds in furtherance of any political object not named in section 3(3), and also on the holding of political meetings and the distribution of political literature, where the main purpose of the meeting and the literature is the furtherance of the trade union's industrial and social objects.   Section 3(3) should be altered so as to secure the result that the political fund alone should be used to pay for the holding of political meetings, or for the distribution of political literature, unless there is *no* political purpose being served, or if the political element is merely incidental and insubstantial.
   Comment.   The Registrar of Friendly Societies observes that the broad principle behind section 3(3) is that election expenditure must always be borne by the political fund, and also expenditure on political propaganda which goes substantially beyond the pursuit of the union's industrial and social objects.   The proposal of the Society of Conservative Lawyers would mean abandoning this principle and making everything which partook partly of politics, and partly of a trade union's industrial and social activities, chargeable to the political fund alone.   He adds that the present principle appears to him to be intelligible and right: and that though section 3(3) presents diffi- culties of construction at times, the same would certainly be true of the proposed amendment.   We agree with these observations, and recommend no change.

6.   *Proposal.*   Section 3 requires expenditure on the distribution of political litera- ture to be paid for out of the political fund.   It should be made clear that " distribution " here includes the cost of writing, preparing, printing and publishing.
   Comment.   If there were evidence that trade unions frequently prepared party

342

political literature and charged the whole cost of writing, preparing, printing and publishing such literature to their general funds, and the cost of distribution alone to its political funds, this proposal would have weight. We have no evidence that such is the case. Trade unions, we understand, usually purchase such documents from a political party and debit the cost to the political fund.

7. *Proposal.* All trade union accounts should be professionally audited.
   Comment. Our report makes a recommendation on these lines (see paragraph 655).

8. *Proposal.* Trade unions should be compelled to itemise payments appearing in their accounts under a general heading such as " Grants to Charities " in order to bring to light any payments which have been made from their general funds but which should have been made from their political funds.
   Comment. In support of this proposal the Society of Conservative Lawyers referred to certain payments made by the Amalgamated Engineering Union, the Draughtsmen's and Allied Technicians' Association and others from their general funds, e.g. to the Fabian Society, the Movement for Colonial Freedom, the Labour Research Department, etc. It cannot be predicated of these payments that they promote " political objects " within the meaning of that term in section 3(3) of the Act of 1913. In 1925 the then Chief Registrar of Friendly Societies in a convincing judgment construed these words as connoting " party political objects "—a construction with which we respectfully agree. More investigation would be needed to establish that the donations in question served party political objects. They might or might not. At the moment registered unions are not obliged to show in their annual returns to the Registrar anything more than totals of expenditure under general headings. The proposal now made would require unions to itemise every payment made by itself and its branches. The burden thus imposed would be heavy on a large union, and we are informed by the Registrar of Friendly Societies that he has seen no evidence suggesting that the absence of such a requirement has encouraged the misuse of general funds. We therefore make no recommendation on the matter.

9. *Proposal.* Under the present law trade unions are free to use their general funds for political meetings or for the distribution of political literature if the *main* purpose of the meetings or the literature is the promotion of the unions' industrial and social objects. Their union journals often contain political matter. The law should be altered so that the cost of such meetings and literature must be charged to the political fund unless the political content is insubstantial or incidental.
   Comment. This is similar to proposal No. 5 above. Again, while under the present law it might be difficult in some cases to determine the main purpose of any such meeting or literature, it would be even more difficult in many cases to decide whether the political content of them was " insubstantial " or " incidental ". We cannot endorse this proposal.

10. *Proposal.* Section 3(2) of the 1913 Act empowers a member of a trade union to complain of a breach of the political fund rules: and the decision of the Registrar upon any such complaint is final. This is unsatisfactory and " the matter should be dealt with by legislation. . ."
    Comment. It is not stated what the provisions of any such new legislation should be. Presumably it is being urged that any member of the public should have the same right of complaint under section 3(2); and that the Registrar's decision should be open to review. We have no evidence of any real need for such legislation.

11. *Proposal.* The auditors of trade union accounts should in future report and certify the accounts not only to the union itself but to the Registrar of Friendly Societies. If the Registrar, having examined the accounts, considered that any item required further explanation, or that expenses have been drawn from the wrong fund, he should have the power to refer the matter to the court for adjudication and decision. Other interested parties should have a similar power.
    Comment. Again we are not aware of such abuses as would justify " other interested parties " having the right to investigate a trade union's accounts and to refer selected entries to a court for " adjudication and decision ". Such a power might lead to much vexatious litigation; and in the absence of proof of its necessity, we cannot recommend such a proposal.

12. *Proposal.* Trade unions should be obliged by law to state on application forms for admission to the union that there is a right to " contract out " of the political levy.

Comment. Trade unions are forbidden by law to make contribution to the political fund a condition of membership (section 3(1)(b)). A reference to the applicant's right to contract out on the application form, followed, as it might well be, by an inquiry whether he wished to exercise the right, would be open to the objection that these matters are irrelevant to admission, and might give rise to misapprehension. On this ground we are not in favour of the proposal. Moreover under the present political fund rules a union is required to supply a new member with a copy of these rules on admission, and these rules will refer to his right to contract out. Any member who does not know that he has this right cannot properly say that the information has been withheld from him.

13. Apart from the foregoing, certain difficulties which arise in cases where the check-off is operated concerning the refund of the political levy to union members who have " contracted out " were referred to by the Society of Conservative Lawyers. The legality of the check-off is referred to in Chapter XII (paragraph 722).

APPENDIX 8

(see paragraph 996)

PAYMENTS FROM STATE SOURCES RECEIVABLE BY WORKERS INVOLVED IN TRADE DISPUTES

Income Tax Refunds

1. Under the PAYE system a wage-earner normally pays at the end of each week tax which takes account on the one hand of his total income since the tax year began and on the other of the appropriate fraction of his tax allowances by then due to him. If for whatever reason he gets no pay during a particular week, his total income will remain the same but there will be one week's additional allowances to set against it and he will therefore be entitled to a refund. (This refund is the individual's own money in the sense that any tax payer has a legally enforceable entitlement to any tax he has overpaid.) Thus a man who gets no pay in a week because he is on strike will be entitled to a refund of tax at the end of that week (provided that there is any tax to refund, which there will not be for example at the beginning of the tax year). If the strike continues further refunds will become due each week until either all the tax paid has been refunded or the end of the tax year is reached.

2. The employer can either make the repayment himself or give the necessary particulars to the Inspector of Taxes to enable him to do it. In practice the employer generally makes the repayment as being the more convenient course.

3. The amount of refunds to be paid will vary according to individual circumstances and the point of time in the tax year at which the strike starts, but hypothetical examples can be quoted. In the tax year 1967-68 a wage-earner with average earnings of £21 a week, and with agreed annual flat-rate expenses deduction for tax purposes of £20, would receive in the first few weeks of the strike (provided it began some considerable time after the start, and before the end, of the tax year) approximately:

if married with two children under 11 years old	£3 10s.
if married with no children	£3 13s.
if unmarried	£2 14s.

Supplementary Benefit

4. Section 10 of the Ministry of Social Security Act provides that " where by reason of a stoppage of work due to a trade dispute at his place of employment a person is without employment, for any period during which the stoppage continues . . . his requirements . . . shall be disregarded for the purposes of benefit except so far as they include the requirement to provide for any other person." In other words supplementary benefit is paid for wives and children (and a rent allowance is made) but not for the breadwinner. Very occasionally single men are given benefit where really urgent need exists. This is done under section 13 of the Act which provides an overriding discretion for the payment of benefit in cases of urgency.

5. The following are average annual figures relating to payment of supplementary benefits (and national assistance previously) for the period 1962-66 inclusive:

Number of workers involved in stoppages to whom payments were made in respect of themselves or their dependants	5,266
Number of payments	13,228
Amounts paid to workers in respect of	
(i) their own needs	£538
(ii) dependants' needs	£64,678

6. It is possible to make a rough and ready comparison between these figures and the Ministry of Labour's statistics of numbers involved in stoppages due to industrial disputes. It may be assumed for the purpose of the comparison that no worker will consider applying for benefit unless the stoppage in which he is involved has lasted more than two weeks. The Ministry of Labour's statistics show that, in the period

345

1962-66, some 62,500 workers were on average involved each year in stoppages lasting more than two weeks. The average annual total number of workers involved in stoppages who received payments in this period (5,266) was approximately 8·4% of this figure.

Sickness Benefit

7. If a man is ill he is not prevented from claiming sickness benefit under the National Insurance scheme because he happens to be on strike. The Ministry of Social Security have a special procedure in force to detect abuse of sickness benefit in connection with strikes. The Ministry's local offices are informed by the Department of Employment and Productivity (and in the case of coalmining, by the National Coal Board) when a strike is taking place and special checks are made, including the reference of claimants to a medical officer for a second examination, if there is any doubt about " incapacity for work ". The Ministry believe that abuse of sickness benefit in connection with strikes is kept to a very low level.

SUMMARY OF INSTITUTIONS CONCERNED WITH INDUSTRIAL RELATIONS UNDER THE COMMISSION'S RECOMMENDATIONS, AND THEIR FUNCTIONS

Department of Employment and Productivity

All existing functions.
Overall responsibility for promoting reform of the collective bargaining system on basis of effective factory agreements.
Encouragement of and guidance to companies in the review of their industrial relations in the light of the Commission's report.
Registration of collective agreements and promotion of good practice through industrial relations officers; reference of difficult cases to Industrial Relations Commission for investigation and report; follow-up of reports.

Industrial Relations Commission	Industrial Court	Labour Tribunals	Registrar of Trade Unions and Employers' Associations	Independent Review Body
Advice to Secretary of State on the reform of the industrial relations system: investigation and report on references by the Secretary of State concerning:	Existing arbitration functions.	Existing functions as industrial tribunals.	Registration of trade unions and employers' associations, including oversight of new requirements in relation to rules.	Adjudication in complaints by individuals of unfair treatment by unions, malpractices in union elections, etc.
(i) problems arising out of the registration of agreements; (ii) problems in companies not covered by obligation to register agreements; (iii) problems of trade union recognition; (iv) general state of industrial relations in a factory or industry.	Provision of unilateral arbitration on selective basis.	Settlement of cases of alleged unfair dismissal.	Advice to individuals in their relations with unions and promotion of amicable settlement of complaints.	Settlement of disputes between Registrar and union as to its rules.
Review by its Industrial Law Committee of industrial relations legislation.	Adjudication in enlarged range of cases arising under s.8 of the Terms and Conditions of Employment Act 1959.	Adjudication (concurrently with ordinary courts of law) in cases arising between individual employer and employee under the contract of employment.	Investigation of alleged malpractices in union elections.	Adjudication (concurrently with ordinary courts of law) in cases based on alleged breach of union rules or violation of natural justice.
			Acting as Registrar to the Independent Review Body.	

347

INDEX

NOTE: Numbers in the index refer to *paragraphs* of the report.

350

Printed in England for HM Stationery Office by Keliher, Hudson & Kearns.
C870 Dd142496 K 240 6/68 51-8541